Ancient Maya Political Dynamics

Maya Studies

UNIVERSITY PRESS OF FLORIDA

Florida A&M University, Tallahassee
Florida Atlantic University, Boca Raton
Florida Gulf Coast University, Ft. Myers
Florida International University, Miami
Florida State University, Tallahassee
New College of Florida, Sarasota
University of Central Florida, Orlando
University of Florida, Gainesville
University of North Florida, Jacksonville
University of South Florida, Tampa
University of West Florida, Pensacola

Ancient Maya Political Dynamics

||||||||||||||||||||||||||||||||||||||||||||||||||||||||||||||||||||||||||||||||||||||||||||||||||||||||||||||||||||||||||||||||

ANTONIA E. FOIAS

Foreword by Diane Z. Chase and Arlen F. Chase

University Press of Florida

Gainesville · Tallahassee · Tampa · Boca Raton

Pensacola · Orlando · Miami · Jacksonville · Ft. Myers · Sarasota

The publication of this book is made possible in part by a grant from Williams College.

First cloth printing, 2013
First paperback printing, 2014

29 28 27 26 25   6 5 4 3 2

Library of Congress Cataloging-in-Publication Data
Foias, Antonia E.
Ancient Maya political dynamics / Antonia E. Foias ; foreword by Diane Z. Chase
    and Arlen F. Chase. pages cm. — (Maya studies)
Includes bibliographical references and index.
ISBN 978-0-8130-4422-4 (cloth)
ISBN 978-0-8130-6089-7 (pbk.)
1. Mayas—Guatemala—Politics and government. 2. Mayas—Guatemala—History.
    3. Mayas—Guatemala—Antiquities. 4. Political anthropology—Guatemala.
    5. Guatemala—Antiquities. I. Chase, Diane Z. II. Chase, Arlen F. (Arlen Frank),
    1953- III. Title. IV.
Series: Maya studies.
F1435.3.P7F64 2013
972.81—dc23
2013007070

The University Press of Florida is the scholarly publishing agency for the State University
System of Florida, comprising Florida A&M University, Florida Atlantic University,
Florida Gulf Coast University, Florida International University, Florida State University,
New College of Florida, University of Central Florida, University of Florida, University
of North Florida, University of South Florida, and University of West Florida.

University Press of Florida
2046 NE Waldo Road
Suite 2100
Gainesville, FL 32609
http://upress.ufl.edu

Contents

Figures

Tables

Foreword

Ancient Maya Political Dynamics is a compelling reconstruction of Classic Period Maya politics. While the primary vantage point for discussion is the decade of excavations undertaken at the site of Motul de San José in Guatemala, Antonia Foias also provides comparisons with other archaeologically known polities and considers theoretical perspectives from areas within and outside of ancient Mesoamerica. Her outlook is particularly valuable in that she views politics from a variety of scales—micro, macro, and intermediate—thus providing balance to her interesting and in-depth discussion. She frames the volume within a reconstruction of Maya culture and history, using this framework as a backdrop for considerations of change in political organization over time. She further focuses on variability within these systems rather than on the establishment of centralized or decentralized units. Likewise, her discussion of political anthropology focuses on the dynamic, as opposed to static, nature of political systems. Comparative examples for the Motul de San José case study are drawn from both the Maya area and broader Mesoamerica as well as from the southeastern United States and Mesopotamia. Foias uses her multi-scaled framework to focus on the kinds of data that can be used in the reconstruction of political organization. Thus, the macro-scale discussion focuses predominantly on polity and interpolity organization, as informed by the study of settlement patterns, epigraphy, and ethnohistory. The intermediate-scale discussion focuses on the internal political dimension, as informed by Maya hieroglyphic texts and reconstructions of tribute, tax, and palace economies. The micro-scale discussion focuses on the politics of individuals, households, and subgroups within the community, especially as expressed on stone monuments and in artifact distributions. Her broader discussions include considerations not only of the political power held by the elite but also of the political power held by commoners—either because of their role in production or their participation in the political process itself. Foias concludes that Maya political organization exhibits very fine levels of variability, especially when all data elements, scales, and comparisons are taken into account.

Ancient Maya Political Dynamics fills a significant void in the literature that often is either site specific or pan-lowland in scope. By focusing on a limited period of time and by using Motul de San José as a base—while at the same time incorporating external comparisons—Foias is able to offer a more nuanced view of the Classic Period lowland Maya, one that emphasizes change and variation, the value of multiple lines of evidence, and the significance of multiple levels of stakeholders in the political process. In sum, this volume is a welcome addition to the Maya Studies series.

Diane Z. Chase and Arlen F. Chase
Series Editors

Acknowledgments

I would like to thank all the sponsors of the Motul de San José Archaeological Project, including the National Science Foundation (grant number SBR-9905456); the Wenner-Gren Foundation; the Foundation for the Advancement of Mesoamerican Studies, Inc.; Sigma Xi, the Scientific Research Foundation; the Fulbright Scholar Foundation; and the home institutions of participants who collaborated on this study: Williams College; SUNY Potsdam; University of Florida; Tulane University; University of California, Riverside. Field seasons sponsored by my National Science Foundation grant took place in 1998–2001, while Matthew Moriarty, Christina Halperin, Crorey Lawton, Jeanette Castellanos, and Elly Spensley undertook field seasons in 2002, 2003, 2005, and 2008. Their work was funded by various means, including National Science Foundation Dissertation Improvement grants and grants from the Wenner-Gren Foundation and the Fulbright Foundation.

The writing of this work was made possible by a sabbatical from Williams College and by a New Directions Fellowship awarded by the Andrew W. Mellon Foundation. I thank both of these institutions for their generosity. I am grateful to Eleanor King, Daniela Triadan, Kitty Emery, Christina Halperin, David Edwards, Norman Hammond, and Olga Shevchenko for their comments on the manuscript. Eleanor was kind enough to read through two drafts and provide extended, thoughtful, and insightful comments. I am immensely grateful for all her insights. The final product was much improved by these conversations, but all errors or omissions are my own.

Additional thanks go to the administrative assistants in the Department of Anthropology and Sociology at Williams College, Donna Chenail and Peggy Weyers, who assisted tirelessly with many versions of the book's bibliography and other segments. Additional assistance with the illustrations came from research assistant Evalynn Rosado.

I thank UPF director Meredith Morris-Babb and copy editor Kate Babbitt, who were patient and encouraging throughout the process of publication. I would also like to express my gratitude to the Departamento de Monumentos Prehispánicos y Coloniales of the Institute of Anthropology and History of Guatemala (IDAEH) for permission to conduct research at Motul de San José, especially to director Hector Escobedo and co-director Erick Ponciano.

Finally, this book would not have been possible without the assistance of all the members of the Motul de San José Archaeological Project and all of the field workers from San José and Nuevo San José, Guatemala. Kitty Emery, Jeanette Castellanos, Matthew Moriarty, Christina Halperin, and José Sanchez as the co-directors and/or senior members of the project deserve the most thanks for all their hard work from fieldwork to laboratory analysis to publication. Other senior members and collaborators were Oswaldo Chinchilla, Ronald L. Bishop, Dorie Reents-Budet, Henry P. Schwarcz, Richard E. Terry, and Elizabeth A. Webb. The student members of the project were Maria Alvarado, Monica Alvarez, Jeff Buechler, Benito Burgos, Jessica Charland, Jessica Deckard, Aaron Deter-Wolf, Julia Drapkin, Megan Foster, Rigden Glaab, Daniel Glick, Emma Golden, Becky Goldfine, Francine Guffey, William Hahn, George Higginbotham, Chris Jensen, Kris Johnson, Erin Kennedy Thornton, Eric S. Kerns, Melanie Kingsley, Anna Lapin, Crorey Lawton, Camilo Luin, Gerson Martinez Salguero, Erin McCracken, Geoff Schoradt, Tirso Morales, Freeden Oeur, Fredy Ramirez, Patricia Rivera, Carolyn Ryan, Anita Sanchez, Elly Spensley, Eliza Suntecun, Yukiko Tonoike, Cathy Warren, Andrew Wyatt, and Suzanna Yorgey. I thank all these individuals for contributing the hard work and intellectual energy that has permitted me to complete this book.

1

||||||||||||

Introduction

This book grew from a question that I pose to my students and that I asked myself when I began to study anthropology in college: What makes humans behave as they do? Social scientists, philosophers, moralists, political scientists, psychologists, and anthropologists have tried for many centuries to understand what makes humans tick: Is it our basic need for food, shelter and respect or efficiency in obtaining these things? Is it morality in the broadest sense, the idea that for most of us being a good person beats being a bad person? Or is it a constant desire for more power? Because the past makes the present and shapes the future, I go back in time to the Classic Maya civilization, one of the best-known and most-celebrated pre-Hispanic cultures of Central America, to investigate the larger question: How much did political power shape the lives and landscape of the Maya people?

The goal of this book is not only to present a review of how archaeologists have reconstructed ancient Maya politics but also to engage with the methods they used to reconstitute politics and the debates they have encountered and tried to resolve. By bringing together all the different approaches and the various bodies of knowledge about ancient politics, I hope to provide the foundation for further studies that open new doors to the past.

Maya culture is celebrated for its majestic ruins now hidden by jungle forests in Guatemala, Belize, El Salvador, and Mexico, for its sophisticated hieroglyphic writing system, and for its artistic masterpieces carved or painted on stone, shell, bone, and pottery. The historical trajectory of Maya culture is generally divided into three time periods from the Agricultural Revolution to the Spanish Conquest of the sixteenth century: the Preclassic, or Formative (1800 BC–AD 250); the Classic (AD 250–950); and the Postclassic (AD 950–1542) (Table 1.1). The most populous polities, the largest cities, and the most intense production of Maya art occurred during the

Classic period. The Classic centuries are the focus of this book because we know most about them from the hundreds of hieroglyphic texts that have now been deciphered and the massive quantities of archaeological materials produced by excavation, surveys, and mapping carried out by numerous archaeological projects. The end of the Classic period is generally described as the Classic Maya collapse, but although this "collapse" involved major societal upheavals and changes, it did not cause a complete demographic collapse or the disappearance of Maya culture. Maya society and culture continued through the Postclassic period and are alive and well today in the flourishing communities of more than 5 million Maya speakers widely dispersed through eastern Mesoamerica (but especially concentrated in the Guatemalan highlands, the Chiapas highlands, and the lowland Yucatan peninsula). Rather than speaking of Maya culture as a "dead civilization," we need to understand the incredible continuities and transformations that connect modern Mayas with their Classic-period ancestors.

We know a great deal about Classic Maya culture and society, but its political sphere remains a contentious topic. It is often presented as polarized between two extremes: the centralized model that envisions regional, large-scale centralized states (Chase and Chase 1996; D. Chase et al. 1990; Haviland 1992, 1997; Marcus 1993; Adams 1986) and the decentralized model that proposes small-scale, weakly integrated polities (Demarest 1992; Houston 1993; Fox et al. 1996; Iannone 2002; Lucero 1997; Sharer and Golden 2004; Foias 2003; Runggaldier and Hammond in press; see also Chapter 4). However, these concerns with absolute classification into decentralized or centralized structures have been surpassed by an increasing awareness that Classic Maya polities were variable not only in size but also in structure (Chase and Chase 1996; Demarest 1996c; Fox et al. 1996; Iannone 2002; Marcus 1993, 1998; Pyburn 1997; Sharer 1991; see Chapter 4). Rather than essentializing the "Maya state," we need to "enter" individual Maya cases and their internal complexities before seeking to understand how and why they differed from each other across time and space. A common adage in twentieth-century politics, "All politics is local politics" (O'Neill and Hymel 1995), has as much relevance for ancient times as it does today: to understand ancient politics, we need to begin from the local and move upward.

Best known among this new scholarship is Joyce Marcus's dynamic model, which argues that not only the Maya but all ancient civilizations cycled between periods of centralized powerful states (or possibly empires) and fragmented landscapes of smaller and weaker states (1993, 1998; see

Table 1.1. Pre-Columbian chronology of the Maya region

Archaic	3400–1800 BC
Early Preclassic	1800–900 BC
Middle Preclassic	900–300 BC
Late Preclassic and Terminal Preclassic-Protoclassic	300 BC–250 AD
Early Classic	250–600 AD
Late Classic	600–800 AD
Terminal Classic	800–950 AD
Early Postclassic	950–1200 AD
Late Postclassic	1200–1542 AD

also de Montmollin 1995; Culbert 1992). Although one may debate if this is a correct view of ancient history,[1] we still need to ask Why these cycles? and Which cycle is the basic one of ancient history, the troughs of decentralization and small city-state units or the peaks of centralized large states or even empires? I will try to answer these queries by carving out a piece of the historical puzzle by considering Maya political dynamics during the Classic period. Here, suffice to say that even though states are lauded for being the most integrated and most centralized of human societies, they can also be the most exploitative and most fraught with major and multiple internal divisions. This makes them most fragile, caught between dominance and resistance, and this leads to cycles of integration and disintegration.

Because this may be a long journey, I first review how political power has been examined by political anthropologists over the last century (Chapter 2) and then how archaeologists across the world have studied ancient political structures and dynamics (Chapter 3). These two short excursions into political anthropology and world archaeology point to three major concerns among anthropologists and archaeologists alike: 1) macro-scale politics (at the levels of polities, regions, and beyond; relations among polities; and international dynamics) (Chapter 4); 2) middle-scale politics (at the intra-polity level, including the internal administrative structure and relations among different political institutions and officials) (Chapter 5); and 3) micro-scale politics (at the level of individuals, including agency as shaped by gender, household, status, class, and community identities and political practice in performances) (Chapter 6). Through this multiscalar analysis of political dynamics, a more comprehensive modeling of ancient polities is possible. We also need to examine the processes and strategies through which the three levels were integrated with each other or rubbed against each other. I use the research I have conducted at Motul de San José,

Guatemala, over the last ten years to shed light on some of these debates (Chapters 4, 5, and 6). One point I hope to impart in this work is that there isn't one Maya political history but multiple histories, that there isn't one Maya "state" but many different polities. The histories of these polities need to be understood from the level of the local and of the lived experience of human beings to the regional and interregional levels of a state and civilization. Rather than thinking of Maya politics as static, we need to envision it as dynamic and treat political structure together with political dynamics.

Some Theoretical Points

As we enter the world of Maya archaeology, we need to sweep aside some unstated assumptions about ancient states. In spite of efforts by anthropologists, social scientists who study ancient states are still caught in the dilemma of the "Other." What I mean is that we often think of ancient non-Western societies or states as characterized by values that are directly opposed to those of our own society and political system—that is, the Western democracy of the United States. Thus, ancient states become the opposite of modern democracies: we see them as completely exploitative and undemocratic, incapable of including any democratic institution (such as councils) and capable only of producing exploitative and absolute kings who were followed by obedient farmers, traders, craft specialists, and so on. This view of ancient states is a legacy of Karl Marx (1966, 70), who described Asian ancient states as the "Asiatic mode of production" or "Oriental Despotism," and later this view was championed by Karl Wittfogel (1957).[2] This mode of production also encompassed the ancient states of the New World (Offner 1981). While the specifics of Marx's "Asiatic mode of production" have been rejected, the overall perspective on ancient states that this model promotes has prevailed (Offner 1981; McFarlane, Cooper, and Jaksic 2005; Blanton and Fargher 2008). Premodern states are often seen as exploitative, but excavations at Motul de San José give a different impression: Maya people lived well at the site during the Late Classic period. For example, most structures were built with walls and roofs of stone, an architectural feature often identified with the elite class only (see Foias et al. 2012; Chapter 5).

Another unfortunate consequence of Marx's ideas about what he called the "Asiatic mode of production" is that until recently, most scholarship on political organization in ancient states focused on the role of paramount rulers as if they are the only ones with agency or political power. This view presents everyone else in antiquity as having a "herd mentality," as people who lacked self-reflection and were completely mystified by the elite ideologies of domination (Blanton and Fargher 2008, 7; see also Chapter 2). But archaeological, ethnohistorical, and ethnographic evidence point to the agency of all groups in human societies, albeit with different degrees of influence (Blanton and Fargher 2008, 7). Thus, we must credit ancient states with as much complexity as we can envision for ourselves today rather than as despotic systems with monolithic politics and economies. As we will see in the case of the Classic Maya and as other archaeologists and anthropologists have found in other civilizations of antiquity, political governments (or states) are not monolithic, operating with one mind and one voice, but rather are fractured into factions and subgroups that may have very different and competing discourses, goals, and intents (Yoffee 2005; Saitta 1994; Offner 1981; A. Smith 2000; see Chapters 5 and 6).

Although the extreme view that sees ancient states as characterized by "unrestricted exploitation of the masses, [and] terroristic methods of control" (Murdock 1957, 546 reflecting on Wittfogel 1957) is inaccurate, the opposite is just as unlikely, and this is the problem with some of the current models of agency theory. Although it may not be intentional, agency models give the impression that there was no exploitation in the past because everyone had less or more agency and therefore those who had less must have agreed to their loss of power (Pauketat 2000, 2007; but see other contributions in Dobres and Robb 2000).[3] This stance is a direct response to the exclusive focus of modernists on political economy and a model of top-down hierarchy in which the power of the state was omnipresent and all encompassing. The reality of the past is that systems were predominately neither hierarchical nor equal; the truth lies somewhere in between, depending on local circumstances and historical contingencies. There is no doubt that there was exploitation in the past, but not to the degree envisioned by advocates of the "Asiatic mode of production" (as shown by the evidence from Motul de San José; see Chapter 5 and 6). However, some institutions in ancient states gave access to political power to some groups more than to other groups, and in that sense, disadvantaged groups were "exploited" by the political elites and the political institutions (Whitmeyer 1997, 222), as we will investigate in several chapters. The role of the archaeologist is to discover how, where, and when power was practiced more inclusively or more exclusively. In this endeavor, though, we also have to be careful not to impose the dominant institutions of today's society on the past: As Mann reminds us, "State, culture, and economy are all important structuring networks, but they almost never coincide" (Mann 1986, 2).

Finally, one more point has to be made about the pre-Hispanic Maya people who populated the Classic period polities. McAnany's *Ancestral Maya Economies in an Archaeological Perspective* (2010) makes a critical point: Ancient Maya people were much more about doing (and being) and less about thinking. They were much less cerebral than us, in the sense that they would not spend most of their time thinking about human behavior, as we social scientists or students tend to do. They would embody their thoughts about how things are done in the way they conducted themselves daily. A second point in McAnany's work is important for non-anthropologists: the critical relationship between tradition, objects, and identity in every human culture. We as members of a modern capitalist and industrialized society often think of ourselves as separate from the objects we use, but what if we had made the objects we used by hand after long hours of labor?[4] Our identity would be much more tied to these objects and to the process of making them. These objects, be they shoes, clothing, hats, houses, would be part and parcel of "us" and our identity. What if the success of our work was likely only if we followed the prescribed or traditional way of doing it and only if we gained the blessings of the right gods? These traditions and rituals would become critical to our identity also. Instead of thinking of production as an economic process driven by calculations of efficiency and least effort (as we do in capitalist societies today), production would be craft work that shaped our identity, interwoven with ritual and tradition.

Extending this argument, all that human beings make (and that later archaeologists encounter as the archaeological record) is a series of discourses (about identity, power, ideology, etc.).[5] By deciding to do anything in a particular manner, each individual is asserting his or her power to do it. The archaeological record accumulates through such decisions and actions and such assertions of power to do something. Figurines are the discourses of their makers, pottery vessels are the discourses of their potters, painted polychrome vases and stone monuments are the discourses of their makers and patrons, the royal elites, and so on.

We can paint a rich picture of Classic Maya politics but it has to be done carefully by combining multiple lines of evidence and multiple discourses. We will need to shift between spatial scales, from small to large sites, and between time scales, from short term to long term, to bring to fruition the comparative approach that archaeologists have used so much and that has recently been championed by Brumfiel (2006) as the heart of anthropology today (see also Pyburn 1997). A point in time and space takes meaning if it is compared with another point in time or space: Patterns bring into relief differences over time and across space, and both similarities and differences are critical to reconstructing the lives of our predecessors.

Overview of Maya Civilization: Preclassic, Classic, and Postclassic

Maya civilization developed in Guatemala, Mexico, Belize, and Honduras in the eastern part of Central America, the part of the word that archaeologists refer to as Eastern Mesoamerica.[6] The Maya cultural heartland encompassed a number of different environments and ecologies, from the lowland and dry northern Yucatan Peninsula to the much more rainy forested southern Maya lowlands of northern Guatemala (the department of Peten) and Belize to the cooler highlands of Guatemala and Chiapas (and Honduras) to parts of the hot and fertile Pacific Coast of Guatemala (and neighboring Chiapas in Mexico to the north and coastal El Salvador to the south, all called the Soconusco area) (Figure 1.1; Table 1.1).

Although other parts of Mesoamerica were first occupied earlier in time (12000–10000 BC), evidence for human hunter-gatherers in the Maya lowlands (particularly, Belize) is dated to circa 5000–3400 BC (Zeitlin and Zeitlin 2000; Rosenswig and Masson 2001; Lohse 2010; Lohse et al. 2006; Hammond 2007). Microfossil and pollen studies (Pohl et al. 1996, 2007; Wahl et al. 2006) have revealed that initial burning of the forests in the southern Maya lowlands and the first appearance of maize and manioc co-occurred between 3000 and 2500 BC. However, no sedentary human settlements (or pottery) have been discovered for these first agriculturalists during the fourth or third millennium BC, and this remains a mystery. One possible explanation is that even though the earliest Maya were experimenting with agriculture, they may have maintained a highly mobile lifestyle. Another possible explanation is that climate and/or cultural changes may have erased or covered these earliest sites (Lohse et al. 2006, 210). Whatever the explanation, sedentism together with agriculture and pottery-making finally took root in the Maya lowlands between 1200 and 1000 BC, 600 years later than in other parts of Mesoamerica (Hammond 1991b, 2007; Lohse et al. 2006; Estrada-Belli 2011). Small to large villages appeared all over the southern Maya lowlands, including Colha, Cuello, K'axob, Blackwater Eddy and Cahal Pech in Belize and Tikal, Altar de Sacrificios, Ceibal, and central Peten lakes sites in Guatemala. Residents of these villages also made the first pottery of the Maya lowlands, but there are a number of styles (called Cunil, Swasey, Eb, and Xe), which show some cultural distinctions between the inhabitants of these zones (Ball and

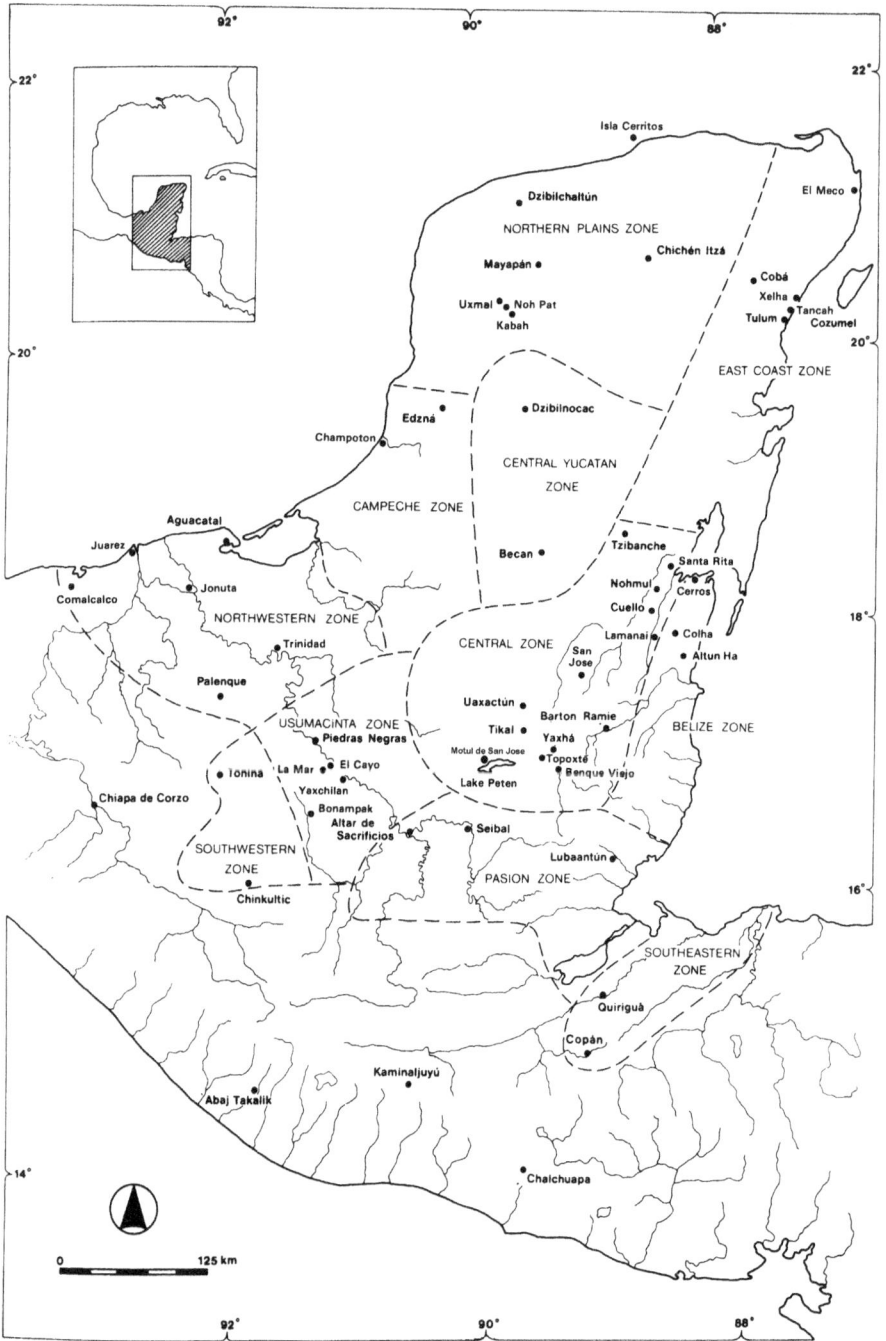

Figure 1.1. Map of the Maya region. After Willey 1986, Figure 2.1.

Taschek 2003; Cheetham 2005; Cheetham et al. 2003; Garber, Brown, and Hartman 2002; Garber et al. 2004; but see Lohse 2010).

Significant social, economic, and political inequality increased rapidly at specific sites, so that by 900–700 BC (or the beginning of the Middle Preclassic period), we see public architecture, including open raised platforms, temple-pyramids, astronomically associated E-Groups and ball courts at such sites as Komchen in northern Yucatan, Nakbe in northern Peten, and Kaminaljuyu in the southern Maya highlands, to name the most famous (Andrews and Robles 2004; Clark and Hansen 2001; Hansen 1998; Hatch 1997; Valdes and Hatch 1996).[7] For example, Nakbe had an 18-meter-high temple-pyramid by 600 BC and exhibited differential access to prestige goods and significant differences in residential mound sizes (Hansen 1998), all markers of considerable socioeconomic inequality and centralized control of human labor, typical features of chiefdoms (Clark and Hansen 2001). Excavations at Cival in eastern Peten also revealed the massive scale of plaza construction, which involved the leveling of a hilltop during the Middle Preclassic, circa 800 BC, a process that required over 1.3 million cubic meters of boulders (Estrada-Belli 2011, 75–77). Even though this type of construction is not as impressive or as visible as the temple pyramids of later times, it involved major amounts of human labor. In spite of these increasing social distinctions, pottery styles across the northern and southern Maya lowlands (the Mamom ceramic sphere) were much more similar than they had been in earlier time periods, suggesting a more unified cultural vision for all Maya sites.

The evolution of the first states marks the major transformation of the Late Preclassic period in the Maya region. Even though scholars have traditionally defined the onset of the Classic period with the appearance of the first Maya states, there is significant archaeological evidence for the emergence of the first cities, writing, and kingship in the last two centuries BC and the first two centuries AD. The site of El Mirador in northern Peten is without doubt the first city in the Maya region and was the capital of a Maya state. At 16 square kilometers and approximately 50,000 residents, it rivaled Late Classic Tikal in overall settlement and population size (Matheny 1987; Hansen 1990, 1994, 1998). Its two largest temple-pyramids, the Danta and Tigre Pyramids, rise 72 and 55 meters high, respectively (Hansen 1990; Matheny 1986, 1987), comparable in height to modern 18-story skyscrapers! The scale of these pyramids is incredible. For example, the Danta complex is larger than the combined size of the North Acropolis, the Central Acropolis, and Great Plaza of later Classic Tikal. Furthermore, many of these massive constructions were built in one phase. Ongoing excavations at the site and its periphery have led to increasing hints about its complexity. For example, field systems at the site were enriched with dark soil from the *bajos* (seasonal wetlands) surrounding El Mirador, and causeways connected the site with other centers such as Nakbe and Tintal, 12 and 18 kilometers away. We also have some clues about the possible causes of El Mirador's collapse at the end of the Preclassic. Massive use of stucco in construction to make 12-centimeter-thick floors and smooth surfaces on structural terraces and walls may have caused insurmountable deforestation (Hansen 1998; Hansen et al. 2002; Hansen et al. 2007; Wahl et al. 2006). The site was mostly abandoned by AD 150, but we need to further investigate the causes of its disintegration. While the production of stucco may have contributed, at the same time, climatic changes caused water sources in northern and eastern Peten to diminish, impacting agricultural systems in the *bajo* swamps surrounding El Mirador (Hansen et al. 2002; Wahl et al. 2006; Estrada-Belli 2011; Scarborough 1993).

Although El Mirador surpassed other settlements in size (and probably influence; see Clark et al. 2000), there are signs of similarly increasing complexity at other centers in the Maya lowlands, such as Tikal, Uaxactun, Cival, and San Bartolo in Peten, Guatemala; Lamanai and Cerros in Belize; Calakmul, Dzibilchaltun, and Komchen in the Yucatan Peninsula; and Kaminaljuyu, Izapa, and Takalik Abaj in the southern Maya highlands and coast. These sites also show monumental temple-pyramids (many decorated with giant stucco masks of different deities), stelae, the first hieroglyphs, and the iconographic symbols associated with Classic Maya rulership (such as the trilobed Jester God and the sign of *ajaw*, "lord") (Laporte and Fialko 1995; Valdes 1995; Estrada-Belli 2011; Pendergast 1981; Freidel 1986; Schele and Freidel 1990; Hatch 1997; Schieber de Lavarreda and Orrego Corzo 2001; Saturno 2006, 2009; Saturno, Stuart, and Beltran 2006; Houston and Inomata 2009). Although they are fragmentary and lack glyphs, Late Preclassic stelae include male figures that may be early rulers or deities, and their style and structure make them clear precursors to the Early Classic stone monuments that center on the images of kings.

The most remarkable recent discovery has been the murals at the site of San Bartolo in northeastern Peten, Guatemala. Dating to the first century BC, these brilliant polychrome murals present scenes dealing with the myth of the creation of the Maya cosmos, involving the Maize God and Hunahpu (one of the Hero Twins, the central characters of the Quiche origin mythology called the Popol Vuh written in the sixteenth century by Quiche Mayas; Tedlock 1986), bloodletting, and even the coronation of a human ruler or paramount god (Saturno 2006, 2009; Saturno, Taube, and Stuart 2005; Saturno, Stuart, and Beltran 2006). The sophistication of the cosmology (and glyphic writing) already present in these murals and their similarity to mythological scenes painted in the Postclassic Maya barkpaper book called the Dresden Codex and to the later Popol Vuh is remarkable: it shows cultural and religious continuity from the Late Preclassic into the Postconquest Colonial period, over almost 2,000 years.

The cultural splendor of the Late Preclassic states in the Maya lowlands was disturbed to some degree as some sites were abandoned, possibly as a domino effect of the collapse of the much larger El Mirador (Hansen et al. 2007; see also an excellent discussion of the Preclassic Maya civilization in Estrada-Belli 2011). However, certain sites benefited; Calakmul, Tikal, Holmul, Rio Azul, and other sites in central-eastern Peten and Campeche (zones that surrounded El Mirador) exploded in the Early Classic period (250–600 AD).

The Early Classic was as tumultuous as the earlier periods. One major political transformation was the centering of public art and writing on the ruler. While monumental art during the Late Preclassic generally depicted different deities[8] that were important in Maya cosmology (e.g., the Sun Jaguar God, the Venus God, and the Principal Bird Deity or Itzamnaaj)[9] as large-scale stucco masks on the facades of temple-pyramids, monumental art in the Early Classic shifted to stelae in which the kings are depicted emblazoned with symbols of supernaturals. These signs of change point to the centralization of the ruler's power: While his claim to power in the Late Preclassic was drawn entirely from the religious sphere, by the Early Classic, he had gained sufficient power that he could depict himself as the intercessor with these supernatural forces. Also noteworthy is that evidence for royal tombs in the Late Preclassic is rare, although this may be caused by the undersampling of such monumental contexts or by a pattern of burial in residences rather than in temples or pyramids (Houston and Inomata 2009; Hansen 1998; Estrada-Belli 2011, 55–64). There is no scarcity of rich royal tombs during the Early Classic period. The most famous ones are those located deep in the North Acropolis at Tikal and the looted painted tombs of Rio Azul (Coggins 1975; Martin and Grube 2008; Adams 1999; see also Krecji and Culbert 1995 for a discussion of Early Classic burials and the significant differentiation between elite and commoner interments that arose in the middle of the Early Classic). Both the art and the tomb evidence highlight that there was a qualitative change in the institution of Maya kingship from the Late Preclassic to the Early Classic. From that point on, Classic Maya art in the southern lowlands (and to a lesser degree in the northern lowlands) was all about the "doings" of the "rich and famous" (Miller 1999).

The role of Teotihuacan (a major city in central Mexico and possibly the capital of a highland Mexican empire; Smith and Montiel 2001; White et al. 2002) at Tikal, Copan, El Peru–Waka, La Sufricaya, Kaminaljuyu, and other Maya sites during the Early Classic has sparked an intense debate among Mesoamerican archaeologists (Braswell 2003; Stuart 2000; Estrada-Belli et al. 2009). The nature of the historical events remains unclear but the story begins with the arrival at Tikal on January 16 in AD 378 of a noble warrior named Sihyaj K'ahk' (Smoking Frog), who wore a costume reminiscent of the attire of Teotihuacan warriors and who had the title of *kaloomte'*, or "great king." On that same day, Tikal's king, Chak Tok Ich'aak I (or Great Jaguar Paw), died (Schele and Freidel 1990; Martin and Grube 2000, 2008; Estrada-Belli et al. 2009, 241). It is unlikely that this was pure coincidence, and thus most scholars attribute the death of Chak Tok Ich'aak I to Sihyaj K'ahk', the newly arrived "great king." However, we still don't know who the latter individual was or where he came from. Contact between the Maya and Teotihuacan civilizations occurred both before and after this day, as reflected in the adoption of the architectural style of Teotihuacan for some structures at certain Maya sites, the use of Teotihuacan symbols and ceramic forms at some Maya sites, and the importation of a few Teotihuacan prestige items (such as green obsidian, Thin Orange and stuccoed pottery, censers and figurines from Teotihuacan) (Demarest and Foias 1993). Scholars debate whether this contact was based on interaction among elites and emulation triggered by intense competition within and between Maya royal houses or whether it involved an actual conquest of Tikal by a Teotihuacan contingent led by Sihyaj K'ahk' (Braswell 2003; Demarest and Foias 1993; Stuart 2000; Estrada-Belli et al. 2009). The solution may be that Sihyaj K'ahk' was accompanying a contender to Tikal's throne, a child named Yax Nuun Ayiin I (or Curl Snout), who became the next ruler of the city (Braswell 2003; Martin and Grube 2000; Laporte and Fialko 1990; Estrada-Belli 2011, 122–26). Most important, though, there is no cultural fracture at Tikal; Yax Nuun Ayiin I married a Maya woman, and his son, Sihyaj Chan K'awiil (or Stormy Sky), became the next ruler and marked himself as the sixteenth dynast in a long line of Tikal kings (Martin and Grube 2000). Furthermore, stable strontium isotope analysis of the multiple skeletons of Burial 10 (the royal tomb of Yax Nuun Ayiin I) has revealed that they are all local individuals, not foreigners (Wright 2005).

There is also a connection between Copan, Tikal, and Teotihuacan. The founder of Copan's royal dynasty, K'ihnich Yax K'uk' Mo', is depicted on Altar Q (a monument that portrays the complete dynastic line of Copan with each ruler seated above his name in the order of his succession) with clear Teotihuacan symbols and is recorded as arriving in AD 426, possibly from Caracol (or via Tikal) (Estrada-Belli et al. 2009; Martin and Grube 2000; Stuart 2007). Stuart (2004) stresses the ritual significance of this arrival event, noting that the Copan artists recorded that he arrived from the "Place of the Reeds" (a mythical location) and was accompanied by the lightning god K'awiil, the patron god of Classic Maya kings.

Another issue with the Early Classic in the Maya lowlands is that artifacts from this period are not found at all sites that were occupied earlier in time. Some sites (e.g. Tikal, Uaxactun, and Holmul) have massive amounts of Early Classic construction, pottery, and other cultural remains, especially in central and eastern Peten, but other settlements seem to have been abandoned or retained and used ceramic styles of the previous Late Preclassic period. Whether this means that the Late Preclassic to Early Classic transition was marked by significant cultural disturbance remains to be resolved by further ceramic studies accompanied by more AMS radiocarbon dates.

The transition between the Early and Late Classic periods across the Maya region exhibits major continuities. Although pottery styles changed, and these are the critical archaeological markers of the onset of the Late Classic (AD 600–800), social, economic, and political institutions appear to have continued mostly unchanged. The Late Classic is the Golden Age of pre-Hispanic Maya civilization, with the most dense, most populous, and most complex cities; thousands of artistic masterpieces (large and small) in stone, clay, bone, stucco, and other materials; and thousands of hieroglyphic texts that have now been deciphered to reveal to us what the Maya world was like through the Mayas' own words (albeit from a very elite perspective) (see recent and excellent overviews in Houston and Inomata 2009; McAnany 2010; Houston, Stuart, and Taube 2006; McKillop 2004; Sharer and Traxler 2006).

Signs of increasing social, political, and economic complexity from the Early Classic to the Late Classic have come to the surface, but these may be due to larger-scale archaeological explorations of the latter time period and the impressive size of Late Classic cities and towns. The institution of kingship developed to its fullest as the Maya rulers of the Early Classic, named *ajaw,* became *k'uhul ajaw* (divine lords) in the Late Classic. Monuments and texts glorify these divine rulers and record their births, accessions, and deaths; their descent from gods in mythological time; their rituals of bloodletting, incense burning, and human sacrifice; and their conquests on the battlefield (Schele and Miller 1986; Schele and Freidel 1990; Freidel, Schele and Parker 1993; Miller and Martin 2004). Socioeconomic differences expanded as the palaces of the rulers of major cities encompassed whole complexes of courtyards and multistoried stone buildings such as the Central Acropolis at Tikal, the palace at Palenque, or the Caana Complex at Caracol. In contrast, farmers in small rural villages lived in small courtyards with houses made of adobe or perishable materials. A middle class of merchants, craft specialists, or low elites may have developed as A. Chase and D. Chase (1996) have suggested for Caracol in Belize. Although disagreements about the nature of Classic economies abound, scholars agree that markets probably existed, as they have been recently identified through archaeological and geochemical soil analyses at Chunchucmil, a major city dating mostly to the Early Classic in northwest Yucatan (Hutson et al. 2006; Dahlin and Ardren 2002; Dahlin et al. 2007, 2009); Sayil, in the Puuc area of northwest Yucatan (Smyth and Dore 1992, 1994; Smyth, Dore, and Dunning 1995); Calakmul (Carrasco Vargas, Vasquez Lopez, and Martin 2009; Boucher and Quiñones 2007); and Motul de San José and its port of Trinidad (Dahlin et al. 2009; Bair and Terry 2012).

The three centuries of the Late Classic also show a slow process of political fragmentation. The elite class grew in numbers and prerogatives as hieroglyphic texts and monuments that had previously been exclusively associated with Early Classic royals became more widespread, especially at the end of this time. More and smaller sites declared themselves independent seats of royal power with their own emblem glyphs (essentially symbols of political independence; see Chapter 4). The extensive noble class and the increasing number of royals must have felt intense competition as areas of possible expansion diminished over time and as warfare continued and intensified (Demarest 2004, 2006; Inomata 2007).

These political processes finally came to a head, causing the Classic Maya collapse in the southern Maya lowlands. We have to use the term "collapse" carefully because we do not see evidence of a complete abandonment and cultural dissolution (Aimers 2007; McAnany and Yoffee 2010; Demarest, Castillo, and Earle 2004). Rather, a great number of political centers and regions in the southern Maya lowlands were generally abandoned, but not all and not completely. For example, some sites such as Ceibal and Altar de Sacrificios in southwest Peten and Uxmal, Kabah, Sayil, and other Puuc sites in the northwest Peten flourished during the ninth to tenth centuries AD, the period generally identified as the Terminal Classic (AD 800–950). In Belize, Lamanai was never abandoned and continued into the Postclassic period (AD 950–1542). The northern Maya lowlands did not suffer such a collapse; although some sites (mostly in the Puuc region) were abandoned, others were founded and grew in the rest of the peninsula.

The Classic Maya "collapse" did not happen suddenly; it was an uneven domino-like dissolution that took place over a century or two. The long duration of the collapse disproves theories that involve sudden epidemics or earthquakes. The collapse entailed the disintegration of the general political system in place during the Classic period—divine kingship and the elaborate rituals and constructions that sustained it. There is little consensus about the causes of the Maya collapse in the southern lowlands. Demarest (2004, 2006) and others support social causes for this political disintegration, while others point to environmental change and degradation, including droughts and/or deforestation, as the primary forces (Gill 2000; see also discussion in Aimers 2007, Lucero 2002). The reason why we cannot point to one cause is that different factors contributed to collapse in the distinct zones of the lowlands. Drought and deforestation may have been important in some regions (such as Copan and Calakmul) but not in all (see the absence of evidence for deforestation or declining health status among Petexbatun populations in Wright and White 1996; Wright 2006). In several recent contributions, Aimers (2007), Demarest et al. (2004), and Lopez Varela and Foias (2005) provide a comprehensive overview of the variability and complexity of the processes involved in the collapse across the Maya lowlands.

Although the southern Maya lowlands were not completely abandoned, the center of activity and power shifted to the northern Maya lowlands and southern Maya highlands during the Postclassic.[10] It is possible that population movements from the southern Maya lowlands into the Yucatan and highlands were part of this transition, as myths about migrations by different ethnic groups are common among the Postclassic Mayas (see, for example, the migrations of the Peten Itza in Jones 1998; Rice and Rice 2009). Furthermore, rapid population growth at both Uxmal and Chichen Itza in Yucatan support such migrations (Dunning 1992; Schmidt 2007).

Two Yucatan cities appear to have dominated the politics of the Postclassic (Chichen Itza and Mayapan), although other sizeable centers in the northern lowlands flourished from the Terminal Classic to the Postclassic (including the Puuc centers and Ek Balam, Coba, and Dzibilchaltun). Chichen Itza became the dominant city from the end of the Late Classic–Terminal Classic (AD 750–950) through the Early Postclassic (AD 950–1100) (Milbrath and Peraza Lope 2003; Kowalski and Kristan-Graham 2007; Cobos 2004), although it was in competition with the other major cities mentioned above (Ringle et al. 2004; Cobos 2004).[11] Traditionally archaeologists thought that Mayapan followed Chichen Itza by a century or so, but recent excavations at Mayapan and chronological reinterpretations of the ethnohistorical documents have pushed the occupation of this site back to the eleventh century AD, thus contemporary with the collapse of Chichen Itza (Milbrath and Peraza Lope 2003; Masson, Hare, and Peraza Lope 2006).

A great deal of debate has surrounded Chichen Itza because of similarities in architecture, art, and layout with the highland Mexican city of Tula (generally placed between AD 900 and 1200) and because of references in ethnohistorical documents written after the Spanish Conquest to the conquest of Chichen Itza by the foreign Itzas and Toltec warriors (Thompson 1970; Schele and Freidel 1990). This interpretation of Chichen Itza as Tula's outpost has been revised by more recent archaeological excavations since the 1980s (for syntheses, see Kowalski and Kristan-Graham 2007; and Boot 2005). Chichen Itza is now seen as a cosmopolitan city that had far-ranging relationships, including with Tula, and therefore produced architecture and art that were more international than the art and architecture of the previous Late Classic period. Furthermore, Mayapan (AD 1050–1100 to 1450), which is often named as an example of the "decadent" Maya culture during the Late Postclassic, is now described as exhibiting innovative art styles similar to the art of Chichen Itza for similar reasons. Milbrath and Peraza Lope (2003) write that "newly discovered murals and sculptures reveal Mayapan's role at the crossroads of cultural contact between the Central Mexican and Mayan areas" (1).[12] Kowalski (2007) suggests that the use of foreign symbols in Terminal Classic to Postclassic Yucatan centers is due to political forces. New elites appear to have founded these cities in the aftermath of the collapse of the southern Maya states and to have searched for new symbols of power as a way of legitimating themselves.

Political structures also shifted during the Postclassic. While Classic Maya art extolled the political and ritual power of one individual, the *k'uhul ajaw*, or "divine ruler," who also built massive temple-pyramids, Postclassic rulers are rarely depicted in art and are even more rarely named, and monumental construction diminished. Instead, large, open, colonnaded halls that hosted reunions of elite lineages or lineage councils were preferred, and Postclassic art became a compendium of humans, gods, processions, warriors, and battles and rarely centered on one larger-than-life ruler (see more discussion in Ringle and Bey 2001; Kowalski 2007; Milbrath and Peraza Lope 2003; and Chapters 4 and 5). The absence of elaborate tombs at Mayapan and Chichen Itza supports this theory of a political shift (Schele and Freidel 1990; Schmidt 2007). Even though there may have been a paramount ruler, elite lineages or houses counterbalanced his power through councils (see more discussion in Chapters 5 and 6).

Although Chichen Itza and Mayapan may have been contemporary, they were not friendly with each other. Instead, there is evidence (albeit ambiguous evidence) that these cities were enemies. The Books of Chilam Balam of Mani state that the ruler of Mayapan, Hunac Ceel, fought and defeated the ruler of Chichen Itza, Chac Xib Chac (Roys 1967, 177–79), but it is unclear when this occurred: "Many scholars now place [the event] . . . early in Mayapan's history and contemporary with Chichen Itza's decline" (Milbrath and Peraza Lope 2003, 37). If this dating is correct, it argues that the fall of Chichen Itza was caused by Mayapan, but since both sites were dominated by Itza families, the political upheaval was an internal struggle between competing "blue-blood" families. Milbrath and Peraza Lope hypothesize that the original founders of Mayapan may have included three groups: Maya groups from Yucatan's east coast, Xius from western Yucatan, and a small contingent from Chichen Itza (38).

Warfare permeates Terminal Classic to Postclassic art in the northern Maya lowlands more than in the south during earlier times (Ringle et al. 2004, 506–11). At Chichen Itza, murals and carvings show battles in progress or processions of warriors. For example, the dozens of warriors carved on the stone columns that allowed entrance into the Temple of the Warriors record processions following victories by Chichen's army (Schele and Freidel 1990) and murals in the Upper Temple of the Jaguars and in Las Monjas show sieges of walled settlements (Ringle et al. 2004). At Mayapan, skeletal figures, some with niches where human skulls would have been placed, have been recently uncovered on an earlier temple within the Castillo, the largest pyramid at the site (Milbrath and Peraza Lope 2003). Defensive perimeter walls are also more common in the northern Maya lowlands; they have been found at Ek Balam, Uxmal, Chichen Itza, Mayapan, Tulum, Yaxuna, Cuca, Chacchob, and Muna, among others (Ringle et al. 2004; Webster 1978; Kurjack and Garza T. 1981), and although their function is not completely clear (Ringle et al. 2004), they may suggest that Postclassic Maya society was increasingly bellicose (Schele and Freidel 1990). The flourishing traffic in slaves (see below) during the Postclassic may be one impetus for this escalation in militarism.

Economic pursuits also appear to be more at the forefront in the Postclassic at Chichen Itza and Mayapan, leading to suggestions that these cities were part of a world system that encompassed most of Mesoamerica during the Postclassic (Kepecs et al. 1994; Kowalski 2007). Chichen Itza was connected to the port of Isla Cerritos and the salt flats along the north coast of Yucatan Peninsula (Andrews et al. 1988), and a similar control over salt production has been suggested for Mayapan (Tozzer 1941; Andrews 1983; Milbrath and Peraza Lope 2003). The white salt produced on these north coast flats was especially desired by the Aztecs (Kepecs et al. 1994). Apart from salt, the Yucatan Peninsula was famous for a number of other goods or raw materials that were highly prized by the rest of Mesoamerica, including blue pigment (found only in the zone of Mayapan), honey, cotton, and slaves (Milbrath and Peraza Lope 2003, 30; Kepecs, Feinman, and Boucher 1994, 149; Tozzer 1941). Both Chichen Itza and Mayapan have revealed evidence of foreign imports from afar, such as obsidian from Veracruz, highland Guatemala, western Mexico, and central Mexico; metalwork from Michoacan; turquoise discs from northwestern Mexico; Tohil Plumbate from highland and coastal western Guatemala; jadeite from eastern Guatemala; and cultural influences from central Mexico (Toltec, Aztec), Oaxaca (Mixteca-Puebla), and eastern Yucatan (Milbrath and Peraza Lope 2003; Kowalski and Kristan-Graham 2007; Cobos 2007; Braswell 1997). As a matter of fact, the cause of the collapse and burning of Mayapan around AD 1430–50 was trade: Bishop Diego de Landa writes that Mayapan was burned and abandoned when the Xiu nobles rebelled against the dominant Cocom rulers; the Cocoms were accused of desiring more wealth through trade with the "Mexicans" (presumably Aztecs) through their allies the Canuls (or "Mexicans"), whom they brought in from Tabasco and Xicalango, a known Aztec trade center and garrison, probably located at the western end of the Laguna de Terminos, Campeche (Tozzer 1941, 32, 36; Scholes and Roys 1968). Thus, Mayapan and probably Chichen Itza were international cities where multiple languages were spoken, including Chol Maya, Yucatec Maya, and probably the Nahuatl language of the Aztecs (Milbrath and Peraza Lope 2003). After Mayapan was burned, the noble families returned to their original provinces or territories, where the Spanish conquistadores encountered them in the sixteenth century. The

Cocoms lived in Sotuta, the Cupuls in the territory around Chichen Itza, the Chels (a third powerful aristocratic family) in the province called Ah Kin Chel, the Tutul Xius at Mani, and so forth (Roys 1957, 1943).

Although Chichen Itza and Mayapan were not unique in size or population, they are seen as special cities in the Postclassic history of Yucatan because they exercised some dominance over parts or most of the northern lowlands (Ringle et al. 1998, 2004; Kepecs, Feinman, and Boucher 1994). How they were able to become such dominant capitals is still debated. Some (e.g., Ringle, Gallereta Negrón, and Bey 1998) see the religious role of Chichen Itza as a pilgrimage and cult center for a new international religion centered on the Feathered Serpent (Quetzalcoatl in Nahuatl, and Kukulcan in Maya) as critical:

> Chichén asserted itself as a transcendent spiritual center. . . . Such ideological authority is one way in which claims of Itzá dominion in Yucatan may be understood, as exerting not direct political control but rather conveying legitimacy and, not incidentally, access to the riches confirming authority. Chichén's increasing success as the fount of legitimacy directly challenged the basis for monumental architecture elsewhere, and one by one these [other centers] . . . were abandoned. (Ringle et al. 2004, 513–14)

Other archaeologists stress the economic role of both Chichen Itza and Mayapan in long-distance pan-Mesoamerican trade networks (Andrews 1990; Freidel 1986; Kepecs, Feinman, and Boucher 1994), but as Ringle and colleagues state above, these two roles may have been intertwined. For example, the island of Cozumel, off the east coast of Yucatan, served such a double duty when the Spanish arrived in the sixteenth century: it was both a well-known trade center, where large canoes heavy with trade goods stopped on their way around the peninsula, and a religious pilgrimage center that was home to a famous oracle.

The Spanish Conquest of the Maya region occurred in several waves known as entradas. Instead of envisioning the Conquest as a rapid event, we now see these multiple entradas, which covered some 20 years, and the continued resistance by some Maya groups over the next centuries as a slower process (Restall 1998, 2003). The Spanish left us important records from their conquest of Central America. Among these, the most famous are Cortes's account of his travels through the southern Maya lowlands (Cortes 1908) and Bishop Diego de Landa's *Relaciones de las Cosas de Yucatan* (Tozzer 1941). The Mayas themselves preserved their histories in the

Books of Chilam Balam that were written in a number of cities in Yucatan (Chumayel, Mani, Tizimin, and so on) and in other types of records and accounts, such as the Popol Vuh, that describes the origins, myths, and history of the Quiche Mayas who flourished in the Guatemalan highlands during the Postclassic (Tedlock 1986). Unfortunately, these varied sources do not always agree, and some give no dates or different dates for Maya historical events (Milbrath and Peraza Lope 2003).

Early explorations of the Yucatan peninsula by the Spaniards Francisco Hernandez de Cordoba and Juan de Grijalva in the first two decades of the sixteenth century revealed impressive cities that were comparable to Seville, but the explorers had little luck in establishing a foothold as the local Mayas resisted them (Restall 1998). Because of the failure of these early explorations, the next attempts began in the northwestern part of Yucatan. These, called the first and second entradas, in 1527–28 and 1531–34, respectively, failed (Restall 1998, 9–13). Not until the third entrada in the early 1540s were the Spanish able to gain control in the northern Maya lowlands, where they established the Spanish town of Merida in 1542 (Restall 1998, 2003). By this time, European diseases that the conquistadores brought had already swept through the Maya region, killing thousands (Jones 1989, 1998; Restall 1998, 2003). The fragmentation of the Yucatan peninsula into small kingdoms after Mayapan's collapse also did not help because the Mayas could not present a unified front against the Spanish. Thus, the Spanish found willing allies among the native states, some of which fought alongside the conquistadores against other Maya kingdoms (Restall 1998).

Definitions of Political Systems, Political Organization, and Political Power

Because politics take center stage in this book, it is useful to define that concept here, although more detailed treatment of political power follows in Chapter 2. Some scholars consider all of human society to be political because power is always at play and in action. However, this definition does not make it a particularly useful concept, and for this reason, I restrict my definition of politics to the political system or the government and its office holders, the use and manipulation of political power by these office holders, and the encounters with and resistance to the political system by those who do not hold political offices. I prefer to frame the discussion of ancient politics following several different perspectives, including Rice's focus on the political system, Wolf's search for the forces and processes behind the political structure, Wolf's and Mann's emphasis on struggles among factions and individuals, and Dobres and Robb's concern for all individuals and their role in ancient politics.

Prudence Rice (2004) has recently defined the political system of a complex society as "1. its *structures*: a. an administrative or organizational sector, usually hierarchical, of policy- or decision-making roles, and b. a 'political' sector where decisions are made and competition for power takes place; and also 2. its *functions*: rules and sanctions that implement policy, maintain societal order, and safeguard territorial sovereignty" (5).

In contrast, Eric Wolf (1964) defines the political as "the struggle of social groups and their dynamic accommodation to one another, and, implicitly, of the emergence, distribution, and containment of power in a system" (61). He argues that if we are to understand politics, primacy must be given to "the forces generating the [political] processes" rather than to the political structure because structure "becomes a temporary accommodation to these forces, which extend their pressures from within or from without the system" (65). He also warns that political power "is not a seamless web of domination but [is] a panoply of processes of varying intensity and scope" (Wolf 1999, 61). Wolf stresses the intertwined nature of power and symbolism because "great collective social myths . . . serve to draw large strata of the population toward collective goals" (1964, 77). In a similar vein, Mann (1986) argues that if we conceive of society as "multiple overlapping and intersecting sociospatial networks of power," the "central problems [of power] concern *organization, control, logistics, communication*—the capacity to organize and control people, materials, and territories, and the development of this capacity throughout history" (2–3; Mann's italics). Thus, for Mann, power requires an infrastructure and scholars can study power through an analysis of the organization of this political infrastructure (10).

Another way to conceive of ancient politics is to begin with the individual rather than with structure or process: Politics can be conceived as the individual's experience of political power and his or her contributions to, support for, or reaction against power. Here I take my cue from Barth's words: "Instead of seeing political organization in the traditional anthropological manner as an 'institution,' based on rules and norms and defined by its function for society, I wanted to describe it as an outcome of the choices and alignments made by its participants" (Barth 2007, 3). Questions that need to be explored are the degree of individual agency (Dobres and Robb 2000): Can a person act as he or she wishes? Does he or she have choices of action? How restricted are these choices by structure and process, be it kinship, neighborhood, community, religion, wealth, status, or competition for political power? Although we may not be able to answer all these questions with archaeological evidence, they should be among our concerns about the past.

Rather than restricting our perspective on ancient politics to one of these definitions, I endeavor to present aspects of all in the following chapters, as I reconstruct ancient Maya political dynamics. Politics were as dynamic in the past as they are today. They were fragmented and constantly in flux as different individuals, institutions, groups, and communities pursued their own goals. My last caveat is that the chapters that follow are to be taken not as the final statement on ancient Maya politics but as the foundation for asking new questions. I hope nevertheless that the following chapters will illustrate that we know much about Classic Maya politics when all the threads of evidence are drawn together.

Notes

1. De Montmollin (1995) correctly takes exception to the idea that Marcus's theory is applicable to the Classic Maya lowlands. He doesn't feel that we see periods of consolidation alternating with periods of fragmentation over the *longue durée* of Maya civilization. He argues that instead, we see "a linear increase through time in the numbers of centers and city-states . . . in Protoclassic through Late-Terminal Classic" (261). He argues that probably small and large states appeared together during the Classic period in separate regions or even in the same region (262), and I agree with him (see extended discussion in Chapter 4).

2. The Asiatic mode of production refers to a vision of ancient states as characterized by exploitative and despotic rulers who controlled a centralized government, obedient commoners, and all land. In essence, this theory argues that the economy was under the complete control of a despot (Murdock 1957, 546; Wittfogel 1957; Offner 1981, 1981; Blanton and Fargher 2008).

3. I agree with Pauketat (2000) and Joyce (2004) that when social scientists examine the reasons for the evolution of complex societies (such as chiefdoms and states), we assign too much intentionality to long-term processes when in reality, the human agents who made changes in their daily practices would not have had in mind such long-term objectives or consequences. Thus, to understand the rise of inequality, we need to focus on daily practices of human agents rather than on the intentions of individuals to form reified proto-institutions that later become states governments.

4. This does not deny that some members of our society are strongly attached to "objects" or "things," so much so that they become packrats or hoarders.

5. Discourse is a presentation of an individual's ideas of how the world should be in an attempt to achieve such a world. This definition of discourse is an expansion of other

scholars' definition of ideology. Miller and Tilley (1984) define ideology as "the representation of the world held by the dominant group" (10). Wolf (1999) writes that ideology is "a complex of ideas selected to underwrite and represent a particular project of installing, maintaining, and aggrandizing power in social relationships" (55). Scott (1990) broadens this definition by arguing that nondominant groups also have their own ideologies and their own discourses. Discourse is more appropriate here because unlike ideology, its use does not imply that all members of a society share it or agree with it. Thus, several discourses may appear in a society, and these discourses may be in agreement or in disagreement with each other.

6. Mesoamerica is a culture area that stretches from central Mexico to central Honduras and northwestern Costa Rica. Within this area, societies have interacted over thousands of years to such a degree that they share many core cultural principles.

7. An E-Group is an architectural complex consisting of a pyramid on the west side of the plaza and an elongated rectangular platform with three small superstructures on the east side of the plaza.

8. Some Late Preclassic stelae include images of early "rulers," but there is some debate whether these are human or supernatural. Estrada-Belli (2011) sees these Late Preclassic stelae, such as Cival Stela 2, as portraying early historical rulers in all the finery and symbolism that is typical of Classic Maya kings. In the San Bartolo murals there is even a coronation scene, albeit a small one (Hammond 2007), but it is unclear if the crowned "ruler" is a human or the Maize God.

9. Estrada-Belli (2011, 84–110) presents an excellent overview of the iconography of these Late Preclassic stucco friezes of deities found throughout the Maya lowlands.

10. Coastal Belize and the Central Peten Lakes also remained vibrant during the Postclassic. In addition, some centers in the northern Maya lowlands suffered collapse and abandonment, such as Ek Balam (Ringle et al. 2004).

11. One clue that Chichen Itza was competing with these centers is that its pottery (called Sotuta) is restricted to its environs and areas it controlled (such as Isla Cerritos off the north coast of Yucatan), while the rest of the Yucatecan sites produced slightly different pottery types, called the Cehpech ceramic sphere (Lincoln 1986; Robles and Andrews 1986; Ringle et al. 2004).

12. Newly discovered murals and sculptures show scenes and individuals that are highly similar to three of the four surviving Maya codices that were painted in Yucatan at different moments during the Postclassic and that survived the Conquest: the Dresden Codex, the Paris Codex, and the Madrid Codex (Milbrath and Peraza Lope 2003, 40).

2

|||||||||||||

Political Anthropology, Archaeology, and Ancient Politics

Archaeological studies of political organization draw paradigms, models, and concepts from political anthropology in order to describe, define, and understand ancient politics in a broad cross-cultural perspective (Kurtz 2001; Claessen and Skalnik 1978, 1981; Claessen and van de Velde 1987, 1991; Claessen, van de Velde, and Smith 1985; Claessen and Oosten 1996; Roscoe 1993; Haas 2001a, 2001b; Vincent 1990). In this chapter, I describe how political anthropologists have approached political power and how their approaches have influenced archaeology. Political anthropology has moved from earlier paradigms of political evolution and political economy to the functional and processual-action[1] paradigms of the early and mid-twentieth century, and finally, to the postmodern approach (Kurtz 2001; Vincent 1990).

Political power within ancient complex societies has come to be seen as fragmentary and as fluid as in today's modern states. Rather than conceiving of elites as the only power holders in ancient societies, anthropologists and archaeologists now argue that all members of a society have some power, even if they have less than the rulers and the political elite. Because power is not considered to be a static quantity that is held by elites only, it is seen as relational and conflictive; leaders and followers are constantly engaged in a virtual tug of war. Legitimacy and authority are at the heart of the relationship between leaders and followers, and recent explorations of political power have moved away from studies of the economic foundations of ancient governments to the study of the ideational means by which rulers, leaders, and governments persuaded their followers to support them. The key to ancient political dynamics was the degree to which ways of establishing legitimacy and maintaining power succeeded or failed.

Current political anthropology also draws attention to political ritual as the locus where power was materialized and embodied. In ancient societies, as Kertzer (1988) underlines, political reality and people's power relations were constructed by and through rituals.

After briefly summarizing the different approaches to political power that predominate in political anthropology, I hope to make several points in this chapter: first, that political power has multiple sources and that to understand how it works, we need to explore the specific sources used in the society under scrutiny; second, that political power is based on the contested relationship between leaders and followers and that political actors will actively pursue strategies that strengthen this relationship; third, that political power is also formed through cooperation and alliance and that "power to" (an individual's ability to do what he or she wants) may be in tension with "power over" (the ability of some to get others to do their bidding) (Miller and Tilley 1984); fourth, these dynamics find form in rituals, discourses, and ideologies promoted by the different active political factions and/or political institutions in any society.

Paradigms of Political Anthropology

Two paradigms that dominated political anthropology at its inception and that continue to flourish in modern archaeology are political economy and political evolution (Service 1975; Fried 1967, 1978; Sahlins 1972; Trigger 1998; Donham 1999; Wolf 1999). Although political theory in cultural anthropology has moved in the direction of both the symbolic and the interstitial workings of power, these two schools of thought have remained very influential in archaeology, providing the theoretical impetus for a predominantly materialist perspective on the past (Conrad and Demarest 1984).

Political economy remains by far the most successful concept in the field. Its central principle addresses how human labor and its products satisfy human needs and wants and how power relations affect the use of resources (Kurtz 2001, 113–31). At its heart, though, the concept of political economy explores the nature of the involvement of state governments in the economic process through political control over production and distribution in order to sustain itself (ibid., 14; Fried 1967; Claessen and van de Velde 1991; Smith 1991). There has also been increasing attention to how political agents even in stateless societies use control over production or exchange to advance their goals and gain more power (Polanyi 1957; Polanyi, Arensberg, and Pearson 1957; Sahlins 1963, 1972; Wolf 1999; Donham

1999). The world-systems model proposed by Wallerstein (1974, 1980, 1989) and modifications of this model to precapitalist societies (Kardulias 1999; Stein 1999; Hall 1997, 1998, 1999; Hall and Chase-Dunn 1993, 1994; Chase-Dunn and Hall 1997; Chase-Dunn and Grimes 1995) remain dominant in studies of political economy. At the same time, Marxist analyses of modes of production that engendered the debates over substantivism versus formalism[2] (Terray 1971; Godelier 1978; Meillasoux 1981; Bloch 1983; Polanyi 1957; Wolf 1982) and cultural Marxism (Taussig 1980, 1987; Godelier 1988; Donham 1999; Kurtz 1996b) have influenced many other studies in political economy. In archaeology, the political economy paradigm has engendered broad studies of regional and/or site-specific economic patterns and of the role of elites in economic systems (Masson and Freidel 2002; Smith and Schreiber 2005, 2006; see Chapter 3 for specific examples). Although all these approaches have made significant contributions, they view political institutions through the lens of the economic structure, so they devote less attention to the details of how political power is manipulated, contested, and reshaped by active human actors or factions (with rare exceptions, e.g. Kurtz 2001, 128–31, Brumfiel 1983). Considerations of political economy provide a useful perspective on political power because they show the movement of economic goods and/or human labor from all members of society to the upper ranks, but they do not give the whole picture.

The second dominant paradigm, political evolution, considers the changes in political systems through time as societies become more populous and more differentiated economically and socially. Studies that focus on political evolution have often paid close attention to political centralization (Feinman 2001; Roscoe 1993) and to differentiation and specialization of political-administrative roles (Flannery 1972). The concept of political evolution has also been tightly integrated with classifications of political systems that began with Morgan's and Tyler's unilineal trajectory of savagery, barbarism, and civilization (which Boas and his students rejected at the turn of the twentieth century). Since the rejection of Morgan's stages, theories of political evolution have identified multilineal evolutionary paths of change from egalitarian political systems such as bands and tribes to more complex ranked or stratified systems such as chiefdoms and states (Haas 2001b; Service 1962, 1975; Steward 1955, 1956; Fried 1967). However, the rather monolithic views of political power held by those who subscribe to versions of the political evolution paradigm and their implicit or explicit typologies of political systems have been criticized for being too simplistic and for devaluing significant differences among the cultures grouped within the same evolutionary type (Feinman and Neitzel 1984; Shanks and Tilley 1987; Trigger 1998; Haas 2001a, 2001b; Kurtz 2001; Smith 2003; Chapman 2003, 42–45; Yoffee 2005; Pauketat 2007; Vincent 1990). Furthermore, an emphasis on a static political structure rather than on the "practices of political agents" (Kurtz 2001, 16; Roscoe 1993; Donham 1999) has hindered this school of thought from explaining more fully the societal transformations of the past.

The political evolution model has also been critiqued for its adherence to functionalist assumptions. The functionalist paradigm that emerged from the work of Malinowski, Radcliffe-Brown, and other British social anthropologists in the first half of the twentieth century envisioned human societies as well-integrated social systems consisting of structures or institutions that function together to maintain the stability of each society and the well-being of all its members (Malinowski 1961; Radcliffe-Brown 1965). In contrast to the functionalist paradigm, more recent perspectives have tended to view states as fluid and fractured entities that are characterized by competition and conflict among different socioeconomic classes, groups, and factions, "formed through differential and constantly shifting patterns of cooperation and competition among emergent elites and other groups" (Stein 1998, 6; see also Brumfiel 1992; Cowgill 1977, 1993). Although the functionalist model has been discarded, it had a significant impact on the last century of research (Kurtz 2001) and continues to be of some descriptive utility in archaeology that is concerned with discerning the functions of the artifacts, buildings, and sites that we encounter.

In the 1960s, the functionalist paradigm was replaced by processual-action models that shifted attention from the political structure to individual political agents whose strategies in the competition for power transformed the static political system of the functionalist school into a dynamic system of alliances, conflicts, and tensions (Swartz, Turner, and Tuden 1966; Barth 1959; Bailey 1969; Kurtz 2001; Donham 1999; Brumfiel and Fox 1994; Vincent 1990). The processual-action models of political anthropology should not be confused with the processual school in archaeology, because its principles are closer to postprocessualism in archaeology. Bailey (1969), one of the political anthropologists who promoted the processual model, argued that the political structure should be seen not as a set of static, functional positions but as a series of flexible rules that guided the "political game," or competition for political power among active political agents, leaders, and factions (see Sewell 1992 for a similar treatment of "structure"). Vincent (1990) distinguishes between action theory and processual theory, although both theories emphasize the individual agent, conflict, tensions, and fractures. While the processual model considers political process as it unfolds in the interactions between "groups, roles, ideals and ideas" (Turner quoted in Vincent 1990, 336–37), action theory is about "individual actors and their strategies within political arenas" (Vincent 1990, 341).

The centrality of political agents and individual action in the political anthropology of the 1960s and 1970s remains at the core of political anthropology and postprocessual archaeology today (Bourdieu 1977, 1990; Giddens 1979, 1984; see also Roscoe 1993; Brumfiel 1992; Cowgill 1993; Haas 2001b; Dobres and Robb 2000). For example, practice theory as proposed by Bourdieu (1977, 1990) converges on the mutually determinative nature of the relationship between the actions or practices of political agents and the political structures of the larger community. Agents are constrained by political rules of the larger community, but their actions also influence and change political structures (Sewell 1992; see also Kurtz 2001, 149–57). According to this view of political action, political systems are fluid and are continuously reconstituted by the practices of competing or allied political agents (or factions), even though human actions are framed and constrained by the political structure itself and by their natural environments (Kurtz 2001; Brumfiel 1992; Cowgill 1993; Dobres and Robb 2000; Pauketat 2007; Sewell 1992).[3] Although political anthropologists currently center their research on the interstitial arenas between formal political institutions (Vincent 1990), archaeologists have stayed close to the more visible political institutions in their exploration of ancient politics.

Thus, the most recent foci of political anthropology have been the fluidity of political power, the heterogeneity and conflictive nature of human societies and political structures, the importance of symbolic ways to negotiate conflicts, and the relational nature of power as it permeates all human relations (Miller and Tilley 1984; Foucault 1978a, 1978b; Wolf 1999; Fleisher and Wynne-Jones 2010; O'Donovan 2002a). Postprocessual approaches in archaeology and anthropology have also shed light on "the association of power and personal identity . . . particularly as they are constructed through symbolic meanings and movements of the body through space and the landscape" (O'Donovan 2002b, 28; Tilley 1994).

Political Power and Sources of Power

All theories that attempt to explain the nature of political systems must come to terms with the concept of "power," which has proven slippery for political anthropologists, sociologists, political scientists, and philosophers alike (Kurtz 2001; Wolf 1990, 1999; Foucault 1979, 1991; Mann 1986; O'Donovan 2002a). The simplest definition is Weber's: the ability to make others do one's will (Weber 1964 [1947], 152). Kurtz (2001) astutely asks "what . . . attribute provides some with the capacity to force others to do things"? (22). According to Kurtz and many other scholars, it is control over resources, both *material* (or *allocative*, to use Giddens's terminology) and *ideational* (*symbolic*, or *authoritative*, to use Bourdieu's and Giddens's terms, respectively) (Lasswell and Kaplan 1950; Earle 1997, 2004; Kurtz 2001; Miller and Tilley 1984; Rice 2009, 73; Bourdieu 1990; Giddens 1984; Foucault 1978a, 1978b, 1979). Mann (1986) echoes Kurtz's definition of power: "the ability to pursue and attain goals through mastery of one's environment." Based on this definition, Mann states that power should be seen as a "generalized means" to attain one's goals (6). Following Giddens (1979, 91) and Mann (1986, 6), Stein (1998) argues that "although power is a very abstract, volatile, and fluid phenomenon, it can be studied through an analysis of its sources, media, and effects" (6).

Mann (1986) identifies four sources of (social) power: ideological, economic, military, and political relationships (2; see also the discussion of Mann's ideas in Whitmeyer 1997). Earle (1997) distinguishes four sources of political power: ideological, economic, military, and social (also see Earle 1991). Finally, Giddens (1981) recognizes four types of power institutions: symbolic orders or modes of discourse, economic institutions, a legal system or modes of sanction or repression,[4] and political institutions. Mann's, Earle's and Giddens's categories can be subsumed under Kurtz's more general classification of material and ideational power (see also Blanton et al. 1996, 3).

Foucault (1978a, 1978b, 1979) sees power present in all social actions and relationships as an all-permeating "force" that defines the most basic ways we see the world and our role in it. This view of power as a diffuse resource is not very useful for understanding how ancient states controlled people and how people affected states. Wolf's (1999) envisioning of power is of more utility here, in particular his definition of structural power: "the power to deploy and allocate social labor" or "the power manifest in relationships that not only operates within settings and domains but also organizes and orchestrates the settings themselves, and that specifies the direction and distribution of energy flows" (5). Mann (1986) also makes a distinction between *diffuse power* (where Foucault's interest lies) and *authoritative power* that is "actually willed by groups and institutions . . . [and]

comprises definite commands and conscious obedience" (8). My interest in ancient Maya politics focuses on authoritative power or the sphere of political power consciously wielded by human individuals, groups, and communities rather than on Foucault's concept of power as something that is diffuse and omnipresent.

Scholars are interested in establishing the foundations of political power, whether the source is material or ideational or both. Material sources of political power include human supporters or followers and tangible resources (such as land, money, cattle, pigs, etc.). Elites can attempt to control land, natural resources, or food sources of particular importance for production or exchange, or the means of production. The decision of which resources to control varies among different societies, depending on a number of factors, and archaeologists can reconstruct material sources of power by recognizing which economic pursuits elites are intervening in as reflected in the productive activities that took place in elite households.

Ideational sources of power include symbols, ideology, ritual practices, moral codes, and information or knowledge (Mann 1986, 22–23). Control of ideas may take many forms: political leaders may control symbols or the exchange of information or access to the supernatural domain. Kurtz (2001) argues that ideational resources were critical because they helped "leaders to convince others of the legitimacy of their authority" and because they promoted "perceptions that the government is just, is concerned with the well-being of its citizens, and protects them from their enemies" (31, 35–36). Ideational resources create emotional as well as metaphysical links between the state and its subjects (Smith 2000). Leaders are constantly in need of more tangible resources to support their political strategies, but the use of coercion to obtain them is too costly, so they often must rely on ideational means (Kurtz 2001; see also Kertzer 1988). Thus, ideational resources are doubly important in the pursuit of political power (Miller and Tilley 1984).

Another important distinction in definitions of power is between "power over" and "power to" (Miller and Tilley 1984). The first term refers to the ability to get others to do one's bidding (as we defined political power above), while the second refers to one's ability to do what one wants (ibid.). While political scientists have traditionally emphasized "power over" others (Mann 1986; Miller and Tilley 1984; Wolf 1990, 1999) and have privileged the elite as the source of all such political power, recent perspectives have shifted attention to the "power to" that emerges from social interactions and relations that involve all members of society, not just elites (Miller and Tilley 1984; Foucault 1979; Wolf 1999; Dobres and Robb 2000). "Power to" can be seen as the positive, enabling power that relies on cooperation and persuasion and develops in alliances between individuals or groups, both non-elite and elite (Miller and Tilley 1984, 7). Mann (1986) defines "power to" as collective power, "whereby persons in cooperation can enhance their joint power over third parties or over nature" (6, following Parsons 1960, 199–225). But "power to" can also be seen as a limiting, negative force that defines the rules of interaction or as the "apparatus of social control [that] permeates and defines every aspect of social life" (Fleisher and Wynne-Jones 2010, 182). This negative version is more closely aligned with Foucault's analysis of modernity. Although "power over" is clearly important in complex societies, we cannot deny the role of "power to." Those who dismiss the concept of "power to" should consider the anti-communist revolutions of 1989 in Central and Eastern Europe in which citizens with "power to" dismantled Communist states and their centralized apparatuses of economic, military, and political "power over" (Whitmeyer 1997, 213). This book aims to examine both "power over" and "power to" among the ancient Maya of the first millennium AD.

No matter how we define it, power now tends to be viewed not as a discrete and quantifiable substance that some people have and others do not but as a shifting relationship among an assortment of individuals that is not imposed exclusively by certain ones who have it over those who don't (Wolf 1999; Blanton et al. 1996; Sewell 1992). Michael Love (2002) writes, "I model the dialectic of domination and resistance as a crucial element of why centralization waxed and waned and propose that elites eventually gained the upper hand by more effectively wielding institutional sources of power" (214–15). Furthermore, because political power is dialectical, "volatile and fluid" (Stein 1998, 6), the events, processes, and means by which it is embodied or materialized (DeMarrais, Castillo, and Earle 1996, 2004) become contested loci for controlling and reproducing political power (Kertzer 1988). It is to these means of maintaining power that I turn next.

Power, Leaders, Followers, and Authority

Power is now understood as a relational phenomenon between individuals or groups interacting with each other. No leader can continue to lead without followers. Supporters provide material and ideational resources to the leader. Thus, the relationship between leaders and their followers is critical in understanding political power. This relationship is founded on reciprocity, which by definition requires the exchange of material resources or services (Kurtz 2001, 32–33; Roscoe 1993; Feinman 2001; Schortman and Urban 2004; Foias 2007; Pauketat 2000; Marcus and Flannery 1996). But it can also center on emotional and ideological links between leaders and followers (Smith 2000; Kertzer 1988). The success of a political leader (or his or her ability to pursue his or her agenda and increase his or her power) is predicated on the size of his or her supporting group, so he or she must spend a great deal of time and energy to attract and maintain the allegiance of followers (Kurtz 2001, 40–41; Roscoe 1993). There are a number of capable individuals who can fulfill the role of political leader in any community, which suggests that competition is at the core of political organization in human societies (Brumfiel 1983, 1992; Brumfiel and Fox 1994; Kurtz 2001).[5] Bradbury (1967) aptly describes this situation for the kingdom of Benin in West Africa during the nineteenth century: "It should . . . be clear that the Oba [king] of Benin was neither a mere ritual figurehead nor a constitutional monarch, but a political king, actively engaged in competition for power" (28).

Because a leader's power depends at least in part on the number of supporters he or she can attract and maintain, the mechanisms that strengthen this relationship become the keys to successful political strategies. Thus, if we are to reconstruct political power, we must study the followers as well as the leaders. Political power has to be understood as a contested relationship between leaders and followers, rulers and subjects, both sides always looking for ways to gain an advantage or maintain a balance (Roscoe 1993; Giddens 1979; Pauketat 2000, 2003; Joyce 2000; Joyce, Bustamente, and Levine 2001).

Authority, a group's public recognition of a leader's right to make decisions on its behalf (Kurtz 2001, 40; Gerth and Mills 1960; Smith 2003), is one of the key strategies for attracting and maintaining followers. Authority and legitimacy are two sides of the same coin. Following Weber, we can divide authority into three ideal types: charismatic, traditional, and legal-rational (Gerth and Mills 1960; Weber 1964). Charismatic legitimacy is based on special "gifts of the body and spirit" of specific individuals who are generally believed to have supernatural powers and who instill in their audience emotions that convince them to follow the leader's vision or mission (Gerth and Mills 1960, 245, 296). Traditional legitimacy draws from "an established belief in the sanctity of immemorial traditions and the legitimacy of the status of those exercising authority under them" (Weber 1964, 328). Finally, legal-rational legitimacy is typical of modern states, which rely on state bureaucracies and impersonal systems of law that are presumably based on rationality. Legal-rational legitimacy is predicated on a rational belief "in the 'legality' of patterns of normative rules and the right of those elevated to authority under such rules to issue commands (legal authority)" (ibid.). These three types of legitimacy are idealized, and in reality, societies and leaders exhibit a combination of them. For example, charismatic leaders are particularly strongly remembered, although their political power may also be sustained by traditional and/or legal-rational authority. Although traditional and legal-rational authority are typically seen as enabling the practice of political power of leaders, they can also be restrictions on the free behavior of these same leaders, as Lombard (1967) has noted in his study of the kingdom of Dahomey in nineteenth-century West Africa: "The [absolute] king's powers were in fact limited by age-old traditions, established by his predecessors and bolstered by their great re-spect accorded the royal ancestors which precluded their violation" (78).

Just as views of power have shifted in the last decades, more recent stud-ies of authority depict it as relational rather than imposed or coercive: the people participate and contribute to the authority of the state (Kus 1989; Smith 2000, 2003; Fleisher and Wynne-Jones 2010). Baines and Yoffee's (2000) definition of legitimacy in early civilizations is especially apt: legiti-macy is "the institutionalization of people's acceptance of, involvement in, and contribution towards order" (15). Adam Smith (2003) writes that both power and legitimacy are necessary ingredients of authority. Emotions and affect are as important in creating political authority as rational persua-sion based on calculations of costs and benefits (Smith 2000; Fleisher and Wynne-Jones 2010). Thus, legitimacy and authority, like power, become collective endeavors that involve both elites and non-elites (Fleisher and Wynne-Jones 2010, 184).

Although the evolution of the institution of permanent leaders in ranked and stratified societies endows political offices with inherent legitimate au-thority, competition for more power among political officeholders, agents, and factions continues, and those who gain more legitimacy will be able to attain more power and a larger following. Because of this continuous competition, political offices are not static and immutable entities; rather, they should be viewed as "inert abstractions, mere niches for incumbents of government" (Kurtz 2001, 176) who are ready to manipulate them. Gailey (1987) also echoes this "non-finality" of political officialdom: "the conflict between producing people [or commoners] . . . and civil author-ity, protecting the classes that siphon off goods and labor is a *continual, ongoing process*" (ix; Gailey's italics). A better way to envision the state, then, is not as "a political form but a process" that is always ongoing and is never final (Vincent 1990, 414). The mechanisms and strategies used to achieve legitimacy and the variable success or failure of these mechanisms and strategies explain at least in part the rise and fall of political leaders and their governments, or, in short, ancient political dynamics.

Legitimacy is most often pursued through ideational mechanisms, although coercive methods are dominant in some societies (e.g., the Neo-Assyrian Empire and Nazi Germany). African archaeologists and anthropologists have also used the terms *creative* and *instrumental* power to define the distinction I use here between ideational-persuasive and coercive means of achieving authority (and power), respectively (Fleisher and Wynne-Jones 2010). Instrumental power is coercive power imposed from above by political elites and political institutions and can clearly be associated with definitions of "power over." In contrast, creative power is based on ideological-persuasive means because it is about "manipulat[ing] and invent[ing] forms of meaning" (Schoenbrun 1999, 139, quoted in Fleisher and Wynne-Jones 2010, 183). Thus, it can be easily associated with positive views of cooperative power as "power to" (Fleisher and Wynn-Jones 2010; Arens and Karp 1989). Fleisher and Wynne-Jones (2010) write: "In many African examples, coercive forms of power and impositional forms of authority are shunned or resisted; instead, power is often constituted through ritual practices and alliance building . . . and authority is made legitimate through the performance and maintenance of these collective actions" (185).

A variety of ideational mechanisms can be used to gain legitimacy, such as naturalizing the political structure of the community and/or the political power of the leaders through rituals (Kertzer 1988), transforming or inscribing the landscape with political symbols of power (Smith 2003), creating a society-wide identity that all members share (Yaeger 2003a; Kus 1989), or forming affective connections between the polity and its members (Smith 2000; Kertzer 1988). The nature of the ideational (and/or coercive) strategies political leaders use to achieve legitimacy can be reconstructed through archaeological means.

Political Rituals: Materializing and/or Embodying Power

As our perspective on ancient political institutions has shifted from the idea that they were unitary well-integrated systems to the view that they incorporated multiple levels of competing and conflicting claims to power, from an emphasis on the economic foundations of power to a focus on ideological means of establishing power and authority, from an etic and large-scale view of societal patterns to a more emic and micro-scale view of individual action within households, genders, communities, or factions, political ritual became the focus of attention as the locus for producing, reproducing, and transforming power. Power came to be seen as embodied, effected, and reproduced in political rituals that were mostly performed in institutions, from the household all the way up to the state government. Although these institutions cannot be observed directly by archaeologists, they "often materialize in specific and recurring ways" in particular physical arenas or landscapes, using specific material equipment, facilities and ritual activities (Kristiansen 2001, 86; DeMarrais, Castillo, and Earle 1996, 2004; Emerson 1997; Smith 2003). Earle (2001) describes institutions as those "that integrate more people in increasingly differentiated ways, but especially they determine rights and compensations within increasingly complex economies" (106).

According to DeMarrais, Castillo, and Earle (1996; Earle 2001), institutions are embodied and materialized through different physical media: built landscapes, writing (including legal contracts), symbolic objects, and ceremonies (or political rituals).[6] For many archaeologists, landscapes are seen as most effective for forming institutions and materializing power: "Construction of the cultural landscape is a means to build large human institutions in the processes of social evolution" (Earle 2001, 107). The built landscape includes not only settlements from small to large, but also walls, trails, roads, and large monumental buildings, such as pyramids, temples, and palaces, all of which embody, represent, and materialize power as control over human labor (Earle 2001; Trigger 1990; Abrams 1994). Earle continues: "The scale and spatial arrangement of monuments show how labor was organized and controlled in the institutionalization of power held by leaders who would be rulers" (2001, 110). Furthermore, these monuments serve a specific role in the institutionalization of power: "monuments . . . are built to define space and restrict rights of access within emerging political economies" (111). Earle applies his model to Hawaiian chiefdoms: "The chiefdoms, created by conquest, were institutionalized by the construction of facilities and monuments that then were the stages for major ceremonies" that embodied these new political institutions (123).

However, most political anthropologists also see the political process materialized primarily in ceremonies or political rituals. To understand this perspective, we need to conceive of political power not as something abstract that is held by certain people in some "bank of political power" but rather as what is seen and heard or embodied and demonstrated in actions and/or rituals. In *Ritual, Politics and Power*, Kertzer (1988) describes the centrality of rituals to all political systems and hence to political power, arguing against the previously dominant idea that "political ritual merely serves to bolster the status quo" (2). Kertzer defines ritual as "culturally standardized, repetitive activity, primarily symbolic in character, aimed at influencing human affairs" and as action "that follows highly structured, standardized sequences and is often enacted at certain places and times that are themselves endowed with special symbolic meaning" (8–9). Symbols are critical as the chief content of rituals, even though their most important features ("condensation of meaning, multivocality, and ambiguity") may seem to make them weak tools (11; here Kertzer is building on the foundational work of Victor Turner). Kertzer describes how rituals and associated symbols build political organizations and legitimacy by guiding how organizations are viewed and by linking people to them (15–21). Rituals can serve to institute the symbols associated with the organization, but at the same time they can themselves be symbols of that organization (21).

Kertzer asserts that "in nonliterate societies, where no written [documents] exist, rituals are especially important" (18) because individuals need them in order to identify with the political regime (see also Kimmel 1989, 1273). Political rituals that relate the local to the national or to the larger polity are critical in the evolution of larger complex societies: "Identification of the local with the national can take place only through the use of symbols that identify the one with the other" (Kertzer 1988, 21). Among such rituals, we find rites of allegiance, the construction of local monuments that symbolize the larger polity, and rituals of royal procession (21–23).

Kertzer writes that political reality is constructed by and through these rituals, engendering both change and stability: "The struggle to elicit political support thus involves the struggle to establish one schema [that of the political elite] as the appropriate one for interpreting experience" (81–82). Rather than dismissing the emotional side of these political rituals, Kertzer stresses the importance of emotions in gaining political support: "The emotional climate that ritual can create is itself a powerful molder of beliefs and perceptions" (86), adding that "if political rites encourage certain interpretations of the world, they do so in no small part because of the powerful emotions that they trigger" (99). Political rituals create power by promoting solidarity around (and hence support for) the leaders who direct or sponsor these ceremonies (ibid.). This solidarity can be achieved even if consensus about the meanings of the symbols or beliefs does not exist (66–71). Furthermore, "ritual can produce a harmony of wills and action as people play out their appointed roles" (71).

Because of their centrality in creating political reality, rituals are seen as loci where political power is produced and contested: "Far from simply propping up the status quo, ritual provides an important weapon in political struggle, a weapon used both by contestants for power within stable political systems and by those who seek to protect or to overthrow unstable systems" (Kertzer 1988, 104). The intersection of the political with the ritual is brought to life in the political structure of the kingdom of Benin in Western Africa during the nineteenth century: "Every political role . . . implied ritual roles. The distribution of rights, duties, and privileges among the complex hierarchies of officialdom received constant expression in an endless series of palace rituals" (Bradbury 1967, 27).

Foucault (1978a, 1978b) has emphasized the importance of spectacle (or performance) in the exercise of power in premodern states (see also Rouse 2005, 98). As just discussed, Kertzer (1988) has used a similar argument for modern states as well. In his review of the importance of performance in premodern polities, Inomata (2006b) echoes Foucault, Kertzer, and others by emphasizing that political power was what was seen: "Subject populations' perception and experience of authorities and national unity were highly uneven, accentuated in the specific temporal and spatial contexts of state-sponsored events such as ceremonies and construction projects . . . , [in] the tangible images of the ruler's body, state buildings, and collective acts" (805). Ritual as performance is doubly important in premodern societies because, as Kertzer states, "*In the absence of writing, it was ritual that defined people's power relations*" (1988, 104, my italics). Therefore, if we are to understand political power in premodern, noncapitalist societies, we must consider both the performances of political power (political rituals) and their contexts in political institutions.

My argument is not that what we see in political ritual is all there is to ancient politics, because clearly plenty of "political deals" happen behind closed doors. Rather, the visible in political performances is just as important as what takes place behind closed doors. The dynamics of political power are caused by both what happens in public political rituals and what happens in private settings. But even decisions reached behind closed doors find public form in that they have to be carried out publicly by political officials and they depend on the obedience (or disobedience) of commoners. To understand political dynamics, therefore, we need to consider the archaeological materials left behind by ancient peoples *not* as pale reflections of political, social, economic, and religious structures but as playing a much more dynamic and active role: they are "the material traces of the process through which power was authorized in different times and places, the objects and spaces that were mobilized in negotiations of authority" (Fleisher and Wynne-Jones 2010, 189; see also Smith 2003). These objects and spaces are tools in the ongoing process of achieving, maintaining, changing, or contesting relations of power: "Just as power is only constituted through its enactment, objects are only powerful through the ways that they are implicated [used] in the activities through which authority is created" (Fleisher and Wynne-Jones 2010, 190; see also DeMarrais 2005; Meskell 2005; Miller 2005).

Because political performances involve large numbers of people and sometimes special clothing and objects, feasting, and music, they require economic resources. For this reason, political elites may be constantly in need of more economic resources. Eisenstadt (1993) and Yoffee (2005) have argued that ruling elites must search for "free-floating resources," or resources not tied to other social structures, such as goods or labor obtained outside the polity through warfare and trade or foodstuffs obtained through the intensification of agriculture on elite-owned lands.

Ancient Politics, Ideology, Dominance, and Contestation

Some scholars have seen ideology as a critical force in providing cohesion for a state because it masks the unequal distribution of power and wealth by creating a false consciousness for the dominated groups and because it naturalizes the power of the elites. In *Domination and the Arts of Resistance* (1990), Scott takes issue with this view and argues instead that the ideology of domination states and their political elites promote through public rituals and documents ("public transcripts") is not shared by the dominated groups (or classes), which develop their own ideologies of resistance in "hidden transcripts" (for example, in myths, songs, and rituals that take place in the household or through practices such as poaching, pilfering, and carnival-like celebrations) (see also Abercrombie, Hill, and Turner 1980).

Rather than arguing about whether there is resistance in stratified social systems, Scott (1990) sees it as always there and argues that any "analysis of forms of domination might well begin by specifying the ways in which the structure of claims to power influences the sort of public transcript it requires." Then we "might . . . examine how such a public transcript may be undermined or repudiated" by the dominated groups (104). Scott contrasts feudal Europe with its warrior aristocrats to the Hindu religious caste system in India to highlight the kind of analysis necessary to understand domination:

> If, for example, we were studying the relation between warrior aristo-
> crats of feudal Europe and their serfs it would be important to under-
> stand how their claim to hereditary authority was based on providing
> physical protection in return for labor, grain, and military service.
> This "exchange" might be discursively affirmed in an emphasis on
> honor, noblesse oblige, bravery, expansive generosity, tournaments
> and contests of military prowess. . . . A parallel kind of analysis might
> be applied to relations between the Brahmin (or high-caste superior)
> and the lower caste [in Hindu Indian society]. Here the basis for the
> claim to power is based on sacred hereditary status, superior karma,
> and on the provision of certain presumably vital ritual services that
> can be performed only by Brahmin due to their status and knowl-
> edge. Discursive affirmations might include all the ritual separations
> of purity and pollution, diet, dress . . . and presiding at key rites of
> birth, marriage, death. (Ibid.)

Each distinct system of domination will encounter specific forms of resistance. Thus, it is important to consider the claims to power or foundations of power of ancient rulers in order to understand both the "public transcripts" promoted by the political elite and the "hidden transcripts" of competing ideologies of resistance among the dominated groups. Emerson and Pauketat (2002) add that resistance should not be viewed in the Western sense of conscious actions: "It is critical that we divorce resistance from its Western foundation of consciously motivated actions taken in opposition to a hegemonic force if the concept is to have utility in the study of the past. Such resistance as we mean . . . here is of the everyday sort" (107).

Political Strategies for Maintaining Power: Exclusionary versus Corporate, Hierarchy versus Heterarchy, and Council Institutions

Until recently, most political anthropologists and political archaeologists perceived political centralization as the core process or strategy through which one or a few "aggrandizers" pursued more power in human societies. Blanton and Feinman and their colleagues have criticized this unitary view of the "political" and, in line with the processual-action paradigm, have encouraged researchers to "abandon . . . static ideal-type stages and instead investigate the varying strategies used by political actors to construct and maintain polities" (Blanton et al. 1996, 1; Blanton 1998; Feinman 1995, 2001). Feinman (2001) also warns that "recent postprocessual and selectionist emphases on individual strategies have further promoted the presumption that highly centralized and personalized leadership, control, and aggrandizement underlie most if not all hierarchical political organizations" (154–55). Instead, these scholars propose two types of strategies political elites use to advance their agendas: the exclusionary (or network) strategy and the corporate strategy (Blanton et al. 1996; Feinman 2001).[7]

In the exclusionary strategy, "political actors aim at the development of a political system built around their monopoly of sources of power" (Blanton et al. 1996, 2). This strategy is characterized by "the development and maintenance of individual-centered exchange relations established primarily outside one's local group" (ibid.). In contrast, in the corporate strategy, "power is shared across different groups and sectors of society in such a way as to inhibit exclusionary strategies." Monopoly "control of sources of power is precluded by restrictions on the political behavior of those vested with power or aspirants to power" (ibid., 4). The corporate strategy is founded on "a cognitive code that emphasizes a corporate solidarity of society as an integrated whole" (6). The pharaonic state of ancient Egypt and the Classic Maya civilization represent the exclusionary political strategy, while the Classic-period Greek poleis, the Indus civilization of South Asia, and Teotihuacan in Central America exemplify the corporate power strategy (Small 2009; Parkinson and Galaty 2007; Blanton et al. 1996; Blanton 1998; Feinman 2001; Stein 2001; Rothman 2004, 90–91).

Blanton et al. (1996) argue that these two strategies are coupled with distinct forms of legitimation, production, and finance. The exclusionary strategy correlates with ruler cults recorded in writing and art, a well-developed economy of prestige goods, and wealth finance (a tribute-tax system based on prestige goods). In contrast, the corporate strategy is associated with a corporate cognitive code that leaves leaders anonymous, a well-developed internal system of intensive agricultural production, and staple finance (a tribute-tax system based on agricultural goods, as originally defined by D'Altroy and Earle 1985; see also Earle 2001). Following a similar line of reasoning, P. Rice (2009) connects the exclusionary strategy with political centralization and the corporate strategy with decentralization. However, Blanton et al. (1996) argue that the corporate strategy is found in "large powerful states, such as Teotihuacan" and empires such as the Mexica of Late Postclassic central Mexico (5).

These distinctions between network and corporate power strategies fail in more detailed examinations. Small (2009) presents evidence that exclusionary and corporate strategies coexisted in ancient Greek poleis in different spheres. Kolb (1996, 59), D'Altroy (1996, 55), and Gilman (1996, 57) concur with Demarest (1996c) who affirms that these two strategies should be conceived as "different aspects of large states rather than the predominant mode in any given state" (56). The distinction between the two power strategies draws heavily from the art of such societies. But instead of providing a record of the full political arena, this art represents the ideology of one powerful group that is promoting their vision of "what should be" (Miller and Tilley 1984; Smith 2000). Finally, the Classic Maya evidence calls into question the association of exclusionary polities with wealth finance and of corporate polities with staple finance. As we will see in Chapter 5, tribute-tax at Motul de San José involved both food and exotic goods. This is also applicable to the tributary system of the Mexica (Aztec) Empire, which combined both wealth and staple finance.

These critiques do not deny that the distinction between exclusionary and corporate strategies has provided critical insights into the process of power dynamics. Blanton and his colleagues overcome the division between materialist and ideational power by showing the interconnections between ideology, legitimation, and economics in corporate or network societies. Distinguishing between these two different strategies has also allowed anthropologists and archaeologists to see that ancient political leaders had at their disposition and pursued a range of strategies to maintain their polities. Blanton et al. (1996) admit that "elements of both [strategies] may coexist" in the same society, although "either the corporate or the exclusionary strategy may dominate the political process . . . at any given time" (5–6). Instead of identifying a society as either network or corporate, I find it more useful to inquire if, when, and why each of these strategies was used by leaders, factions, or institutions as they pursued their political goals (see Chapter 6). Furthermore, other political strategies were used in the past beyond these two (Clark 1996, 52), and my interest is to explore the various mechanisms the Maya used to gain power.

This envisioning of alternative power strategies has also enabled scholars to consider shared power, collective action ("power to") and council institutions in ancient state societies (Blanton and Fargher 2008; see also Chapter 6). Elite councils, non-elite assemblies, and limits on the ruler's behavior in premodern societies are often dismissed as unimportant, but they are more common than we suspect. In their cross-cultural survey of premodern, noncapitalist states, Blanton and Fargher have found many examples of societies with collective institutions that they call "collective polities": "a complex society in which the government (we'll call this 'rulers' for now) provides services ('public goods') in exchange for the revenues (including labor) provided by compliant taxpayers" (13). These authors suggest that collective polities develop when significant bargaining occurs between rulers and taxpayers: "Taxpayers are endowed with resources placing them in a position to make demands on rulers to the degree that rulers depend on them to achieve their revenue goals" (14). When rulers depend significantly on internal revenues controlled by the taxpayers, the latter tend to be able to bargain, make demands, and have a voice in the government of the polity. Councils are thus important institutions in such polities. When rulers depend mostly on external revenue (income not controlled by taxpayers), such as revenue from state-controlled land, external warfare or trade, taxation of international trade, or state-owned labor (slaves, serfs, etc.), they are less inclined to bargain with the taxpayers, who then have less voice in the government (112–16). In these polities, councils and assemblies will be lacking. In Chapter 6, I will apply Blanton and Fargher's argument to Classic Maya states to ask whether they could have been collective polities.

The distinction between network and corporate power strategies parallels the dichotomy between hierarchy and heterarchy proposed by Crumley (1979, 1987, 1995, 2001) and her colleagues (Ehrenreich, Crumley, and Levy 1995). Hierarchy is the ordering of elements of a society "on the basis of certain factors [which] . . . are subordinate to others" (Crumley 1979, 144). Crumley (1995) defines heterarchy as "the relation of elements to one another when they are unranked or when they possess the potential for being ranked in a number of different ways" (3). The heterarchical model contributes to a better understanding of ancient power because it allows us to conceive of politics not as a monolithic whole but as different arenas in which power may be held by distinct individuals and may be founded on the basis of different sources. In this model, relations between different individuals, factions, or institutions may be hierarchical, but they could also be heterarchical, and the nature of these relationships is varied (in terms of economic, ritual, social, or political factors). In the context of ancient societies, these relations should be explored instead of assuming that they were hierarchical. For example, Wailes (1995) documents multiple distinctions of social status based on a lay-civic hierarchy, a religious hierarchy, and a professional-crafting hierarchy described in legal documents in Early Medieval Ireland. These hierarchies generally operated independently in the context of a heterarchical system (64). Nevertheless, Ireland's heterarchical system was full of intrigue and competition, at least at the highest levels of the social scale, according to extant historical documents. Archaeologically, the heterarchical structure of Early Medieval Ireland is reflected in the existence of two main types of large sites, lay residential ringforts and Christian monasteries, each of which had a "comparable range of wealth, status, and importance" although their functions at the top of parallel civic and religious hierarchies were quite distinct (68).

The concepts of heterarchy and the corporate mode of political organization both emphasize political power that is shared by groups, factions, federations, or coalitions and is not wielded by individual rulers (Crumley 1995, 3; Crumley 2001, 32; Feinman 2001). Parkinson and Galaty (2007) make such a distinction among Bronze Age societies in the Aegean world, finding that societies with large corporate kin groups and indirect interactions with foreign stratified societies tended to develop into heterarchical, corporate systems of political organization. Just as with exclusionary and corporate strategies, hierarchy and heterarchy can coexist in the same society in different spheres or even in the same sphere at different moments (Crumley 1979; Chapman 2003; Small 2009). For example, Plog (1995) details the coexistence of an egalitarian ideology and hierarchical relations in the Pueblo societies of the American Southwest.

Both the network-corporate and the hierarchy-heterarchy dichotomies are useful constructs, but they do not go far enough. We need to consider in more detail when network or corporate (as well as other) power strategies are used and by whom. We also need to ask what the relations between different political institutions, factions, and/or agents may have been. Were they heterarchical or hierarchical, were they supportive or conflictive, and were they based on economic, social, ritual, or political power (see also Schortman, Urban, and Ausec 1996, 62–63)?

Conclusions

This chapter has explored how views of power (specifically political power) have changed in political anthropology. Power and politics are now seen as in flux rather than as constants. Instead of discussing static political structures, we need to examine political dynamics. Vincent (1990) summarizes this overarching principle when she writes that the state should be viewed not as "a political form but a process" (414).

Political power is held by all groups in human societies, albeit to different degrees. Commoners can and do contest requests by elites for labor, tribute, or military service by delaying payments, disappearing into the "wilderness," migrating, poaching, gossiping, and so forth (Scott 1985, 1990; see also Chapter 6). We now understand power as relational, situational, and conflictive. The nature of the power both elites and commoners held needs to be understood.

Elites use different strategies to ameliorate conflict and to bolster support, including controlling particular institutions, gaining more legitimacy and authority, promoting corporate identities or exclusionary ruler cults, and inscribing the landscape with symbols of power and arenas for political rituals. Similarly, commoners and middle-rank groups may also promote their own strategies, ideologies, and identities and may build their own arenas of power (see Chapter 6). The success or failure of these different strategies is the key to the political dynamics of ancient societies.

Because political power is now seen as conflictive and situational, current anthropologists and archaeologists conceive of political rituals as the most important locus for embodying, reproducing, contesting, and changing politics. Thus, we cannot disentangle the political from the ritual. In premodern states, political reality is established through political ceremonies or rituals because other means of communication with a wide range of commoners are underdeveloped or nonexistent. Ritual is materialized archaeologically because it requires specific built arenas, material paraphernalia and symbols, and the same repeated activities.

A final point in this review of current paradigms in political anthropology is that material resources are always involved in the pursuit of political power: we cannot deny that food and labor are required to create pyramids or palatial residences for the rulers or to hold any kind of ritual. We cannot disentangle the material from the ideational in the formation of political power, and both elements must be followed if we are to understand ancient politics. In the following chapters, I will try to pursue some of these threads. What did the ancient Maya rulers choose to control economically, politically, socially, and ideologically? How did the ancient Maya rulers legitimate themselves vis-à-vis the much larger number of commoners? What were the ritual and political roles of ancient Maya rulers and aristocrats? What kind of political rituals did Maya rulers carry out? Did the commoners support or contest such attempts at political control? Did the commoners and other middle-rank groups pursue their own alternate strategies, identities, and rituals?

Notes

1. As described below, the processual-action paradigm in political anthropology is very distinct from processualism in archaeology.

2. This debate questioned whether premodern precapitalist economies were qualitatively distinct from modern capitalist economies. Formalists suggested that there were no differences beyond scale, while substantivists perceived a major disjuncture between earlier economies and capitalist economies.

3. O'Donovan (2002b, 25) critiques the assumption of agency theories that some individuals have an innate or biological drive to attain power and status (Clark and Blake 1994; Earle 1997; Hayden 1995), not only because of lack of biological evidence but also because these power seekers are always assumed to be male, leaving out the other half of the human species (O'Donovan 2002b, 26). However, I would argue that in complex societies, many individuals (both men and women) strive for higher status and/or power. Other scholars have disagreed with the view of human agents as driven by tactical concerns rather than by moral obligations. While morality must have been important, so were strategies for gaining advantages. Barth (2007) describes the Swat in this manner: "Society is no doubt a moral system, but the political alignment of the persons within the polity in Swat could be shown as the aggregate result of myriad individual tactical decisions" (3).

4. The law system can encompass both the military and police institutions. Unfortunately, although law studies are a major component of political anthropology (Vincent 1990), they are of little assistance to archaeologists because premodern societies do not have texts, or if they do, laws are rarely encoded in them.

5. This is also the case for the Classic Maya (Culbert 1991; Demarest 1992; Hendon 1991; Sabloff 1986).

6. I limit my discussion to the built landscape in this work, but anthropologists conceive of the cultural landscape much more broadly. Knapp and Ashmore (1999), Smith (2003), and Ashmore (2002) stress that the cultural landscape includes the perceptions, concepts, and experiences of members of human society of their surroundings as they try to make sense of their world.

7. This dichotomy between exclusionary and corporate strategies is similar to Renfrew's (1974) description of individualizing and group-oriented chiefdoms in ancient Europe (see also the discussions in Blanton et al. 1996; Stein 1998; and Pauketat 2007).

3

||||||||||||

Archaeological Studies of Ancient Politics

Archaeologists have been interested in political power for many generations (see Trigger 1974). In this chapter, I present archaeological studies
from outside the Maya world that focus on ancient politics. The discussion
is not meant to be an exhaustive review of the literature, which is extensive,
but rather is a review of major trends in archaeological studies of political power, highlighted by case studies. My concern in this chapter is with
political power in complex societies that we call "states." These will serve as
comparisons with Classic Maya polities, such as the one centered at Motul
de San José, where I have worked for the last decade. My goal is to understand how archaeologists approach the issues and problems involved in
reconstructing power in archaeological societies for which few or no written historical records have survived.

The archaeology of political power has been heavily influenced by the
paradigms of political anthropology. Until the 1980s, the paradigms of neo-
evolutionism and political economy were dominant. Archaeologists were
most concerned with macro-scale political processes and institutions, and
more often than not, they viewed political power as state power through
the lens of economics. Beginning in the 1990s, the focus shifted and archaeologists began to inquire about political processes rather than about origins
and causes of political complexity. Instead of viewing political power as
resting exclusively within the hands of state governments, archaeologists
began to consider the middle and micro scales of ongoing political processes, focusing on individuals, households, and communities and the actions that create, change, or reproduce norms, customs, and structures of
the larger society. Archaeologists have now begun to incorporate the roles
of ideology, religion, and rituals in their assessments of political processes,
institutions, and power instead of viewing political power as an economically driven machine.

The Sociocultural Evolution and Political Economy Paradigms: Case Studies from the Near East

In the mid-twentieth century, archaeologists were concerned with political organization as a long-term process of social change within the perspective of sociocultural evolution (Trigger 1998; Steward 1955; White 1959; Sahlins and Service 1960; Service 1962; Fried 1967, 1978; Johnson and Earle 1987; Haas 2001b). Following the classifications of human societies promulgated by Service (bands, tribes, chiefdoms, and states) and Fried (egalitarian, ranked, and stratified societies), archaeologists hoped to identify the complexity of political systems on a general level so they could categorize the societies they studied in one of Service's or Fried's ideal types of society.

Archaeological studies for most of the rest of the century engaged with the evolutionary model that focused on chronicling the transformation from small-scale, egalitarian societies to large-scale, urban polities with significant social, economic, and political inequality and a centralized government (Flannery 1972; Johnson and Earle 1987; Upham 1990; Price and Feinman 1995; Manzanilla 1997; Trigger 1998; Marcus and Feinman 1998; Haas 2001a). These studies have tended to be highly materialistic (see a critique in Conrad and Demarest 1986) and too focused on classification (see critiques in Upham 1990; Earle 1991; Feinman and Neitzel 1984; A. Smith 2003; Yoffee 2005). Often the concept of political centralization is at the core of investigations of how highly complex societies or states have evolved politically (Haas 2001b). However, recent work questions the existence of a single type called "the State" (A. Smith 2003; Yoffee 2005) and the usefulness of a single definition of "political centralization" that applies to all ancient states (Blanton et al. 1996; Feinman 2001; Stein 1998). In other words, states are variable, and so are their political institutions.

Nevertheless, the evolutionary paradigm has made significant contributions to our understanding of ancient politics by identifying large-scale patterns of political organization. Stein's (1994) research in Northern Mesopotamia is an excellent example. Like many Maya archaeologists of the 1980s and early 1990s, Stein is primarily interested in characterizing Mesopotamian states as either unitary or segmentary (or as either highly or weakly centralized, concepts that were originally proposed by Southall [1956]). Stein argues that ancient states should be viewed along the three main axes of scale, complexity and integration. Unitary states are at the high end of these axes and segmentary states are at the low end. Stein identifies segmentary states by the presence of administrative staff in both the capital center and in subsidiary administrative nodes (or centers), where they had the same political powers as in the capital. This feature of segmentary states is called replication. Furthermore, the central authority of a segmentary state has only limited control over its periphery, so its influence declines with distance from the center, as does its ability to extract tribute from peripheries farther away from the capital (Southall 1956, 260–61). Stein (1994) argues that rural settlements in segmentary states would have "few positive or negative incentives impelling them toward economic specialization in the sense of surplus production and exchange. Instead, villages would maintain a generalized, flexible subsistence system aimed at preserving a high degree of local political and economic autonomy" (12; see also Stein 1998). In contrast, the greater territorial scale, complexity, and integration of centralized or unitary states would push the rural economies of such states "toward the specialized production of large-scale food surpluses" that could then be extracted as tribute and used by the state government (Stein 1994).

Stein's study is also concerned with the intersection of political power with economics. For example, he provides estimates of the minimum agricultural area needed to sustain each settlement in the Tell Leilan zone of the Khabur Plains of northern Mesopotamia using reconstructed population densities for rural and urban sites and data about agricultural productivity in this zone (14). The overlap of the sustaining agricultural area required by Tell Leilan with those of neighboring communities suggests that this newly urbanized center was not self-sufficient and needed to extract agricultural surplus from the surrounding villages and secondary centers (ibid.). Furthermore, Stein uses site rank-size distributions to assess regional political and economic integration following geographical approaches (see Johnson 1980, 1987; Christaller and Baskin 1966; Haggett 1966). The regional rank-size distribution of settlements exhibits a straight-line pattern (in log-linear or log-normal space) if there is a great deal of political and economic integration, but the distribution will deviate from the log-linear straight-line pattern when there is less regional integration (Stein 1994, 15). Based on this macro-scale approach, Stein was able to reconstruct the change in the regional settlement around Tell Leilan from one with little integration to one with high integration. Although agricultural tribute extraction is indicated by the settlement study, the state did not control all economic systems: ceramic production and exchange were localized and took place at all levels of the settlement hierarchy, as shown by the broad distribution of kiln wasters across the region.

Stein's work is a sophisticated analysis of Mesopotamian political systems using the paradigms of political evolution and political economy that focus on political structures at the large-scale or societal level. His study exemplifies archaeology's concern with political economy as the lens through which political power can be queried. Even recent reviews of the political organization of ancient states and empires use this framework: Smith and Schreiber (2005, 2006), Feinman and Nicholas (2004), M. Smith (2004), and Stein (1998) find economic organization a useful way to reconstruct the nature of state politics because they see economic control as the most important foundation of political power.

Postprocessual Case Studies from the Near East and North America

In the 1990s, archaeological studies of ancient politics shifted to a conflict-based model that examines organizational dynamics of complex societies instead of exploring state origins (Stein 1998; Stein, 2001, 214; Stein and Rothman 1994; Brumfiel 1992, 1994; Ehrenreich, Crumley, and Levy 1995; Mann 1986; Eisenstadt 1993). Moving away from generalized typological discussions of political organization, archaeologists have been drawn to micro-scale analyses of political dynamics. These studies have been deeply influenced by post-processual approaches in archaeology and in the social sciences in general (Hodder 1986; Giddens 1979, 1984; Bourdieu 1977, 1990; Foucault 1991) and have therefore emphasized the role of individuals, gender, households, and factions in manipulating, reacting to, and resisting political power within specific ecological, cultural, and historical contexts (Arnold 1995; Brumfiel 1992; Brumfiel and Fox 1994; Chapman 2003; Cowgill 1993; Dobres and Robb 2000; Haas 2001b, 13–16; Preucel 1991; Stein 1998, 2001; Stein and Rothman 1994).[1] Rothman (2004) describes the theoretical shift in the paradigms of political archaeology: "With a concentration on the administrative, centralizing core largely rejected, these researchers propose that administrative organizations are one of a number of sometimes competing, and sometimes cooperating, institutions" (88; see also Smith 2003; Pollock 1999).

The Political Landscapes of the Urartian Empire

Adam Smith (2003) has made a case for a new approach to understanding political authority in early complex societies that focuses on the political landscape, or the spatial dimension of political life where relationships are created and reproduced. Instead of emphasizing on the "polarized concepts of coercion and consent" to account for integration in ancient states, he proposes authority as the crucial concept: "The central pillar of any political community is authority, the asymmetric, reciprocal public relationships where one actively practices a power to command that is confirmed by another as legitimate" (26). For Smith, "politics is not directly about territory, or urbanism, or architecture. It is about the production and reproduction of authority" (280).

He envisions a framework for understanding ancient politics that is predicated on four sets of relationships: 1) between polities; 2) between subjects and regimes within each polity; 3) between "power elites and grassroots organizations that produce regimes"; and 4) between "institutions within a governing apparatus" (26, 104).[2] However, at all four levels, the landscape is critical in creating legitimacy: "Political authority is constituted through the making and transformation of landscapes by the governing bodies" (5). Thus, Smith argues that political power is materialized in the landscape and that the landscape in turn generates and legitimates political power. For Smith, landscape and therefore space are defined in a recursive manner through the interaction between space and individuals: "space, defined as the relationships between [human] bodies, forms and elements, is a product of negotiations between an array of competing actors with varying practical capacities to transform these relationships" (72). By placing relationships, authority, and landscape at the core of political systems, Smith incorporates the dynamic nature of political institutions in his analysis.

Authority as the central pivot of ancient politics is recursively constituted of power (the ability to direct the action of others) and legitimacy, which Smith defines as "the ability . . . to synchronize practices that perpetuate the existing political order within a discursive framework that generates the allegiance of subjects" (2003, 105–8). Smith argues that the "central spatial problems for constituting authority within polities" are "the delineation of a bounded territory within which a sovereign regime rules a community of subjects integrated by a shared sense of identity that binds them together in place" (151). He maintains that the "practical relationships between regimes and subjects . . . were constituted within the experience, perception, and imagination of political landscapes" (153). Regimes make up the political structure involving varied power blocs or factions: "Regimes are located in the intersection of a power elite that controls critical institutions of governance (the political apparatus) and grassroots coalitions of 'like-minded' subjects committed to sociopolitical reproduction" (155). The political apparatus is recognized archaeologically in the built environment of political centers, fortresses, palaces and administrative structures, monuments, the living space of the power elite, and so forth. The connections between these built features are mapped out across the landscape, especially in urban settlements, and are produced and reproduced through the imaginations, perceptions, and experiences of the grassroots subjects and political elites who live within these political landscapes (202–31).

Smith is also interested in the dialectical relationships between the multiple political institutions (which existed in all ancient states), which he sees "as both privileged sites of political action (or inaction) and arenas for contending social forces" (235). Rather than envisioning the "state" as one unitary institution, Smith constructs it as a number of institutions that at times work together and at other times work against each other. Echoing some of the processual-action theorists, Smith defines a political institution as "less a formal structure than a set of enduring procedures, routines, and values that establish the frameworks within which social and political relationships proceed" (ibid.). Institutions in a political regime are also manifested in the landscapes, primarily but not exclusively in the constructed locales of these institutions: "Political institutions are profoundly sited in place within an architectural landscape that draws together not only discourses on appropriate action but also physical demands on inter-institutional ties and imaginings of the governmental apparatus as a whole" (ibid., 235).

Smith uncovers the political institutions of the Urartian landscape of the Ararat plain during the eighth and seventh centuries BC by following the regularities in the siting, design, and architecture of Urartian political centers or fortresses. He analyzes how humans experienced the Urartian fortresses through the architectural organization, symmetry and distribution of access of these sites. He also examines how these fortresses are depicted clothed in religious symbolism in Urartian art. His analysis highlights that by the seventh century BC, the institutions of king and temple within the Urartian imperial administration had differentiated and were probably competing against each other, weakening the whole empire (254–63).

Archaeology of Power at Cahokia

Another important postprocessual (or historical-processual) approach to the archaeology of power is Pauketat's analysis of Cahokia (2000, 2001, 2003, 2007). Pauketat, who is critical of debates that centered on whether

Cahokia was a chiefdom or a state, pursues the historical process of changing political relations by analyzing the practices of individuals rather than
analyzing reified (or objectified, abstracted) institutions. For Pauketat, state
formation is the process of creating one unitary identity through place and
community: "It's all about building collective memories and group identities into landscapes" (2007, 199). Rather than focusing on causes, he delves
into the process: "Urbanization, landscape, and polity were inextricably
wrapped up in the historical process whereby people were 'gathered' and
their cultural practices and embodied identities and labor appropriated for
the greater good" (177; see also Pauketat 2001, 2003). In other words, the
pyramids and palaces that are at the apex of state political power "were
not simply *reflections* of political institutions. Mounds and mound building were the [political] institutions *coming into being*" (Pauketat 2007, 42,
Pauketat's italics). Rather than debating whether coercion or persuasion
was more dominant in the rise of chiefs, rulers, or kings, Pauketat asserts
that both the non-elite and the elite had agency in the process: "The strategies of 'the few' matter little, after all, if 'the many' refuse to heed them
or accommodate them; power and hegemony are clearly 'relational' if not
'consensual'" (Pauketat 2003, 56). But when the proto-elite and proto-com-
moner groups came together to build mounds, temples, pyramids, or palaces, they may not have predicted that the consequence of these construction projects would be social, political, or economic inequality. This is what
Pauketat calls the "tragedy of the commoners" (2000).

Emerson (1997) also pursues a practice-oriented approach in his study
of Cahokia's political structure from the perspective of its rural settlements in the Midwest United States. Like Adam Smith, Emerson stresses
that coercive power (what he calls political power) is always intertwined
with persuasive-emotional power (what he calls religious power) because
of the importance of authority and legitimacy. Drawing upon Bourdieu's
practice theory and Giddens's structuration theory, Emerson argues that
material culture should be seen as an active "medium of discourse" that
recursively forms and reshapes social practices of the individual (26–30;
see also Shanks and Tilley 1987).

To identify political structures and power dynamics at the rural tier of
Cahokia's settlement, Emerson pursues a dual approach by differentiating
between the material culture associated with political (or coercive) power
and the material culture associated with religious (or ideological) power
(Emerson 1997, 37–67). Political power is manifested in the construction
of an architecture of power, control over prestige/wealth items, and control

over differential mortuary treatment (37–38). The architecture of political power is represented by "elaborate [elite] domestic structures, storage facilities associated with the elite accumulation of comestibles and goods, [other specialized architectural facilities such as meeting houses,] or ritual facilities that indicate [elite] access to supernatural power" (36–37). Religious power is manifested in the construction of religious architecture and a sacred landscape and through control over religiously charged artifacts, symbols, and cults (39–40). The architecture of ideological power is identified as "temples, [sweat houses], priest houses, and specialized elite mortuary facilities" (39).

Through this dual approach that considers the distribution of material markers of political and religious power across the landscape, Emerson is able to show that the Stirling phase (AD 1100–1200) was the apogee of political centralization at Cahokia and of its control over the periphery (167). At this time, ceremonial nodes (centers of religious power) were separate from civic nodes (centers of political power), showing a degree of functional differentiation or specialization in the rural tier of Cahokia's settlement hierarchy that had not been seen before (ibid.). Elite roles also show specialization into separate political, religious, and mortuary functions (178). Emerson is also able to chart transformations in political leadership as storage shifted over time from the civic to the ceremonial nodes and as sweat houses were introduced into civic nodes. These changes may suggest a transition from civic-dominant authority to religious-dominant authority.

Power, Discipline, and Dynamics on the Pacific Coast of Guatemala

Our final case study comes from a region closer to the Maya lowlands: the early center of Ujuxte on the Pacific Coast of Guatemala. Michael Love (2002) explores the dimensions of power at Ujuxte during the Middle to Late Formative Period (600 BC to AD 100), when it was the seat of a complex chiefdom or early state (219–22).

Love is interested in "aspects of disciplinary power that are not institutional but concern daily social practice, particularly the organization of space" (216). Like Foucault, Love sees this disciplinary power as lacking a locus because it appears "through collections of practices shaped by the material world and [because it] pervaded all social relationships" (ibid.). According to Love, two aspects of this type of disciplinary power are important: first, it is hard to resist because it lacks a specific locus; second, it affects everyone but not equally because the dominant groups are not controlled to the same degree as the dominated groups (216–17). Love argues that "discipline of the body was a vital part of governance and . . . one of its principal forms was the control of people's movements through space and time" (217). He asserts that the central feature of early states is that they involve a tug-of-war between dominance and resistance: this feature makes them such fragile societies that they cycle between periods of integration and disintegration (or "political dynamics"). Resistance is only rarely successful because the "networks of power and institutions controlled by elites are simply too much a part of the structure of society for resistance to succeed" (219). But although resistance may not succeed, it does affect and shape the state and its political institutions. For example, Love suggests that elites learned from episodes of resistance or from episodes of political disintegration and that they sought "new and enhanced means of grasping power" (ibid.).

Love explores how more institutional forms of power (economic and ideological) are integrated with the more diffuse form of disciplinary power (222–33). He begins with economic power: elites at Ujuxte had more control over subsistence production and in particular over food processing and storage technology, as is evidenced by the greater numbers of ground stone tools and large storage vessels found in elite architecture (223). Members of elite households also had more control over exchange; they consumed more imported obsidian and foreign pottery than members of lower-status households. But non-elites resisted this economic control. Elites and non-elites used two distinct ways to obtain obsidian needed to create all sorts of tools: while elites used mostly percussion blades (which were probably imported in finished form from the highland quarries), the non-elite obtained small nodules and spalls separately from the highland quarries and created their own small flake tools (224–25).

Elites at Ujuxte also had more control over the ideological realms than earlier elites. First, they "appropriated ritual functions" from the non-elite, and second, they "asserted an ideology that reinvented the basis of chiefly power" (226). While earlier commoners had numerous figurines and ceramic feasting equipment, Ujuxte non-elite households are devoid of figurines and large feasting vessels. To highlight the tremendous change in the frequency of household rituals involving figurines, we can compare the frequencies of figurines uncovered at Ujuxte and at the earlier site of La Blanca in the same region. Excavations at the earlier site of La Blanca produced approximately one figurine for every five ceramic vessels, but at Ujuxte, excavations produced only one figurine for every 2,500 ceramic vessels. At the same time that we see this decline in household rituals, there was "a dramatic new emphasis on public ritual [at Ujuxte], which was manifested in the construction of planned ceremonial groups" including a temple-pyramid over 20 meters tall, a ball court, and several plazas with formally arranged structures around them (227). Even more significantly, the new architectural ritual construction was replicated at Ujuxte's subsidiary centers. Based on these multiple lines of evidence, Love concludes that "it is likely that rites and 'official' religious practices were usurped by the elite during the Caramelo phase [when Ujuxte flourished] and that household ritual waned in importance" (228).

Love uses the iconography of stone monuments and other art media to suggest that the elites of Ujuxte made new ideological claims that were very different from the claims of earlier chiefs. Previous coastal leaders "derived their identity and power by linking themselves to . . . powerful and dangerous [natural forces like lightning and earthquakes, and] animals, such as serpents" (228). In contrast, Ujuxte's leaders made much stronger claims that they controlled the order of the whole universe by planning the entire city in alignment with astronomical directions of importance and placing symbols of cosmic order in numerous caches buried in the Central Plaza along the east-west axis of the site (228–29). One example of such symbols is the cross representing the World Tree that connected the different levels of the multilayered universe that Central American civilizations envisioned. At Ujuxte, the site itself represented a World Tree and the elite controlled this axis mundi. Love argues that we see at Ujuxte the beginning of the same claims to divinity that are characteristic of the Maya lowlands in the Classic period: "It was the ruler who maintained cosmological order through shamanic prowess and blood sacrifice" (228). This new ideological claim that the Ujuxte lords made "goes far beyond the ideology of earlier chiefs and their claims to control natural forces and spirits. The new ideology posited that without the ruler the world would fall into chaos" (229). Thus, all of a sudden, Ujuxte's rulers claimed to be the center of the universe rather than just shamans who were able to control part of the universe. According to Love, this new claim to ideological power transformed Ujuxte's lords into divine or semi-divine beings who were different from the commoner populace (ibid.).

In spite of this all-encompassing new ideology and even though the elite at Ujuxte appear to have usurped household rituals involving figurines and feasting, the commoners at the site resisted by elaborating other rituals, in particular those surrounding the dead. So in the ideological realm, again, we see that the commoners had sufficient power to resist in some way the attempts of the elite to control all ritual life.

Finally, Love asserts that the elite at Ujuxte developed a new type of power, disciplinary power, through the extensively planned orientation of the site in which structures, open space, and lines of access were oriented along the same approximately east-west and north-south axes (230–31). Daily social practices became highly spatialized, limiting contact between elites and non-elites to the moments the elites chose. More important, this spatial control regularized "people's daily paths to a high degree, thereby promoting disciplined social actors more likely to comply with the desires of centralized institutions" (231). Ujuxte is indeed a special site because it is built on a grid, a feature found at few other sites in Mesoamerica. Teotihuacan is the only other planned site that is organized along a grid system, which is usually interpreted as evidence that a powerful political elite could impose its ideas about urban planning. Love goes beyond this explanation to show how Ujuxte's urban planning could change daily practice for the whole population, creating more obedient "subjects": "Such regulation of movement, I suggest, disciplines actors in the same way that the regimes of schools, prisons, and clinics discussed by Foucault do," but to a lesser degree (232). Although elites may have not intended to instill such new disciplinary practices, the effects on people's movements and social practices were exactly that. Love affirms that a second consequence was "to create actors unsuited to active resistance . . . [although] they may have utilized the 'weapons of the weak'" including hidden resistance such as poaching, pilfering, and delayed payment of taxes (ibid.; Scott 1990).

Conclusions: Toward an Archaeology of Power

This chapter presented four archaeological case studies that explored ancient politics: at Tell Leilan in northern Mesopotamia in the Near East; in the Urartian Empire of the first millennium BC, also in the Near East; at Cahokia in the southeastern United States, and at Ujuxte on the Pacific Coast of Guatemala in Central America. These studies are representative of the major theoretical shift in political models that occurred in archaeology in the late 1980s and 1990s.

The four studies also illustrate the types of evidence and methodologies used by archaeologists interested in power and the epistemological issues these scholars encountered in their attempts to reconstruct political dynamics in premodern societies. In the absence of ancient texts, archaeologists rely heavily on settlement patterns to understand many aspects of ancient states, including their extent and boundaries, population density and the scale of monumental construction, the number and distribution of first- , second- , or third-order centers. Archaeologists have also used the distribution of artifactual evidence (be it administrative records, political insignias, or evidence of economic or religious activities) to reconstruct the locales of political activities, the foundations of political power, and the identity of political actors. The decisions ancient states made about what to depict in their monumental or public art provides another window into how political actors constructed power in these societies.

An important point to be drawn from these studies is that we need to continue to pursue the study of political power and its dynamics by considering in detail the manifestations of political power in the material world of archaeology at all the levels of each polity, from the commoner individual and household to the village or local community, the district or larger communal hinterland, and the polity and suprapolity levels. Because all "politics is local politics" (O'Neill and Hymel 1995), we need to reconstruct political power along these multiple levels of human societies, from the local to the suprapolity.

Although the micro-scale studies presented in this chapter may appear to be the most promising new arena for providing insights into political dynamics, we cannot lose sight of the political macro-scale because it is the one that provides the structure, institutions, or rules and possibilities for social encounters (Bourdieu 1990; Stein 1998; DeMarrais 2005; Barrett 2000). Rather than placing the macro scale (or "power over" arena) in opposition to the micro scale (or "power to" arena), these two social realms should be seen as complementary. Therefore, I will pursue the threads of political dynamics at three scalar levels: the macro level of the polity and its supra-polity interactions, the middle level of the internal complexities of the polity, and the micro level of individuals, households, and small communities that interacted with each other and with political elites in the capital in a tug-of-war of dominance and resistance.

In the following discussion, Chapter 4 presents the macro-scale analysis of Classic Maya polities and Chapter 5 addresses the middle scale of the internal political structure of these kingdoms. Finally, Chapter 6 endeavors a micro-scale exploration of the discourses of political power from different political factions including commoners. All three scales of the political arena contribute important threads to our understanding of ancient Maya societies because the flow of power from the individual upward to the Maya ruler was shaped, enabled, and/or restricted by the structure of the interactions among individuals, administrators, leaders, and factions. Such an approach to Classic Maya political structure envisions a plurality of political forms and political dynamics. At any one time, there were probably different kinds of Maya polities, some that could be easily envisioned as states and others that probably could not (Scarborough, Valdez, and Dunning 2003), some large and complex, others smaller and simpler, some more theocratic, others less so.[3] In the following chapters, I will explore the critical aspects of these complexities and dynamics of Classic Maya polities.

Stein (1998) calls for a new "archaeology of power" that can be pursued by integrating textual, iconographic, and archaeological evidence of claims to power with regional analyses of political economies that examine "variation in 'nodes of power' across the landscape" by recording "the behavioral correlates of the exercise of power . . . [or the] variation in patterns of production, exchange, and consumption of different goods or forms of value (such as labor)" (26–27). I would add to this definition the importance of political rituals as the embodiment of political power, authority, and legitimation (as I explore in Chapter 6).

Notes

1. Also see critiques of structuration and practice theories for their overemphasis on individual action (Gillespie 2001; Pauketat 2000; McGuire 1992) and their deemphasis of the processes of cultural transmission (Earle 1991; Meskell 1999).

2. The first and second sets of relationships are similar to the relationships between leaders and followers discussed in Chapter 2, while the third and fourth relate to a society's political structure of governing institutions with their attendant hierarchies of officials. This will be discussed in greater detail in Chapter 5.

3. I will use the term "polity" rather than "state" because some of the smaller Classic Maya polities may be closer to the "chiefdom" ideal societal type in terms of their population scale and internal sociopolitical complexity. However, see critiques of the classification schemes developed by the evolutionary school and of the debates about whether we should categorize some societies, such as the Maya or Cahokia, as chiefdoms or states in Pauketat (2007) and Yoffee (2005).

4

||||||||||||||

Reconstructing Classic Maya Polities

The Macro Scale of Political Analysis

Our interpretations of Classic Maya politics have changed tremendously over the last half-century. Until the 1960s, Maya civilization was conceived as a peaceful Eden dominated by priests who devoted their time to the esoteric arts of calendar-keeping, astronomy-astrology, and mathematics. This view has been completely overturned, and in this chapter, I consider how Maya states have been reconstructed at the macro scale by different scholars and from different perspectives since the 1960s. Archaeologists have used a combination of archaeological, epigraphic, and ethnohistorical data to reconstruct Classic Maya polities, and I follow how these sources of information have contradicted or supported each other.

Although Classic Maya polities clearly varied in structure and size, as most recent scholarship has highlighted (Marcus 1993, 1998; Pyburn 1997; Haviland 1997; Chase, Chase, and Haviland 1990; Demarest 1996a; Lucero 1999a; Iannone 2002; Munson and Macri 2009; Borstein 2005), previous (and sometimes current) discussions of the Classic Maya have engaged with two polarized models: the centralized model that envisions regional large-scale centralized states (A. Chase and D. Chase 1996; Chase, Chase, and Haviland 1990; Haviland 1992, 1997; Marcus 1993; Adams 1986) and the decentralized model that proposes small-scale weakly integrated polities (Demarest 1992; Houston 1993; Fox et al. 1996; see also reviews in Iannone 2002; Lucero 1997; Sharer and Golden 2004; Foias 2003; Runggaldier and Hammond in press). This debate has so dominated Maya archaeology in the last decades that I first explore its impact on our views of Classic politics.

The Old Debate: Centralization versus Decentralization

The centralized (or strongly centralized) and decentralized (or weakly centralized) models provide an entry into the points of contention surrounding ancient Maya politics. Toward the decentralist end of the spectrum lie various applications of cross-cultural political models, such as the peer-polity model (Renfrew 1982; Renfrew and Cherry 1986; Freidel 1986; Sabloff 1986), the segmentary state (Southall 1988; Fox 1987; Fox et al. 1996), the "theater state" (Geertz 1980; Demarest 1992; Hammond 1991a), the "galactic polity" (Tambiah 1976, 1977; Demarest 1992; Houston 1993; Hammond 1991a), the regal-ritual centers model (Fox 1977; Ball and Taschek 1991; Ball 1993), and the city-state model (Grube 2000). Although they vary in detail, all these constructs relate to a model that sees the state as weakly centralized. The main features of such a state are: 1) the polity consists of a capital city and its hinterland, which includes weakly controlled secondary and tertiary centers where the structures and functions found in the primary center are clearly replicated; 2) the power of the ruler is predicated on his personal charisma and his success in warfare, rituals, and marriage alliances that enhance his prestige; 3) a general lack of economic control by the state government that underscores its ritual legitimation (Demarest 1992; Iannone 2002; Rice 2004). These authors pay little attention to the smaller settlements on the lower levels of the political hierarchy beyond noting that they replicate the functions and structures of the capital. But these middle-size centers would have been important in the extraction of resources and the management of conflict within the polity (Stein 1994; Marcus 1993; Pyburn 1997; Iannone and Connell 2003).

At the other end of the spectrum, the centralized state model (A. Chase and D. Chase 1996; Marcus 1993; Adams 1986; Haviland 1992, 1997; Chase, Chase, and Haviland 1990; Rice 2009) proposes that the largest Maya cities—Tikal, Calakmul, and Caracol (and possibly others)—were characterized by rulers who were able to amass considerable political power, as reflected in their ability to construct massive nonritual public works such as the extensive causeways and standardized terrace systems at Caracol (A. Chase and D. Chase 1996; Chase, Chase, and Haviland 1990) and the water catchment reservoirs and possible *bajos* drainage systems at Tikal (Haviland 1997; Culbert 1992; Chase, Chase, and Haviland 1990; Vilma Fialko, personal communication, 2000; Scarborough 2003; Lucero 2006). Centralized states are thus seen as able to control economic systems to a great degree or completely. Supporters of this model also argue that the middle and lower centers in the political hierarchy were tightly controlled and integrated with the capitals because some of the middle-rank centers that have been excavated, such as the causeway termini complexes at Caracol, replicated neither the structure nor functions of the capital (A. Chase and D. Chase 1996; Iannone 2002). The centralized state model also presupposes a much more complex social system based on differentiated socioeconomic classes (and not exclusively on kinship) and an extensive middle class, as is evidenced at Caracol (Chase and Chase 2003). Nevertheless, the "centralists" do not present a well-articulated model for the structure of these polities beyond assuming the presence of a well-developed bureaucracy (see the excellent discussion and historical overview in Runggaldier and Hammond in press).

More recent scholarship has seen this dichotomy between centralized and decentralized power as false or nonexistent. For example, Arens and Karp (1989) write: "The key question is not how power is centralized; it isn't. The key question is how the illusion that power organizes a social formation composed of a center and periphery emerges and acts in society" (xvi).

Another critique by Elizabeth Graham (2012) contrasts modern states with the Maya polities and shows how even modern states that are often seen as centralized are not. Even though modern states do not control the economy completely, wealth accumulates to an incredible degree among a small group of elites. This doesn't deny that modern states have economic power, because all of them have central laws and regulations that pertain to the economy and to the (sometimes massive) budgets of the central government.

The postmodernist and post-processual schools in archaeology and more generally in the social sciences also question the dichotomy between centralized and decentralized polities because these are static models and power is not static. It is continuously reproduced, resisted, or changed through the actions of humans and institutions. Marcus (1993, 1998) has been the champion of this perspective through her "dynamic model" that argues that pre-Hispanic Maya civilization, like many other ancient societies, vacillated between periods of empire building and periods of political fragmentation (see an early intimation of this theory in Sharer 1991). Demarest (1996a) and Lucero (1999a) have also pointed to the "noticeable amount of variability that existed" (ibid., 211) among the Classic Maya states and to the need to understand this variability.

Nevertheless, some important points of contention have emerged from this "old" debate, and these appear as threads in models that have been used in recent scholarship to portray the variability that existed among Classic Maya polities. These include the scale or size of political units (states, polities) during the Classic period; the degree of intensification of agricultural, craft, and exchange systems in Classic Maya polities; the nature of Maya urbanism; the differences in the functions of smaller subsidiary centers and the dominant major centers; and the size, organization, and nature (bureaucratic or not) of the administration of each polity.

In this chapter and the next, I explore these points of contention and the methods and evidence through which archaeologists have attempted to reconstruct Classic polities. Finally, I will consider how these questions are actually answered by specific archaeological projects, including studies of the Greater Rosario polities in Chiapas, Mexico; the Xunantunich state of central Belize; and the Classic Maya polity centered on Motul de San José in northern Guatemala. This chapter is dedicated to the macro-scale analysis of Classic Maya polities, from relationships between states to the extent and scale of these kingdoms to the general pattern of their settlements, forms of subsistence, and administrations. Because of the nature of the case studies, I also examine other aspects beyond the macro scale.

Landscape and Settlement Archaeological Approaches

Archaeological approaches to ancient politics have relied heavily on settlement hierarchies, using them as direct correlates of political administrative structures. Thus, the largest Maya centers have been interpreted as independent political capitals, sites of the second size rank have been seen as secondary administrative centers, sites of the third rank as tertiary administrative centers, and so on (Bullard 1960; Flannery 1972; Marcus 1973, 1976, 1983, 1993; Adams and Jones 1981; Turner, Turner, and Adams 1981; de Montmollin 1989, 1995, 72–76; Laporte et al. 2004). Such analyses of settlement size have identified four to eight major cities in the top rank: Tikal, Calakmul, Palenque, Copan, Yaxchilan, Rio Bec, Coba, and possibly Uxmal (Adams and Jones 1981; Turner, Turner, and Adams 1981; Hammond 1975a; Culbert 1991; Marcus 1973, 1993; Lacadena García-Gallo and Ciudad Ruiz 1998).[1] These have been interpreted as capitals of sizeable regional states across the southern and northern Maya lowlands. According to proponents of this perspective, these major cities controlled significant territories of around 30,000 square kilometers and were supported by a hierarchy of four tiers of centers of decreasing size (de Montmollin 1995, 249). These scholars view Classic polities as large-scale regional states with centralized political power that enabled their rulers to manage such large territories. In contrast, archaeologists whose scope is intraregional (e.g., de Montmollin 1989, 1995; Laporte et al. 2004) perceive the Classic Maya landscape as dominated by peer-polity systems of small-scale polities averaging 2,000–3,000 square kilometers or even smaller (those that were 50–200 square kilometers are called microstates) that did not have generally hierarchical connections with major cities elsewhere (de Montmollin 1995, 249).

Numerous scholars have pointed out the problems with directly correlating large settlement size with primary political power and have emphasized the need for additional sources of political evidence to supplement the settlement data, such as historical texts.

Settlement studies have also borrowed from geographical or locational models (e.g., central place theory, nearest neighbor analysis, Thiessen polygons) to reconstruct the internal political hierarchy of Classic Maya states (Marcus 1973, 1976, 1983; Flannery 1972; Inomata and Aoyama 1996) or the extent of their territories (Hammond 1972, 1974; Laporte et al. 2004). Because these locational models assume the unity of political, religious, and economic hierarchies, these authors generally align themselves with the centralist camp (see the discussion in Potter and King 1995, 21–22). Studies that apply such locational theories to the Maya case (see Christaller and Baskin 1966) or any archaeological case also suffer from a number of important limitations because they assume that cost-benefit calculations were the most important factors in determining the location of human settlements (Crumley 1976; Smith 2003, 35–45; Hammond 1991a, 276). This is not the case; the size and location of Maya sites was heavily influenced by Maya cosmological concerns or cosmologies (Ashmore 1991, 1992; Brady 1997; Brady and Ashmore 1999; Houk 2003) rather than solely by political or economic factors.

In spite of the limitations of these landscape and settlement approaches, they are used to provide first estimates of the scale of ancient states. Although most of us envision ancient states as encompassing large territories, in fact there was tremendous variability in scale in terms of both territory and population (Chase, Chase, and Smith 2009; de Montmollin 1995; Feinman 1998; Hansen 2000; Hare 2000). Renfrew (1975, 1986) has reconstructed the average size of early states as 1,500 square kilometers. This number agrees well with the size estimated for the Sumerian city-state of Lagash during the Early Dynastic period (2,000–3,000 square kilometers) (Adams 1966; Diakonoff 1974; Flannery 1998; Yoffee 2005). But, there were much smaller states than this average, and some much larger (Feinman 1998). Some scholars have argued that the minimum scale in population and territory for archaic states should be placed at approximately 2,500 people and 625 square kilometers (an area with a radius of around 14.1 kilometers) (Renfrew 1975, 1982, 1986; Feinman 1998). However, we know that there were much smaller Greek poleis, some of which covered only 25 square kilometers and included only 1,000 people (Hansen 2000).

For the Classic Maya lowlands, Mathews (1985, 1991) has reconstructed the average polity size at 2,500 square kilometers based on the distribution of emblem glyphs (glyphs associated with independent capitals; see definition below) and using Thiessen polygons to estimate territorial extent of each polity. Hammond (1991a) has reached a similar estimate of 2,000 square kilometers based on evidence of conflict in hieroglyphic texts. Chase and Chase (1998; Chase, Chase, and Smith 2009) use similar data on the size of arenas of warfare but reach a different conclusion than Hammond does.[2] They argue that the regional-state model is more applicable to Classic Maya geopolitics because it fits considerations of military marching distances and epigraphic records of conflicts between different Maya polities: "The optimum Maya polity size . . . [was] limited by a military marching distance of 60 km . . . meaning that the physical territory directly controlled by a single Maya polity could approach, but was likely not to be much larger than, 11,333 km²" (Chase and Chase 1998, 14; see also Chase, Chase, and Smith 2009). These authors also distinguish between primary capitals located approximately 60 square kilometers from each other and border centers located around 30 kilometers from the primary centers (Chase and Chase 1998, 24–25).[3] These border centers are identified by the fact that they exhibit "variable histories": they switched alliances, achieved independence, and then reverted to dependency on another primary center (ibid.). The political volatility of the border towns not only underscores the intense competition among polities but also suggests that border centers may have had a role that was closer to that of client states instead of being directly and territorially controlled by primary capitals such as Tikal. Rather than seeing these highly divergent reconstructions of Maya state size as contradictory, we should accept that Classic kingdoms varied in size depending on the success of their rulers, their governments, and their armies.

Case Study: Settlement Pattern Studies in the Upper Grijalva Basin, Chiapas, Mexico

De Montmollin's research (1989, 1995) in the Greater Rosario Valley and Upper Grijalva tributaries in Chiapas, Mexico, is an excellent example of the settlement approach in reconstructing ancient polities. The Grijalva drainage is located along the southwestern periphery of the southern Maya lowlands (Figure 1.1). Because Late Classic monuments with hiero-glyphic texts were few and far between (and this is typical of many other Maya sites and regions), de Montmollin identifies polity capitals in the region based on the scale, number, and types of monumental civic archi-tecture (1995, 52). He notes the limitations of this approach: "The austere prehistoric context [where only settlement surveys have been conducted] prevents any tracing of fluid power relationships of dominance and subor-dination among rulers at [these] different centers" (53). No one center had substantially more civic architecture than others, so de Montmollin con-cludes that this drainage was divided into small peer polities of relatively equal power and standing (Figure 4.1). The boundaries of each polity were

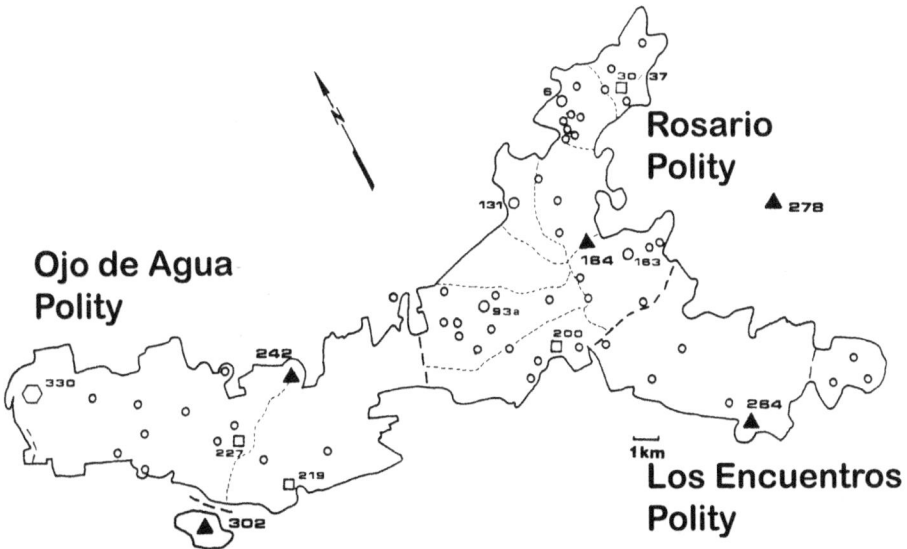

Figure 4.1. The three polities of Late Classic Greater Rosario Valley, Chiapas, Mexico. Legend: triangles = political capitals (Tenam Rosario is 164, Ojo de Agua is 242, and El Zapote is 264); square = district capital; large circle = subdistrict capital; small circle = local center; hexagon = anomalous center; light dashed lines = district boundaries; heavy dashed lines = polity boundaries. After de Montmollin 1995, Figure 14.

defined (in a sense arbitrarily) by geographical features such as rivers, hills, valley edges, but these are likely possibilities for the actual ancient frontiers.

Based on the scale of monumental civic architecture, de Montmollin identifies three small peer polities in the Greater Rosario Valley: the Rosario polity with its capital at Tenam Rosario (Site 164), the Ojo de Agua polity with its capital at Ojo de Agua (Site 242), and the significantly smaller Los Encuentros polity with its capital at El Zapote (Site 264) (Figure 4.1). The size of these three polities is quite small; they average 41.71 square kilometers and 10,428 inhabitants (55, Tables 9–10).

De Montmollin then explores the political hierarchies in each of these small polities through the settlement lens: rather than using calculations of the volume of architecture or numbers of plazas for each site, he argues that the architectural diversity of civic buildings is a better index "of different intensities and kinds of political activities" (76). This index reveals significant differences in the political administrative hierarchies of the three polities. The Rosario polity had four civic levels above the basal village: the polity capital; the district capital (with at least one plaza with more than one pyramid and one ball court); the subdistrict capital (with plaza with only one pyramid and one ball court); and the local center (with some civic buildings but no plazas with more than one pyramid and no ball courts) (79) (see Figure 4.1). In contrast, the Ojo de Agua civic hierarchy was simpler, with three levels above the basal village: the polity capital, the district capital, and the local center. However, the Ojo de Agua district capitals exhibit a higher level of public architecture complexity, unlike the district capitals in the Rosario hierarchy (83). The third polity, Los Encuentros, was much smaller and was the least complex politically: above the basal village, there were only local centers and the large polity capital at El Zapote. No district or subdistrict capitals have been discovered in this polity. De Montmollin also identifies similarities in the civic architecture of the capital sites and their subsidiary district capitals, which suggests a replication of functions between the top tier and the second tier of the political hierarchy in these small peer polities (83). Putting together these pieces of evidence, de Montmollin concludes that the Rosario polity may have had a more centralized political structure than Ojo de Agua, but the overall replication of civic architecture in all polities brings them close to the decentralized political "type" (84).

Examination of the structure of Tenam Rosario, the capital of the largest and most centrally located polity in the Greater Rosario Valley, reveals more details about the political organization of this small Maya polity

(Figure 4.2). Tenam Rosario had as many public plazas as the number of districts in its realm, and the layout of the plazas is similar to the layouts found at the district centers in its hinterland (de Montmollin 1988, 1989). In other words, the internal organization of the capital appears to be a microcosm of the whole polity. Furthermore, de Montmollin (1988) finds that Tenam Rosario's civic center was divided into two halves, one to the north of the Acropolis (which was the royal palace) and one to the south (see Figure 4.2).[4] These halves consisted of similar large plazas (Plazas 3 and 6) with pyramids on three sides, a range structure (a palace built of stone on a

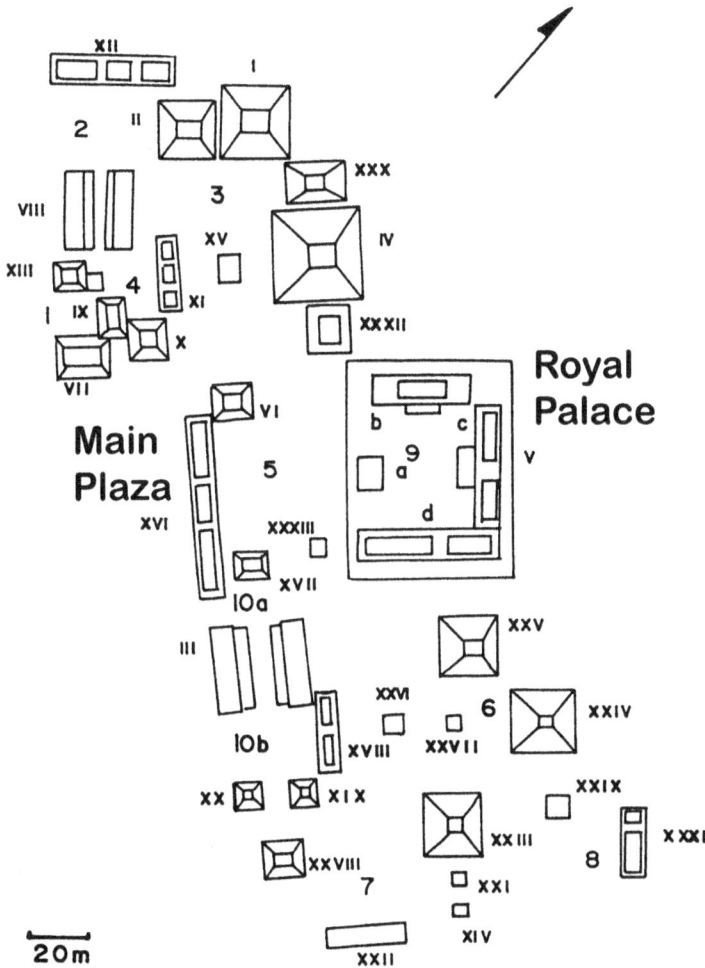

Figure 4.2. Map of the core of Tenam Rosario (RV164), the capital of the Rosario polity in the Greater Rosario Valley, Chiapas, Mexico. After de Montmollin 1995, Figure 20.

low platform) on the fourth side, and a ball court tucked in the northwest corner (de Montmollin 1995). These main plazas may correspond to the two major divisions in the polity: upper districts to the north of Tenam Rosario and lower districts to the south, each with its own district capital. De Montmollin suggests that the shaping of the capital site as a political microcosm of the whole polity would have served as a mechanism of political integration for the whole polity: the capital plazas would have served as the arenas for rituals involving the elite (and maybe the non-elite) from all the districts and subdistricts of the realm (365).[5] Other known Maya capitals also served as political-ritual microcosms of their hinterlands, including Utatlan in the Late Postclassic K'iche state (Carmack 1981), Mayapan in Middle Postclassic Yucatan (Proskouriakoff 1962), and San Gervasio on Cozumel Island (Freidel and Sabloff 1984).

The duality of the major plazas at Tenam Rosario contrasts with the apical position of the Acropolis and its associated Plaza 5 (de Montmollin 1988, 361) (Figure 4.2). The fact that there was only one acropolis in the center of the capital led de Montmollin to conclude that the Rosario polity had a centralized political system in which the dynastic ruler and his kin group formed the apex. Furthermore, the developed four-tier site hierarchy (including Tenam Rosario at the top) and the general lack of replication in civic plaza forms in the lower levels of the hierarchy support the suggestion that the Rosario state had a more centralized political system. Even so, the scope of power of the Tenam Rosario elites was limited: they did not attract a large proportion of the subject population to the capital. De Montmollin writes, "Tenam Rosario has only six percent of the total number of housemounds from the valley . . . [so its power] does not entail a particularly high degree of 'forced' settlement for the population at the capital" (364).

The presence of ball courts at many sites (small to large) in the Greater Rosario Valley speaks of a more decentralized system overall (de Montmollin 1995, 158). The discovery of ball courts at both district and subdistrict capitals (and not just at polity capitals) contrasts with the rarity of ball courts in the central Maya lowlands, where they are almost always found in the polity capitals (160).[6] Because of this contrast, de Montmollin suggests a different function for the Upper Grijalva ball courts: they were used to manage internal conflicts between "proliferating and continuously fractious junior elite groups" (ibid.). This implies that the ball game was a substitute for war or other status-reinforcing rituals.

De Montmollin (1995) also examines political organization by considering the degree of concentration or dispersal of commoner residences in polity capitals and subsidiary civic centers. Archaeologists generally associate population concentration in major centers with political centralization (175–77). But it is important to consider that there were alternative strategies for maintaining control over a subject population without resettling everyone in the political capital (177). For example, another strategy would have been to bring into the capitals only the secondary elites to make it easier for the royal elites to monitor them and transmit political decisions to them (ibid.). Such an approach to population nucleation was present in many ancient empires: all provincial elites had to maintain residences in the imperial capital and send their offspring to be schooled there (e.g., the Inca and Aztec empires). Another political strategy for maintaining control over the subject population was to disperse the ruling elites among the commoners; in this configuration, elite residences were found in hinterlands and in small noncivic centers.[7] We see this pattern in feudal Europe and Japan (ibid.; Adams and Smith 1981). However, in this strategy, elites had a different type of control: the primary link was between members of the lower elite and commoners rather than between members of the upper and lower elites. In all strategies, the chief concern of the upper elites was controlling or at least monitoring whoever the primary political actors or contenders were, whether they were secondary elites or commoners or both. De Montmollin (1995) finds disparities in the nucleation of elites and commoners in the three polities of the Greater Rosario Valley.[8] Surprisingly, only the smallest and least hierarchically complex Los Encuentros polity had a high degree of nucleation of elites and commoners in its capital: 60 percent of the elite and 36 percent of the commoners lived in its capital El Zapote (ibid., 180). In contrast, the larger and more hierarchically complex Rosario and Ojo de Agua polities had lower nucleation indices, although elites were more nucleated there than commoners: 18 percent and 16 percent for elites and 4 percent and 9 percent for commoners, respectively (ibid.). Thus, the greater investment in or greater success of nucleation of elites (rather than nucleation of commoners) in these two polities may suggest that the second strategy of nucleation (described above) was pursued by Greater Rosario Maya elites or that secondary elites had reasons for wanting to live in the polity capitals.

There are also distinctions in nucleation in sites at different levels of the civic hierarchy in these polities. The Rosario polity shows bottom-heavy nucleation, while Ojo de Agua shows top-heavy nucleation (182).[9] According to de Montmollin, this is a clear sign that the Rosario polity was more decentralized because "more people [residing] outside civic centers . . . [would be] unreachable by agents of the political regime" (ibid.). Notice that this feature stands in contrast to the more developed civic (and presumably administrative) hierarchy that was in place in the Rosario polity! In other words, the Rosario polity embodies features of both the "centralized-state" and the "decentralized-state" models, showing that the dichotomy between unitary and segmentary states is false.

The distribution of civic or public architecture can also shed light on the concentration of political events at the capital or their dispersal across the landscape (de Montmollin 1995, 198). In the Greater Rosario Valley (as in most of the rest of the Maya lowlands), civic architecture was dispersed across the landscape. De Montmollin argues that there are two reasons for the dispersal of civic plazas: "so that officials based at the plazas can keep an eye and an obsidian-spike club on the restive commoners" and because "the presence of government officials and plazas close to them increases the commoners' contentment" (198–99). Therefore, rather than considering dispersal of public architecture as a sign of political decentralization (or weakness), it can be seen as a different type of political control. On this dimension of political organization, the Ojo de Agua polity scores higher than the Rosario polity because its capital had a higher concentration of plazas than outlying civic centers did (ibid.). But further "down the hierarchy, both polities have near identical proportions of plazas in district capitals vs. local centers" (200). However, the much smaller Los Encuentros polity has an even higher concentration of plazas in its capital. It thus ranks as the most politically "centralized" polity along this dimension.

More controversially, de Montmollin asserts that pyramids denote political offices, while elite residences identify possible "contenders for office" (197). It is hard to justify such one-to-one correspondence for pyramids or elite residences because we don't know the specifics of how pyramids related to political institutions and we don't know if every member of the elite could compete for political offices. Whether de Montmollin's one-to-one correspondence is valid or not, we can still gain some insights into Maya politics by considering how tribute burdens on the commoners as represented by civic constructions were distributed within each polity. The scale of such civic constructions presumably reflects the ability of rulers to extract labor from commoners. Since excavations have not been done that would allow us to reconstruct phases of construction, de Montmollin uses the total volume of public architecture and the number of commoner families[10] in each polity to gauge how much labor was needed per family to construct the buildings. The Ojo de Agua polity required the most labor (around 31–41 cubic meters per family). In the Rosario polity, the tribute labor burden was 19–23 cubic meters per family, and in the Los Encuentros polity, the burden was significantly lower at 7–8 cubic meters per family (205). De Montmollin sees these as relatively low burdens, and indeed they are if one considers that these tribute demands could be paid over the several hundred years that these polities lasted. When civic construction burdens for polity and district capitals are compared with the burdens in lower-level centers, it becomes clear that rulers or officials of the upper-level centers could command much more tribute labor than lower-level centers. As the ability to extract human labor correlates well with political power, this suggests that much more political power was concentrated in the hands of the upper-level rulers and administrators and hence that the political structure was more centralized (de Montmollin 1995, 206).

De Montmollin is also interested in estimating the burden on commoners for the "feed[ing], fan[ning] and flatter[ing]" of officials (208). He breaks the scale of pyramid construction into six size classes and arbitrarily assigns three official positions for the pyramids in the top three size classes (1 to 3), two official positions to pyramids in middle-size classes (4 and 5), and one official position to the smallest pyramids in the lowest-size class (6; 209). Although we don't know how these pyramids of religious function tie into the political structure, we can still follow de Montmollin's argument here. His goal is to gauge how many elite contenders for political offices and how many tribute payers or possible supporters existed in each polity. Surprisingly, all three polities have similar numbers of elite families contending for political offices, around nine to ten (210).[11] When the number of commoner supporters of each political office is calculated, differences come to the surface: while Rosario and Ojo de Agua polities had relatively similar levels of tribute payers supporting each official (30–35), the Los Encuentros polity had many more supporting each official (67). This means a much higher tribute burden for each commoner in the first two polities and much less of a burden in the third polity. According to de Montmollin, this implies more significant political power in the hands of the Rosario and Ojo de Agua elites who extract more from their commoner populations (ibid.).

We can draw several lessons from this case study. First, although there are significant limitations to the use of survey data for reconstructing ancient politics, de Montmollin's research illustrates the richness of possible details that can be drawn from such data. Second, de Montmollin returns throughout his study to the question of whether Maya polities were centralized or decentralized, illuminating how this intense debate dominated 1980s and 1990s research. Third, the centralized/decentralized dichotomy is false and needs to be abandoned: some features of the Greater Rosario polities were more similar to the centralized state model, while other features were more typical of the decentralized state model. Instead of discovering centralized or decentralized states, de Montmollin's work suggests that Classic Maya elites used a number of strategies for maintaining political power, such as establishing administrative centers in the hinterland, concentrating the commoners and/or subsidiary elites in the larger centers, and building the capital as a microcosm of the larger polity. De Montmollin finds that different elites chose different strategies based on local conditions.

Environment, Agriculture, and Urbanism

Another debate about Classic Maya political organization at the macro scale pivots on the nature of its urbanism. This debate was engendered by Sanders and Price's (1968) distinction between highland civilizations in Mesoamerica characterized by "true" urbanism based on intensive agriculture (e.g., Teotihuacan and Tenochtitlan) and lowland civilizations characterized by more dispersed settlement and non-intensive subsistence agriculture (e.g., Maya and Olmec polities). Although the most recent settlement surveys in the Maya lowlands have clearly demonstrated that some Maya cities were urban, with dense populations surpassing 50,000 (Rice and Culbert 1990), this distinction between highland and lowland urbanism has continued with Sanders and Webster's (1988) application of Richard Fox's cross-cultural urban typology to the Classic Maya. Sanders and Webster write that most Maya cities are regal-ritual centers in Fox's classification system, while the highland Mexican cities (such as Teotihuacan) fall in the category of administrative cities. Smith (1989) and Chase, Chase, and Haviland (1990) have critiqued Sanders and Webster for assuming that there is only one kind of Maya city. In the last decades, we have attained increasing awareness (and evidence) that both Maya and highland Mexican political centers varied in size, density, complexity, and function (Chase, Chase, and Haviland 1990; Chase, Chase and Smith 2009; Hare 2000; King and Potter 1994; Potter and King 1995; Smith 1989, 2008).

Evidence from excavations at a number of centers does not support the argument that all Maya sites were regal-ritual centers. These sites include Chunchucmil, a very densely occupied site in northwest Yucatan located in an agriculturally poor environment (Dahlin and Ardren 2002; Dahlin 2003; Hutson 2010; Hutson, Magnoni, and Stanton 2004; Hutson et al. 2007; Hutson, Dahlin, and Mazeau 2010). The soils at Chunchucmil cannot support agriculture (Beach 1998; Dahlin et al. 2005), so what were the residents doing there? Mounting evidence suggests that the city specialized in trade, especially of salt produced at the nearby flats of Punta Canbalam (Dahlin et al. 1998; Dahlin et al. 2007; Dahlin et al. 2009). Some centers may have been only ritual sites: for example, King and Shaw (2003) describe Maax Na in Belize as a possible pilgrimage center because its major temples are all tied to caves, which the ancient Maya saw as sacred entrances to the Underworld.

Recent Maya ecological studies have outlined the complexity and intensity of Maya agricultural systems, including swidden agriculture, which may have been the dominant practice in this region (Atran 1993; Fedick 1996; Gómez-Pampa, Flores, and Aliphat Fernandez 1990; Reina and Hill 1980; Whitmore and Turner 1992; Zier 1992). Johnston (2003) argues that swidden agriculture may have been an intensive system. Ford and Nigh (2009) have described the Maya as managers of the tropical forest because they maintained forest gardens that required much more work than current Peten agriculture where plots (known as milpas) are completely cleared of trees and burned for maize monocropping. Thus, Sanders and Price's suggestion that Maya lowland agriculture was not intensive is not supportable. However, we do not know how widespread intensive agricultural systems were, if they were responses to increased demands from political elites, whether the elites controlled the most intensive systems, and whether all these systems were sustainable over the long term.

Sanders and Webster's classification of Maya cities as regal-ritual centers also has important implications for our understanding of rural settlements in the Maya lowlands. They envision rural communities as urban settlements writ small and see few functional differences between rural and urban settlements (see a critique of this view in King and Potter 1994, 65–66). In contrast to Webster and Sanders, Potter and King (1995) have argued quite forcefully that a heterarchical approach, one that is "concerned with functional complexity along both vertical and horizontal dimensions" (17), should be applied to Classic Maya political structure.[12] This approach hypothesizes that Maya power hierarchies along the political, religious, and economic dimensions were partially or completely disarticulated. Thus, it assumes variability in the functions of Classic Maya settlement over time and space, in both small and large sites. Like McAnany (1993b) and Ford

(2004), Potter and King (1995) suggest that in the mosaic environment of the Maya tropical lowlands, small communities near raw material sources specialized in extracting and producing these resources (19; see similar studies in Scarborough, Valdez, and Dunning 2003). In this view, the economic hierarchy was tied to the distribution of raw materials across the landscape, but it was at least partially disarticulated from the political and/or religious hierarchy. I agree with Potter, King, McAnany, Ford, and Scarborough that the Maya lowlands were characterized by multiple hierarchies, not one hierarchy, and that it is important to investigate at the local level where these nodes were and how they intersected.

Hieroglyphs and Classic Maya Polities

The decipherment of the Maya hieroglyphic writing system began in the 1960s and has developed rapidly in the last thirty years. This advance ushered in a new era that provided a historical and emic perspective on Classic Maya political organization and the royal personages involved.

Maya hieroglyphs have contributed to macro-scale political reconstructions in three ways. First, their focus on the ritual life of the royal elites has enabled Mayanists to understand that divine kingship was the overarching political institution of the Classic Maya states (see detailed treatments in Schele and Miller 1986; Schele and Freidel 1990; Schele and Mathews 1998; Freidel, Schele, and Parker 1993; Houston and Stuart 1996; and Sharer and Golden 2004). At the heart of Classic Maya polities was the divine ruler, or *k'uhul ajaw*, who lived in the royal court in the epicenter of an independent political capital, from which he conducted the affairs of the state. Based on the Classic period hieroglyphic texts, Houston and Stuart (2001) see the divine king as an individual who is marked as different from everyone else: "For the Classic Maya, power was almost a unilateral quality of the lord, a fiery essence, hotter than the hearth, coursing through the blood and scorching the breath" (55; see also Houston and Stuart 1996). Through ritual, the kings could become the gods whose appearance they took on through costuming: for example, the Palenque ruler Ahkal Mo' Nahb (grandson of the famed Pakal) is recorded in the texts on the monolithic stone platform of Temple XIX as becoming "fused" with the deity GI, the principal god of the Palenque Triad, while his main priest Janab Ajaw is "fused" with the Creator God Itzamnaaj (Stuart and Stuart 2008, 226–27, Figure 76).[13]

Second, emblem glyphs in Classic hieroglyphic texts have provided the information that is most relevant to political reconstructions (Berlin 1958; Mathews 1985, 1991). Emblem glyphs are the personal titles carried by rulers of an independent Maya polity (Mathews 1991; Martin and Grube 2000; Graña-Behrens 2006).[14] Each emblem glyph consists of three parts: 1) a prefix, called the "water group," which can be translated as k'uhul, or divine; 2) a superfix that translates as ajaw or ruler (reinforced sometimes by the subfix syllable -wa); 3) the main sign, which varies with each city-state and is generally a feature or place-name within the capital of that polity (Mathews 1991; Stuart and Houston 1994; Tokovinine 2008). The first and second parts are fixed, and the third is variable. Putting these elements together, we can translate the meaning of the emblem glyph as a dynastic title along the lines of "Divine Lord of X-place."

Because the title places all who carry it in the same rank, Mathews (1991) concluded that all 30 or more sites that had an emblem glyph in the southern Maya lowlands during the Late Classic were autonomous realms in a landscape of small-scale independent polities (Mathews 1985, 1991). However, similar to the international political system of today, these states, although nominally autonomous, would have varied greatly in political capital because of their different sizes and resources. Compare, for example, the United States with Ghana. The identification of the main symbol of an emblem glyph with a specific location in the capital city of each polity (Stuart and Houston 1994; Houston and Stuart 1996; Tokovinine 2008) has pushed Mathews (1985, 1991) and Martin and Grube (2000) to suggest that the city-state model is the most applicable to Classic political entities, although Classic Maya cities generally lacked the economic functions that were part of the Classical Greek city-states, or poleis (see also Ball 1993 and Hammond 1991a, 277–80).

Third, Classic texts record a number of subsidiary political titles and provide insights into the variability in internal structure of Maya states (Inomata 2001a; Houston and Stuart 2001; Sharer and Golden 2004; Parmington 2003; Foias 2003). These titles will be discussed in detail in Chapter 5, but suffice it to say for now that these titles are few and rare, suggesting a small administrative cadre.

Tokovinine's (2008) research on emblem glyphs confirms that the Classic Maya conception of polity was not tied to territory but to specific spatial locations that were generally associated with gods and/or ancestors. Hammond (1991a) provides support for the argument, which is based on the archaeological evidence of the Classic period, that territory and frontiers were relatively unimportant in Classic Maya conceptions of polity. He argues that the absence of frontier markers (with a few exceptions) and the focus of inscriptions on polity capitals and subsidiary centers suggest that the Maya were not very concerned with boundary maintenance or territorial integrity.[15] Archaeologists often use living non-Western traditional societies to gain insight into the past cultures they study. Maya archaeologists are no exception, and they have sought similar societies from many parts of the world to compare with the Classic Maya. For example, southeastern Asian "galactic" polities have a similar focus on the capital center and not on bounded space (Hammond 1991a), and as Demarest (1992) elaborates, this is predicated on the rulers' desire to control labor rather than land (either because land is abundant or because a large amount of human labor is required to work the land). Hammond brings in Moertono's Javanese metaphor of a torch as the perfect image for the "galactic" polity and for Classic Maya states: "Territorial jurisdiction could not be strictly defined by permanent boundaries, but was characterized by a fluidity or flexibility of boundary dependent on the diminishing or increasing power of the center" (Moertono 1968, 112, quoted in Hammond 1991a, 277). Hammond argues that Maya states may have followed patterns that were similar to thirteenth-century Thai and fourteenth-century Javanese polities: the "galactic" polity was constructed of "circles of leaders and followers that form and reform in highly unstable factions . . . [in] a political-economic system premised on the control of manpower as its chief resource" (Tambiah 1977, 92).[16] Factionalism between elites was a significant characteristic of these societies (Tambiah 1977), as it was in medieval Europe (Fourquin 1978; see also Hammond 1991a, 274) and in Contact period Yucatan (Restall 1997). Similar fractures are in evidence in the Classic period and may be the leading cause of the Classic Maya collapse (Culbert 1991; Demarest 1992, 2006; Fash and Stuart 1991; Fash 1991; Hendon 1991; Pohl and Pohl 1994; Demarest et al. 2004). Because factionalism was such a significant force in Maya polities, trade, markets, religion, and elite marriage alliances were manipulated to cement political ties, as they were in feudal polities and "galactic" polities elsewhere (Hammond 1991a, 275).

Variation in Political Structure from the Emblem Glyphs

Emblem glyphs are a crucial piece of the political puzzle and give hints of differences between kingship in the southern lowlands and the northern lowlands and between the Early and the Late Classic periods.

The three-part emblem glyph (described above) appears only in Late Classic times and most often in the southern Maya lowlands. During the Early Classic, the emblem glyph lacked the water group prefix, and therefore didn't carry the k'uhul, divine, adjective that modified the title ajaw, or lord (Houston and Stuart 1996, 295). It is hard to discern if the addition of this adjective in the Late Classic marked an important transformation in the institution of rulership from secular to divine kingship (Houston and Inomata 2009). To follow the hypothesis that it marked the advent of divine kingship, we need to consider in more detail how the title of ajaw originated and how it was treated before the Late Classic in inscriptions and art. The linguistic origins of the title may lie with the verb for shouting, *aaw (Kaufman and Norman 1984, 139; Houston and Stuart 1996, footnote 3). Thus, ajaw means "he who shouts," a title associated with rulers in other cultures. Although the glyph for ajaw first appears in the third century BC at San Bartolo in the southern lowlands (Saturno, Stuart, and Beltran 2006, 1282), its meaning at that time is unclear (Houston and Inomata 2009, 132). The title appears in scenes in the San Bartolo murals that depict myths of creation; it is used to name one of the gods in these scenes (Saturno, Taube, and Stuart 2005; Saturno 2009). Thus, the title from its earliest use had religious associations or supernatural connotations. During the Early Classic, when it appears together with the emblem glyph or adjectives that mark age, it refers to rulers depicted usually holding holy objects such as the double-headed serpent bar. These Early Classic rulers, like their Late Classic descendants, claimed a long dynastic line all the way back to original gods (Houston and Stuart 1996). In other words, the sacred quality of the ruler named as ajaw was already there in the Early Classic but did not become formalized in the writing system until the Late Classic, when the k'uhul prefix was added to the emblem glyph (Houston and Inomata 2009). It is noteworthy that when a divine ruler was captured in war, he was stripped of the k'uhul prefix and was named only as ajaw of his home polity (Miller and Martin 2004, 183).

The emblem glyph was used in various ways across the Maya lowlands during the Late Classic, intimating possible differences in the institution of rulership. Several sites used the same emblem glyph, including Dos Pilas and Tikal, Calakmul and Dzibanche, and Palenque and Tortuguero. It seems that the meaning of these ambulatory emblem glyphs was changed from "place" to "descent from place" such that the Dos Pilas dynasty claimed descent from Tikal's royalty, Calakmul's dynasty from Dzibanche's royalty, and so on (Tokovinine 2008).

In the northern Maya lowlands, the use of the prefix *k'uhul* was rare even in the Late to Terminal Classic, and kings took only the *ajaw* title. These titles, which are sometimes called problematic emblem glyphs (Houston 1986), are also found at Altar de Sacrificios, El Chorro, Rio Azul, Xultun, and Zapote Bobal in the southern Maya lowlands (ibid.; Fitzsimmons 2006). Most interestingly, though, this pattern is dominant in the northern Maya lowlands (Graña-Behrens 2006; Lacadena García-Gallo 2004). The absence of the *k'uhul* prefix in emblem glyphs of the northern Yucatan is coupled with a different placement of the emblem glyph in the northern hieroglyphic texts: they generally precede the individual ruler's name instead of following it, as is always the case in the southern texts (Graña-Behrens 2006). Can we understand this difference between the emblem glyphs of north and south as a difference in the way northern Maya rulers saw themselves—as "mere mortals" rather than "divine beings"? Graña-Behrens (2006) intimates such a possibility in his study of emblem glyphs of northwestern Yucatan but leaves open the possibility that we are seeing only the Early Classic title that northern dynasts retained.

Maya Superstates

More recent epigraphic treatises (Grube 2000; Martin and Grube 1995, 2000, 2008) have introduced another element of complexity in the Classic Maya political landscape: the existence of superstates (or hegemonies) centered on Tikal and Calakmul that were involved in a bipolar system of international politics.[17] These superstates are manifested in the hieroglyphic texts through expressions such as *y-ajaw*, or "the lord of," followed by the name of the paramount king, or *u-kabjiiy*, translated as "he supervised it," followed by the name of the paramount king (Martin and Grube 2008, 18–21). It is possible that the title of *kaloomte'*, loosely translated as "king of kings," or a divine ruler who has conquered others of his rank, is associated with these superstates or hegemonies (see Figure 5.1a). Although this title was generally carried by the powerful rulers of Tikal, Calakmul, and other such superstates, a cautionary note is in order here. The early Late Classic ruler Tayal/Tayel Chan K'inich of Motul de San José (which was clearly not a superstate) calls himself *kaloomte'* on a unique square polychrome platter with four supports that was discovered in the tomb of Dos Pilas Ruler 2 (Itzamnaaj K'awiil) (ibid., 58–59; Tokovinine and Zender 2012). Because the style and chemical profile of this special plate suggest that it was made at Tikal by royal scribes (Reents-Budet et al. 2012), this title may have been given to Tayal by the Tikal *k'uhul ajaw*.

Martin and Grube assert that Maya superstates existed based in part on the archaeological evidence that the two sites of Tikal and Calakmul were much larger in settlement size and scale of public construction than most other capital centers. They argue that such major construction projects "would have required centralized planning and the control of substantial manpower," which was achieved through the formation of hegemonies. However, they describe the political structure of these hegemonies as decentralized; there was no military occupation or central administration of the vassal states (Grube 2000, 550; Martin and Grube 2008, 20). The vassal states probably paid some type of tribute to the superstates, which also dominated the external affairs of the states under their hegemony (see Martin and Grube 2008, 21). This description of Tikal and Calakmul as hegemonic powers hints that they were not highly centralized bureaucratic polities, even though there was substantial power in the hands of their divine rulers. The organization of these hegemonies needs to be explored in much greater depth, though, through targeted projects such as the work at Xunantunich.

Case Study: Archaeology, Integration, and Hegemony at Xunantunich, Belize

Xunantunich was one of the dominant centers in the Upper Belize Valley in western Belize during the Late Classic. Its largest pyramid, the Castillo, is an impressive edifice that rises 45 meters tall and is visible for kilometers. The Xunantunich Archaeological Project, which was directed by Richard Leventhal and Wendy Ashmore, conducted extensive excavations and surveys at this center. The project also explored a number of secondary centers and intersite settlements along the Mopan and Macal Rivers (LeCount and Yaeger 2010a; Leventhal et al. 2010).

Although some doubts remain, it is very likely that Xunantunich was conquered by and incorporated into the hegemony of Naranjo (which was in turn part of the larger Calakmul superstate described above). LeCount and Yaeger (2010b) prefer to call hegemonies "multipolity networks" because they consist of one state that begins to expand and conquer other polities, incorporating these newly acquired territories in diverse ways, from very loose attachment to direct control and/or annexation. Many ancient empires were indeed hegemonies, and of these, the Aztec (Mexica) Empire is probably the best known (Conrad and Demarest 1984; Smith 2008).

LeCount and Yaeger (2010b) consider the different types of incorporation strategies in the better-known empire-hegemonies in order to understand how Naranjo incorporated and controlled Xunantunich during the Late Classic. Their approach can shed light on how other Classic Maya hegemonies were organized. They define three types of incorporation strategies: 1) patron-client relations; 2) alliances (with independent allies or dependent allies); and 3) formal control or direct annexation (30–39, Table 2.2). Both patron-client relations and alliances are indirect forms of control because they are based on the cooperation of the leaders of the subsidiary polity, who maintain at least nominal political independence from the hegemon. Under formal control, subordinate polities lose their independence and are territorially annexed; their internal and external affairs are directed by the hegemon (31; Doyle 1986).

Patron-client relations were the most loose and most unstable strategy of incorporation: leaders of the dominant state were patrons of the subordinate polity and obtained services or support from these clients in exchange for gifts. The services the clients provided were intermittent or a one-time event and generally consisted of military contingents to defend the frontiers of the hegemon (Doyle 1986; Luttwak 1976; M. Smith 1996; LeCount and Yaeger 2010b). They are often called "client states" in the Roman Empire (Luttwak 1976) or "strategic provinces" in the Aztec Empire (Smith 1996). LeCount and Yaeger (2010b, 40, Table 2.2) detail the material implications or archaeological markers of this patron-client strategy: although gift exchanges are central, tribute payments are nonexistent; foreign symbolism, marriage alliances, and war events are rare; and there is no restructuring of the client polity politically, economically, or demographically. Gifts from the patron hegemon to the rulers of the client polities may have ranged from land to valuables to special statuses (32). Therefore, patron-client relations are reflected in "the presence of a few rare items in elite contexts at a site that otherwise lacks evidence of extensive interaction or contact" with the hegemon (39).

Alliances were tighter integration strategies and can be subdivided as independent and dependent (32–35). All allies, whether independent or dependent, maintained political independence in theory and at least to some degree in practice. For LeCount and Yaeger, the important distinction between independent and dependent allies is "whether or not the ally had been subjugated by an act of war. Subjugation [through war] always resulted in the imposition of regularized tribute payments and other forms of servitude" (33). Thus, these two subtypes are distinguished by the degree to which the hegemon intruded into and reorganized the subordinate polities. LeCount and Yaeger illuminate the nature of such alliances through a description of dependent allies of the Aztec Empire that are known ethnohistorically: "Local rulers maintained considerable autonomy, including command of their own military . . . so long as they capitulated to imperial demands" (ibid.). Dependent allies paid tribute to the hegemon, while independent allies made such payments only irregularly (ibid., Table 2.2). Although war events connected both independent and dependent allies with the hegemon, such events were more common with dependent allies than with independent allies (34–35). The dominant power also imposed marriage alliances and foreign symbolism. In addition, the hegemon reorganized the highest levels of the political hierarchy of dependent allies by imposing a collaborator as the local ruler or by some restructuring of the land tenure or economy (34–35). LeCount and Yaeger note that "as the degree of intrusion by the dominant polity into the affairs of its allies grows," so does the level of political and military conflict or unrest within these dependent allies (35). Rebellions would occur, especially at times of transition in imperial rulership, such as the death of the hegemon.

The third type of incorporation strategy, formal control, is the most intrusive because it involves the territorial annexation of conquered polities and the reworking of their sociopolitical, economic, and demographic structures (35–39). In each newly annexed polity, the hegemon would build a provincial capital and name a nonlocal provincial governor, although smaller local communities may have remained under the same local leaders (37). The economies of these annexed polities would generally intensify to respond to the new tribute demands. The hegemon might seize and redistribute land belonging to the previous ruling elites. The dominant polity would also impose state ideologies expressed through art and architecture on these newly acquired territories (39).

We can understand the relationship between Xunantunich and Naranjo (which was only 13 kilometers east) more deeply by examining it in the context of LeCount and Yaeger's analysis of incorporation strategies. When Naranjo resurged in the late seventh century AD under Lady Six Sky and her son K'ahk' Tiliw Chan Chaak (Martin and Grube 2000, 2008), Xunantunich experienced its great florescence and growth, in the phase locally called the Hats' Chaak, between AD 670 and 780 (LeCount and Yaeger 2010a, 2010c). Naranjo's influence on Xunantunich was profound. The site was rebuilt at this time in the image of the core of Naranjo (esp. group B) and Calakmul (Ashmore 1986, 1998, 2010; Ashmore and Sabloff 2002). The massive scale of construction at Xunantunich at the beginning of the Hats' Chaak phase contrasts with the low population density around the site, suggesting that a source of manpower was brought in from elsewhere, presumably from Naranjo. Such major intervention at Xunantunich is evidence that Naranjo intruded into the internal affairs of this center in significant ways, suggesting Naranjo controlled Xunantunich either formally or by making it a dependent ally.

A new palace complex (Plaza A-III) was built at this time at the north edge of the Xunantunich central group, again pointing to a reworking of the local political institution by a foreign force from elsewhere (Yaeger 2010). Yaeger, who excavated this new royal palace, suggests that it was a dependent court (presumably under Naranjo) because it did not represent the full set of activities typical of an autonomous royal court. Here, Yaeger relies on Martin's (2001) argument that independent royal courts have the following set of components:

(1) residential quarters of the royal family;
(2) facilities for the offices and officers of the state bureaucracy;
(3) workshops where artisans created sumptuary goods under royal patronage;
(4) space for storing tribute goods;
(5) facilities for housing foreign dignitaries and other visitors. (Yaeger 2010, 153–54)

Xunantunich's new royal court differed significantly from Martin's description. It included no artisan workshops, and its small size and simple layout most likely could only have hosted a small resident group (the extended family of the ruler).[18] Furthermore, no royal throne (a stone bench with armrests) was discovered in the royal palace, even though the palaces at nearby sites of Cahal Pech and Buenavista del Cayo have thrones (154). The ability of Xunantunich rulers to carry out ambitious new architectural programs such as the new royal court contrasts sharply with their inability to acquire sumptuary goods from Peten or farther afield: little jade or other exotics and few elaborate Peten polychromes were found in caches or burials at Xunantunich (Jamison 2010; LeCount 1999; LeCount and Yaeger 2010c).[19] This may be due to the fact that their overlords forbade Xunantunich rulers to make such displays of wealth or that the wealth of the Xunantunich rulers was being transferred to Naranjo as tribute (LeCount and Yaeger 2010c, 353–54, 359). All in all, these varied pieces of evidence suggest that the newly built royal court in Plaza A-III represents a dynasty dependent on its overlords at Naranjo.

Connell (2010) explores Xunantunich's integration with and/or control over its hinterland from the perspective of a small settlement, Chaa Creek, some six kilometers east of this center. Xunantunich's rise to regional prominence in the Hats' Chaak phase (AD 670–780) was accompanied by significant changes at Chaa Creek. The middle-elite groups at Chaa Creek felt these changes more than the commoner ranks did. The first significant change is that Type VII minor centers, or the compounds of the top leaders of this community, were abandoned at the beginning of the phase (302–5). Instead, smaller Type VI minor centers were rebuilt with more lavish dimensions and accoutrements but with some important differences from the earlier Type VII groups. For example, the Plantain Type VI Group was rebuilt to be oriented toward Xunantunich. The group's impressive offerings and rich architectural details were clearly drawn from Xunantunich, but it had no temple-pyramids (in contrast to the Type VII minor centers, which always included temple-pyramids) (305–6). The absence of temples in these newly refurbished groups may indicate that the wealth of the minor elites at this location was attributable not to local kinship ties and ancestor veneration but to political connections to the powerful ruler of Xunantunich (ibid.).

These connections could have been through alliances or direct control by the Xunantunich ruler. To distinguish between these two types of integration strategies, we need to consider the level of intrusion into the social, economic, demographic, and land tenure institutions of the Chaa Creek community (as outlined by LeCount and Yaeger 2010b). The continuity in commoner households through this time period suggests that there were no disturbances in demography or land tenure at Chaa Creek. However, there were some changes in the pottery assemblage that both commoners and the middle elite of Chaa Creek used (Connell 2010, 308–12). Black-slipped pottery that is dominant only at Xunantunich and its hinterland (LeCount 2010) also became most frequent in Chaa Creek household assemblages during the Hats' Chaak phase, reaching almost 74 percent of the monochrome pottery of this time period. This change in pottery use was strongest among members of elite groups, who intensified their consumption of black-slipped pots from 35 percent (in earlier times) to 81 percent in the Hats' Chaak phase. In contrast, black-slipped pottery accounted for only 65 percent of what was used in commoner households in the Hats'

Chaak phase, compared to 52 percent in earlier times (Connell 2010, 311). The differential investment commoners and elites made in the Xunantunich "identity" as marked by use of black-slipped pottery (LeCount 2010) speaks of integration strategies that involved the elite rank to a higher degree than the commoner stratum and may indicate that Xunantunich incorporated Chaa Creek as an ally rather than as a directly controlled community (Connell 2010, 313; see also LeCount and Yaeger 2010c, 349–61).

Xunantunich's history highlights the dynamics of Classic politics. Its fortunes fluctuated from a small independent center in the seventh century to incorporation into the Naranjo hegemony, followed by its resurgence as an autonomous state when the Naranjo realm fragmented and then its decline and collapse in the Terminal Classic (LeCount and Yaeger 2010c). Xunantunich's fate was driven by its role in the complex politics of the Maya lowlands that involved not only the two superpowers at Tikal and Calakmul but also the intrigues and machinations of the superpowers' strong allies at Caracol, Naranjo, and Dos Pilas (Martin and Grube 2000, 2008; Ashmore 2010; LeCount and Yaeger 2010c). To understand these hegemonies, we need to examine the capitals of these polities as well as their supporting hinterlands and their rulers as well as the commoners and middle elites from a number of different perspectives, as the Xunantunich Archaeological Project did. The evidence the Xunantunich archaeologists have gathered suggests that this center was incorporated into the Naranjo hegemony for a short time (perhaps from AD 680 to 750) as either a dependent ally or as a directly controlled province (LeCount and Yaeger 2010c, 349–61). LeCount and Yaeger note that "evidence for escalating economic production or exchange networks indicative of regularized tribute demands . . . is limited" (357), perhaps making the first scenario more likely. However, Schortman (2010) sees the rapid increase in population in Xunantunich's hinterland and the associated construction of agricultural terrace systems as evidence that Naranjo attempted to transform this zone into its breadbasket.

Religious Cosmologies, Ethnohistory, and Political Organization

While the view that Maya civilization was a peaceful theocracy has been overturned by the decipherment of Maya glyphs that revealed historical kings whose lives and conflicts were recorded again and again on stone monuments (Houston and Inomata 2009), the role of religion in Classic politics is still being scrutinized. Most Maya archaeologists agree that divine kingship was the central institution of most if not all Classic Maya polities, but how other religious concepts impacted political organization has not yet been ascertained.

The importance of religious cosmologies in political organization has resurfaced as a central concern in several recent studies of the Classic and Postclassic Maya. In *Maya Political Science*, Prudence Rice (2004) argues that Classic Maya political organization "was structured by Maya calendrical science" (xv), especially by the sacred calendrical cycle *may* of 256 years, or 13 *k'atuns*. Edmonson (1979, 1982, 1986) first described this cycle for the Postclassic Yucatan. According to Rice (2004), Classic Maya major cities took turns hosting the *may* for a period of 256 years, for the first half alone and for the second half together with the next hosting capital. Rice sees the rise and fall of Tikal's political fate as best explained by the rotation of the *may*. This interpretation recasts the conflicts recorded in Tikal's stelae as ritual events that marked the points of transition in the *may* cycle. Although there may have been a sacred cycling of the *may* among Maya cities, the wars among numerous competing polities that were recorded in stelae suggest that these polities were independent players and were not subsumed under a unitary religious and political structure. Houston, Stuart, and Taube (2006) underscore that the Maya wanted to link "their models of political reality with the order of time itself" (95), but they meant that the rulers attempted to increase their supernatural status through such links, not that the international politics of the Maya lowlands were dictated by the *may* cycle. Hammond (2005) also finds that the archaeological and epigraphic evidence falls short of supporting a purely ritual organization for Classic Maya lowland politics.

Nevertheless, Rice's analysis may apply to the internal organization of Maya polities, where cosmological views of time and space may have impacted political organization, at least during the Postclassic, if not earlier. Postclassic Maya kingdoms were divided into four sections, and the capital city was the fifth section in the middle of the state (see also Marcus 1993, 126–33). Grant Jones's (1998) ethnohistorical study of the Itza state in the Central Peten Lakes region has confirmed a quadripartite organization of provinces and the existence of 13 settlements within the Itza realm among which the *k'atun* seating rotated. Ciudad Ruiz (2001) provides ethnohistorical evidence from Chiapas and from Tipu, Belize, that a hegemonic quadripartite political organization was characteristic for the Maya of these regions in the Postclassic to Contact period. Freidel and Sabloff (1984, 158–62) also show that Cozumel Island during the Late Postclassic was divided into five sections. In her overview of Classic period political organization, Marcus (1993, 132–33) discusses the abundant ethnohistorical evidence from sixteenth-century Yucatan that the quadripartite model of the cosmos was the foundation of territorial divisions into four quarters or provinces (even if they were not equally sized or ideally positioned according to the cardinal directions). In contrast, Restall (1997) sees little evidence for quadripartite divisions in the Yucatan communities that he studied, so variation in the territorial organization of Maya states is again apparent.

The quadripartite view of the cosmos may have also impacted Classic period political institutions and/or organization of sites, as is suggested at Ek Balam (Ringle et al. 2004), Dzibilchaltun (Coggins 1983), Coba (Folan, Kintz, and Fletcher 1983), La Milpa (Tourtellot et al. 2000; Tourtellot et al. 2003), and Xunantunich (Keller 2010). For example, Tourtellot and his colleagues have found four secondary centers around La Milpa, Belize, situated approximately three kilometers from the center in the north, south, east, and west (Tourtellot et al. 2000; Tourtellot et al. 2002; Tourtellot et al. 2003). These secondary centers each had a large plaza and a small pyramid but no residences, except for La Milpa North, which had two palace courtyards. These cardinally oriented minor centers may have functioned purely as religious locations, but they are part of a network of 18 centers in La Milpa's hinterland that had a similar plaza organization called Plaza Plan 2 (plazas defined by low structures along two or three of the center's sides and a pyramid or shrine on its eastern side, as originally defined by Becker 1971). Tourtellot and colleagues (2002) interpret these Plaza Plan 2 centers as "local control facilities at a level below the palace and noble houses of La Milpa Centre." It is also notable that these Plaza Plan 2 sites "correlate well with hill shoulders and sub-maximal altitudes, placing them in an advantageous position between hill and valley resources and settlement" (634). The initial findings at these Plaza Plan 2 centers around La Milpa are very intriguing, and the sites need further investigation. Their functions may be more complex than has been suggested to date. The Three Rivers Region, where La Milpa is located, was densely occupied, and relatively major centers such as La Milpa were spaced as close as six kilometers from each other (Eleanor King personal communication, 2012). La Milpa was crowded by nearby Dos Hombres, Gran Cacao, Great Savannah, and Maax Na (ibid.). In such a closely packed landscape, La Milpa North, La Milpa South, La Milpa East, and La Milpa West could just as well be border centers and not secondary centers (ibid.). But even as border centers, their quadripartite organization shows the impact of the Maya religious cosmovision on political organization.

Case Study: Settlement Patterns, Hieroglyphs, and Hegemony at Motul De San José, Peten, Guatemala

In this section I want to illustrate how the different methodologies Maya archaeologists use to extract political information at the macro scale are being applied in an ongoing archaeological project at the site of Motul de San José, Peten, Guatemala.

Motul de San José is located approximately three kilometers north of Lake Peten Itza, the largest in a series of lakes in the Central Peten region of northern Guatemala (Figures 1.1 and 4.3). It is a small center, and according to Hammond's (1975a) classification of Maya settlements in Belize, it would fit in the category of "Level 9, regional ceremonial center" (Moriarty 2004a). Only 32 kilometers southwest of Tikal, Motul was fully immersed in the hegemonic politics of Tikal and Calakmul.

I have worked at Motul since 1998, when the Williams College Motul de San José Archaeological Project began investigating the site and its periphery (Foias and Emery 2012; Foias 2003; Emery 2003a; Moriarty 2004a; Halperin 2004; Halperin et al. 2009). Test pitting and more limited clearing excavations provided a general sample of architectural and material culture from small, medium, and large households in the monumental core of Motul and in its less dense North Zone. Explorations beyond Motul at peripheral centers such as Trinidad de Nosotros, Akte, Buenavista–Nuevo San José, Chakokot, and La Estrella (Figure 4.3) sought to better understand pre-Hispanic occupation and the relations between Motul's residents and environmental resources in this region (Foias and Emery 2012; Moriarty and Wyatt 2001; Moriarty et al. 2001).

We have learned a great deal about the macropolitical organization of this polity through the hieroglyphic texts available, even though only a few have survived and they are quite eroded. We know that Motul de San José was the seat of an independent royal court because it had its own emblem glyph (identified by its central symbol called Ik', or "wind"). However, in the early Late Classic, Motul de San José became Tikal's vassal as documented by the *y-ajaw* expression in the hieroglyphic text on Stela 1. On this stela, Motul's ruler Yeh Te' K'inich I celebrates his accession in AD 701 to the position of *k'uhul ajaw* as a subordinate of Jasaw Chan K'awiil I, Tikal's most famous Late Classic ruler (Foias 2000; Tokovinine and Zender 2012). Motul was thus part of the Tikal hegemony, and the research at this site contributes to our knowledge of the organization of Late Classic superstate entities (or multipolity networks). Motul can also be seen as a border polity of the Tikal

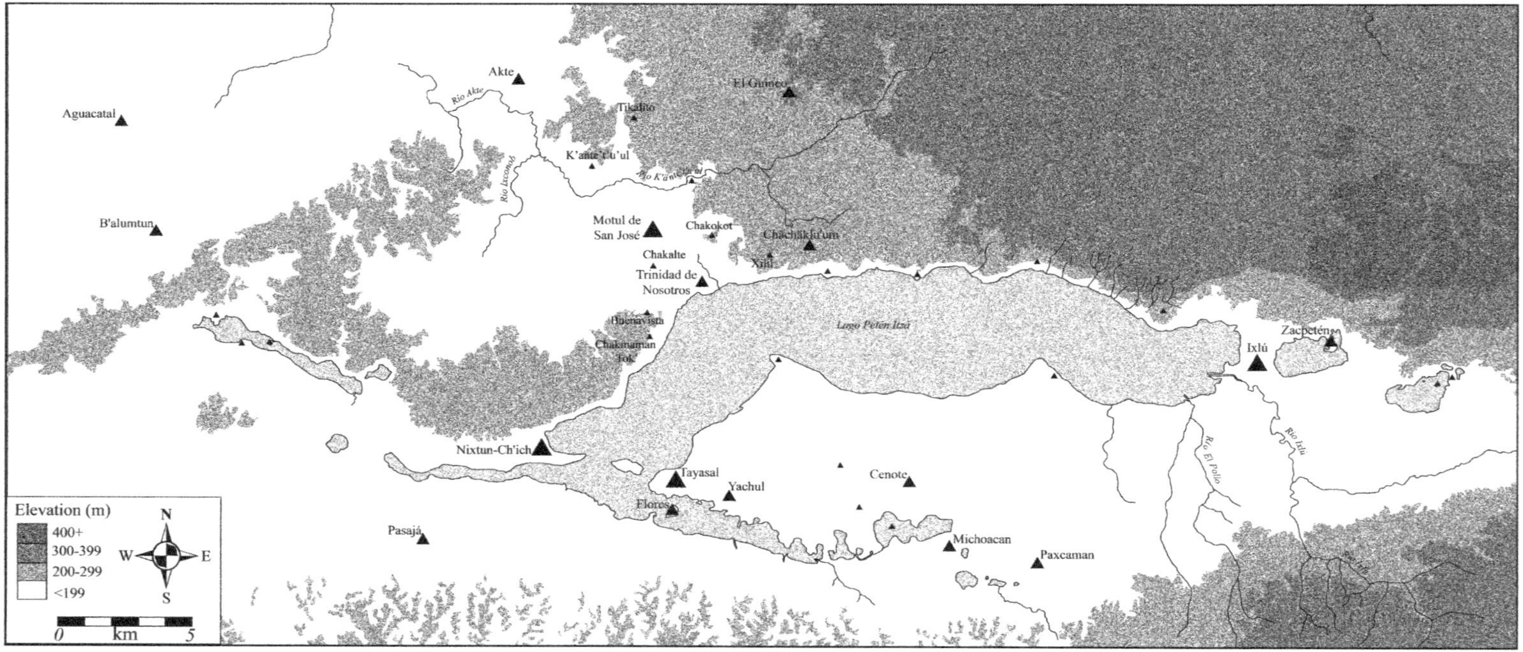

Figure 4.3. Location of Motul de San José and nearby sites in the Central Peten Lakes region, Guatemala. Drawn by Elly Spensley Moriarty; after Foias and Emery 2012, Figure 1.4a.

state if we accept the Chases' view that some Classic Maya states, including Tikal, extended 60 kilometers from their capitals. Motul appears to have switched allegiance between Tikal, Calakmul, and Dos Pilas and was involved sequentially in wars or alliances with these primary centers. These events are recorded in stone monuments as well as on polychrome vessels of the Ik' Polychrome Style that were produced at Motul (Tokovinine and Zender 2012; Reents-Budet, Ball, and Kerr 1994; Reents-Budet et al. 2012; Halperin and Foias 2010).[20]

Although Tikal dominated Motul's rulers at the end of the seventh and the beginning of the eighth centuries AD, the Ik' *k'uhul ajaw* had a number of liberties, including the right to raise stelae and the right to carry the title of *kaloomte'* (loosely translated as "king of kings"). As mentioned above, this title was carried by the ruler Tayal/Tayel Chan K'inich, who succeeded Yeh Te' K'inich I, Tikal's vassal, in the early eighth century (Tokovinine and Zender 2012). Tayal/Tayel Chan K'inich displayed his title of "king of kings" on a unique square tetrapod plate produced in the Tikal area (Reents-Budet et al. 2012), suggesting that he received it as a gift from Tikal and therefore was probably still under Tikal's dominion. The relationship between the rulers of Tikal and Motul was maintained not only through gifts of special vessels but also through marriage alliances: Tayal/Tayel Chan K'inich appears to have taken two consorts from the Tikal royal line (shown on vessels K2573 and K4996, Tokovinine and Zender 2012).

The stormy geopolitics of the eighth century AD allowed Motul to become independent from Tikal during the third or fourth decade (at the latest) of the eighth century, and its most famous (and hence most successful) rulers (Yajawte' K'inich, or Fat Cacique, and his successor K'inich Lamaw Ek', or Lord Completion Star) reigned during this time of independence (Tokovinine and Zender 2012; Reents-Budet et al. 2012). These two kings were especially adept at forming alliances with rulers in the Pasion region in southwestern Peten (they gave gifts of Ik' Style polychromes to the royals of Altar de Sacrificios) and with the San Pedro Martir River polities of La Florida (ancient Namaan) and Zapote Bobal–El Pajarral–La Joyanca (ancient Hix Witz), with whom they painted themselves on polychrome vessels (Tokovinine and Zender 2012; Halperin and Foias 2010). Yajawte' K'inich also contracted marriage alliances with the Yaxchilan royal dynasty in the western lowlands; he sent two Motul princesses (possibly daughters or sisters) to marry Bird Jaguar IV of Yaxchilan (Tokovinine and Zender 2012; Martin and Grube 2008). Most spectacularly, Yajawte' K'inich and K'inich Lamaw Ek' (and possibly their predecessors Yeh Te' K'inich and

Tayal/Tayel Chan K'inich) built all of the surface monumental architecture that archaeologists have tested at Motul de San José during one major building episode in the eighth century AD.

Like Xunantunich, Motul experienced a short and explosive period of growth in the eighth century AD (Foias and Emery 2012; Foias et al. 2012). In contrast to Xunantunich, whose golden age is attributable to its absorption into the Naranjo hegemony, the golden age at Motul appears to have been fueled by its rupture with Tikal and its allegiance with Dos Pilas, Yaxchilan, and/or Calakmul (Tokovinine and Zender 2012). Motul was farther away from its powerful neighbor, Tikal (31 kilometers) than Xunantunich was from Naranjo (13 kilometers), and this may have led to this instability.

Additional data on the macropolitical structure of the Motul polity can be gathered from settlement patterns. The distribution and sizes of sites allow us to estimate the scale and population levels of this kingdom. The population in the center of Motul surpassed the population of the smallest Greek polis; Motul hosted between 1,200 and 2,000 people (Moriarty 2004a; Foias and Emery 2012). This estimate of the capital's size was calculated using the procedures recommended by Rice and Culbert (1990). The approximate size of Motul is 4.18 square kilometers, as is suggested by a contiguous settlement found in three controlled survey transects (Moriarty 2004a, 30). This total size was then converted to a population estimate by multiplying the number of mounds found or estimated from surveys within this area (an average of 159.72 structures per square kilometer) by the number of individuals we expect to have lived in each structure (five, based on ethnographic analogy with modern Maya), then applying a reduction factor of 30 percent. As Rice and Culbert (1990) discuss, this reduction is necessary because some mounds were likely not used, others are not necessarily contemporaneous, and some mounds were probably nonresidential. Motul's population has been estimated at 1,200–2,000, suggesting that it was not a huge metropolis. It was quite small compared to Tikal (60,000) and Copan (5,000–8,000) but was comparable in size to Quirigua (427–2,223) and Seibal (2,974) at their apogees.

Maya archaeologists are also particularly interested in the scale of the polities that capital centers such as Motul de San José controlled. We suggest that the territory Motul controlled at its height (between approximately AD 700 and 830) must have extended beyond the three-kilometer radius of the smallest Greek polei, possibly between five and seven kilometers (Emery 2003a; Foias and Emery 2012).[21] We estimate this radius based on a few pieces of evidence. Emery (2003a) uses the area in which all the animals that were exploited at Motul were found: around 5 kilometers. A second method (Thiessen polygons) assumes that Motul controlled half the distance between it and the next major site, in this case Nixtun-Ch'ich'. Because Nixtun-Ch'ich' was some 9.4 kilometers southwest of Motul, Motul's maximum radius of control could be 4.7 kilometers (see Figure 4.3).[22] Finally, excavations at Akte, located 7 kilometers northwest of Motul, have found enough ties with Motul to suggest that at one point it was under Motul's control (Yorgey 2005; Yorgey and Moriarty 2012; Moriarty et al. 2002; Tokovinine and Zender 2012). If we envision this territory as a circle (for the sake of this discussion), the reconstructed size of the Motul de San José polity at its apogee is between 79 and 154 square kilometers and the estimated radius of control was between 5 and 7 kilometers.

Although we can't give accurate population estimates for the whole polity because we don't have complete surveys of the zone, I make an educated estimate here only for illustrative purposes. If we use a conservative settlement density of 50 structures per square kilometer (taken from the density of settlement in two transects surveyed north and south of Motul de San José, 52 structures per square kilometer and 56 structures per square kilometer, respectively; Moriarty 2004a) and the estimate of Motul's territorial extent (79–154 square kilometers), we obtain a population range between 13,000 and 27,000 people (after the 30 percent reduction).

Thus, the Motul polity at its Late Classic apogee was quite small compared to even the average size of Classic Maya polities of 2,000–2,500 square kilometers (a radius of 25–28 kilometers from the capital city) or the maximum size of 11,333 square kilometers envisioned by the Chases (as discussed above). However, Motul's small size is not exceptional for early states or for pre-Hispanic polities in Mesoamerica. There are many examples of similar-sized polities from the Postclassic Mixteca (where polities were 30–50 square kilometers large and hosted some 10,000 individuals; Spores 1984), the Postclassic Basin of Mexico (80–200 square kilometers and 5,000–10,000 people; Hodge 1984, Hare 2000), and the Classic Maya southwestern periphery (polities of 78 and 166 square kilometers; de Montmollin 1995, 260). The Aztec city-states (called *altepetl*) of Postclassic central Mexico averaged 90 square kilometers (Smith 2008). The point of this discussion of Motul's size is not purely theoretical: polity size matters in terms of the scale of resources the state can draw upon to establish its political power vis-à-vis other states. Motul's small size clearly suggests that it was overshadowed by its neighbor Tikal, and it was probably easily influenced by the demands or wishes of Tikal's rulers.

This small size belies internal complexity. Within this area, regional surveys have identified minor centers located between 2 and 5 kilometers from Motul: Jobonmo', 2 kilometers northeast of Motul; Chakokot, 2 kilometers east of Motul; La Trinidad de Nosotros (Trinidad), 2 kilometers southeast of Motul; Buenavista–Nuevo San José, 2.5 kilometers southwest of Motul; Tikalito, 3.5 kilometers north of Motul; and Kante't'u'ul, 2.5 kilometers northwest of Motul (Moriarty et al. 2001; Moriarty 2004a) (Figure 4.3). This configuration of minor centers located between 2 and 3 kilometers from a center that are oriented toward the cardinal and/or intercardinal directions is similar to the settlement patterns around La Milpa (discussed above) and Caracol (A. Chase and D. Chase 2003).

Among these subsidiary centers, only Chakokot, Trinidad, Buenavista–Nuevo San José and Akte have been tested (Moriarty 2012; Yorgey and Moriarty 2012; Moriarty et al. 2007; Castellanos 2007). These consist of at least one temple-pyramid, a major residential plaza group, and a dozen (more or less) small plazuela groups. The overall settlement of each site was larger than 10 hectares (Moriarty 2004a, 32–37). Trinidad is the exception; it is much larger than the other secondary centers (Moriarty 2012) and may have been the first of the secondary centers (for reasons detailed below).

A second issue in macropolitics is whether political centers (the capital and subsidiary centers) were also nodes of economic or religious power. The recent volumes edited by Iannone and Connell (2003) and Scarborough, Valdez, and Dunning (2003) highlight the presence of specialization in minor centers in Belize, and A. Chase and D. Chase (1996) have long discussed the specialized administrative roles of the causeway termini sites around Caracol. Excavations at Cancuen by Demarest and his colleagues have found no temple-pyramids, but they have discovered flourishing production and trade activities at this center in the foothills of the Guatemalan highlands (Kovacevich 2007). This recent research supports the principle that in some cases, religious, economic, political, or administrative roles were separated and specialized, a key feature of the heterarchical perspective on Maya political organization (Potter and King 1995; Scarborough, Valdez, and Dunning 2003).

At Motul de San José, we turned to the activities that took place in each settlement to understand whether they were nodes of religious, political, and/or economic power. The presence of multiple temple-pyramids in the capital center, some reaching as high as 20 meters, suggests that its role was clearly within the religious sphere, although it also had administrative and economic power. Although the secondary centers in Motul's periphery had fewer and smaller temple-pyramids, the presence of the pyramids suggests that these settlements were nodes of both ritual and political power. The excavations in Motul's monumental core revealed that numerous economic activities were carried out in the royal and elite households, such as polychrome pottery production, figurine crafting, making and painting paper, and textile production (Foias et al. 2012; Halperin and Foias 2010, 2012; Halperin 2008, 2012; Emery 2012; see also Chapter 5). The great majority of lithic tool and general pottery production took place elsewhere in the Motul realm (Lawton 2007; Halperin and Foias 2012) as researchers found little evidence of these crafts in the capital. Significant lithic tool manufacture was discovered along the north shore of Lake Peten Itza because of the nearby chert sources: Buenavista–Nuevo San José, Chak-Maman-Tok' (La Estrella–Nuevo San José), and Trinidad (Moriarty 2012; Lawton 2007; Castellanos 2007) were heavily involved in the extraction of chert and the manufacture of chert blanks and/or tools. Trinidad fulfilled another important economic role as the lake port of the Motul polity (Moriarty 2012; Thornton 2012). Furthermore, the only ball court in the Motul kingdom was found at Trinidad: Maya rituals carried out in ball courts could take place only at Trinidad, not at Motul (Moriarty 2012).

Additional evidence for economic specialization among Motul's secondary centers comes from the ethnoarchaeological survey and geochemical studies of soils across this zone (Moriarty 2001, 2004a, n.d.; Bair and Terry 2012; Jensen et al. 2007; Webb et al. 2007; Webb and Schwarcz 2012). Stable carbon isotope soil studies found that little maize was cultivated within the confines of the capital center, indicating that Motul was economically dependent on foodstuffs produced by peripheral villages and secondary centers such as nearby Chakokot (Webb et al. 2007; Jensen et al. 2007; Webb and Schwarcz 2012). Terry has hypothesized that the absence of maize cultivation in Motul (in spite of the richness of its soils) may have been due to the maintenance of this zone as a forest hunting preserve or as gardens with mostly fruit trees (Bair and Terry 2012; Emery and Foias 2012). The soils of the savannas that dominate the landscape some two kilometers east of Motul are called *chachaklu'um*, or "red earth," by local Itza informants. They are known to be of low fertility for agriculture but quite good for fruit trees (Moriarty 2004a). The site of Chachaklu'um, approximately five kilometers east of Motul, is named for these soils. Initial soil testing has revealed that little corn agriculture took place there (Bair and Terry 2012). Since the site is quite large, this suggests an alternative specialization for its inhabitants, possibly growing tree fruits (Emery and Foias 2012). Another of Motul's secondary centers, Kante't'u'ul, is located some three kilometers northwest of Motul in well-drained and moist soils ideal for growing cacao trees (Moriarty 2004a). However, this site has not been submitted to soil testing to pursue the possibility that it specialized in cacao cultivation. Each of these secondary centers had a temple-pyramid, so it is clear that they also functioned as nodes of religious power (or ritual political power).

These settlement investigations have revealed at least two levels of political and ritual centers, with Motul de San José at the top of the hierarchy and a set of secondary centers below it. Although Motul's subsidiary centers exhibit some functional redundancy with the capital, variability is more characteristic. Sites to the south of Motul along the shore of Lake Peten Itza appear to have specialized in the extraction and exploitation of the nearby chert, while Chakokot and Chachaklu'um to the east of Motul were producers of agricultural or possibly horticultural surplus for the capital at Motul de San José, which was not self-sufficient. In the following chapters, I will pursue the details of Motul's political dynamics as we shift from the macro level to the middle and micro levels of politics.

Political Organization and Maya Royal Courts in the Ethnohistorical Record

To better understand Classic political organization, Maya archaeologists have turned to the testimonies and accounts of the Contact and Conquest periods in the sixteenth and seventeenth centuries when the last indigenous Maya states were still functioning in northern Yucatan, in the Guatemalan highlands, and in the Central Peten Lakes region. The best analogies for Classic Maya polities are drawn from the same cultural tradition, the polities of the Postclassic period that the Spanish conquistadores, friars, and colonists encountered and described from the sixteenth through the nineteenth centuries (for excellent summaries of ethnistorical studies, see Marcus 1993 and Rice 2004). Although I present here how these ethnohistories saw the political macro scale, I will also include some details about internal matters in sixteenth-century politics so that later chapters can be devoted more fully to the archaeological record.

Northern Yucatan

Spanish conquistadores, friars, and settlers described the political geography of Yucatan at the time of the conquest as consisting of multiple polities

Table 4.1. Titles associated with administrative positions from Postclassic–Contact period Yucatan, seventeenth-century Peten Itza and possible equivalencies from the Classic period

	Postclassic Yucatan	Seventeenth-Century Peten Itza	Classic Period
Suprapolity			kaloomte' (king of kings) (see Figure 5.1)
Top tier	halach uinic, ahau (regional ruler)	ajaw (top ruler)	k'uhul ajaw (divine ruler)
		aj k'in (top priest)	
Second tier	batab (cah ruler)	ajaw b'atab', ajaw noj tz'o kan, or kit kan (senior provincial governor)	sajal (governor of secondary center)
		b'atab' (junior provincial governor)	ti'sakhuun (king's speaker, prophet, oracle)
			ajk'uhuun (high priest, scribe, court chaplain)
Lower tiers	ah kulel, ah can (deputy, council member, "he who speaks")	ach kat (representative of conquered town; council member)	yajawk'ahk' (fire's vassal, warrior, fire priest?)
	nacom (special warlord and/or priest in charge of sacrifices?)		lakam (ward representative?)
	ah cuch cab, holcan, chunthan (council member, ward representative, "chief speaker")		
	holpop ("head of the mat," council member in charge of festivals, lineage head)		

of variable extent and structure (Roys 1943, 1957; Marcus 1993; Rice 2004; Restall 1997, 2001). Roys's work (1943, 1957) is still the foundation for reconstructions of the political geography of Yucatan in the Contact period, although several scholars (Restall 1997, 2001; Quezada 1993; Williams-Beck, Liljefors Persson, and Anaya Hernadez in press) have critiqued some of his interpretations.

Roys (1957) identified 16 "native states" (which the Spanish called *provincias* but the Yucatec Maya called *cuchcabals*) in northern Yucatan.[23] Roys recognized three types of political organization among these 16 *provincias*. The most centralized states were ruled by a lord called *halach uinic* who resided in the major regional center and capital of the *cuchcabal*. He was still called the *ahau* (or lord) of that native state, just as the Maya nobles were called during the Classic period (Table 4.1). The *halach uinic* dominated a network of dependent communities, called *batabil*, each ruled by a *batab*, or local ruler-governor.[24] A second type of state, less centralized, had no *halach uinic* but was organized as a confederacy of communities ruled by related *batabs* who belonged to the same lineage (or patronym group, *chibal*, following Restall 1997).[25] A third type of *provincia* was much looser and smaller in scale, consisting of a few towns or settlements allied together (each ruled by a distinct *batab* of different lineages). These were usually found on the edges of the more centralized states.

Quezada's and Restall's critiques of Roys's three polity types go in separate directions. Quezada (1993) argues that there was only one type of state in sixteenth-century Yucatan: the first of Roys's types, the regional polity headed by a *halach uinic*. However, he recognizes some variation in the political organization of these regional states. In some *cuchcabals*, the *halach uinic* filled the top political, religious, judicial, and military positions, but in others, separate officials from the *halach uinic* performed the top religious and military functions.

In contrast, Restall argues that only the third and smallest type of Roys's typology existed, the basic community (or town) that he calls the *cah*, ruled by a *batab*. For Restall (2001), the *halach uinic*, or regional overlord, was mostly a honorific title with little real political power: "Pre-Conquest polities [were] . . . loosely organized, with subject communities governed neither directly from the center nor by representatives sent from the center but surviving as self-governing entities [the *cah*] whose subordination was expressed through tribute relations. There were multiple layers of subordination, and all were potentially open to negotiation" (349).[26] This assessment of Yucatan polities is reminiscent of Grube and Martin's description of the hegemonies of Tikal and Calakmul during the Classic period. Quezada's conclusions concur with those of Restall, and he also notes that the *batabs* appear to have been relatively autonomous within their subject communities (Quezada 1993, 52–53). However, I see the ability to impose and collect tribute as real political power that should not be discounted. Therefore, in my view, the *halach uinic* had political power in Postclassic Yucatan. I conclude from Restall's, Quezada's, and Roys's ethnohistorical analyses that there was variation in political organization in sixteenth-century Yucatan (in agreement with Marcus 1993 and Rice 2004). Although the *cah* appears to have been the most enduring political entity over the long term, these communities were sometimes incorporated into larger units dominated by a *halach uinic*. As both Quezada and Restall note, this potentate was in charge of a state that he controlled only loosely because the *batabs* had considerable power in their local communities. In other words, the *halach uinic* was a hegemon, possibly similar to the hegemons at Tikal, Calakmul, Naranjo, and other powerful cities during the Classic period (Martin and Grube 2008, 21).

According to Restall (2001), the *cah* (the basic Maya municipal community consisting of both the residential site and the territorial lands controlled by the town) was "the principal focus of Maya self-identity, loyalty, organization, and activity" (349). Restall equates the *cah* with the Mexica or Aztec *altepetl*, which is usually envisioned as a city-state that varies in size from small to large (Hare 2000; Smith 2008). This adds more complexity to the *cah* and seems to transform it into a polity.

Restall (2001, 350) argues that the "patronym groups" (*chibal*) of the ruling families were the second most important integrative social unit in Maya society. The legitimacy or authority of the royal families (or *chibal*) came from their assertion of higher status based on four elements: "social differentiation; an oligarchical monopoly over political activity; group hereditary status; and the perpetuation of dynastic origin mythology" (352, 371). Restall contends that the foreign origins the Yucatec elite families claimed have no basis in historical fact but served (successfully) to separate the elites from the commoners (370). This mythology of "stranger kings" (Sahlins 1985, 73) allowed the royal elites to assert "a sacred and celestial connection to distant places and ancestors" (Restall 2001, 373; see also Helms 1993, 1998, McAnany 2008, 2010).

Yucatan's noble class can also be considered the political elite because they had an oligarchical monopoly over political offices (Restall 2001, 359; Restall 1997, 65). Although lower-level elites and high-status commoners also held lower positions at court, the dynastic elite can be said to have controlled government, not through the construction of a centralized government but based on "the control of cah governorships (*batabilob*) by members of the dominant dynasty or their allied kin" (Restall 2001, 365). It is worth pointing out that Contact period Maya politics were much more participatory than most of us suspect, as Restall underscores: "No one man, or even one family, ruled a Maya community or polity alone; the members of the court, to degrees depending on their rank, participated in rulership" (364). This is what Restall calls "factional rule" (387n25; Restall 1998, 141), in contrast to the *multepal* (joint rule) that some scholars argue was the dominant form of government at Chichen Itza and Mayapan (see Schele and Freidel 1990). Restall (2001) describes "factional rule" as dominated by "negotiation and persuasion" rather than by hierarchy and "power over," and argues that this type of rule provided the motor for political dynamics during the Postclassic (370).

For the Yucatec Maya of the century before and after the Spanish Conquest, the court surrounding the *halach uinic* was the heart of the polity as shown by the fact that the court came together to face the Spanish threat (Restall 1997). The court included "previous rulers; relatives of the ruler eligible to succeed him; prominent members of allied or competing noble families; the rest of the general pool of principal men, including those with specific offices; representatives of commoner families holding lesser offices; and non-office-holding servants and dependents, including in pre-Colonial times, slaves" (Restall 2001, 359). The average size of the royal court of a Yucatec *cah* just before the Spanish Conquest was around 50; an example is the court of the *halach uinic* Nachi Cocom, which gathered for a summit in 1545 to review the territorial boundaries of the Sotuta polity (364). This is hardly large enough to be called a bureaucracy, especially because it was tied to specific elite families (see further discussion in Chapter 5).

Restall (1997) uses ethnohistorical documents to detail the size and structure of the government of the *cah*, which consisted of the *batab* and his council (*cabildo* in Spanish) (51). While the *cabildo* was clearly a Spanish concept that the Spaniards imposed on Maya communities, the ease with which the Maya adopted, transformed, and used it suggests pre-Hispanic roots, and I suspect that these roots lie in the royal court and/or council of pre-Columbian times (as suggested by Restall's description of Nachi Cocom's royal court).

Although the Spanish required that particular administrative positions be filled, the Maya created as many positions as they needed (ibid., 65–71). These numerous political offices were ranked and elite males advanced through the junior offices to the more senior positions such as *batab, escribano* (notary), *teniente* (interim governor), *alcalde* (judge), and *regidor* (councilman or ward representative; 71–72). Classic-period titles suggest a similar pattern of political advancement from lower to higher positions in the hierarchy (see Table 4.1 and Chapter 5). A clear consequence of "the creation of a ladder of offices . . . is the minimalization of specific functions, and the flexible usage of titles"—a process that worked against specialization within official political positions and therefore against bureaucratization (77). The establishment of all these political positions was driven by the desire of the Maya to include all principal men (called *principales* in Spanish and *kuluinicob* in Yucatec Maya) in the affairs of the *cah* (70–71).

These *principales* were men of status and/or wealth but not necessarily of noble blood; thus, they formed a middle-rank group.

Roys (1957) also describes the town governance of the *cah* (see Table 4.1). The *batab* fulfilled generally executive, judicial, and military functions. He also led the local council, which could impose limits on his power (7). He generally did not extract tribute but depended on an estate ("farm") that townspeople operated on his behalf. Although the position of *batab* was generally hereditary, some *batabs* received their office from the *halach uinic* if one existed in their *provincia*. Special war chiefs, called *nacom*, carried out military campaigns, even though the *batab* was the nominal head of the warriors. *Ah kulels*, the *batab*'s deputies, delivered and carried out his orders. *Ah cuch cabs*, officers slightly higher in rank than the *ah kulels*, were in charge of the wards or barrios of towns. The *ah cuch cabs* were elected by their wards and were probably respected commoners (Roys 1943; Ringle and Bey 2001). The *ah kulels* and the *ah cuch cabs* formed the town council (Ringle and Bey 2001). In the province of Ah Canul, the deputies of the *batab* were called *ah canob*, or "speakers," rather than *ah kulels* (Roys 1957, 12). Another post was that of the *holpop* ("head of the mat"), the head of the council (the mat was the symbol of both political power and councils in the pre-Hispanic Maya region). Roys (1957) mentions that in pre-Hispanic times, the *holpop* replaced the *batab* in some *cah* communities. In other documents, the *holpops* are the heads of important lineages. In the provinces of Hocaba and Sotuta, the functions of the *holpops* were parallel to those of the *ak kulels*: "This lord [*halach uinic* of Hocaba] governed and ruled his people in this province with his caciques, whom they called holpops, who were like regidors or captains; and through these [officials], they [the people] negotiated with the lord for what they desired" (Roys 1957, 55). After the Spanish Conquest, the *holpops* appear to have been stripped of their political duties and remained as the chief organizers of festivals, dances and the music at such events (Roys 1957, 7). In his study of the province of Chakan (where modern Merida is located), Roys finds that Ah Kin Euan, the ruler of the Maya *cah* of Caucel, was both the *batab* and head priest, which was not typical (35). Ringle and Bey (2001) describe the administration of the *batab* of Chicxulub, a lord named Nakuk Pech: "Despite what would seem to be a rather humble noble rank, Nakuk Pech briefly mentions a full complement of his own officers, including two ak kulelob, two holpopob, and two ah kinob [priests], as well as several nacomob/holcanob" (272).

Postclassic Guatemalan Highlands

Braswell (2001) and Carmack (1981) bring to life the Postclassic K'iche'an (K'iche'/Quiche and Kaqchikel) Maya states and the royal courts at their centers in their respective capitals at Q'umarkaj and Iximche' in the highlands of Guatemala. The K'iche' capital at Q'umarkaj and other large towns in the K'iche'an states "were sacred sanctuaries for gods and lords," and commoners "were too profane" to frequent these locations (Carmack 1981, 183).

Nobles (*ajawa'*), their slaves (*mun*), and attached commoners (vassals, *alk'ajola'*) lived in palace structures in the core of Q'umarkaj (Braswell 2001, 309–10). Warriors of both noble and commoner *estate* also resided in the court.[27] Merchants of different kinds (lower-status *ajk'ay* or *k'ayil*, "people of the market," and higher-status *b'eyom*, or *ajb'eyom*, "people of the road," who sold long-distance valuables) also passed through the royal courts, although maybe not as residents. Commoners who became musicians or specialized artisans were attached to the royal court, although they may not have lived full time in the royal palaces either (310–11). The high esteem and status some musicians reached underscores the importance of performance and the materiality of power in Maya courts. The positions held by the lords of the royal court are detailed in perhaps ambiguous ways by a wide range of titles, including Ambassador (*lolmay*), Great Giver of Banquets or Spokesmen–Town Criers (*nim ch'okoj*), Councilman (*popol winaq*), Lord Sweatbath (*tuj*) (311), Tribute Officer (*k'amahay, lolmet*) (Braswell 2001: 311; Recinos and Goetz 1953, 52; Carmack 1981, 175). As Braswell notes, many titles point to the importance of councils in the governance of highland Maya polities during the Postclassic. Certain priestly positions were also of high rank and were inherited by the elites, such as Aj Tohil, Aj Q'ukumatz, and Aj Awilix (Carmack 1981).

Rulership among both the Kaqchikel and K'iche' was shared among two lords in Kaqchikel (Ajpop Sotz'il and Ajpop Xajil) or among four high nobles in the latter (Ajpop, Aj K'amja ["king-elect"], Nima Rajpop Achij [major war captain], and Ch'uti Rajpop Achij [minor war captain]) (Braswell 2001, 312). This shared power is evidence against models of autocratic kingship and provides alternative models of rulership for the Classic period (see for example, the exploration of dualism at the site of La Milpa, Belize, in Tourtellot et al. 2003). Although dual or quadripartite rulership involved power sharing, it is not clear that power was equally divided between these co-rulers. For example, Schele and Mathews (1998, 300) note the association of the title Ajpop Sotz'il with the name of "firstborn child" (*nab'ey al*), hence a more powerful position, and the title Ajpop Xajil with the name of "last-born child" (*chipil al*), hence a less powerful position. Carmack (1981) argues that rulership was shared because representatives of powerful factions (or lineages) were present in these K'iche'an kingdoms, although the Ajpop was indeed the supreme ruler. Alternatively, Braswell (2001, 313) suggests that power was shared because of the two contradictory principles seen in divine rulership among the Postclassic Maya: "the preservation of power and the maintenance of sacred authority." Nevertheless, Braswell asserts that K'iche'an rulership "was based more on military prowess and threat than on any ritual authority" (322), and Carmack (1981) writes that militarism was so central to the K'iche' that all political positions were both administrative and military (152). Even though the K'iche'an rulers claimed divine powers, their creation myths as recorded in the Popol Vuh (Tedlock 1986) state that commoners and lords were created at the same time from the same materials of water and white or yellow corn (Braswell 2001, 324).

Just as in the Postclassic communities of northern Yucatan, factional competition between the various social, territorial, and kinship groups was a central feature of K'iche'an politics (327): political power "was neither absolute nor organized in a simple hierarchical fashion. Principles of aristocracy, based on both ascribed and earned status, were used to determine the occupants of high-status roles" (327). Thus, competition for political positions was continuous (313), and we even know of rebellions, some led by commoners (Carmack 1981, 173, 156).

Carmack (1981) has reconstructed the political organization of the K'iche' (or Quiche) kingdom, which controlled a large part of the Guatemalan Highlands at the time of the Spanish Conquest. The Quiche recognized four major noble lineages (the Cawek, Nijib, Ajaw Quiche, and Sakic) at the capital at Q'umarkaj, and these controlled the official political positions. Within each of these major noble lineages there were subdivisions, called principal lineages, and each of these principal lineages ruled over large land tracts (estates), or *chinamits*. The head of the principal lineage was the chief of each *chinamits* (164). Each *chinamit* was "the basis for tribute and service obligations, judicial and ritual processes, and recruitment of soldiers to fight with their lords" (165). The various *chinamits* also formed the core of the Quiche kingdom, as they encompassed the lands surrounding the three major Quiche towns (Q'umarkaj, Pismachi, and Mukwitz Pilocab) (ibid.). The *chinamits* intersected with larger territorial or social divisions called *calpules* that spread throughout the Quiche basin. Each was under the control of one of the three major towns (166). The *calpul* consisted of several commoner lineages that intermarried; members of the same *calpul* could be vassals of different *chinamits* (165-66). Beyond the basin, conquered areas were organized as provinces (*ajawarem*) outside the *chinamit* and *calpul* structures (165). Approximately 30 provinces are known; they were named after the major towns where the Quiche military governors lived, such as Chichicastenango, Zacualpa, Sajcabaja, Totonicapan, Huehuetenango, and Quetzaltenango (185–86).

Although quadripartite rule was a central political principle among the Quiche, how this worked out in practice is a little more difficult to reconstruct. The Caweks, the dominant major lineage in the Quiché capital of Q'umarkaj, controlled all four positions that Braswell sees as representing "co-rulers" (Ajpop, Aj K'amja, Nima Rajpop Achij, and Ch'uti Rajpop Achij). In theory, when major affairs of the state took place, the heads of the four major lineages were supposed to be the central actors. They received the following four titles: Ajpop, Ajpop k'amja, K'alel, and Atzij winak (Carmack 1981, 169). However, the practice was different from the theory; the Caweks controlled both of the first two positions, the Nijib major lineage controlled the K'alel position, and the Ajaw Quiché major lineage controlled the fourth position, leaving out the Sakic major lineage completely. Carmack asserts that the Ajpop was the supreme ruler because he was the only one who could wear a nosepiece and whose throne could be covered by four canopies. The other three named "lineage heads" or "co-rulers" were his assistants in different capacities, as counselors, judges, and the like (170).

Below the king Ajpop, a number of officers served as judges and were part of a council that managed the political affairs of the state (168). The council included both the judges and tribute collectors (174). Another group of officials (governors and such) ruled over the provinces and were appointed and removed by the king. All these officials were of noble blood and were close relatives of the king (168). But, outside the capital, commoners filled political roles. For example, "vassal lineage heads served as justices of the peace" (174). Although priests were highly respected, they did not hold political power beyond two arenas. First, as the keepers of the ritual calendar and divination cycles, they were called into council to interpret the will of the gods. Second, the two highest priests, Tepew (or Aj Tepew) and K'ucumatz (or Aj Q'ukumatz), were the keepers of the state treasury (174–75).

A third level of Quiché political offices were held by officials who managed the *chinamits* of the principal noble lineages. They carried titles such as Utzam Chinamital ("head of the estate members") or Aj Tz'alam ("wall officials"; each estate was separated by walls). However, they "were not considered officials of the state" even though the roles they filled could be characterized as something less than those of state administrators and something more than those of vassals and serfs. Carmack remarks that these officials became militarized over time because they were given the newly created military rank of *achij*. These positions were filled by young members of the aristocracy or by older commoner warriors (177).

Central Peten Lakes: Itza Polity

The third region from which we have substantial ethnohistorical documents about pre-Hispanic Maya political organization is the Central Peten Lakes, where the last Maya kingdom (the Itzas) were conquered almost 200 years after the kingdoms of northern Yucatan. Grant Jones (1998) is the principal source on the political organization of the Itza Maya just before the Spanish Conquest, and Caso Barrera (2002) adds an important new study. Jones (1998) describes Itza governance as "a complex system grounded in principles of dual rulership, a quadripartite division of elite governance over territories, and a crosscutting system of representation on a ruling council from outlying towns and regions" (60).

The Itza state was divided into four quarters (arranged approximately according to the cardinal directions); the capital was located on the island of Nojpeten (modern Flores) as a fifth province. The rulers of the whole polity were called Ajaw Kan Ek', and the high priest AjK'in Kan Ek' (the cousin of Ajaw Kan Ek'). A pair of rulers (senior and junior members) governed each quarter but lived at Nojpeten. The senior governors were called Ajaw B'atab', Ajaw Noj Tz'o Kan, or Kit Kan (or *reyezuelo* in Spanish), while the junior rulers of the provinces were called simply B'atab' (or *cacique* in Spanish) (92–93).[28] The sources provide evidence of the dual religious and political roles of these rulers, and some may have also taken on military duties. Finally, these five pairs of rulers were complemented by 13 officials with the title of Ach Kat who fulfilled religious and military functions (61, 83, 87). The Ach Kat officials appear to have represented towns that were mostly in the periphery of the Itza realm (61).

Political and religious institutions were closely connected, not only because of the dual rulership that Ajaw Kan Ek' and the high priest AjK'in

Kan Ek' shared.[29] For one thing, the quadripartite division of the realm was dictated by Maya views of the universe, and Maya rulers tried to bring the order of the cosmos onto the earthly plane. The Ach Kat officials may have also been tied to the ritual cycling of the 13 *k'atuns* (forming the *may* cycle; Rice 2004) because the communities or provinces they represented served as *k'atun* seating centers. The Spanish Franciscan missionary Fray Andres de Avendaño y Loyola, who visited Nojpeten in 1696, recorded that the seating of each new *k'atun* rotated among 13 communities throughout the Itza kingdom (Jones 1998, 102). This religious-political structure served well to integrate the Itza state: "Newly conquered population centers could have been incorporated directly into the central ruling council at Nojpeten by adopting them not only as symbolic elements of the Itza historical and ritual record but also as part of the military structure" (103).

Jones sees the Itza political system as segmentary but believes that it preserved centralized political power in the hands of a small group of elite lineages (who controlled the senior governorships of the four quarters as well as the dual kingship) (83). This small elite group managed to overcome the weaknesses of segmentary organization through conquest and expansion during the 1500s and 1600s before the arrival of the Spanish in 1697 (450n68): "This system coalesced through a policy of integration by conquest, in which the Itzas incorporated newly dominated groups by marrying them to existing elites and granting them positions on the ruling council as Ach Kat military-religious leaders" (83). However, Jones believes that these same elements caused the instability of the Itza polity, concluding that the "rulers . . . were always at risk of rebellion by war captains [the Ach Kats]" (106). Caso Barrera (2002) also discusses the role of Ajaw Kan Ek' in the Itza political organization: "In spite of the fact that Canek was the central figure of the Itzá political system, we can say that his power was rather more symbolic as he could not make important decisions without consulting the other lords and *principales* [important people]" (219, translated from Spanish).

Jones (1998) also stresses the importance of councils in the Itza government (105). The two rulers of the Itza polity, the four pairs of rulers of the provinces, and the 13 Ach Kats formed the council of the state, and the Itza ruler Ajaw Kan Ek' had to answer to it (106). Jones argues that this council rule was different from *multepal* (joint rulership by multiple kings, or confederacy) which some have argued was the dominant structure of all Postclassic states (Schele and Freidel 1990). Jones (1998) believes that Itza rulership should be seen as shared by principal lords and subsidiary lords (via the council) but "tempered by a strong principle of lineage domination by a single group of closely related males" (105–6).[30]

One final aspect of the Itza kingdom is relevant to our discussion. The Itza elites who were interviewed by the Spanish made a clear distinction between the core of the polity (Nojpeten/Flores and the lands surrounding Lake Peten Itza), and the hinterland, or peripheral provinces. The core of the Itza kingdom was strongly tied to the capital at Nojpeten and was generally under its control. In contrast, lands farther away from the polity's core were gained or lost depending on the ability of the Itza kings to maintain allies and strong armies. These peripheral provinces were far away (as far as Tipu, Belize, for example; Ciudad Ruiz 2001), and this distance may have affected both the ability of the center to maintain control over them and the nature of that political control. Restall (1997) speaks of a similar conceptual distinction among the *cah* polities of Northern Yucatan.

Conclusions

In this chapter, I have painted Classic Maya states with broad strokes using settlement, epigraphic, and ethnohistorical data. Archaeologists have at their disposal both direct evidence and indirect evidence about the macro level of political organization from these three sources of knowledge.

Direct evidence from settlement pattern studies has allowed us to envision the scale of the Classic period states. Reconstructions of polity size vary from as low as 80 square kilometers to an average of 2,000 square kilometers and up to a maximum of 11,333 square kilometers. These estimates are not contradictory but rather capture the variability in the size (and power) of Classic polities both at the same time across the mosaic landscape of the Maya lowlands and through time as different rulers and different polities grew through conquest and alliance and then declined. Such discrepancies in size and political power suggest that the international system of the Classic period was very unstable, and this is confirmed by the epigraphic evidence. Nevertheless, in spite of the richness of settlement pattern data as exemplified by de Montmollin's study in the Upper Grijalva Basin, questions remain about whether settlement size correlates directly with political power and whether settlement distribution can clearly point to the frontiers between separate polities. To reconstruct the sources of power and the extent of political, economic, and religious power, we need to consider closely the activities that took place at each settlement in each polity (see Chapters 5 and 6).

Direct evidence from the hieroglyphs of the Classic period have not only told us the names and lives of the kings and queens who ruled these states but have also revealed the nature of the institution of divine kingship at the heart of Classic polities and the complexity of the international system that engulfed all lowland Maya states. Although all polities with emblem glyphs may have been independent at some point in their history, the smaller ones such as Motul de San José and Xunantunich must also have experienced intense pressures from larger and more powerful neighbors. It is likely that sometimes they were pressured into alliances and other times were conquered outright. Recent decipherments reveal the formation and re-formation of superstates or hegemonies and the playing out of wars and alliances between large and powerful cities, such as Tikal and Calakmul, and less powerful ones, such as Dos Pilas, Naranjo, and Yaxchilan, and small polities, such as Motul de San José and Xunantunich. In spite of the richness of Classic Maya texts, they have significant limitations: they only discuss the affairs of the "rich and famous" and give little or no attention to the lower levels of the socioeconomic ladder or to the economic affairs of any group. To gain the perspectives of all members of Classic states, we need to look at the archaeological remains left behind by all Maya individuals (as I will do in the following chapters). We also need to correlate the few hieroglyphic titles for lower-level political officials with the archaeology of small subsidiary centers.

Indirect evidence from the Spanish conquistadores, friars, and colonists who witnessed Maya polities in the fifteenth and sixteenth centuries has also underscored the variability in size and structure of Maya native kingdoms. Postclassic Maya states ranged from the small Yucatec *cah* ruled by a *batab* to regional polities ruled by a *halach uinic* to the militarized and expanding states of the K'ich'ean kingdoms of highland Guatemala and finally to the hegemony of the Itza in the Central Peten lowlands. These ethnohistories reveal that factional rule and councils were important political institutions. However, despite the richness of the ethnohistorical documents, it is unclear if we can directly apply Postclassic conditions to the Classic period.

All in all, the settlement patterns and epigraphic and ethnohistorical studies presented in this chapter have highlighted that Maya archaeology must shift its perspective from the "old debate" of whether Classic polities were centralized or decentralized and focus on the variability in the different aspects of these ancient complex societies. In addition to great variation in size, Classic Maya states exhibited variation in their political institutions, including that of divine kingship. These institutions include the possibility of single or multiple rulers and range from far-flung hegemonies to tiny microstates (or city-states). They are organized using quadripartite or dual internal divisions, and various combinations of agricultural, religious, commercial, and political power characterize their capital cities and secondary centers. All of these features contributed to the political dynamics of the Classic period. To understand the causes of these dynamics, we need to turn to the internal structure of Maya polities, the topic of the next chapters.

Notes

1. However, more recent surveys have shown that additional sites in the lowlands had substantial population densities and/or monumental construction and may belong in the first size-rank. These include Caracol, Naranjo, Yaxha, Ek Balam, and possibly Chunchucmil and Dzibilchaltun (Chase and Chase 1996). This shows that settlement hierarchy studies require detailed and complete regional surveys. To date, these only exist for some parts of the Maya lowlands.

2. The authors also couple archaeological data on population density with the presence of causeways in the largest states, such as Calakmul, Coba, and Caracol (Chase and Chase 1998, 14–17).

3. Hammond (1991, 277) gives similar numbers (a mean distance of 49 kilometers between polity centers involved in conflict), but he reaches the opposite conclusion. He argues that the typical territory of Classic Maya polities extended halfway, to 25 kilometers, leading to estimates of about 2,000 square kilometers for the size of polity territories.

4. Interestingly, Tourtellot and his associates (1993) have suggested a similar dual division at La Milpa in northwest Belize.

5. Each plaza may have been maintained by the elite of its corresponding district or subdistrict and by commoner groups drawn from the hinterland population (de Montmollin 1995, 124). If that is the case, the periphery groups would have had a stake in and an arena for political and ritual engagement (or competition) in the capital of the polity (ibid.).

6. Nevertheless, ball courts have been found at some small sites that lack other major architecture. For example, Chawak But'o'ob in the Three Rivers Region of northwestern Belize is a small village that had a ball court but no public architecture (Walling 2005; Walling et al. 2006; Eleanor King personal communication, 2012).

7. De Montmollin (1995, 178–79) warns that this same pattern of elite dispersal can be caused by resistance. In this scenario, the commoners resist the political policy of resettle-

ment and disperse over the landscape and the secondary elites are then sent out to live among them.

8. Commoner and elite populations are reconstructed based on the number of elite and commoner dwellings. Elite mounds are defined by size and location: "Elite dwellings are from housegroups with at least one dwelling nine meters or longer and/or from housegroups oriented onto civic plazas" (de Montmollin 1995, 170–71).

9. The same settlement pattern can be caused by two very different political processes: "1. A problematically low degree of political control at the top and center" or "2. A policy of spreading civic facilities around in relation to a dispersed subject (and elite?) population, as argued in feudal . . . models" (de Montmollin 1995, 198). Nevertheless, we can distinguish between these two processes archaeologically by considering whether the commoners were distributed in a way that followed the best agricultural land or if they were distributed in a way that followed elite residences and hence for political reasons (ibid.). This brings to the forefront the importance of studying the environment and ecological resources at the same time that we are following human settlement.

10. The number of families is estimated by correlating one commoner housemound with one family (de Montmollin 1995, 205).

11. An alternative interpretation of this calculation is that nine to ten families worshipped at a temple and that larger temples attracted more worshippers (see Lucero 2007). A similar interpretation can be given for the number of "commoner supporters": this could be the number of commoner individuals who worshipped at that temple.

12. A similar approach to rural-urban relations in ancient civilizations is presented in Schwartz and Falconer (1994).

13. It is also noteworthy that the *k'uhul ajaw* was not the only one who could embody gods, as this example shows. An earlier example also comes from Palenque: on Pakal's throne from Palace House E, the artist portrays two figures on the throne's supports who are important courtiers and who embody two aquatic deities (D. Stuart and G. Stuart 2008, 157–158).

14. Recent research by Tokovinine (2008) has altered this understanding of emblem glyphs because in some cases more than one lord (such as those of Dos Pilas and Tikal) carried the same emblem glyph. This suggests that they were claiming common origins as well as making a statement of political independence.

15. Golden and colleagues (Golden et al. 2008; Scherer and Golden 2009) have documented the fortified border between the city-states of Yaxchilan and Piedras Negras along the Usumacinta River. In this highly militarized zone, borders were very important and "related to needed resources" (Chase, Chase, and Smith 2009, 181).

16. Most Maya archaeologists agree that control over labor rather than control over land was the primary concern of Classic period Maya rulers, just as it was in the Contact period (Restall 1997).

17. But see the critique of epigraphic evidence of Calakmul's role in the Tikal-Caracol wars in the Middle Classic in Chase and Chase (2008).

18. However, it should be noted that Xunantunich's Group D housed elite craft specialists who produced fine slate items. These individuals were of high status, and the group

was clearly of importance to the royal family because it was connected to the central group by a causeway, Sacbe 1 (Braswell 2010).

19. Robin, Yaeger, and Ashmore (2010), Jamison (2010), and Schortman (2010) observe that these exotics appear in caches or burials in Xunantunich's hinterland. Presumably they were gifts from the ruling elite to local leaders or powerful families to encourage or reward their support.

20. The Ik' Polychrome Style is a particular style of polychrome pottery that uses pink slip and pink glyphs to depict court or ritual scenes involving Ik' elites (see an extended definition and study of the Ik' Polychrome Style in Reents-Budet, Ball, and Kerr 1994). I discuss this style further in Chapter 6.

21. Foias and Emery (2012) present the results of the research carried out at Motul de San José from 1998 to 2003. The apogee of the site occurred in the period known cerami-cally as Tepeu 2. In the Maya lowlands, pottery is used to date archaeological remains in the absence of radiocarbon dates. The Tepeu 2 ceramic sphere is generally dated to be-tween AD 680–700 and 800–830.

22. We know little about Nixtun-Ch'ich beyond its size and the length of its occupa-tion, which was very long, from the Middle Preclassic until the Colonial Period (Rice et al. 1996). Continued research has been blocked by the owners of the land on which the site is located.

23. Ringle and Bey (2001, 268–69) prefer a different translation of *cuchcabal* as the "jurisdiction [that was] subject to a particular town or city." According to this translation, the *cuchcabal* usually was not a whole *provincia*.

24. Thompson (1970), Tozzer (1941), and Zender (2004), among others, remark that the *halach uinic* and his subordinate *batabs* appear to have had very similar, if not identical, civil and religious duties.

25. I have chosen to pluralize Maya words by adding an "s" rather than the Maya plural suffix "*ob*" or "*tak*" because linguists still argue which of these suffixes was used during the Classic period.

26. Restall (2001) also emphasizes the importance of texts for the royal court: "Docu-ments were not simply kept where the court was located; these texts *were* the court, just as the basis of the court's legitimacy, its history, was kept *as* text" (343). This suggests that many more texts were kept by the Maya elites but did not survive into modern times.

27. I define the term *estate* as the status, rights, duties, and responsibilities given at birth to a child because of his or her parents or kin group.

28. Caso Barrera (2002, 354) notes that this political organization was so ingrained in the Itza Maya society that even in the eighteenth century, the reconstituted communities organized themselves in a way that was similar to the pre-conquest political organization: the caciques of the San Joseph, San Andrés, San Jerónimo, and San Bernabé towns called themselves *batabs*. These communities called the governor at Nojpeten (modern Flores) *halach uinic*.

29. The nature of this dual rulership is ambiguous because the high priest (AjK'in Kan Ek') is not included in Itza testimonies about the political organization of the Itza polity, except when the high priest himself was interviewed (Jones 1998, 94).

30. Much less is known about the Kowojs, the main enemies of the Itza. The Kowojs controlled the northern and northeastern shore of Lake Peten Itza (Rice and Rice 2009; Jones 2009). From the few ethnohistorical sources available on Kowoj political organization, Jones (2009) has concluded that the Kowoj realm was more centralized than the Itza polity (64). The fact that the Kowoj ruler is consistently called "Captain" in the Spanish documents suggests that the military function superseded the religious role in Kowoj governorship (65). Unfortunately, few other details have been preserved because of the tremendous disruptions of the Spanish Conquest and the Colonial period (see also Caso Barrera 2002).

5

|||||||||||||

Internal Dynamics, Bureaucracy, and Political Centralization

The Middle Scale of Political Analysis

In this chapter I explore Classic Maya political dynamics by scrutinizing the internal organization of Maya polities, or the middle scale of political analysis. One of the key variables may be the presence (or absence) of a bureaucracy. The existence of a bureaucracy is tied to the old debate about the degree of centralization in Classic Maya states; Chase and Chase (1992) argue that "centralized bureaucracies were clearly in evidence at sites like Tikal and Caracol" (309). More important, though, the existence of a Maya bureaucracy relates to the nature of internal political processes and human agency in Classic Maya polities.

To better understand the connection between centralization and bureaucracies, we need to reflect on what anthropologists mean by centralization. While definitions abound, we can take Roscoe's definition (1993) as a useful starting point: political centralization is the concentration of decision-making in the hands of a few or as few as possible. Thus, political centralization requires a cadre of officials or administrators who carry out the political decisions of the few and who monitor the populace to ensure that these decisions are followed. Maya scholars often envision this body of officials as a bureaucracy, but in this chapter, I argue that this name might not be appropriate for Classic Maya administrations.

The potential existence of a Classic Maya bureaucracy also relates to new perspectives on power dynamics, as articulated by Stein and Rothman in their "organizational dynamics of complexity" model for the Near East (Stein and Rothman 1994; Stein 1994b, 1998; Rothman 2004) and by Marcus (1998) in her "dynamic model" for the Maya area (see also Iannone 2002;

Demarest 1992, 1996c; Foias 2003, 2007). Following these new perspectives, our discussion must change from whether or not a polity is centralized to how centralized a polity is and from whether or not a bureaucracy is present to the degree of bureaucratization. Because power is now seen as always in flux, political analysis must better define political processes and strategies that are the ongoing attempts of rulers and other active political factions or actors within Maya polities to centralize power.[1]

Most sociologists view bureaucracy as a central feature of modern industrial societies (beginning with Weber 1964 [1947]), and some historians argue that the first centralized bureaucracies appeared in European states during the eighteenth or nineteenth centuries (Kiser and Cai 2003). However, there are earlier examples, including the Qin Chinese Empire (221–206 BC) (Kiser and Cai 2003) and some ancient Near East civilizations. Sumerian city-states of the Early Dynastic periods (ca. 2900–2350 BC) and later empires of the Near East also had proto-bureaucratic administrations, but these may not have been centralized under the state, and seemed to have operated as parallel organizations in temples and royal palaces (Liverani 1996; Maisels 1999; Rothman 1998, 2004; Wiesehofer 1996). Maisels (1999) locates the beginning of bureaucratization in ancient Sumer and describes the Lagash temple functionaries from the Ur III period (the late third millennium BC) in the following manner: "Here we find 'high managerialism' of an order that did not appear until the twentieth century AD" (167). In other words, although bureaucratization reached its maturity in modern times, the process evolved in some states in earlier periods. It is also important to note that these ancient bureaucracies (or administrations) may be political, military, or ecclesiastical.

While I begin this chapter by exploring whether Maya polities had bureaucracies, I consider other issues of the internal organization of these kingdoms, such as the nature of their administration and finance institutions. Variations in internal political organization as seen in the examples I describe below highlight that politics is a result of the interplay of local circumstances, successful and unsuccessful strategies by leaders and factions, alliances or compromises among these individuals or factions, and the material resources at the disposal of these individuals or factions.

Bureaucracy and the Qin Chinese Empire

Kiser and Cai (2003) outline why the process of bureaucratization begins at such an early date in the earliest Chinese Empire, the Qin Dynasty (221–206

BC). Based on their cross-cultural analysis, Kiser and Cai argue that two factors cause the beginning of bureaucratization. The first is intense warfare because "military competition and war force states to adopt more efficient bureaucratic forms," and the second is "improved monitoring capacity arising from technological advances in communications, transportation, and record-keeping" (512). The authors write that because monitoring technologies were not developed until the industrial revolution, warfare was the most important driver of the development of bureaucratic structures in antiquity. To understand why constant and intense war leads to bureaucracies, we should consider the multiple consequences of conflict in ancient times. The aristocracy is usually weakened (because they are the ones that generally die on the battlefield) and the political field is thus opened up for innovations and attempts by the ruler to control more of the state affairs; models of bureaucratic organization develop in the successful military and then political institutions adopt them; roads are built for transportation of armies and supplies, and this improved communication system enhances monitoring of the populace by other groups; and, personnel trained in the military within a developing bureaucratic framework can transfer their expertise to the political institution (ibid.).

To show that bureaucratization develops only in civilizations with significant conflict, Kiser and Cai take a broad perspective, comparing the intensity and frequency of war and the degree of bureaucratization in China during the Qin Dynasty, the Neo-Assyrian Empire (883–608 BC), Persia during the Achaemenid Dynasty (559–330 BC), ancient Greece in the time of the Delian League (478–404 BC), Rome during the time of the Republic (509–44BC) and the Empire (27 BC–AD 476), the Ottoman Empire (1453–1918), early modern England (1485–1640), and early modern France (1515–1789) (Kiser and Cai 2003, 513). They indeed find that the civilizations with most intense warfare, such as Qin Dynasty China, also have most bureaucratic political systems.

Kiser and Cai's analysis can help us reflect if the Maya also developed a bureaucratic administrative structure during the Classic period because of high levels of conflict. Webster's (2000) review of Classic Maya warfare provides preliminary evidence about its frequency using data compiled by Mark Child (1999, quoted in ibid.). One hundred seven war events (marked by the glyphs "to chop," "to fall," and "to capture") involving 28 centers are recorded for the period from AD 512 to AD 880. Webster emphasizes that this is "a biased and extremely incomplete sample" because Childs's data included only 28 centers and only a subset of all glyphs possibly associated with warfare (96). Keeping in mind this bias, the data indicates that a war took place approximately every 3 years, or 29.1 percent of the time. Evidence from the center of Yaxchilan indicates that it was involved in a war every 13 years, or a much lower 7.7 percent of the time. When we compare these numbers with the frequency of war among the Qin Dynasty state and empire, Assyria, Persia, Rome, and so on, (Kiser and Cai 2003, 523, Table 1), it becomes clear that the level of Classic Maya warfare was lower than in the other civilizations. The Qin State and the Greek Delian League experienced warfare for 75 percent of the period of the study, and the Ottoman Empire, early modern England, and France experienced war around 50 percent of that time (AD 1100–1800). Kiser and Cai use other measures such as the duration of war, the rate of military drafting, and casualties per year to compare levels of conflict, but such information is hard or impossible to come by for the Maya because they did not keep such records in the hieroglyphic texts that have been preserved (see the discussion in Webster 2000). The overall picture Webster (2000) and other scholars (Demarest 1997; Inomata and Triadan 2009) present is that prior to the Terminal Classic, the Classic Maya generally experienced a less frequent, less intense, and less destructive form of warfare than the Qin Empire or the Greek Delian League did. This is not to deny that in some cases war was destructive, for example the burning of Aguateca (Inomata 2008) or the sacrifice of an entire dynastic family at Yaxuna (Suhler, Ardren, and Johnstone 1998; Freidel, MacLeod, and Suhler 2003). Nevertheless, the lower overall incidence of war among the Classic Maya compared to Qin China seems to suggest, according to Kiser and Cai's model, that it is unlikely that the Maya would have developed a bureaucratic administration.

To extend the comparison between ancient Chinese bureaucracy and Classic Maya administrative structure a little further, by the middle of the Han Empire (AD 2), the successor to the Qin Empire, the Chinese bureaucracy had between 120,000 and 150,000 officials for a population of almost 60 million people (Kiser and Cai 2003, 532n42; Loewe 1986, 120, 206). Another example of massive administration comes from the Mughal Empire, where there were as many as 309,000 officials for an estimated population of over 100 million around AD 1595 (Blanton and Fargher 2008, 74). Scholars estimate that the Classic Maya population in the lowlands (several million people) was much lower than in Han China or Mughal India (Rice and Culbert 1990). If we take the Han number of officials as an estimate for the size of a bureaucracy in relation to population size, we would expect to see some 5,000 officials among the many Classic Maya city-states of the lowlands. Considering that the number of Classic Maya polities varied over time from 12 to some 30 small to large units, we are talking about 167 to 417 officials per state. As mentioned in Chapter 4, Restall (2001, 364) estimates that the size of a typical royal court in Yucatan at the time of Spanish Conquest was about 50 (specifically this is the court of Nachi Cocom of the Sotuta polity). Taking into consideration that the Sotuta polity was probably smaller than some of the Classic period states, it is conceivable that large hegemonies such as those controlled by Tikal, Calakmul, and Caracol may have had more than 417 officials.

Regardless of how large the Classic period officialdom was, bureaucracies are more than large numbers. More important, bureaucracies incur great expenses. Kiser and Cai (2003) emphasize that they are inefficient in premodern polities because of low monitoring and sanctioning capabilities and hence will only develop under extreme circumstances of frequent conflict. Yoffee (2005) observes that in ancient Mesopotamia, heavy bureaucracies rapidly depleted their polities financially. Furthermore, bureaucracies are defined by specific means of recruitment and payment, a hierarchical organization, a public (rather than a privatized) administration, and an impersonal ethos among officials (Weber 1964 [1947]; Kiser and Cai 2003; Jackall 1988).

Description of Bureaucracies

Weber (1964 [1947]) is the foremost scholar of bureaucracies because he analyzed the features and conditions necessary for their development in the early part of the twentieth century. Building on Weber's insights, Kiser and Cai (2003) combine elements of comparative-historical sociology and agency theory to define the structural and organizational determinants of bureaucratization at both the micro and macro levels (513–15). They define a bureaucracy by the following features: 1) a method for recruiting bureaucrats/officials (based on merit or other factors); 2) methods of payment (salaries, land grants, or usufruct rights to estates); 3) forms of monitoring; 4) types of sanctions; 5) hierarchical organization; and 6) public or private administration (514, 534–35).[2]

Generally speaking, bureaucrats in modern or early modern states were recruited based on merit rather than their position in society. This meant that the officials drew their political power from their office in the bureaucracy rather than from their social or economic status and thus could be more easily controlled by the top leaders. In the same vein, it was preferable to pay bureaucrats salaries rather than land grants because land grants would give them a separate source of economic and political power and would work against centralizing political power in the hands of a few at the top.

The third and fourth characteristics of bureaucracies, monitoring and sanctioning, are closely related:

> The type of administration rulers choose depends primarily on their monitoring capacity. When monitoring is poor, agent compliance will be low unless strong sanctions are used to compensate. . . . Because bureaucracy relies on fairly weak positive and negative sanctions (fixed salaries and the threat of dismissal), it will be efficient only when monitoring capacity is well developed. (514–15)

Thus, bureaucracies will generally appear only when monitoring is strong because of developments in technologies of communication, transportation and/or record-keeping. Kiser and Cai note that even in ancient Qin China, bureaucratization was not as complete as in modern state bureaucracies because of low monitoring capacity even though some advances had occurred, such as the construction of roads for rapid movement and a common script. To offset the absence of rapid monitoring, the Chinese used severe negative sanctions for disobedience: death was imposed for the most minor infractions. In addition, Qin regional inspectors were named to monitor local officials closely. A third method of monitoring in ancient China was "intentionally introduced redundancy . . . by giving officials overlapping jurisdictions and duties" (such as the placement of two individuals, an "official of the right" and an "official of the left," in the same position) (532–33). Kiser and Cai remark that because of low levels of monitoring capabilities, bureaucratization first occurred "at the top of the administration and in central areas" (518). This has significant implications because we would expect to see more bureaucratization in the large cities such as Tikal than in minor regional centers such as Motul de San José. Finding evidence for bureaucratic development at a small site such as Motul would suggest that the larger sites have even more significant developments of bureaucratization.

Modern bureaucracies are hierarchically arranged, meaning that several levels of decision making exist and that each group of officials is under the jurisdiction of a higher-ranking bureaucrat, who will be under the direction of another even higher rank of administrators. Beyond that, Kiser and Cai define a system as "hierarchical if there is uniform central control of provinces (not feudal, prebendal, or delegation to local notables)" (534).

The final characteristic Kiser and Cai use to characterize bureaucracies is the presence of public (rather than private) administration. The administration is considered public if it is separate from the king's private household and private if it is integral to the king's household. Private administration also refers to tax farming, by which the function of tax collecting is given to specific, private individuals as their business rather than controlled by state officials. Weber (Gerth and Mills 1960) also defines bureaucracies by their impersonal ethos because bureaucracies are predicated on legal-rational authority: "Submission under legal authority is based upon an *impersonal* bond to the generally defined and functional 'duty of office.' The official duty . . . is fixed by *rationally established* norms" (299, their italics).

Armed with this definition, we can now turn to the Classic Maya to see if the administration of lowland polities fits Weber's and Kiser and Cai's description of bureaucracy.

Where Is the Maya Administration or Bureaucracy?

Classic period hieroglyphic texts are one important source of information for the existence of a political administration, whether or not the administration is bureaucratic. Several subsidiary titles have been identified to date: *sajal, ajk'uhuun, yajawk'ahk'* (Sharer and Golden 2004; Inomata 2001a; Houston and Stuart 2001; Houston 1993; Grube in Coe and Kerr 1997; Jackson and Stuart 2001), *lakam* (Lacadena 2008), and *chak tok wayaab'* (Beliaev 2004; Estrada-Belli et al. 2009) (Figure 5.1). However, *yajaw k'ahk'* and *chak tok wayaab'* may be purely religious offices.

The title *sajal* (Figure 5.1c) refers to a subsidiary noble who governed a secondary center, so the title can be translated as provincial governor. The depiction of *sajals* in battle scenes suggests that they also fulfilled military roles as commanders (Webster 2000). The second title, *ajk'uhuun* (Figure 5.1d) has been interpreted variously as "keeper of the sacred books," "royal scribe," "keeper of tribute" (or of sacred/special objects), or "venerator" of specific rulers (Jackson and Stuart 2001). Although the specific meaning of this title has been debated, scholars agree that the contexts where the title of *ajk'uhuun* appears indicate that they are "owned" by their superior

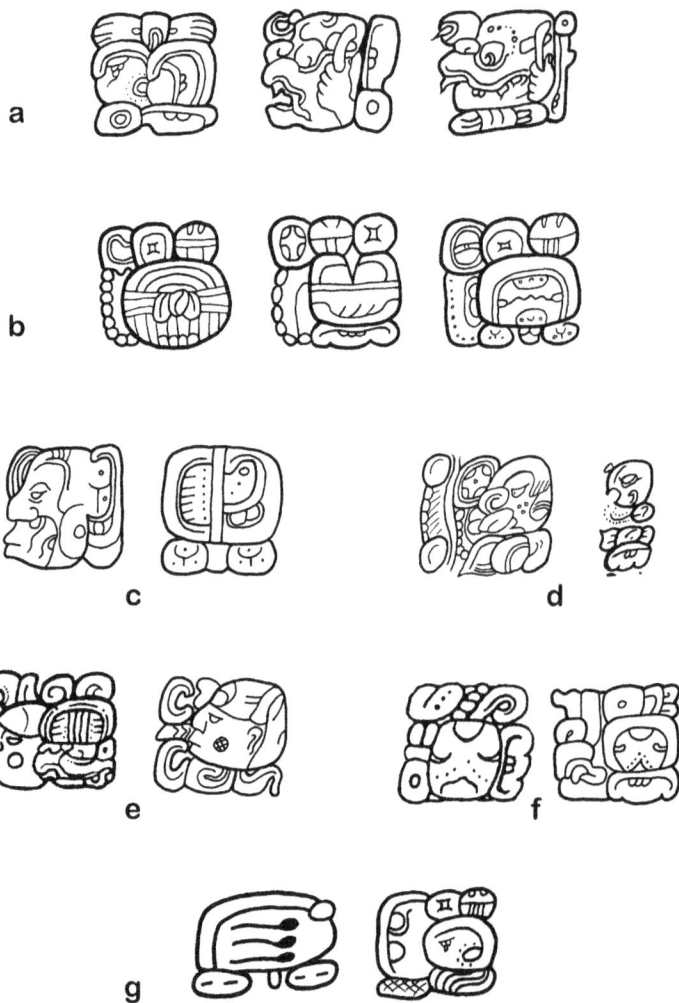

Figure 5.1. Classic Maya political titles: a. *kaloomte'* (after Coe and Van Stone 2005, 76); b. emblem glyphs for *k'uhul ajaw* of Tikal, Yaxchilan, and Palenque (after Coe and Stone 2005, 69, 70); c. *sajal* (after Miller and Martin 2004, Figure 12); d. *ajk'uhuun* (after Miller and Martin 2004, Figure 12; and Zender 2004, Figure 28); e. *yajawk'ahk'* (after Miller and Martin 2004, Figure 12; and Zender 2004, Figure 36); f. *ti'sakhuun* (after Zender 2004, Figure 38; and Houston and Inomata 2009, Figure 6.6); g. *lakam* followed by an emblem glyph (after Lacadena 2008, Figure 8). All drawn by Evalynn Rosado.

lord, the *k'uhul ajaw*, and that this ownership continues beyond the death of the particular *k'uhul ajaw* (ibid.; Houston and Inomata 2009). The common portrayal of *ajk'uhuuns* in court or palace scenes painted on polychrome vessels (including the Ik' Style polychromes produced at Motul de San José) suggests that they had multiple and central roles. Maybe they were the Maya version of the Near Eastern scribe who was the quintessential administrator (Coe and Kerr 1997; Halperin and Foias 2010). The third title, *yajawk'ahk'* (Figure 5.1e), can be translated as "the fire's lord" and may be a religious rather than an administrative position (Houston and Stuart 2001; Sharer and Golden 2004). Hierarchical ordering of these positions were sometimes made among these titles, for example, using the modifier *ba* ("first" or "head of") in terms such as *ba-sajal* ("first governor") (Sharer and Golden 2004; Houston and Inomata 2009).

Two additional titles have been more recently deciphered: *lakam* (Figure 5.1g) and *chak tok wayaab'*. The administrative title of *lakam*, which appears in only a few polychrome vessel texts from Peten, may have applied to non-elites. The duties of this office possibly involved the collection of tribute and military contingents from intrasettlement districts or neighborhoods (Lacadena 2008). Finally, Beliaev (2004) and Estrada-Belli et al. (2009) have translated another title, *chak tok* (or sometimes *k'an tok*) *wayaab'*, as "red cloud [or yellow cloud] dreamer/priest" (246–48). Whether this is purely a priestly position or may have had dual civil-religious duties remains to be seen (ibid.; Beliaev 2004).[3] This title appears in the Usumacinta Basin and at Tikal, Holmul, and Naranjo (Estrada-Belli et al. 2009, 246–48; Beliaev 2004). The holders of this title were clearly of high rank because they commissioned "palaces, temples, ball courts, and monuments, albeit in the presence of a higher political authority" (Estrada-Belli et al. 2009, 246). Beliaev (2004, 127) notes that in the Usumacinta region, *chak tok* (or *k'an tok*) *wayaab'* is a title carried by nonroyal nobles, most commonly by the *sajals*, suggesting a combination of civil with religious roles. If the colors in the *wayaab'* titles are indeed associated with the cardinal colors, it is possible that there were four such *wayaab'* title holders, which reminds us of the quadripartite organization recorded in some Postclassic Maya states, such as the Itza kingdom. Beliaev theorizes that this title may have marked a particular elite rank rather than an actual position in a priestly institution.

These administrative titles appear uncommonly, mostly in the western lowlands (Houston and Stuart 2001; see the distribution of these titles in Houston and Inomata 2009, 170, Figure 6.4). The fact that the holders of these titles were closely linked to an individual ruler who owned them (as specified by the possessive prefixes "u-," "ya," or "y-" that precede the title) argues for a tight patrimonial relationship between the ruler and his administrators rather than a more impersonal bureaucratic connection (Houston 1993; Stuart 1992; Jackson 2004; Houston and Inomata 2009). We know that this relationship continued beyond the death of the ruler or patron, because several texts refer to these officials as owned by a ruler who had already died (Houston and Stuart 2001; Zender 2004; Houston and Inomata 2009). Golden (2003) stresses that the k'uhul ajaw and the sajal were not completely interchangeable posts because the position of the divine ruler was much more complex than the administrative position of the sajal (see also discussion in Houston and Inomata 2009, 174). Jackson (2004), Zender (2004), Houston and Inomata (2009, 174) all add that hieroglyphic texts that record accession to these various titled positions make clear that they were recognized as formal offices. In contrast, additional titles appear in the Bonampak murals but do not correlate with accession, suggesting honorifics rather than actual positions: baah took' ("head person of the flint"), baah pakal ("head person of the shield"), baah tz'am ("head person of the throne"), and baah te' ("head person of the tree-staff"; "head bailiff")(Houston and Inomata 2009, 182–87, Figure 6.13; Houston 2008, 2012). Houston and Inomata (2009; Houston 2012) believe that although the functions of these four titles are not clear, the first two may relate to military officials, and the second two to poorly known functionaries or courtiers in civil service. The problem is that these titles appear so rarely and it is hard to decipher their meaning (Houston and Inomata 2009; Houston 2008, 2012).

Recently, Zender (2004) has re-translated the most common of these administrative titles, the ajk'uhuun title, as a priestly position of high rank. This new translation strongly supports the interpretation that the Classic Maya political administration was a theocratic one. Zender identifies three priestly offices in a "ranked ecclesiastical bureaucracy" (78–79) (with ties to secular administration): 1) ajk'uhuun, the "worshipper" of deities (priest), keeper of codices, and/or court chaplain; 2) yajawk'ahk', or "fire's vassal," a warrior priest in charge of incense ceremonies;[4] and 3) ti'sakhuun, "speaker of the white headband," a prophet, oracle, or speaker for the king (see Table 4.1 and Figure 5.1 in this volume).

Zender draws upon ethnohistorical documents from Late Postclassic Yucatan to decipher the roles of these Classic Maya priests. As mentioned in Chapter 4, the ruler in Late Postclassic Yucatan kingdoms (called the *halach uinic*) was at the top of a three-level political hierarchy, followed by secondary elites (who were the regional or municipal governors, called *batabs*) in the second level, and the priesthood who acted as advisors in the third level. These priests "had by all accounts a great degree of influence [because of] . . . their role as producers . . . of written documents, teach-ers, community leaders, and intermediaries between humans and the gods" (80). The *ajk'uhuun*[5] title has been identified in Late Classic inscriptions on stone monuments and on pottery from various sites, including Comal-calco, Copan, Palenque, Piedras Negras, Tonina, Yaxchilan, and Motul de San José (Zender 2004). These inscriptions highlight the importance of high-ranking priests during the earlier Classic period.

The three main priestly titles (*ajk'uhuun, ti'sakhuun,* and *yajawk'ahk'*) and two other possible priestly offices (*baah ajaw* and *anab*) are ranked in Classic hieroglyphic texts. Although their meanings are still opaque, *baah ajaw* and *anab* (phonetically a-na-b'i) appear to be the lowest priestly positions. *Yajawk'ahk'* and *ajk'uhuun* are ranked above these (*ajk'uhuun* is the more prestigious) and *ti'sakhuun* is the highest rank (Zender 2004). Such a hierarchical statement is carved on the Group IV head from Struc-ture J1 at Palenque. The head probably depicts the nonregnal lord Aj Sul, who was both a *yajawk'ahk'* and an *ajk'uhuun*. The text begins not with Aj Sul but with the most important event in the life of his superior, the lord K'ab'is Uchih Aj Sik'ab, and the latter's accession to the priestly position of *ti'sakhuun*, which in turn is overseen (or sponsored) by a highly ranked noble or royal named Janaab' Pakal (306, Figure 108). The text then tells us that the new *ti'sakhuun* K'ab'is Uchih Aj Sik'ab has under his jurisdiction several *sajals* who became *yajawk'ahk's* in AD 610, including Aj Sul (307). (The life story of Aj Sul continues below.) This interweaving of administra-tive positions with ecclesiastical positions (*sajals* became *yajawk'ahk's*) is similar to the civil-religious cargo system of the Colonial Maya highlands and Yucatan (which continues in some areas into modern times) (Farriss 1984; Restall 1997). Similar to the civil-religious cargo system, Classic Maya lords rose through the hierarchy of positions described above, as a few ex-amples below will show.

The presence of an ecclesiastical hierarchy in which nobles progressed (or were promoted) from a lower to a higher position is clear from the Clas-sic Maya texts. These titles are tied to the verb for accession; thus, individ-ual nobles acceded to these positions under the auspices of a higher lord, but not always the *k'uhul ajaw*. For example, Aj Sul from Palenque was first a *sajal* for an unknown length of time, then a *yajawk'ahk'* for 44 years. For the last 20 or so years of his life, he was an *ajk'uhuun* (Zender 2004, 295). Another Palenque noble, Chak Suutz' was instated as a *baah ajaw*, then as a *yajawk'ahk'* and then as a *sajal*. Here the order of "promotion" from *sajal* to *yajawk'ahk'* is reversed from the order in which Aj Sul progressed, a fact that suggests that there was flexibility in the civil-religious hierarchy. After he was elevated to the position of *sajal*, Chak Suutz' had his own subordinate *ajk'uhuuns* (300; see also Jackson 2004). We have other evidence that Chak Suutz' was an important political figure at Palenque: his residential group, Group IV, had a throne room (just like that of the most famous of Palenque's rulers, Pakal) that included the famed Tablet of the Slaves (Stuart and Stuart 2008, 223). Although the text records Chak Suutz's successes in battle, the Tablet of the Slaves depicts the Palenque ruler Ahkal Mo' Nahb receiving the crown, flint, and shield of rulership from his parents (ibid.).

We also need to inquire whether the individuals who held these priestly positions also fulfilled administrative duties beyond religious ones. The actions and events in which these priests are depicted can tell us about their roles in Classic Maya states. Coe and Kerr (1997) first observed that *ajk'uhuuns* are commonly seen in many scenes on pottery vessels, murals, and (to a much less degree) public stone monuments (see also Zender 2004; Halperin and Foias 2012). *Ajk'uhuuns* and/or *ti'sakhuuns* are depicted in scenes of tribute offering, such as the Structure XVI Panel fragment at Palenque (Zender 2004, Figure 120) and Vessel K8089 (ibid., Figure 123). They are also depicted in court reunions, feasts, and dances, all of which may have involved foreign ambassadors or representatives from local subsidiary centers, such as the El Señor del Peten Vase (ibid., Figure 40), the Bonampak Structure 1, Room 1, North Wall, Medial Register (ibid., Figure 44), and the Piedras Negras Panel 3 (ibid., 324–26, Figure 125). *Ajk'uhuuns* appear to have been scribes, messengers, tribute recorders, and teachers of young nobles (Coe and Kerr 1997; Zender 2004).[6]

Zender (2004) writes that in contrast to the *aj k'uhuuns*,

the *ti'sakhuun*, as the most prominent of the Classic priests, also discharged a series of important political duties. Foremost among these was spokesmanship for the royal family and particularly for its apical head, the *k'uhulajaw*, and may have included the entertaining of foreign dignitaries to the court (as at Calakmul) and the collection of tribute from dependencies (as at Palenque and Pomoná). At a number of sites, *ti'sakhuun* apparently served as regents for young monarchs. (374–75)

Moving down the priestly hierarchy, the *yajawk'ahk'* was closely tied to the command of the army; they are depicted as warriors, captors, or, in unfortunate cases, captives. So, these priests discharged both civil and religious duties.

Was Maya Administration Bureaucratic?

To understand if the Classic Maya political administration was bureaucratic or not, we can examine if it had the characteristics of the early modern to modern bureaucracies described above: hierarchical organization, payment of officials through salaries, strong monitoring systems and/or strong sanctions against disobedience, recruitment based on merit, public administration, and an impersonal ethos.

Epigraphy and art has enabled us to understand that the Classic administration was both civil and ecclesiastical and that it was hierarchical. The hierarchy consists of the following political titles, from the highest to the lowest: *k'uhul ajaw* (the divine lord), *ti'sakhuun* (highest priest and speaker of the ruler), *ajk'uhuun* (royal priest, scribe, teacher), *yajawk'ahk'* (fire's lord, warrior, and fire priest), *sajal* (governor of secondary center), and *lakam* (collector of tribute and of military contingents in towns and/or cities) (see Figure 5.1). But is this administration bureaucratic according to the definitions of Weber and Kiser and Cai?

First, I consider the recruitment methods Classic Maya polities used. Ideally, bureaucracies will select officials based on merit only. But because the hieroglyphic titles for Maya subsidiary administrative positions name elites (Houston and Stuart 2001; Sharer and Golden 2004; Zender 2004), it is clear that recruitment was patrimonial rather than based on merit. This does not mean that merit could not enter into the decision process; rather, it means that individuals had to be chosen among candidates within a particular elite rank, if not of a particular elite lineage or house. This type of administration was likely hard to control and it would have been difficult to centralize power because the officials (whether they were secular—for example, *sajals*—or ecclesiastical, for example, *ajk'uhuuns*) are lords (for example, Aj Sul and Chak Suutz') who had a great deal of power based on their social status and economic wealth (Foias 2007; Foias and Emery

2012). For one thing, they didn't have to obey their overlord unless it was in their interest to do so or unless heavy negative sanctions existed to ensure that the *k'uhul ajaw* was not disobeyed.

This does not deny that merit also played a role in the selection of ancient Maya administrators because, for example, the accession to the position of *yajawk'ahk'* was closely tied to the capture of one or more opponents on the battlefield. However, eligibility for the higher ecclesiastical offices (*ajk'uhuun* and *ti'sakhuun*) was not explicitly tied to merit, and favoritism seems just as likely. The archaeological and epigraphic evidence from Palenque and Copan speaks to long traditions of priests from the same elite families beginning in the Middle Classic and continuing to the end of the Classic period, which weighs in favor of the importance of inherited status in recruitment (Zender 2004). But nepotism did not rule recruitment completely either, because officials such as *sajals* were generally not selected from the ruler's direct family. This is suggested by the findings of Munson and Macri's (2009) network analysis of Late Classic Maya political relationships: "Lineage-based relations are significantly inversely correlated with subordinate statements" (433). However, once an individual was named to a particular political position, that office remained with his or her lineage for a long time, as suggested by a shell plaque whose owner exalted himself as the 19th sajal of a small subsidiary site somewhere in the region of the Usumacinta River and the Lacandon rain forest (Miller and Martin 2004, 191–92, Plate 107).

Another feature of bureaucracies as defined by Weber and Kiser and Cai is a powerful form of monitoring and strong sanctions for wrongdoing or disobedience. The ability of rulers to control their bureaucracies increases with better monitoring technology, and strong sanctions discourage wrongdoing among members of bureaucracies. Without modern communication technologies such as surveillance cameras, radios, television, and satellites, monitoring among the Classic Maya was low. Obedience could be checked through the frequent visits of the kings to their secondary centers or by frequent communication between the capital and secondary centers. We have some evidence for royal visitations of administrative centers, including the celebrations of rituals at close intervals at Dos Pilas, Aguateca, and Seibal by the Late Classic rulers of Dos Pilas in the Petexbatun region. The establishment of twin capitals in the Petexbatun region (first Tamarindito and Arroyo de Piedra in the Early Classic and then Dos Pilas and Aguateca in the Late Classic) may have served the similar purpose of increasing the ability of the ruler to monitor the doings of the members of the state administration (Houston 1993). However, we don't have evidence that visits or written communication between the *k'uhul ajaws* and his *sajals* and other lower administrators were frequent. It is possible that such communication did take place but was written on materials that would not survive the tropical climate of the Maya lowlands. Unless such paper documents existed, the Classic Maya kings did not put much emphasis on monitoring.

When monitoring technology is weak, bureaucratic obedience is generally reinforced by heavy sanctions or punishments, as was described for the Qin Empire. However, in the case of the Maya, we have no evidence for heavy sanctions (such as the death penalty for disobedience or loss of socioeconomic status through imprisonment), at least in the hieroglyphic texts that survived. Heavy negative sanctions are closely tied to coercive means of control and they often turn out to be double-edged swords that cause unrest, disenchantment, and possibly rebellion (as it happened in the case of the Qin; see Kiser and Cai 2003). It seems unlikely that they would have been very common among the Classic Maya because we have no evidence for prison facilities, major groups of slaves, or individuals with major loss of socioeconomic status.

We know little about the type of payment Maya officials received. Scholars even argue whether the Classic Maya used a type of currency. During the Postclassic, Yucatecan Maya may have used cacao beans or marine shell pieces or beads as money. A more bulky form of currency (and hence less useful) could have been a particular length of cloth. Bundles of cacao beans or cloth are depicted or named as tribute payments in the Bonampak murals (Miller 1999, 172) and on polychrome vases (Stuart 1995; Foias 2002); these may represent Classic period forms of currency. However, it is difficult to extend these hints about the currencies used in the tribute/tax system to the manner of payment of Maya administrators. There is no statement in the hieroglyphs of salary payments to any of the subsidiary officials. Taschek and Ball's (2003) interpretation of the minor center of Nohoch Ek as a lord's manor suggests that land grants rather than salaries may have been used. Additional research is needed, especially in view of the fact that elaborate elite plaza groups such as Nohoch Ek were common across the Maya lowlands.

A third feature of modern bureaucracy is its hierarchical organization. The hierarchical distribution of Maya settlement has already been mentioned as the first hint that political organization during the Classic period was hierarchical (see Chapter 4). For example, the settlement patterns in the Motul de San José polity exhibit a ring of minor centers at two to five kilometers away from the capital, suggesting that they functioned as secondary administrative centers that reported directly to the Motul rulers. Although this is not a very developed hierarchy, Motul itself is only a small center in Central Peten and may have not needed an extensive hierarchy to administer its small territory.

When we shift our focus to larger centers, such as Palenque, the complexity of the political hierarchy, as reconstructed from hieroglyphic inscriptions, is distinct. Here, we have significant epigraphic evidence to help us. The Palenque texts refer to at least four levels in the political hierarchy. Below the divine lord, or *k'uhul ajaw* (level 1) is the *ti'sakhuun* (level 2), who has jurisdiction over several *sajals* (level 3), who in turn have several *ajk'uhuuns* (level 4) (Zender 2004). Zender's deciphering of these ecclesiastical titles is key to reassessments of the Classic Maya political-ecclesiastical administration, which now appears to have been more hierarchical than was previously thought.

The fourth characteristic of a modern bureaucracy is the presence of public administration. This is difficult to discern in the Classic period. Here, I can only make an impressionistic evaluation and point to assessment of this issue as a future research goal. One way to gauge whether or not an administration is public is the presence and scale of storage facilities in central state locations. We see such central storage facilities in the sacred precincts of fourth-millennium Sumerian city-states, in the Inca provincial capitals, and at Cuzco itself. But in spite of decades of scientific archaeological excavations in the Maya lowlands, no large facility has been found at a Classic center (Triadan 2000). Rather, storage is small scale and occurs at the level of the household, both large and small. This suggests that administration, or at least the intake of tribute, was integrated with the affairs of the ruler's household.

Another way to assess the presence of public administration is by looking at the degree of separation between the state administration and the king's household. Webster (2001), Houston and Stuart (2001), and Prudence Rice (2009) view the royal household as the core of the political administration, suggesting that there was little to no separation between the public arena of state administration and the private arena of the ruler's family. But a final clue suggests that some aspects of Maya administration were public. Tribute payments (or gifts?) are associated with the priestly offices of *ti'sakhuun* and *ajk'uhuun* (who may or may not have been members of the ruler's direct family) in carved or painted images on stone monuments and pottery vases. This suggests that tribute collection was at least in part a public event that was witnessed by individuals outside the ruler's household. All in all, the evidence here, meager as it is, is quite mixed.

My comparison of Classic Maya administrators with early to modern bureaucracies shows few similarities, although more research is clearly needed. Unlike modern bureaucracies, recruitment among the Classic Maya was mostly based on descent, and positions were awarded to aristocrats (with the possible exception of the *lakams*). As we saw at Palenque, titles remained within the same noble families for generations. However, like modern bureaucracies (and many nonbureaucratic political administrations), the Classic Maya administration had a hierarchical organization. It is unclear, however, how well developed this hierarchy was. We recognize four levels at Palenque but only two (or possibly three) at Motul de San José (see further discussion for this site below). Unfortunately, we have very little or mixed evidence about the other features of modern bureaucracies (types of payment; monitoring and sanctioning; public versus private administration), so these characteristics may have been undeveloped or underdeveloped in Classic period administration.

New evidence about two central features of Classic Maya administration provides support for the argument that it was nonbureaucratic. First, it was a political-ecclesiastical administration in which priestly titles were interwoven with political positions. As described above, several *sajals* at Palenque became *yajawk'ahk's* in AD 610 under the sponsorship of their superior, the *ti'sakhuun* K'ab'is Aj Sik'ab (Zender 2004, 307). Second, the relationship between officials and their superior patron was very personal and extended beyond the death of the patron. Both of these characteristics contradict arguments that Classic Maya administration was bureaucratic.

Was Bureaucratization a Strategy of the Classic Maya?

Although the evidence presented above suggests that the Classic Maya political administration was not bureaucratic, bureaucratization could be seen as a process rather than as a fait-accompli. Bureaucratization could have been a strategy used by political actors (elites and less likely nonelites) to promote their interests and power. Kiser and Cai (2003) note that bureaucracy (once developed) is "partly a strategy for rulers to increase their power in their ongoing struggle with aristocrats" (517; see also Eisenstadt 1993).

Here, I define the process of bureaucratization as the creation of new political offices to administer and maintain control over state affairs. By placing non-elite or low-elite individuals in these new positions instead of older or more established aristocrats, the ruler creates for himself a new group of followers, clients, and supporters. This strategy is found among other ancient states and empires (Eisenstadt 1993), such as in the shift in ancient Egyptian bureaucracy from the exclusive arena of the elite class to commoners. Another example comes from the Roman emperor Augustus, who began to rely on equestrians (lower elites) rather than senators (high elites) for his officials (Doyle 1986; Garnsey and Saller 1987).

LeCount (2004, 2005) has argued that we can see such a strategy archaeologically in Actuncan in Belize. There, large plaza groups, presumably the residences of members of dominant elite lineages or houses, declined at the same time that new courtyards were established and flourished. This happened at the time of the evolution of Maya kings in the Protoclassic period during the first two centuries AD. The owners of the new households probably flourished because they were given political power by the rising kings, presumably as his officials.

The most significant evidence for bureaucratization comes from the subsidiary titles that concentrate in the Late Classic (the apogee of Maya civilization in the southern lowlands). The variety of such titles suggests that rulers were creating new offices, perhaps in an attempt to garner a loyal following (Houston 1993; Houston and Stuart 2001; Foias 2007; Houston and Inomata 2009, Figure 6.5; Munson and Macri 2009). Alternatively, Houston and Inomata (2009, 172) posit that we find concentrations of subsidiary titles in the Late Classic because subsidiary lords had acquired sufficient power and wealth by the Late Classic to give them the right to immortalize themselves in texts and art. The rarity of such titles at Tikal and Calakmul may be because "sumptuary codes and their enforcement were particularly strong" in these cities (ibid.).

Lacadena (2008) has suggested that the rare Late Classic title of *lakam* may refer to new political positions, and possibly positions for non-elites, and may also signify the beginning of a process of bureaucratization during the Late Classic. However, there are not many occurrences of this title, although interestingly enough, one of them refers to the Motul de San José ruler Tayal/Tayel Chan K'inich (ruled ca. 720–740), who is depicted with three *lakams* on vessel K4996 (Tokovinine and Zender 2012; Lacadena 2008) (see Figure 5.4).

I have argued elsewhere that the florescence of artistry in the Late Classic that is seen in elaborate polychrome vases, carved stone monuments, and other carved, incised, or painted artifacts was partly because of the rulers' attempts to gain more power by sponsoring artists from loyal lineages to create more of the accoutrements needed to sustain power or to give as gifts at political events (Foias 2007; Halperin and Foias 2010). From the perspective of the newly appointed artists and officials, their status increased because of the masterpieces they created or the positions that they held. But these positions or titles also tied them to or made them dependent on the political system. In other words, the new officials and artists gained more political influence and status by accepting the new posts. The ruler also created future competitors for himself with these new appointments, a process that could have led to increasing competition, conflict, and political fragmentation. These are precisely the processes that were responsible for the Classic Maya collapse in the southern lowlands (Fash 1991; Houston and Stuart 2001; Demarest 2006).

Adánez and colleagues (2009, 2011) have proposed that Maya states may have moved toward bureaucratization during the Late Classic because this is when we see architecture dedicated only to administrative functions (called basal platform groups) for the first time. These basal platform groups consist of small to quite large platforms on top of which one or a few non-religious structures are built. These groups involved additional labor investment because they sit on platforms. Also, these platforms do not include many structures, which may suggest that most of the area on the basal platform was reserved for political rituals or for perishable structures (possibly for storage of tribute).[7] Adánez and colleagues associate basal platform groups with the newly deciphered title of *lakam* because that title may have referred to low-level officials of districts or neighborhoods. Using Tikal as the example, Adánez et al. (2009) contrast basal platform groups with plaza groups that include shrines, generally on the east side (called Plaza Plan 2). As these shrines are usually dedicated to the burials of important ancestors, possibly lineage founders, the authors argue that the second type (Plaza Plan 2) were the residences of the heads of lineages, clans, or houses, the basic social units of Maya society. Ninety-six of these Plaza Plan 2 groups were found in the nine-kilometer-square area of central

Tikal. In contrast, Adánez and colleagues identified only 28 basal platform groups, which they feel were solely administrative in function. The distribution of the basal platform groups shows that their possible area of influence (or control) encompasses between three and six Plaza Plan 2 groups, using the Thiessen Polygon approach (Adánez et al. 2009, 15). The area of influence of each basal platform group may represent a small neighborhood or district within Tikal.

Surprisingly, no basal platform groups have been excavated at Tikal, but outside Tikal six examples have been explored at Chau Hiix in Belize. They appear to have been occupied by middle-status groups that were involved in crafting activities, not administrative functions (Cook 1997; Adánez et al. 2009). Thus, these groups do not support the hypothesis of Adánez et al.

Supporting evidence comes from minor sites in the Belize Valley: X-ual-canil, Nohoch Ek, the Plantain Group at Chaa Creek (Iannone 2003; Connell 2003, 2010), and Group Atayala at Baking Pot (Conlon and Moore 2003; Adánez et al. 2009), all of which can be considered basal platform groups.

To bring into relief the likely administrative role of X-ual-canil, Iannone (2003) compares it with Zubin, another nearby middle-level site. Zubin was a typical minor center with several temple-pyramids (including an eastern ancestor shrine with as many as 10 graves) arranged around two large open plazas and a smaller and more private residential palace with several lower multi-room elite buildings (which Mayanists call range buildings). In contrast, X-ual-canil's center consisted exclusively of low buildings, some residential and some possibly administrative, but no temple-pyramids. However, X-ual-canil had a ball court and a causeway with an attached terminus complex, where politico-ritual activities or performances would have taken place. As Iannone points out, these are "features more commonly associated with upper-level settlements" (16–19). The causeway terminus complex includes "a relatively small performative platform (15C) fronted by both a stela (Stela 1) and an altar (Altar 1)" (19). Iannone underscores the architectural distinctions between Zubin and X-ual-canil:

> Zubin's emphasis on rituals associated with an eastern ancestor shrine therefore allies it with many other social groups that were striving to initiate and maintain ties to lineage land holdings [during the Late Classic]. . . . In contrast, the failure to exhibit an eastern shrine structure [at X-ual-canil] . . . implies that ancestor-related ritual activity was not imperative to X-ual-canil's claim to land. Rather, the absence

of these features and activities suggests that the inhabitants of X-ual-canil were sanctioned by another, more firmly established political unit. (Ibid.)

The inhabitants of X-ual-canil drew their power over land not from ancestors who had lived in the same area before them but from the rulers of a nearby polity (presumably Cahal Pech, according to Iannone). X-ual-canil's residents would thus function as attached personnel or low-level officials for the ruler of the primary polity. This scenario is supported by the fact that the architecture of X-ual-canil is surprisingly massive considering the sparse supporting population around the core. This suggests that labor was extracted from beyond X-ual-canil and supports the theory that the role of this site was administrative (25).

Iannone argues that X-ual-canil had several administrative structures in its core, Structures 1A and 4A on the Main Plaza (20). For example, Structure 4A has a broad frontal staircase and two small interior rooms (one anterior and one posterior) with large "throne-like" benches. In contrast, Zubin may have only one such building (A3) that is located in a structurally similar position as X-ual-canil's 4A. However, the administrative function of these structures is still questioned as only two features suggest it: the extremely small size of the interior rooms and the broad exterior staircases.

The residential groups in the core of X-ual-canil and Zubin also show contrasts. In X-ual-canil's south palace group, only one structure had features that would indicate that it functioned as a residence, while the other three lacked internal divisions, artifacts, or benches and may have had played an administrative role. (Iannone postulates that these may have been storage facilities, but the absence of artifacts speaks against such a hypothesis [19]). In contrast, Zubin's residential structures (Structures A4 and B8) lie at the north end of its core and frame the eastern shrine. The major difference between the residential "palaces" of these two sites is that X-ual-canil's are completely separate from the public spaces of the core, while at Zubin they are tightly connected to the public spaces. Iannone concludes that X-ual-canil exhibits "a distinction between the institutions of kinship (residential) and kingship (administration, processions, and the ball game)" (20).

The differences in the functions of the two sites are reflected in their divergent artifact assemblages. X-ual-canil has a "significantly smaller number of artifacts" than Zubin, evidence of less intense, shorter, and more restricted activities at the former site (21). In addition, Zubin has both caches and burials, while X-ual-canil does not. The offerings found in the caches and burials at Zubin suggest a sub-elite status for its inhabitants, while the absence of such deposits at X-ual-canil supports the interpretation that its residents drew their power not from kinship but from their position in the political administration. Iannone comments that "although . . . great effort [was made] to create the stage for large processions and ceremonies at X-ual-canil, the normal practice of conducting dedicatory and termination rituals to sanctify this sacred space does not appear to have been required" (ibid.).

A final feature of X-ual-canil also suggests that its role was administrative: a complex drainage system, consisting of reservoirs, check dams, and drainage channels used to accumulate water for irrigating agricultural land at the bottom of the hill on which the site sits. This system originates close to the ball court and the causeway terminus (23). Phosphate testing has confirmed that this zone was used for agriculture; it revealed high levels in the soils. Single housemounds are found in association with large water reservoirs that contained more water than the small resident population needed, so "it seems plausible that the mounds housed individuals specifically involved in the controlled collection and diversion of stored water" (24). The absence of extended family households (evidenced by very few plazuela groups with multiple housemounds) at X-ual-canil also suggests that this settlement had a distinct function. It is possible that the solitary housemounds are what is left of the homes of individuals brought to X-ual-canil for the express purpose of managing the water system built at this site as part of an attempt to control local agricultural production (24–25). Iannone and his team have documented agricultural terraces along the northwest base of the site hill, evidence that fits well with the theory that the water system was used for agricultural production (24).

To summarize, Zubin and X-ual-canil are very different sites. Zubin provides "a quintessential example of a residential corporate group . . . or heterogeneous household" that was mainly involved in agriculture. X-ual-canil was an administrative site "built to integrate an already extant farming population into a broader microregional alliance, possibly the one centered at Cahal Pech" (25). The integration of the population around X-ual-canil was done on two levels: on the political level through administrative personnel and on the ideological level through ritual. Iannone notes that "the two primary ritual features at the site, a stela/altar complex at the [causeway] termini and a ballcourt, are associated with the heads of two principal drainage channels. It seems plausible that fertility rituals were carried out in association with these features . . . [creating a] sacred landscape" (ibid.). Iannone contends that the upper elites from Cahal Pech (or whichever capital controlled X-ual-canil) visited the site frequently and that the permanent residents were sub-elite administrators (or managers): "It seems plausible that the inhabitants of X-ual-canil were full-time, or even part-time (rotating), site managers who were primarily responsible for the collection, storage, and redistribution of agricultural produce, and that the more courtly administrative and ritual tasks were conducted by [higher] elite authorities who did not inhabit the site" (ibid.).

The special features of X-ual-canil are very reminiscent of the causeway termini complexes around Caracol, which have also been described as administrative in purpose (A. Chase and D. Chase 1996, 2003; see also the discussion in Iannone 2003, 25). X-ual-canil is also similar to the Plantain Group at Chaa Creek, a minor center in Xunantunich's periphery (Connell 2003, 2010). The basal platforms and elaborate architecture both at X-ual-canil and in the Plantain Group at Chaa Creek required substantial labor investment. They both lack pyramidal shrines where ancestor veneration could take place (see Connell 2003, 39). Connell argues that Nohoch Ek, another minor center a few kilometers west of Zubin and X-ual-canil, also functioned administratively.[8] It was characterized by the same features: "collections of low structures, a few narrow-range buildings on raised platforms, a lack of pyramidal temples, and low densities of both ritual and domestic items" (ibid.). Another feature most (but not all) of these allegedly administrative groups shared is the presence of small rooms that are cell like and that have been called *audiencias* in the archaeological literature (39; see also Taschek and Ball 1999; Yaeger 2010).[9] Yaeger (2010) also mentions such *audiencias* in the royal palace compound in Plaza A-III at Xunantunich. These archaeologists generally interpret these small rooms as storage spaces for goods that were received as tribute or were to be given as gifts (Connell 2003; Yaeger 2010), but they could have served other functions, such as offices for *sajals* or *ajk'uhuuns*.

Although more excavations of the basal platform groups need to be done, the evidence from these examples suggests that the Classic Maya had a specific type of architectural plaza that may have had administrative functions. These examples are all from the Late Classic, supporting an argument that the complexity of Maya administration was increasing over the course of the Classic period.

Case Study: Blue Creek, Belize, and Archaeological Studies of Internal Political Organization

Many Maya sites do not have hieroglyphic texts that offer insights into internal political hierarchies, so we can explore how archaeological evidence can shed light on these issues. Blue Creek is a small Maya center in northwestern Belize close to the headwaters of the Rio Hondo (which had tributaries that reached into Guatemala, passing close to important sites such as Rio Azul) (Guderjan 1996, 1998; Guderjan, Baker, and Lichtenstein 2003; Guderjan, Lichtenstein, and Hanratty 2003). Environmental and subsistence diversity, including ditched fields, gave the site a distinct advantage in wealth in agricultural and other resources (Guderjan, Lichtenstein, and Hanratty 2003). We can consider Blue Creek a minor center during the Late Classic based on its settlement size. Sometimes it was independent and sometimes it was secondary; Guderjan and colleagues suggest that it was conquered around 500 AD and incorporated into a larger polity (Guderjan, Baker, and Lichtenstein 2003; Guderjan, Lichtenstein, and Hanratty 2003).

Guderjan's study of Blue Creek offers an example of how archaeological evidence alone can enable us to reconstruct political administrative hierarchies. This evidence can complement, support, or contradict epigraphic sources. Guderjan and his team examined the relationship between human occupation and the local environment. They also considered the distribution of lower-status and higher-status residential plaza groups in order to distinguish between several levels of elites and the degrees of political and economic power among these various levels (Guderjan, Baker, and Lichtenstein 2003; Guderjan, Lichtenstein, and Hanratty 2003).

The widely dispersed distribution of residential clusters at Blue Creek is typical of many Maya sites (Figure 5.2). At the center of the site, the monumental core includes multiple temple-pyramids, several royal palaces, and two large zones of subroyal elite residences. One of these zones, the Western Group, was exclusively elite. It had no surrounding smaller residences and no constructed agricultural features such as the terraces, check dams, or ditched fields that are common in the rest of the site (Guderjan, Baker, and Lichtenstein 2003, 85).

The Western Group contrasts with another elite group, Nukuch Muul, located 1.6 kilometers northwest of the core and the Western Group (see Figure 5.2). Nukuch Muul is centered on an elite residential plaza group built on top of a hill. The homes surrounding this wealthier plaza were

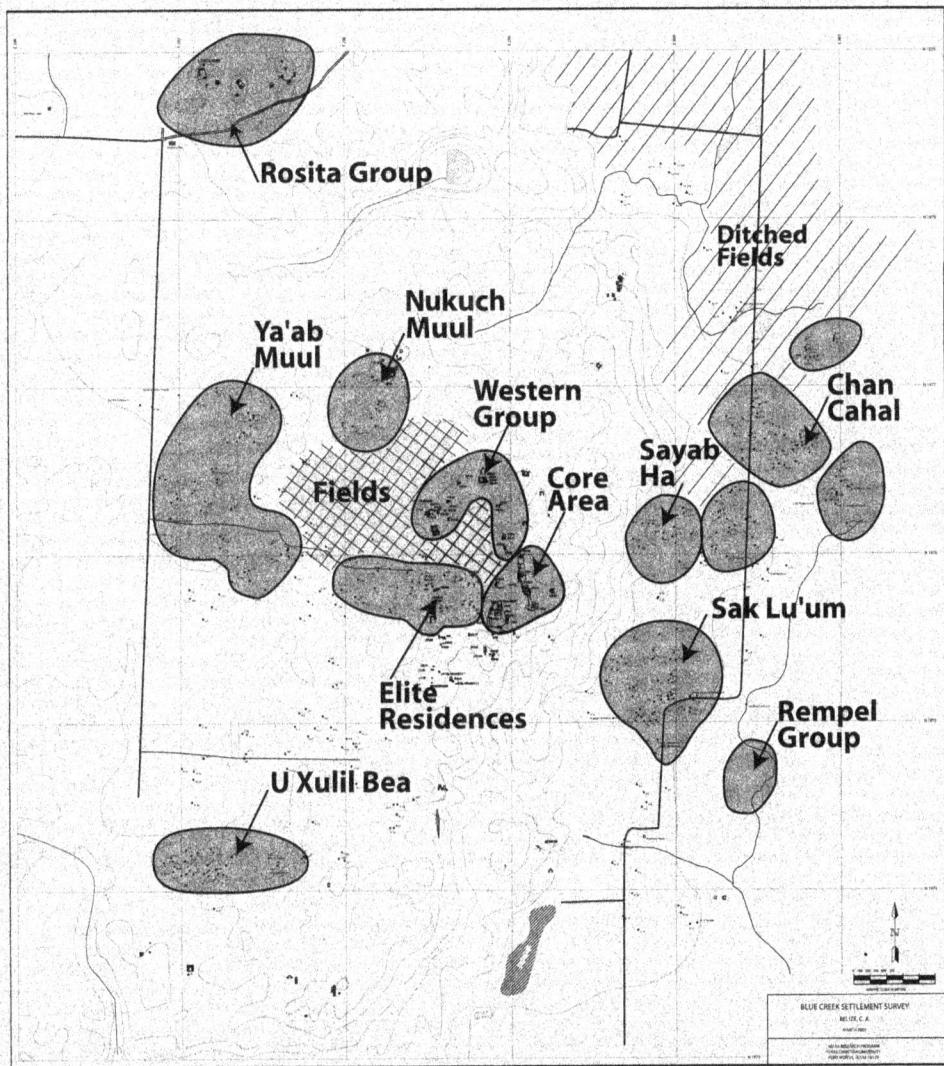

Figure 5.2. Map showing the site components of Blue Creek, Belize. Figure from Guderjan, Baker, and Lichtenstein 2003, Figure 7.2, in *Heterarchy, Political Economy, and the Ancient Maya: The Three Rivers Region of the East-Central Maya Lowlands*, edited by Vernon Scarborough, Fred Valdez, and Nicholas Dunning, © 2003 The Arizona Board of Regents. Reprinted by permission of the University of Arizona Press.

smaller, and their inhabitants "may have been lower-status members of the same lineage or non-lineage members in the service of the [elite] plazuela residents" (85). In contrast to the Western Group, Nukuch Muul was heavily invested in agricultural pursuits, as is shown by the multiple water control features and agricultural terraces along the adjacent Rio Bravo escarpment. Guderjan, Lichtenstein, and Hanratty characterize the contrast between the Western Group and Nukuch Muul thus: the residents of the Western Group "did not seem to require the support of a local 'service' community, nor were they going to any effort to utilize as much of the agricultural potential as possible" (ibid.). We can then intimate that the Western Group's "wealth and authority was based less on control of agricultural resources than on their role in the centralized authority and with the nobility of Blue Creek" (ibid.). The absence of adjoining lower-status residences in the Western Group suggests that these elites relied on tributary labor or services, reinforcing the hypothesis that those who lived in Western Group structures had political power. The residents of the Western Group can be conceived as representing a second level of political power below the level of the high elite in the monumental core.

A third scenario occurs in the Chan Cahal cluster, which was also removed from the core of Blue Creek some three kilometers to the east (86). The 28 mounds of Chan Cahal were all modest houses built of perishable materials, except for one: Structure U-5, a double-vaulted edifice built of stone on a stone platform that was attached to a much larger open platform (2,000 square meters) (86). Structure U-5 clearly fits the basal platform group type (discussed in the previous section). Excavations have revealed that this building was a Late Classic elite residence, and the adjacent platform may have had additional public or administrative functions. Like the residents of Nukuch Muul, the Chan Cahal residents were heavily invested in agriculture; they tended 6–12 square kilometers of adjacent ditched fields. Thus, we can say that they were farmers who produced agricultural food for local residents and for regional trade (87). The construction of the opulent Structure U-5 during the Late Classic suggests that the Blue Creek royalty or upper elite was creating a special relationship with the Chan Cahal commoner-farmers. This special relationship is attested to by the discovery of more than 200 jade artifacts discovered in the area, albeit "of low grade materials and workmanship" (ibid.). Presumably these were gifts for the Chan Cahal residents. The elite residents of Structure U-5 were latecomers to the Chan Cahal cluster, and therefore their power came not from land ownership or kinship relations but from their role in the political administration. They may have been a third level of political power below the level held by the residents of the Western Group.

The Blue Creek research reveals how archaeological evidence can answer questions about political and economic power. Details of the relationship between agricultural resources, human settlement, and status can point to different types of ties between political elites, economic elites, and commoners in Maya states. The top of the political hierarchy, or Rank 1 elites, were the royal residents at the site core (Guderjan, Baker, Lichtenstein 2003). The residents of the Western Group can be considered the political elite of Rank 2 because they were not tied to intensive agricultural systems and did not have servant housing components in their residential clusters. Hence their source of power, status, and wealth came through their role in the political administration of Blue Creek. They could be the *ajk'uhuuns* and *sajals* and other such elite officials named in the Classic period hieroglyphic texts (even though we do not have such texts from Blue Creek itself and do not know if such positions existed there). The secondary elites of the Western Group were probably sustained by tribute-tax labor and services because they had no service housing components in their clusters. This second level of political elites is distinct from the nobles who lived outside the core of Blue Creek, in clusters such as Nukuch Muul or Chan Cahal. Surrounded by agricultural systems and lower-status residences, the Nukuch Muul elites were directly invested in farming and supported by the labor of the lower-status kin or non-kin individuals residing in their respective cluster. Thus, they represented economic elites whose wealth was based on land. At Chan Cahal, the only elite residence (Structure U-5) and its aberrant large platform may hint at the administrative role of the nobles who lived there, tying the tax-paying commoners to the royal elite of Blue Creek. The Chan Cahal aristocrats might, therefore, exemplify a third level of political elites in the Blue Creek polity. Guderjan and his colleagues (Guderjan, Baker, and Lichtenstein 2003; Guderjan, Lichtenstein, and Hanratty 2003) also entertain the possibility that the Nukuch Muul elites were the same as the elites residing in the Western Group. These elites could have had dual residences and have moved between the core of the site and their houses (or estate manors?), which were located farther away, as required by their political, social, and/or economic duties.

The excavations at Blue Creek support interpretations that Classic Maya political power was hierarchical. Three levels of political power were revealed, beginning with the royal family of the monumental core, the secondary elites of the Western Group, and the tertiary elites of the Chan Cahal cluster. Guderjan and his team reconstructed this political hierarchy from archaeological evidence alone—from the distribution and interrelationships of human settlement, agricultural land, and social status.

State Finances: *Oikos* and Tribute

Classic Maya polities were dynamic not only because of the changing composition of the group of elite officials involved in their administration, but also because of the amount of resources each polity could extract through two institutions of state finance: the tribute-tax system and the *oikos*.

Two recent publications have described Maya state finances, or the political economies of Classic Maya states: Rice's (2009) article "On Classic Maya Political Economies" and McAnany's (2010) monograph *Ancestral Maya Economies in Archaeological Perspective*. Both agree that royal power is underpinned by the ideological-religious sphere. Rice proposes that "the foundation of royal . . . legitimacy was an illusion of 'control' over time and the cosmos, achieved through the strategic deployment and manipulation of calendars embodying the accumulated knowledge of astro-calendrical cycles" (70; see more extended treatments in Rice 2004, 2008). Although most scholars would agree with Rice that time, calendars, and temporal cycles were of prime importance to the ancient Mayas, some disagree that time was an independent variable that determined political structure pan-regionally across the lowlands (Hammond 2005; Houston and Inomata 2009; McAnany 2010).

Because Maya political power was grounded in a religious foundation, McAnany describes Classic Maya political economy as "ritual economy" and Rice calls it a "cosmopolitical economy." In other words, because Maya rulers were seen as gods or demi-gods (Houston and Stuart 1996), the state finance system that supported them may have been conceived as a "ritual economy" that produced for the gods. Both Rice and McAnany use the concept of "ritual economy," which Wells defines as "the materialization of socially negotiated values and beliefs through acquisition and consumption aimed at managing meaning and shaping interpretation" (2006, 284). Rice and McAnany emphasize that in the ritual economy, production cannot be seen as an economic process but must be seen as a ritual process consisting of "the production and reproduction of social and cosmic order" (Rice 2009, 72; see an extended discussion in McAnany 2010, 199–211).

What did the cosmopolitical or ritual economy of Classic Maya states look like and how substantial was it? Rice (2009) identifies three institutions in the cosmopolitical economy: 1) a palace economy (what has been called the *oikos* in other archaeological studies); 2) feasting; and 3) periodic markets (75). I would add a fourth important institution: the tribute-tax system.

In the following section, I discuss the importance of the palace economy (the *oikos*) and tribute-tax systems, leaving for later the issues of feasting and markets and their roles in the Classic period (see Chapter 6).

The first major institution that underwrote the Classic Maya polities was the royal court (*oikos*), which consisted of the palaces occupied by the ruler and his family, attached lesser nobles, and other elite or non-elite individuals who served the *k'uhul ajaw* in multiple roles (as servants, cooks, servers, washers, musicians, administrators, diplomats, scribes, craft specialists, guards, etc.) (Inomata and Houston 2001b, 6–7; McAnany and Plank 2001, 86; Rice 2009, 76). These large households (*oikoi*) were the heart of the Classic Maya polity for two reasons: first, because the "administration of the polity is in many respects an extension of [the royal] household administration" (Inomata and Houston 2001b, 10; Webster 2001, 144–48), and, second, because significant production (and reproduction) occurred in these courts (McAnany 1993a, 81; see below).

The Classic Maya royal court parallels the role of the palaces or *oikoi* of the rulers of Early Dynastic Sumer of third century BC (Pollock 1999). In Sumerian Mesopotamia, the royal or kingly households were organized around large heterogeneous estates that formed independent units called *oikoi*, from the Greek word for "great households" (Pollock 1999; Stein 1994b, 1998). Stein describes them as: "the palace sector appears to have operated as a large, autonomous household, producing its own crops, animals, and utilitarian craft goods through its control over 'attached specialists'" (Stein 1994b, 13; see also Zagarell 1986). Like Rice (2009, 77), I see the Maya royal *oikoi* as controlling tracts of land that we could call estates, just like in ancient Mesopotamia. These Maya royal *oikoi* estates may have been dispersed across the landscape, and the many goods and foodstuffs that were produced there were brought into the capital to sustain the royal family and court. The presence of estates in the Maya lowlands is suggested by the identification of residences that were used by rulers as their "summer" palaces or as lordly manors (Ball and Taschek 2001; Taschek and Ball 2003; Tourtellot et al. 2003).[10] Rice (2009) affirms that *oikos* production was "primarily focused on the creation of status-reinforcing elite/luxury/prestige goods" (77), but evidence from Motul de San José suggests that both utilitarian and luxury goods were produced within the royal residences in the Acropolis (see below). However, the overall pattern is that most craft production of utilitarian goods occurred in small village communities dispersed over the landscape, not in the royal households (or on *oikoi* estates).

The second major institution of state finances during the Classic period was the tribute-tax system. I call this system tribute-tax because it included taxes levied on surplus from the population within a polity and tribute obtained through warfare when a polity defeated another. As explored below, different items given in tribute may have been distinct from those that were extracted as tax.

D'Altroy and Earle (1985) defined two distinct types of tribute: wealth finance and staple finance. Wealth finance relies on the production and acquisition of prestige items or social valuables (goods that become prized because they consist of rare or nonlocal raw materials or because they are created with a difficult or extensive production process). In contrast, staple finance involves tribute or tax levied in staples such as agricultural products (crops or meat). Blanton et al. (1996) and Rice (2009) connect these two tribute types with different kinds of polities: exclusionary political systems tend to have wealth finance, while corporate political systems tend to have staple finance. Thus, the study of state finances has the potential to help us better understand the political strategies the rulers of Classic Maya states used. However, both wealth and staple finance were important to the Maya (as described below).

Several authors have drawn attention to the tribute-tax institution of the Classic period (McAnany 2010: 269-304; Foias 2002, 2004, 2007). Based on David Stuart's hieroglyphic decipherments (2005), I have suggested that Classic Maya tribute arrangements were alive and flourishing (Foias 2002, 2004, 2007). A number of glyphs associated with tribute-tax have been deciphered: *patan* (tribute), *u-tohol* (his payment), *yubte'* (tribute mantle), and *ikats* (cargo or burden) (Stuart 1995; Reents-Budet, Ball, and Kerr 1994; Foias 2002; McAnany 2010, 275). Based on Classic glyphic texts, depictions on Classic artifacts and monuments, and ethnohistorical texts from Yucatan, I and McAnany argue that tribute and/or tax from the Classic into the Postclassic consisted of both valuables and subsistence goods: textiles,

Figure 5.3. K1728, the Tribute Vase of the Ik' Style, depicting Motul's ruler K'inich La-maw Ek' receiving tribute from a *sajal*. Photograph © Justin Kerr.

corn, turkeys, beans (cacao and/or regular beans), feathers, and jade (Foias 2002; McAnany 2010). This brings into relief the absence of a clear dichotomy between wealth and staple finance in the Maya case. There was variation in the goods paid in tribute-tax over time, since ethnohistorical documents from Conquest period Yucatan name more agricultural products or foodstuffs (Foias 2002), while Classic period painted scenes and texts name prestige items more often. Five items are specifically depicted or named in tribute-tax presentations on Classic murals and vessels: cacao, jadeite, Spondylus shells, quetzal feathers, and cloth (McAnany 2010). However, it is hard to consider cloth a prestige good unless one assumes that the *yubte'*, the tribute mantle, was of the finest quality and/or was embroidered with exotic goods such as rare quetzal feathers, jadeite beads, or marine shells. We also have to be aware that this textual evidence and associated iconography from the Classic period give us a biased perspective because they provide evidence that relates only to the elite. We need to look to the archaeological evidence to complement the epigraphy (as I do in the case of Motul de San José, below).

One of the vessels crafted at Motul de San José (K1728, sometimes called the Tribute Vase; Figure 5.3) is a good example of the Classic period scenes of tribute-tax presentation: cloth tribute (named *yubte'*), shown as bundles to the far left of the scene, is presented here by two nobles, who are seated on the ground, to the lord, who sits on the bench or throne (Houston, Stuart, and Robertson 2006). Notice also the two males standing behind the visitors. The first one is called *ajk'uhuun* in the two glyphs below his extended left arm, while the second one is identified as "he of the tribute mantles" (Stuart 1995; Zender 2004). The first seated individual is described as the *muut* ("bird" or "messenger") and *u-tojil* (his payment of debt) of another *muut*. This second-named *muut* is a *sajal*, presumably of Motul's ruler K'inich Lamaw Ek', who is named as the owner of this vase in the rim text[11] and is shown as the main figure seated on the bench (Houston, Stuart, and Robertson 2006; Tokovinine and Zender 2012). Therefore, the individuals presenting the tribute-tax to the main lord are the messengers or representatives of one of K'inich Lamak Ek's vassals or secondary governors (*sajals*).

McAnany (2010, 278–83) demystifies the role of *muut*[12] messengers in tribute presentation scenes by hypothesizing that the culture of Classic Maya elites was dominated by an ethos of captive taking and demanding ransom for these captives through the payment of tribute. McAnany suggests that because the *k'uhul ajaw* was afraid of being taken captive, he sent subsidiary elites as messengers to other courts instead of appearing in the flesh at these foreign locales. Although such a scenario is both viable and intriguing, Houston, Stuart, and Taube (2006) propose another explanation for the existence of *muut*. These messengers could be seen as the embodiments of the promise of the human labor that was owed to conquerors and overlords: "The notion that human beings could be as much tribute or payment as cloth or bundled chocolate beans is increasingly evident in Maya texts and imagery" (243; see also Graham 2012). Could we understand this, as McAnany does, to mean that the messenger was held as a captive until the ransom of tribute goods or tribute labor was paid off by the ruler of the defeated polity? Yes, but another interpretation is that the noble messenger (*muut*) represents a particular amount of labor or goods through the estates that he controlled or through the amount of tribute-tax that he received from his commoner taxpayers (Graham 2011, 2012). Rather than seeing *muuts* as captives held for tribute ransom, we could see them as the embodiments of the labor force or tribute-tax that they had command over and therefore owed to the *k'uhul ajaw* who had defeated them.

Regardless of how *muut* messengers should be understood, the direct connection between warfare and tribute is made evident in some cases by the association of the glyph for axe-war events (defeat in war) with the step-glyph verb (likely translatable as "to ascend/present in tribute"), usually accompanied by the Maya terms *patan* (tribute) and *ikats* (cargo or burden) (Stuart 1998, 410–16; McAnany 2010, 275; see also Graham 2011, 40–42). A few Classic period texts hint that in some cases tribute may have been paid for years after defeat on the battlefield (McAnany 2010, 279). Take, for example, the fragment of a wall panel (now called the Tribute Fragment) found in the fill of Temple XVI at Palenque. The fragment appears to depict the ruler (Akul) Ahkal (Anab) Mo' Nahb III helping to carry an immense bundle that presumably holds tribute meant for Tonina, which had defeated Palenque possibly two decades earlier (Stuart 1998, 413–14; McAnany 2010, 279; Stuart and Stuart 2008, 217 and 224, but also see 257n8).

As mentioned above, Classic period hieroglyphic texts and painted scenes tell us that five materials formed the core of the tribute-tax system: cacao, green stone (jade-jadeite), Spondylus shells, quetzal feathers, and cloth (Foias 2002, 2004; McAnany 2010, 286–302). These materials were most desired by the Classic Maya royal courts because they were emblematic of the "performance of nobility, [of] power and [of] supernatural intercession" (McAnany 2010, 291). They were also rare. For example, greenstone and marine shell were rare because they came from faraway regions. Even local cacao, cotton, and quetzal feathers were rare because they could be produced only in areas with specific soil, forest, and climate conditions. Most of these items were also rare because the crafts associated with them involved a great deal of labor (what Clark and Parry 1990 call hypertrophic labor) or required highly restricted knowledge. The nature of the crafting process of each of these five materials intersected with their origins and their distribution across the landscape to produce very different histories, which are explored in detail elsewhere (McAnany 2010, 286–302). But because these items represented great value in small volumes, they may have been strictly associated with a tribute system, goods that a defeated polity owed to the victorious one. Aside from these valuable and rare materials, subsistence goods may have been extracted as tax from the commoners in the core of each polity, as the archaeological evidence from Motul de San José shows (see below).

Masson, Hare, and Peraza Lope (2006, 204–5) suggest that site settlement patterns can also provide a window into the nature and importance of the tribute-tax system. Tourtellot (1988) originally noted that single or two-mound groups predominate at Postclassic Mayapan and Classic Dzibilchaltun, in contrast to the plazas with three or more mounds that were found in Late to Terminal Classic Seibal. His explanation for these divergent settlement patterns is the existence of corvee tribute-tax at Mayapan and Dzibilchaltun: individual nuclear families may have been brought into these cities for short periods of time every year (or every couple of years) to do their military service or corvee labor (on coastal salt beds) at both Dzi-bilchaltun and Mayapan (339–41). Masson and colleagues (2006) provide supporting evidence for this scenario from recent excavations at Maya-pan, although they also note that some isolated structures show evidence of craft manufacture. Masson and her team excavated two small isolated houses (i.e., one-mound groups) at Mayapan that showed no evidence that their inhabitants pursued agricultural subsistence or craft production. Both houses also indicated short occupations but produced higher proportions of projectile points than the site average, "which could imply [that these individuals were residing at Mayapan to perform their] military service" (205).

The juxtaposition of tribute (through images of bundles) with feasting and dance performances in the murals of Bonampak and in scenes on poly-chrome pottery (Looper 2009, 64) reveals the close links between these activities, but it also illuminates the importance of public witnessing of political affairs in the Classic Maya world (see further discussion in Chap-ter 6). Looper writes, "The dressing and performance of dancers using cos-tume elements derived from tribute . . . may have been a ritual procedure by which the royal court acknowledged the receipt of these luxury goods" (ibid.).

Case Study: Political Administration and State Finance at Motul de San José

We now reenter the Classic world of Motul de San José to delve further into the internal institutions of political administration, tribute-tax, and *oikos*, as made visible by the epigraphy and archaeology of this small polity of the Central Peten Lakes zone.[13]

Tokovinine and Zender (2012) have deciphered the hieroglyphic inscrip-tions from Motul, and from this it is possible to reconstruct its political administration. Most of these texts are found on polychrome vases of the Ik' Polychrome Style rather than on stone monuments. The Ik' Style is a particular type of polychrome painting characterized by the use of glyphs outlined in pink or red and/or filled with pink slip; the Ik' emblem glyph of Motul in the Primary Standard Sequence or in shorter hieroglyphic texts; historical court scenes; fine and careful portraiture of elite nobles; black scallops on the interior of the rim; and (often) the use of specular hematite. Ik' Style vessels were made at Motul de San José and probably at several

Figure 5.4. K4996, showing Motul's ruler Tayal/Tayel Chan K'inich receiving tribute from three *lakams*. Photograph © Justin Kerr.

sites in its vicinity (Reents-Budet, Ball, and Kerr 1994; Reents-Budet et al. 2012; Halperin and Foias 2010).

The texts on these vessels name a number of titled officials but show a different political hierarchy from the one described for Palenque (see above). No *ti'sakhuun* appears. Instead, the pots often depict the ruler with one or two *ajk'uhuuns* (Tokovinine and Zender 2012). Only one Ik' pot (the Tribute Vase, K1728, Figure 5.3) names a *sajal* in the Motul de San José polity, and he (or rather his *muut* messenger) brings tribute directly to the divine king of Motul (Tokovinine and Zender 2012; Houston, Stuart, and Taube 2006). The title *lakam* also appears on a vase (K4996), which shows the Motul court, although it is not of the Ik' Style (Figure 5.4): Three individuals (possibly nobles) with a *lakam* title bring tribute to the seated lord who is named as the *k'uhul ajaw* Tayel Chan K'inich of Motul de San José (Lacadena 2008; Tokovinine and Zender 2012). Based on these titles, we can reconstruct at least three levels in Motul's administrative hierarchy: The *sajal* and the *ajk'uhuun* form the second level below the *k'uhul ajaw*, and the *lakams* are a third level. What is also noteworthy here is that the lower officials, be they the *sajal*, the *ajk'uhuun*, or the *lakam*, are always depicted directly with Motul's king, as if they reported directly to him. This choice of depiction may suggest that the political hierarchy at Motul was rather shallow. It is possible that the individuals who held the three named positions specialized in different spheres of administration but were always under the direct jurisdiction of the divine ruler. The possibility of a shallow political hierarchy is also supported by the archaeological settlement in this zone as described in the previous chapter: surrounding Motul, we see a number of secondary centers at a distance of 2 to 3 kilometers, and of these, Trinidad is the largest. As such, it may have been the seat of the *sajal*. However, because of the absence of hieroglyphic texts from Trinidad, this supposition should be considered tentative at this time. The known *sajal* centers around Palenque are Miraflores (15 kilometers west-northwest) and Xupá (12.5 kilometers east-southeast), a significantly farther distance away than Motul's secondary centers were (Stuart and Stuart 2008, 164).

Archaeological excavations at Motul have provided us with a parallel window into the political hierarchy, especially its finances during the Late Classic. A short description of Motul will serve as introduction to these excavations. Like Blue Creek, it has relatively dispersed settlement, with a monumental core of four groups, Groups A to E, surrounded by smaller residential compounds in the North and East Zones (Figure 5.5) (Foias 2003; Foias and Emery 2012). Groups A to E are arranged in a west-to-east direction, and Group C (at the western end) is the largest and most elaborate. Group C had the largest two plazas at the site: Plaza I, or the Main Plaza (which had 5 stelae), and Plaza II (a likely marketplace; Bair and Terry 2012; see also next chapter). The north and west sides of the Main Plaza are framed by the Acropolis (the likely royal court during the Late Classic, where *k'uhul ajaws* such as Tayel Chan K'inich, Yajawte' K'inich, and Lamaw Ek' lived), and the south and east sides are defined by the three largest temple-pyramids (around 20 meters tall) at the site.

The Motul de San José Archaeological Project excavated large to small plaza groups at the site and within its close periphery to query the relationship between economic and political power (Foias and Emery 2012; Foias 2003; Emery 2003a; Moriarty 2004a; Halperin 2004, 2009; Halperin and Foias 2010). We used architectural volumetrics to define socioeconomic ranks or strata at the site and identified three such divisions (see an extensive discussion in Foias et al. 2012). Rank 1 encompassed only the five major architectural groups (Groups A to E), possessing volumes greater than 6,797 cubic meters. A natural break occurs between Ranks 1 and 2 as the volume of Rank 2 groups ranges only from 4,443 to 1,100 cubic meters (see

Foias et al. 2012, Figure 4.1.). In contrast, there is no natural break in the distribution of volumes between Ranks 2 and 3, so the division is arbitrary: Rank 3 groups are defined by volumes less than 1,100 cubic meters and a general absence of vaulted stone architecture (based on surface evidence gathered during the mapping of the site).

My colleagues and I propose that Rank 1 represents the royal elites, the *k'uhul ajaw* and his family (Foias et al. 2012). The fact that five Rank 1 groups are present in the Late Classic to Terminal Classic periods may suggest that the most successful of its eight Late Classic rulers built their own court complexes or that the royal elite encompassed several powerful branches (possibly lineages [see McAnany 1995] or houses [see Joyce and Gillespie 2000; Gillespie 2000]).[14] Groups A to E within Rank 1 were not only larger and more internally elaborate but were also integrated with the major temple-pyramids and public plazas of the site, marking in permanent form the royalty's tremendous power to transform the landscape (Foias et al. 2012).

Rank 2, the most common rank (accounting for around 50 percent of all the groups at the site), were houses of substantial construction, with stone vaults, interior benches, heavy use of stucco, and frequent supporting platforms (Foias et al. 2012). We had trouble understanding the social status of this middle rank: Were they of the elite *estate* or were they high-status commoners?[15] This question could not be answered with the architectural volumetric analysis, but our excavations gave us other hints (as described below). Finally, Rank 3 groups had small volumes and unassuming surface architecture; they were clearly the commoner stratum.

I now turn to the excavations to underscore the range and type of economic pursuits found in the households pertaining to each rank (see Foias et al. 2012 for more detailed descriptions). The households of royal elites (Rank 1 groups) were actively involved in significant economic activities, including food preparation (evidenced by the presence of equipment such as *metates* and *manos* used for grinding maize), textile production (evidenced by spindle whorls; Halperin 2008), figurine production (evidenced by figurine molds and figurine repeats; Halperin 2007, 2009, 2012), paper making (Foias et al. 2012), and polychrome pottery manufacture (Halperin and Foias 2010, 2012). This active involvement of the royal elite households in economic activities illustrates that production in the royal *oikos* contributed significantly to the wealth (and power) of these elites. The food prepared by members of these royal households (whether they were servants,

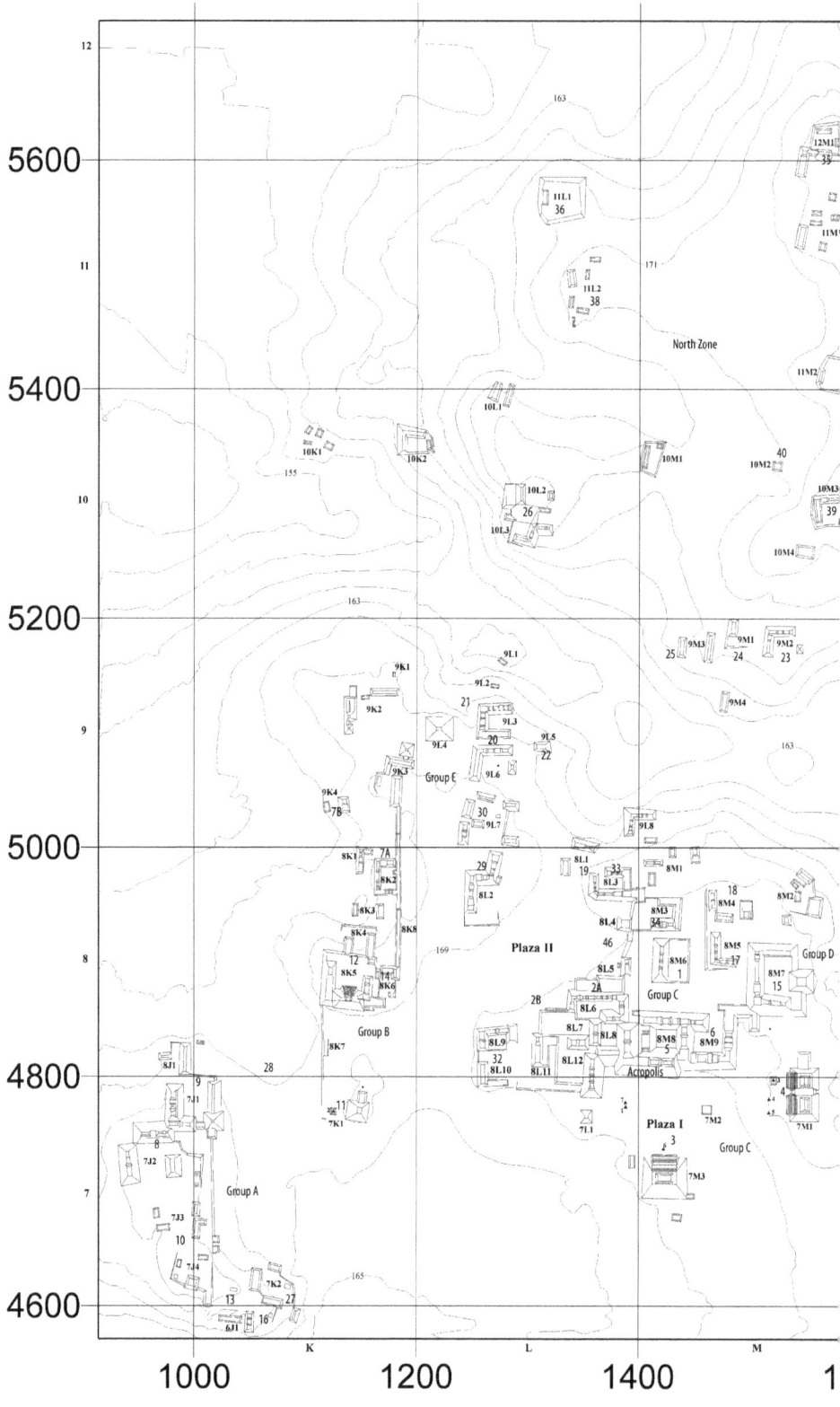

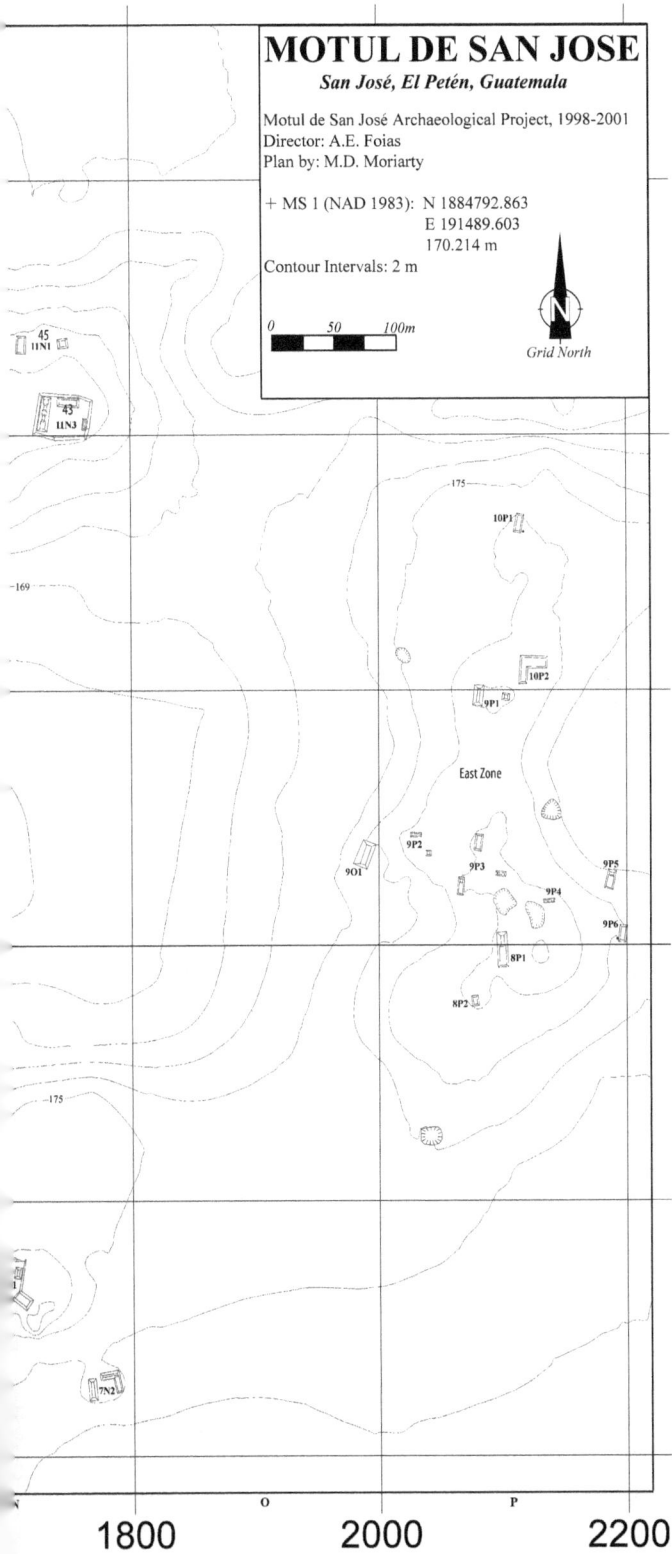

MOTUL DE SAN JOSE

San José, El Petén, Guatemala

Motul de San José Archaeological Project, 1998-2001
Director: A.E. Foias
Plan by: M.D. Moriarty

+ MS 1 (NAD 1983): N 1884792.863
                    E 191489.603
                    170.214 m

Contour Intervals: 2 m

0   50   100m

N

Grid North

45
11N1

43
11N3

175

10P1

169

10P2

9P1

East Zone

9P2

9O1   9P3

9P4

9P5

9P6

8P1

8P2

175

7N2

1800   O   2000   P   2200

Figure 5.5. Map of Motul de San José, Peten, Guatemala. Drawn by Matthew Moriarty; reproduced with permission from Foias and Emery 2012, Figure 1.2.

attendants, "ladies-in-waiting," or the royal ladies themselves) may have been intended for feasts as well as for everyday meals. The textiles created in Rank 1 groups were of finer quality than those produced by other social strata at Motul because the spindle whorls found in these compounds were generally smaller in size (Halperin 2008) and because tiny shell ornaments, which were probably sewn onto textiles, were much more frequent there than in other households (Emery 2012). This evidence brings to mind images of the queens, princesses, and attendant ladies of Medieval Europe who spent long hours weaving intricate textiles.[16] This is not far from the case of the Classic Maya: fine weaving needles made of bone discovered in female tombs are carved with the glyphs *upuutz' b'aak*, "the weaving bone of," followed by the name of a royal lady (Miller and Martin 2004, 94; Houston and Stuart 2001, 64; McAnany 2008, 233–35). Figurines (almost all which are musical instruments) at Motul de San José (Halperin 2007) were also made in the royal court in the Acropolis and must have been important for musical accompaniment during feasts. The discovery of a bark beater and several pigment balls or blocks in one of the royal compounds, Group D, marks papermaking as another activity in royal households (Foias et al. 2012). Papermaking was ritually important because paper was used in bloodletting as well as for scribal recordings of matters of the state and religion. Finally, polychrome pottery with simple geometric designs and complex historical court scenes (typical of Ik' Polychrome Style vessels) was also fashioned in the Acropolis (or nearby; see Foias 2003; Halperin and Foias 2010, 2012). Since polychrome pottery was often presented as gifts to feast participants, the vessels would have also been significant in the ritual economy of the royal elite.

The economic activities that took place in Rank 3 households provide the best evidence that a tax system existed at Motul de San José. The frequency of ground stone implements (used to grind corn into flour) was highest in Rank 3 residences, and it was lowest in Rank 1 royal palaces (Foias et al. 2012). This skewed distribution suggests that members of royal elite households processed less maize than the lower two strata, a surprising finding considering that Rank 1 groups probably included more individuals and were involved in more consumption than the lower ranks. The only way to explain this is to argue that the royal requirements for processed maize (which was important for alcoholic drinks as well as food) were fulfilled through taxation: commoners (and possibly Rank 2 groups) processed the maize in their households and then delivered it to the royal palaces. Zooarchaeological evidence also hints that Rank 3 groups (and possibly

Rank 2 groups) were the taxpayers (Emery 2012): the number of bones of preferred species for hunting, such as deer, in commoner structures (Rank 3 groups) represented more meat than the commoner household could consume. This suggests that members of Rank 3 households were hunters who processed the carcasses and then delivered deboned meat to the royal households. Postclassic documents also speak of commoners providing the elite with meat from wild animals as a type of tax (Thornton 2012).

While the identities of the residents of Ranks 1 and 3 structures are relatively clear, that of the residents of Rank 2 groups remains more opaque. To better contextualize the functions of this rank, I draw upon Hammond's (1982, 1991a) work. Hammond proposes that Classic Maya elite were subdivided into three tiers of decreasing political power, based on both archaeological evidence and direct analogy with Conquest period Maya. As discussed in the previous chapter, the uppermost level consisted of the *k'uhul ajaw* and his kin group and was similar to the *halach uinic* level in sixteenth-century Yucatan (see also Table 4.1). Below him, the second rank was "an aristocracy, the *ahau* class . . . which acted as ambassadors and probably as the administrative class" (Hammond 1991a, 270). Within this second rank would fall the titled positions such as the *ajk'uhuun*, the *ti'sakhuun*, and the *sajal*. Hammond compares the *sajals* with the Postclassic and Colonial-era second-tier political position of the *batab* (as discussed in Chapter 4). He notes that "the presence of funerary pyramids and richly stocked burials in small sites suggests that nobles [of the *sajal* level] were present not only in the polity capital, but formed the top tier of provincial society also" (ibid.). Finally, the third and lowest rank of the elite class consisted of the "gentry, the colonial *principales*, rulers of perhaps only a few square kilometers, local administrators, and denizens of the minor ceremonial centers outside the main population concentrations" (ibid.), including possibly the *lakams*. These three levels of political power may be reflected in the extraordinary murals of Bonampak (Miller 1986, 2001). In Room 1, the whole royal court of Chan Muan (the ruler of Bonampak) is portrayed. Using the elaborateness of the costume of these lords and their vertical position in the mural, Hammond distinguishes at least three ranks: The royal *ajaws* are positioned at the highest level in the mural and wear the most elaborate costumes (including white robes[17] and Spondylus-shell pendants); second come individuals named *ah nab* (or *anab*, the lowest priestly title, according to Zender 2004) who also wear fancy accoutrements, including "jade jewelry, elaborate individualized headdresses and elaborate loincloths . . . of rich fabric" (Hammond 1991a, 271). Members of the third (and possibly the fourth) rank are positioned lowest in the murals, wear the most standardized and simplest headdresses and loincloths, and have no jade jewelry (271–72). The evidence from this mural combined with the elaborateness of the Rank 2 plaza groups at Motul would suggest that Rank 2 could be identified as Hammond's second and/or third-tier elites (the *ahaus* or *principales*).

Zooarchaeological analysis supports this interpretation of the identity of the residents of Rank 2 structures (Emery 2012; Emery and Foias 2012). Emery has found evidence of the manufacture of bone tools and ornaments in seven residential groups at Motul, and the Rank 2 groups are the most common. Thus, these middle-rank households were heavily involved in craft production, but the finished products were concentrated only in the Rank 1 compounds, supporting the theory that the members of Rank 2 households were producing goods for the royal houses (Emery 2012). This evidence should be juxtaposed with another finding of the zooarchaeological analysis: Like the Rank 1 royal families, members of Rank 2 households had significant access to ritual animal species; Rank 3 commoners did not (ibid.). This piece of information implies that Rank 2 groups participated in ritual activities alongside the royal elites and that Rank 3 commoners were excluded. If that was the case, then Rank 2 individuals had a social, political, or economic position that allowed them to participate in royal rituals. Such access makes them political and/or religious elites (or both) who were perhaps similar to the *sajals* and *lakams*[18] of Classic times or the *principales* of Colonial times.

However, the population of Rank 2 seems too numerous (around 50 percent of all the groups at Motul proper) to have been part of the *ajaw* "class." In preindustrial agrarian societies, the nonfarming, tribute-receiving upper "class" (the *ajaw* class in the Maya case) can reach a maximum level of only 10 percent of the total population (Webster 1992; Kai Lee personal communication, 2006). Emery and Foias (2012; see also Chapter 4) calculated the likely population of the Motul de San José polity at its Late Classic apogee as being between 13,000 and 27,000, and they argue that at the most, 10 percent (or 1,300–2,700) could have been maintained as nonproducing elite. The lower end of this range is close to what the Ranks 1 and 2 groups could house. This suggests that Rank 2 households were indeed elites of secondary status. D. Chase and A. Chase (1992) encountered a similar situation at Caracol: they remark that the middle groups at the latter site "are far more numerous than would generally be expected of any elite grouping" (314).

The small number of commoner households at Motul (i.e. Rank 3) and at Caracol implies that most commoners were dispersed, living in smaller centers and villages beyond these large centers.

We can draw a number of conclusions from the evidence at Motul de San José. First and foremost, based on the evidence of significant production in Rank 1 households, we conclude that the Motul royal elites formed large *oikoi* in which ritual economic pursuits were important. These activities created basic goods (food and cloth), but most important, they created social valuables (fancy cloth, paper, musical instrument figurines, elaborate polychromes) that could be easily used as gifts in the feasting cycles of the elite class (Halperin and Foias 2010; see also Chapter 6). These items formed a "fund" of ritual-economic power in the hands of royal families. This scenario does not imply economic centralization, because other households were also involved in the ritual economy (see further discussion in Foias et al. 2012). Similar levels of involvement in the ritual economy have been identified at other medium-sized royal courts, such as at Aguateca in the Pasion region (Inomata 2001b, 2007; Inomata and Triadan 2000; Inomata et al. 2002; see also Halperin and Foias 2010).

Second, a tax system existed at Motul that tied the commoners to the royal households. Members of Rank 3 households prepared maize flour and wild animal meat, which they then gave to the Rank 1 royal compounds.

Third, both architectural volume and consumption patterns unmask a complex and stratified social system in which the major distinction was between the royal elite and everyone else (Foias et al. 2012). However, significant variability within the second and third strata paints a picture of variable histories and trajectories for Motul's households; some were more adept at accumulating wealth and/or controlling labor and others were less so. This variability also suggests that individual choices and capabilities as well as political maneuvering played a significant role in increasing or decreasing the social, economic, and political status of a household. It is also important to remember that political power must have varied greatly even within the elite *ajaw* "class" (D. Chase and A. Chase 1992a; Schele and Freidel 1990; Inomata and Houston 2001; Foias and Emery 2012). The political power of the divine ruler (*k'uhul ajaw*) of Tikal, who controlled over 60,000 subjects, would have been of a different scale and scope than that of the Motul de San José king, who would have had some 13,000 subjects, or of a Motul de San José *sajal* who had control over a secondary center such as Trinidad.

Variation in Internal Political Administration

Variation in the internal structure of Classic Maya polities across different regions and times also needs to be explored. These internal variations supplement the evidence that the scale of territory, population, and therefore power differed considerably among polities. These internal variations also support the presence of a range of administrative hierarchies in different polities, as indicated by the presence or absence of subsidiary political titles and of smaller or larger subsidiary centers near or far from the capital of the polity.

The use of the title *sajal* varies considerably in the lowlands. We know of *sajals* as governors of second-tier centers in the polities of the Usumacinta Valley and the western lowlands in general, for example at the site of La Pasadita under Yaxchilan's control, and the site of Lacanha under Bonampak's control (Hammond 1991a, 280) or at the sites of Miraflores and Xupa within Palenque's realm (Stuart and Stuart 2008, 164; see also Houston and Inomata 2009, 175). But the *sajal* title is completely absent at Tikal and many other central Peten and Belize sites. This may not necessarily imply that such subsidiary political positions did not exist, only that we don't have evidence for these titles in the extant hieroglyphic texts for the Peten and Belizean states. Motul de San José is an exception in Central Peten, as vase K1728 names a *sajal* (see Figure 5.3 and discussion above). But this is the only mention of this title. Does this mean that it was a rare or unique position in the Motul administration or that it was a new administrative office adopted from Yaxchilan after two Motul princesses married the Yaxchilan king?

Instead of *sajals*, *ajk'uhuuns* are most commonly portrayed on the Ik' Style vases painted at Motul de San José (Tokovinine and Zender 2012). Although *ajk'uhuuns* appear at other sites, they are much more visible at Motul. So the Motul political administration seems to have relied heavily on these ecclesiastical positions. It is possible that the absence of the title of *sajal* at Tikal or Calakmul may be due to the greater power invested in the divine kings of these two "superstates." There may have been no need to have the *sajals* displayed in monuments or mentioned in texts because Tikal's (or Calakmul's) divine kings did not depend as much on their support as the kings in other polities did, such as Palenque and Motul de San José (see also discussion in Houston and Inomata 2009, 172).

In several cases, rulers of subsidiary secondary centers are of higher rank than *sajals*. For example, Arroyo de Piedra, a secondary center under

Dos Pilas in the Pasion region, was ruled by an *ajaw*-rank elite (Hammond 1991a, 280; Houston 1993), probably because Arroyo de Piedra was incorporated into the Dos Pilas polity through a marriage alliance and its rulers were able to sustain their higher status in spite of their subordination to the Dos Pilas king. The rulers of Arroyo de Piedra were also the original ruling dynasty in this region before the new Dos Pilas/Aguateca dynasty arrived from Tikal (Houston 1993). So this may also be a recognition that the *ajaw* of Arroyo de Piedra (or his predecessor) originally ruled over an independent polity.

Another possible variation in political structure is dual rulership or co-rulership. Velásquez (2010) has proposed that two rulers may have governed Motul de San José since several Ik' Style vessels record two *k'uhul ajaws* (Yajawte' K'inich and K'inich Lamaw Ek') in the same scene, both carrying the emblem glyph of Motul. This proposal remains hypothetical, though, because we have no accession or death dates for these two rulers. In addition, there are alternative explanations for these pottery scenes. Because K'inich Lamaw Ek' was not the son of Yajawte', he may have acceded to the throne in an irregular manner (should I say as a usurper?). It may be that to gain legitimacy, he depicted himself with Yajawte' on these Ik' vases to suggest that Yajawte' chose him as his rightful successor. Reents-Budet et al. (2012) have made a slightly different argument based on the presence of two emblem glyphs in the hieroglyphic texts of Motul de San José that suggest that a confederacy of several holy lords made up the polity. However, dual emblem glyphs appear elsewhere in unitary polities, such as Yaxchilan (Mathews 1991). Even if there wasn't a confederacy, it does appear that secondary elites, such as *ajk'uhuuns*, had considerable political clout in the Motul polity because they are depicted so often on the Ik'-Style polychrome vessels (see Chapter 6). Stuart and Stuart (2008) have also discussed the possibility of co-rulership at Palenque for the eighth-century kings Ahkal Mo' Nahb and his possible brother Upakal K'inich; both held the title of *k'uhul ajaw* of Palenque (230). However, this may be a compromise in the later years of an older dynast who wanted to smooth over the transition to his heir before his death.

Chase, Grube, and Chase (1991) have also hypothesized that dynastic rulership at Caracol during the Terminal Classic may have changed from life terms to 20-year terms based on the length of time that each Terminal Classic ruler is mentioned in stone monuments from this site. Restall (1997) also finds evidence for 20-year rulerships in the Yucatan polities, the *cah* or *batabil*, of the Postclassic period. Rulership of finite duration would imply a major ideological reworking of the monarchical kingly institution during the Terminal Classic and Postclassic (Chase, Chase, and Smith 2009, 181). Future studies may provide more evidence to support this type of rulership.

Lucero (2006) has proposed that there were three types of Maya polities during the Classic period in the lowlands: 1) independent minor centers or local communities (such as Saturday Creek, Barton Ramie, and Cuello in Belize) that had no political leaders or had communal leadership; 2) local polities focused on secondary centers (such as Altar de Sacrificios, Dos Pilas, Yaxchilan, and Piedras Negras); and 3) integrative polities, or regional polities that coalesced around major centers (such as Tikal, Calakmul, Caracol, Palenque, and Copan).[19] Lucero makes an ambitious proposal that the variations between these three types of polities had to do with the distribution and availability of water and fertile agricultural land. The difference between local and regional polities is that the former are located along rivers or other reliable sources of water while the latter are in areas with no easy water sources. Hence, Lucero proposes, rulers of regional centers amassed control over water by investing in the construction of massive reservoirs and water catchment systems. Because the rulers of regional centers controlled water, they had much higher levels of political power than local polities and could demand tribute in exchange for water (154). Although this scenario may be true for some urban centers, it seems completely contradictory to the situation at the regional centers of Palenque and Copan, where water sources were plentiful. Furthermore, since large polities would have needed more water, locating them away from naturally occurring water sources would not have made sense. Although Tikal and Calakmul may have no clear water sources today, in the Classic period they may have been sustained by shallow lakes that have now become *bajos*, low areas that become flooded only during the rainy seasons. Isendahl (2006) questions whether Classic Maya royal political power can be reduced to such an economic contract (459). Furthermore, it remains unclear what mechanisms would have prevented commoners from moving away from these cities to avoid the royalty's monopoly over water. Although Lucero's original classification of Maya polities (small communities, local polities, and regional polities) probably captures the variation in the scale and complexity of Classic states, the connections she makes between the distribution of water and political power appear to be weaker.

Several scholars have pointed out political differences between the northern and southern lowlands in both the Classic and Postclassic periods (in addition to the differential use of the title *k'uhul ajaw* in the northern and the southern lowlands as discussed in Chapter 4). Krochock (1988) first suggested that the political structure at Chichen Itza, the major city in northern Yucatan in the Terminal Classic to the Early Postclassic, was different from the structure that was dominant in the Classic period in the southern Maya lowlands. She calls the northern structure "councilor government" because brothers (hieroglyphically, *yitaj*[20] or *yitah*) carried out most of the deeds recorded in Chichen's hieroglyphic texts together (see also Grube 1994). Schele and Freidel (1990) pursued this hypothesis and called the political system *multepal* (a Maya term mentioned in the Contact period ethnohistorical documents), or joint rule by a council (see also Schele and Mathews 1998, 197). However, Stuart (in Houston, Stuart, and Robertson 2000, 335) and Boot (2005) identified many of the figures in the *yitah* relationships as deities: in other words, the ruler is not acting together with other individuals or brothers but with gods who presumably were his patron deities. Since these latest epigraphic decipherments, scholars have tended to move away from the *multepal* hypothesis (see Cobos 2007; Grube and Krochock 2007; Plank 2004).

Lincoln (1990, 1994), Wren (1994), Cobos (2007), and Grube and Krochock (2007) have brought evidence to support the existence of a monarchy at Chichen Itza from a variety of sources, including ethnohistories that name one king at Chichen Itza and hieroglyphic texts that describe rituals known to be at the heart of Maya accession to kingship. Grube and Krochock's latest analysis of the Chichen Itza texts (2007) points to K'ak'upakal as the paramount ruler, but the overall impression from reading their translations of Chichen's texts is that gods and rituals (and not K'ak'upakal) dominated the inscriptions of the site (and presumably the imagination of Chichen's ancient Maya inhabitants).

In their review of royal courts of the northern Maya lowlands, Ringle and Bey (2001) reach a similar conclusion: "*Mul tepal* refers not to joint rule but a type of court composed of powerful 'vassals' who, although acknowledging subservience to a paramount, nevertheless retained considerable holdings and rights" (275; see also Plank 2004, 215–18). Reflecting on the political organization of Mayapan, Masson and colleagues (2006) use Postclassic art to support the importance of councils at Mayapan but do not deny the possibility that a paramount ruler had higher power: "Recent multiactor art programs found in the two colonnades flanking the

Castillo . . . reflect the multiple patron gods or ancestors of members of Mayapan's ruling council (*multepal*), which was dominated by members of one paramount family at a time" (194).

Thus, we cannot dismiss the fact that the art and texts of Chichen Itza and other northern lowland centers are different from the Classic corpus of the southern Maya lowlands. The carvings and wall paintings found at Chichen Itza represent many individuals, and no one figure emerges as the most important, as happens in the southern lowland texts and art. Terminal Classic texts at Chichen Itza also tend to include groups of individuals (rulers and gods, rulers and possibly other more mortal companions[21]) who together perform fire ceremonies and other rites that are usually tied to the dedication of buildings or shrines (Grube 1994, 325; Grube and Krochock 2007, 230; Plank 2004, Chapter 6). The lives of the individuals named in these texts are not described in the details that are omnipresent in Classic period monuments in the southern lowlands (Grube and Krochock 2007). In other words, there are no ruler cults in most sites in the northern lowlands. The focus on the many in the art and texts of most Yucatan sites implies a shift away from exclusionary power strategies (to use the terminology of Blanton et al. 1996) beginning in the Terminal Classic. The emphasis of the art in the northern lowlands is on the collective or the community rather than on the singular king that the art of the southern Maya lowlands emphasizes. We see a change in the balance of power, with the community (and/or elite groups) becoming stronger than the monarchy or divine kingship.

A similar situation to that at Chichen Itza is found at Xcalumkin, another Yucatecan center that flourished earlier in time, during the Late Classic (Grube 1994). Over a period of 40 years for which we have hieroglyphic texts, some 14 individuals are named, none of whom is the supreme ruler (320). Rather, the title most commonly associated with Xcalumkin lords and with lords from other Puuc sites in northwestern Yucatan is *sajal*, not *k'uhul ajaw*. Although this may suggest that the Puuc lords were vassals of divine kings from elsewhere, there is no mention of any local or foreign *k'uhul ajaw* in the texts (321).

As discussed in Chapter 4, Graña-Behrens (2006) finds a similar pattern more broadly applicable to the whole northwestern Yucatan, where either the title of *sajal* by itself is present or where the title of *ajaw* is used without the modifier *k'uhul* for "divine" (see also Houston and Inomata 2009, 135–37). Should we conclude that northern Yucatan rulers had a more mortal view of themselves than the southern Maya divine kings? The uneven use of the modifier *k'uhul* at several other sites (in the south, Itzan and Zapote Bobal, or ancient Hix Witz; in the north, Ek Balam) prompted Houston and Inomata to muse: "This leads to the unanswered question of how such epithets [*k'uhul*] were acquired or assigned and whether they corresponded to some subtle hierarchy of rulers" about which we know nothing (ibid., 135). Whether or not the prefix *k'uhul* is present, it seems likely from the art programs of the northern lowlands that there was a qualitative change in the ideology of kingship that became instituted in the north after the Classic Maya collapse in the south. Rulership may have become disassociated from divinity and ruler cults. Instead, rulers became more tied to council organizations (see further discussion of Maya councils in the next chapter).

Liendo Stuardo (2003), using evidence from elite architecture, also concludes that political organization in the northern lowlands was distinct from that of the southern lowlands. He considers changes in elite architectural space and access to and movement within the royal palaces from seven sites, three in the south (Palenque, Tikal, and Uaxactun) and four in the north (Sayil, Labna, Kabah, and Uxmal) (188). Liendo Stuardo finds that the northern palaces "show much simpler access" but that the access was more restricted than it was in the south (ibid.). The northern courts also had more shallow access; that is, it took less time to get to the deepest room in the complex than it did in the southern royal palaces.

He also underscores other architectural changes in northern Yucatan in the Terminal Classic (800–950 AD) that imply political changes. Plazas "are larger and more open," while colonnaded structures surrounding these plazas become more frequent, both changes "suggest[ing] wider participation in ritual [and presumably political] events" (194).

Another architectural change that may show political transformation during the Terminal Classic and Postclassic is that central palaces (such as the Nunnery Quadrangle at Uxmal) became nonresidential and began functioning in purely political and administrative ways (Liendo Stuardo 2003; Webster 1989; Ringle and Bey 2001, 281). Ringle and Bey also note that quadrangles (probably buildings for assemblies or councils) in the epicore of northern Maya centers were nonresidential: "This would suggest some separation between the social spheres of the paramount's household and the court"—that is, public administration rather than private administration (Ringle and Bey 2001, 297). However, we cannot be sure that all Yucatan sites made such a separation. For example, Boot (2005) suggests that the Temple of a Thousand Columns at Chichen Itza was both the ruler's residential palace and the administrative court.

Liendo Stuardo (2003) argues further that the shallowness of access to the northern palaces "indicates an apparent functional specialization among buildings" (199) that may suggest increasing bureaucratization. Based on these architectural differences between the two zones, Liendo Stuardo proposes that the northern polities had a more bureaucratic political organization than the southern states.[22]

Although I agree with Liendo Stuardo that architectural changes in plazas, palaces, and public buildings occurred during the Terminal Classic and Postclassic in northern Yucatan, I am disinclined to see this as evidence for a bureaucratic system in the northern lowlands. For one thing, increased bureaucratization would have been accompanied by political centralization, but widespread evidence suggests that instead participation in ritual-political affairs increased in the north during this period. I would argue instead that during the Terminal Classic and into the Postclassic there was more open access to the royal families for the whole populace, including (and maybe especially for) the aristocratic rank, possibly through the increasing importance of councils that met in nonresidential palaces-quadrangles such as the Nunnery Quadrangle at Uxmal (Ringle and Bey 2001; see also next chapter). If indeed these nonresidential palace-quadrangles housed councils, we can suggest that the administration of these northern polities was more public than the private administration of the southern polities.

Conclusions

Like all other premodern complex societies, Classic Maya polities had an internal administration that varied across time and space. Although many scholars argue that this administrative structure was bureaucratic, my survey of the literature has demonstrated that there were few similarities between Classic Maya political organization and early modern to modern bureaucracies. How then can we describe Maya internal political institutions and dynamics?

Three features characterize Classic Maya political structure. Maya administration was political-ecclesiastical; nobles were promoted from lower to higher positions during their lifetimes. Second, it was hierarchical; there were from two to four levels of elite officials. The divine ruler *k'uhul ajaw* was at the top, and the hierarchy descended through the *ti'sakhuun*, the *sajal*, the *ajk'uhuun*, and the *yajawk'ahk'* to the *lakam* (the only possibly non-elite post) at the bottom (although some of these positions were present in only some polities). Third, it was intensely personal; superior elite patrons "owned" the lower officials or priests, even after death.

Two institutions supported this political administration: the *oikoi*, or great royal households, which varied in composition and size in each polity; and the tribute-tax system, which consisted of staple goods levied from commoners as tax and wealth items (or social valuables) extracted possibly from conquered or defeated polities as tribute.

Archaeological evidence from Maya sites, including Blue Creek and Motul de San José, also shows hierarchically arranged elites with variable political and economic power, some with political power that relied on taxes and some with economic power that relied on the work of smaller *oikoi* to sustain them. At Motul de San José, for example, we found three social ranks: Rank 1 royal elites, Rank 2 secondary elites, and Rank 3 commoners. A number of ritual economic activities took place in all households, but they were most pronounced in the royal houses and attached courts (Rank 1), or royal *oikoi*. The evidence from Motul de San José suggests that the royal *oikoi* generally produced social valuables, while staples (such as corn flour and wild animal meat) were obtained through taxation of the commoner stratum.

Surprisingly, Classic Maya polychrome vases depict tribute-tax as almost completely made up of valuables (Foias 2002; McAnany 2010), while the archaeological evidence from Motul suggests that the tribute-tax system was dominated by staples. This contrast between image and practice at Motul may indicate two separate components of this institution (tax and tribute). But it may also hint that rulers prided themselves on their control over valuables that were possibly obtained through warfare or conquest.

The discussion presented in this chapter has shed light on the presence of multiple layers of political, economic, and ritual power among the elite of ancient Maya society who were members of the political institutions at the core of Classic polities. Governments of complex societies fulfill a number of functions and perform various activities. The scope of their administration ranges from external affairs between the polity and outside actors and internal affairs such as managing the borders of the polity, seeing to the well-being of the polity's inhabitants, keeping order and peace, developing the infrastructure and production, and extracting resources for its own support.

Rather than seeing state political institutions as frozen in time, we need to conceive of them as involved in constant rearrangements, compromises and conflicts with active factions, both elite and non-elite. To see how these political institutions could and did fluctuate, I considered the variation in time and space in the southern Maya lowlands and compared such variations in the southern and northern lowlands from the Late Classic to the Postclassic.

Because political power is not frozen in time, the strategies Classic Maya power holders and factions used to achieve their political goals are pieces of the puzzle of the dynamics of Classic Maya polities. We saw that bureaucratization (or rather increased administration) may have been one such strategy; elites at Actuncan, X-ual-canil, Motul de San José, and northern Maya centers tried to create more administrative positions and to fill these with non-kin loyal office holders. Another strategy of the Classic Maya royals was the use of the ritual economy, in which they sponsored members of their *oikoi* to craft social valuables for use as gifts in grand pageants and feasts. This strategy is seen at Motul de San José, Aguateca, and other centers. In the next chapter I turn to other strategies Classic Maya elites and other power groups pursued to reach their political goals.

Notes

1. I am not arguing that the centralization of power is the only or even the foremost concern of rulers and other active political factions, but rather that it is one strategy that leaders pursue.

2. Written texts can be a form of monitoring. Examples include the small cuneiform tablets that are so common in ancient Near Eastern civilizations from the third millennium BC that were basically confirmations of delivery and receipt of goods.

3. Beliaev (2004) explores the possible nature of this priestly position or status: the color denominations (red-east; yellow-south) may relate to the cardinal directions, which were important in calendrical year-bearer rituals at the end of the solar year. The word *wayaab'* (dreamer) may be associated with shamanistic rituals of communication with gods and ancestors through dreams.

4. Grube (1994, 331–33) writes that the title *yajawk'ahk'* also appears at Chichen Itza, but in relation with other titles that may translate as "the decapitator, the ballplayer." Fire priests-warriors are also found among the Aztecs (Zender 2004).

5. Mixtec priests also functioned as political advisers and keepers of the royal treasury (Lind 2000, 571; Pohl 1994). The priesthood included a group of priests called the *yaha-yahui*, or eagle–fire serpent priests. (See also Spores 1984, which argues that Mixtec administrations were not bureaucratic.)

6. A few were also sculptors, such as the sculptor who signed Bonampak Panel 4 (Zender 2004, 230; Figure 43).

7. With some exceptions: Group 6B-II (Barringer Group) has eight stone-vaulted structures (Adánez et al. 2009, 14, Table 2); Group 6D-XI has five stone-vaulted structures; and Groups 5B-VIII, 6E-XIII, and 7F-I have two stone-vaulted structures each.

8. Connell's interpretation of Nohoch Ek does not necessarily contradict Taschek and Ball's (2003) views that it was a lord's manor since the lord would not have lived there full time and therefore the site would not have eastern shrines, important burials, or heavy artifact density.

9. *Audiencia* is a term used in South America for U-shaped single-room buildings that are generally found at the entrance to storage rooms. Because of this location, they are usually interpreted as checkpoints. This is not the function of these rooms as Maya archaeologists understand it, so *audiencia* might not be the best word for them.

10. In Southeast Asian "galactic" polities, the provincial administration consisted of elites who were rewarded with similar land estates (prebendal assignments, or appanages) (Tambiah 1977; Hammond 1991, 274).

11. This rim text is called the Primary Standard Sequence because of its standard sequence of glyphs that form an extended name tag that identifies not only the shape and function of the vessel but also its owner or elite patron and sometimes the scribe who painted it (Reents-Budet, Ball, and Kerr 1994).

12. The other implication of this scene on vase K1728 is a three-tiered political hierarchy at Motul in which the *muut* depicted in front of the bench represents the lowest tier, his "superior" (the *sajal* who is also a *muut*) represents the second tier, and his superior, the divine ruler of Motul de San José, represents the third and top tier. Although I am not advocating here that this hierarchy was bureaucratic, I do suggest that the Maya conceived of their political administration as hierarchical. The Maya were also aware, at least linguistically, that the *k'uhul ajaw* owned representatives in the form of *muut* bird-messengers and that those representatives could have or own their own messengers.

13. This section draws from Foias et al. 2012, in which we present more details about the archaeological evidence.

14. Tokovinine and Zender (2012) have reconstructed eight successive rulers at Motul beginning around 680 and ending in the early ninth century AD: K'inich, White Bird, Yeh Te' K'inich I, Tayal/Tayel Chan K'inich, Sihyaj K'awiil, Yajawte' Kinich, K'inich Lamaw Ek', and Yeh Te' K'inich II.

15. Here I am using the term *estate* to mean the birthright or inherited social status of individuals who are born of elite parents. At birth, these individuals inherit a number of rights as well as duties and responsibilities (see Garraty 2000; D. Chase and A. Chase 1992; see also discussion in Foias et al. 2012).

16. In the sixteenth century, Bishop Diego de Landa observed gatherings where elite ladies wove fine textiles on backstrap looms in northern Yucatan (Tozzer 1941, 127).

17. See an alternate interpretation of the white-robed nobles in Room 1 as *muut* messengers bringing tribute to the ruler (who could be from either Bonampak or Yaxchilan) in Houston, Stuart, and Taube (2006, 244–47).

18. The presence of grinding stones in Rank 2 households suggests that the residents were heavily invested in the production of ground maize. This can be interpreted in two ways: They were paying tax in corn flour to the royal households or they hosted many feasts.

19. Lucero (2006) distinguishes between integrative and centralized polities. Centralized polities are "possible when critical resources are concentrated, leading to nucleated, dense settlements" (145). Integrative polities such as the Maya regional centers had to deal with widely dispersed critical resources such as fertile agricultural lands and water sources (148–49). The contrast in the distribution of critical resources (land and water) is also reflected in another aspect of the political organization: centralized polities have one primary ruler, but integrative polities have "several relatively autonomous ones" (148).

20. Kelley (1962) identified the glyph *yitah* as a relationship glyph; then Stuart deciphered it as "the sibling of," and MacLeod broadened it to "the companion of" (Grube 1994, 326; see also Cobos 2007). MacLeod and Stone (1995) have translated it as simply "with, and" (175; see also Grube and Krochock 2007, 220).

21. Grube (1994, 326) mentions that some of the individuals who were connected through *yitah* glyphs were clearly mortals and were full brothers who had the same mother.

22. Liendo Stuardo (2003) believes that the elite class in the north became wealthier and more powerful during the transition from the Terminal Classic to the Early Postclassic because there were more elite residences in the north (palaces) during this period than in the Classic period. According to Liendo Stuardo, this greater wealth and power can be explained only if the residents of these households had acquired greater political (bureaucratic) functions than in earlier times (191). However, there is no consensus among Maya archaeologists that there were more elite groups in the Postclassic than in the Classic. For example, royal and subroyal elites appear to have formed as much as 50 percent of the plaza groups at Motul de San José and Caracol (both in the southern lowlands), and Tourtellot et al. (1992) suggest a similar ratio for Sayil, a northern lowland site that dates to the Terminal Classic.

6

‖‖‖‖‖‖‖‖‖‖‖

The Flow and Use of Power

The Micro Scale of Political Analysis

Up to now, I have considered politics from the perspective of Maya states and their rulers and political elites. This has placed undue emphasis on political power emanating from the top levels of society, or from the political institutions in which individuals interact. But recent scholarship has underscored that power is more fluid and more contingent on actors and situations. Because political power is dynamic, what matters is not only how much power individuals have but also how this power is materialized in interactions between all participants (elite and non-elite). Emerson and Pauketat (2002) summarize this new perspective: "We argue for an archaeology of power that holds that people's practices, embodiments, and interactions are generative, power-laden, historically situated, and contingent. . . . We should not remove and segment power from the theater of practice where it was enacted and embodied by all people" (118–119).

In ancient states, the political power of the state was what was seen in state-sponsored rituals or spectacles that included feasts, construction projects, receptions for foreign ambassadors, and presentations of tribute and captives (Inomata 2006b). In these rituals, the position and behavior of the different political actors and factions made their relations of power with the others visible, but the responses by some factions or actors, which ranged from acquiescence to resistance, could affect the whole ceremony, adding to or decreasing the power of the host. Thus, resistance is as much a part of ancient politics as obedience to the state (Scott 1990).

In this chapter I want to follow some of the theoretical threads introduced in Chapter 2 by examining the foundations of Classic Maya political power, the processes of establishing authority and legitimacy and their contradictions, the performances of power and the dynamics of those performances, and the role of commoners in Classic Maya politics. I use Motul de

San José as the central case study, but I compare it with other Classic Maya polities.

Foundations of Classic Maya Political Power

Kurtz (2001), Mann (1986), Earle (1997), and Yoffee (2005), among others, note that political power derives from multiple sources. While the Classic Maya appear to have defined political power in religious terms as divine kingship, we need to go below the surface of this dominant ideology (which the rulers presented in the "public transcript") to look at what they did in practice. As in all other societies, Maya political power likely came from more than one source (economic, social, religious, and military), and as archaeologists we need to ask which sources of power existed on a case-by-case basis. Furthermore, we need to ask if these sources of power were restricted to particular groups. For example, it is possible that elites with social power (or religious power) may not have been allowed to be involved in economic pursuits. Elites who chose to practice such economic activity may have lost social status (or social power) even as they were gaining economic wealth or economic power. Incongruities between these sources of power would have impacted the success of some polities and may have caused their collapse. Alternatively, different sources of power may complement each other and lead to the success of a state. The variety of sources of power Maya elites drew upon leads one to consider that there must have been multiple hierarchies of social, economic, political, and religious power in the Maya lowlands. This theory is congruent with the heterarchical propositions that Potter and King (1995) and King and Shaw (2003) put forth.

Military strength underpins coercive power, the power achieved through the threat of bodily harm. As Foucault (1979, 1991) has stressed in his work, the degree of coercion possible in premodern states was of a very different kind and scale from what is possible in present-day modern states in which communication, transportation, and monitoring (or surveillance) technologies are much more developed. So it is likely that coercive or military means of achieving political power were less significant in premodern states such as the Classic Maya. However, I think we understate or negate the role of military power in some of these ancient polities. For example, the leaders of Teotihuacan appear to have resettled a large portion of the valley population into that city's apartment compounds early in the polity's history (Millon 1981). During the fourth millennium BC, early in its history, Uruk carried out the same kind of resettlement (Rothman 2004; Stein

1994). Tikal also may have resettled nearby population into the urban center at the beginning of the Late Classic (Chase, Chase, and Haviland 1990).
Unless these population movements were due only to the attractions of
city life, an element of coercion backed by military power must have been
involved.[1] Beyond this population movement at Tikal, evidence for direct
coercion by Maya rulers over their subjects is not clear (Inomata 2004),
and many Maya archaeologists believe that these demographic shifts are
attributable to the commoners' freedom to vote with their feet (Ashmore,
Yaeger, and Robin 2004; Inomata 2004; Robin, Yaeger, and Ashmore 2010;
Yaeger 2003b).

The theory that Maya rulers were partially sustained by military power is
supported by the frequent depiction of captives under the feet of kings and
the enumeration of war events in hieroglyphic texts throughout the Classic
period (Houston, Stuart, and Taube 2006; Demarest 1978; Webster 2000,
2002; Brown and Stanton 2003). Some rulers adopted titles that named how
many warriors they had captured in battle (for example, "he of X captives")
(Houston, Stuart, and Taube 2006, 204).[2] The evidence for titles related to
captive-taking is concentrated at smaller sites and has not been found at
Tikal or Calakmul (ibid.). Thus, we conclude that the declaration of martial
prowess served to enhance the social status (and power) of rulers of smaller
sites. Houston, Stuart, and Taube write that the shaming and dishonor-
ing of captives was an important element of warfare and of elite and royal
culture in general, suggesting that Classic Maya society may have been a
timocracy like early Classical Greece, in which "a sharp sense of personal
value ('pride' [and honor]), especially among men, played a marked role in
face-to-face interaction" (ibid., 202–26, quote on 202). Houston and colleagues argue that this system of personal pride and honor was the root
cause of the political fragmentation of the Classic Maya, who were un-
able to end long-term feuds or vendettas against each other caused by the
"loss of face" on the battlefield or in captivity afterward. If Houston, Stuart,
and Taube are correct, then Classic Maya society was a warrior society, although the militaristic tones became stronger in the Terminal Classic and
the Postclassic, when scenes of dozens of warriors and battles appear more
frequently (Baudez and Latsanopoulos 2010). However, we have to keep
in mind that most Classic Maya warfare involved only elites, so any coercive elements would have involved the upper class more than commoners
(Webster 2000; Inomata and Triadan 2009).

Although most Maya warfare during the Classic period may have been
limited in scope (Demarest 1978; Webster 2000),[3] entire sites were burned

and abandoned in some episodes (e.g., Aguateca). In others, rulers and their gods and families were imprisoned or killed (e.g., Yaxuna, Cancuen, Palenque), and in others, only the milder sanction of tribute was imposed (Freidel, MacLeod, and Suhler 2003; D. Chase and A. Chase 2003; Bey 2003; Ambrosino, Ardren, and Stanton 2003; Webster 2000, 2002; Inomata 2007; Martin and Grube 2000; Stuart and Stuart 2008, 191). Because of this variability in the consequences of warfare, we need to explore the impact of individual cases of Maya warfare on both the conquerors and the losers. Victorious centers that benefited substantially from these conflicts embarked on major construction projects and may have attracted more population, as in the case of Caracol during the Middle Classic (A. Chase and D. Chase 1996; D. Chase and A. Chase 2003). In contrast, the losing side could sustain short to long periods of little architectural activity and/ or more substantial disturbances.

Even though military power was one aspect of political leadership, Classic art centers on the Maya rulers' display of ritual power. Late Classic period kings called themselves divine rulers, k'uhul ajaw (Houston and Stuart 1996; Zender 2004; Schele and Freidel 1990; McAnany 2008; McAnany 2010, 158–98). They are most often portrayed enacting religious rituals, such as bloodletting, burning incense at specific calendrical/ritual points, and communicating with or materializing ancestors, gods, and other supernatural beings (Schele and Miller 1986; Schele and Freidel 1990; Demarest 1992; Sanchez 2005; Lucero 2006).[4] Most scholars agree that the basic foundation of the power of Maya rulers was their control over the supernatural sphere through shamanistic rituals (but see the critique of this view in Zender 2004; and Klein et al. 2002). As described in Chapter 4, the religious sphere was clearly important; it even affected the political structure by dictating the quadripartite organization of some realms. There is no doubt that the Late Classic k'uhul ajaw drew most of his power from his control of the religious sphere. There is even evidence from some Late Classic sites that ruling elites may have attempted to control the ritual sphere even more tightly by restricting access to the central plazas where the royal family and priests held the most important state rituals. Joyce and Weller (2007) describe how the main plazas of Caracol, Tikal, Xunantunich, Altun Ha, Baking Pot, and Blue Creek were closed off by new construction that transformed them from public ritual space to royal residential space by the end of the Late Classic (155–60). However, we have to turn to the archaeological record to move beyond the "public transcripts" of these monuments and plazas and consider whether Maya rulership was also founded on economic and/or social power.

Social power may also come into play if the royal elite were seen to be of a different origin from the rest of society. This is true for the Postclassic and Contact period Maya of the Yucatan Peninsula and for other Postclassic societies, such as the Mixtecs and Aztecs. For example, in the Mixtec area, the rulers traced their descent back to 11 divine couples "who were born supernaturally from trees, rivers, or mountains" (Lind 2000, 571). In Postclassic times, the Maya lords also claimed faraway origins in the supernatural realm (Restall 1997, 2001). In the Classic period, Maya rulers claimed descent back to mythical times and major gods, such as the Palenque Triad (of gods GI, GII, and GIII) (Schele and Freidel 1990; Houston and Stuart 1996). Social power among the Classic Maya, then, was predicated on the divine descent of the noble rank (or *estate*), which contrasted with the mortal origins of the commoner rank (or *estate*).This distinction in the origins of the two ranks was also surely accompanied by an acute sense of difference between noble and commoner that translated into social power for the elites. Because social power is tied to the divine origins of the noble rank, it is also religious power. However, the presence of a moral code of conduct similar to the European aristocratic principle of noblesse oblige (Houston and Stuart 2001) probably limited the social power of Maya elites.

Scholars debate whether Classic Maya political power was based on economic power, probably because economic power varied considerably among the many lowland polities. Economic power in premodern, precapitalist, agrarian societies is predicated on control over land, production and/or exchange, or human labor (McAnany 1993a). For the Classic period, control over land has been difficult to ascertain, although large-scale agricultural projects (where they have been found) have been interpreted as being under state supervision. Here I am referring to the standardized system of terraces at Caracol (Chase and Chase 1996) or the possible drainage system and raised fields in *bajos* around Tikal (Grazioso Sierra et al. 2001). However, these large-scale agricultural projects are limited in number and extent, and archeologists believe that most land was held by families, lineages, "houses," or communities (Lohse 2004). This does not deny the possibility that the elites held large tracts of land as their private estates (Taschek and Ball 2003; Foias 2002).

Another source of economic power may have been control over water (specifically fresh or pure water) by constructing reservoirs and other water control systems or by conducting water purification rituals (Scarborough 1998; Lucero 1999b, 2006). Again, this applies to some Classic Maya centers but not to all. Water control systems have been documented at Tikal and Calakmul, but none have been found at Motul de San José, Aguateca, Dos Pilas, or Seibal.

When we turn to elite control over production and/or exchange, mixed results appear, as only some rulers controlled markets in the core of their sites (e.g., Chunchucmil) and a few others may have controlled some workshops where obsidian was processed and pottery was made (e.g., Quirigua). The variation in elite control over production and exchange is quite likely one of the causes of the political dynamics of the Classic period (Foias and Emery 2012). Generally, the elite seem to have managed only the production and distribution of valuables that had meaning in terms of ideology or status (e.g., carved jade, marine shells, or elaborate polychrome pots). Sometimes the elites themselves crafted these items in palace workshops, as at Aguateca and Motul de San José (Foias and Emery 2012; Halperin and Foias 2010, 2012; Inomata 2001b, 2007; Inomata and Triadan 2000; Inomata et al. 2002).

Another way to gauge economic power is to consider differences in control over human labor, as reflected in the volume of constructed architecture (Abrams 1994). Royal palaces at Copan involved almost 500 times more labor than housing for low-status commoners living in outlying villages, which consisted of perishable houses made of wood, adobe, and thatch: royal palaces required approximately 25,000 person-days to build, while commoner houses required only 50 person-days. Architectural volume analyses at Copan and at Motul de San José (Foias et al. 2012; see also Chapter 5) shed light on the hierarchical nature of Maya society and the higher control over human labor by the elite rank (or *estate*).

Pyburn (1997) advocates an architectural and material approach to understanding the foundations of Classic Maya political power. She argues that the scale of temple-pyramid architecture provides an estimate of elites' ideological power and that the size of residential elite architecture (e.g., stone palaces) marks the royalty's political and economic power (162).[5] She also proposes that if elites drew most of their power from agricultural resources, we should expect them to have lived close to these resources and therefore that we should find more elite structures in rural areas. Pyburn also feels that the quantity of imported objects is further evidence of the degree to which elite power was based on economics (163). Using this approach, Pyburn compares the investment of elites at Albion Island

and Nohmul (both in Belize) in the construction of temple-pyramids and/ or elite residential structures and the rate at which elites imported exotic goods. She finds a decline in temple/shrine construction during the Late Classic, or "a shift to more centralized religion and more government involvement" (165–66).

All of the evidence above makes it clear that rulers depended on distinct constellations of a variety of sources of power, including religious, military, social, and economic power. For example, Lucero and Scarborough have pointed to the intersection between ritual and economic power. Lucero (2006) emphasizes that the rituals for water purification that Maya royals conducted were crucial for extracting surplus, which she finds to be the economic foundation of political power.[6] Both Scarborough (1993, 1998, 2003) and Lucero (1999b, 2006) focus on the importance of water to the ancient Maya: seasonal and long-term fluctuations in rainfall could be a matter of life and death. The Maya lowlands are characterized by a dry season from November to May when there is little to no rain. In addition, surface water sources are few and far between on the karstic landscape of the northern and southern lowlands. According to Lucero (2006), Maya kings not only performed water purification rituals, rituals of "life, death and renewal," but also helped build and maintain systems for catching water, including major reservoirs next to royal courts at Tikal, Calakmul, and Caracol (2; see also Lucero 1999a, 1999b). However, at other Maya centers, for example Motul de San José, Seibal, or Palenque, water was plentiful, and Maya rulers did not invest in water-catching systems. Therefore, the kings of the latter polities derived power from other sources.

The articulation and interplay of these different sources of power provides insight into political dynamics because they may work against or complement each other. We can learn about which of these sources of power were most important in each Maya polity if we view material culture as a discourse about power between individuals, factions, communities, and polities.

Leaders, Followers, Authority, and Legitimacy

Archaeologists and ethnographers of Africa make an important distinction between material wealth (wealth in things) and people wealth (wealth in people) (Guyer and Belinga 1995; Nyerges 1992; Fleisher and Wynne-Jones 2010; Robertshaw 2010). Robertshaw (2010) observes that material "wealth (wealth-in-things) may not have been particularly valuable in tropical

Africa, where potential agricultural land was generally abundant but labor was often in short supply" (264). Demarest (1992, 151) has made a similar point about the Classic Maya, but his observation is based on ethnographic evidence from Southeast Asia (relying on Geertz 1980 and Tambiah 1977). Control over human labor was of great importance for the Classic Maya, as it was for tropical Africa and tropical Southeast Asian states (see also Lucero 2006; Chase, Chase, and Smith 2009). Chase, Chase, and Smith (2009) reach a similar conclusion: Mesoamerican polities "were defined not on the basis of land or territory, but on the basis of personal ties to a ruler" (181). Graham (2011) also concurs with this conclusion from her reassessment of Maya states in Belize on the eve of the Spanish Conquest: rather than focusing on the territorial state model, we should envision Maya states as a set of relationships of allegiance and tribute centered on the ruler. This has implications for political dynamics.

In the tropical African context, a powerful ruler was one who attracted many followers or dependents, forming extensive networks of clients or allies (Robertshaw 2010, 264). Fleisher and Wynne-Jones (2010) describe the political implications of a system of wealth in people: "The need to attract and retain followers or clients is a never-ending process, during which allegiance must be continuously deserved and re-enacted. The impermanent state of power derived from wealth-in-people means a constant situation of performance, through which society is composed and authority is constituted and understood" (189). Thus, in tropical Africa and probably in the Classic Maya lowlands, political power was predicated at least in part on the number of followers that a leader could attract and the degree to which that leader could sustain the loyalty of followers through constant political performances.

One of the key strategies for attracting and keeping a loyal following is maintaining a convincing claim to authority and/or legitimacy.[7] Legitimacy means that leaders are seen as the rightful holders of power and therefore are entitled to exercise power. But even in complex societies such as the Classic Maya, where the political hierarchy was institutionalized and different offices were invested with legitimacy, likely candidates competed for political positions and had to work continuously to maintain their legitimacy and authority. Without legitimacy, power is diluted or entirely lost. Even today in U.S. politics, particular offices (including the presidency) are sometimes described as "losing authority," which impedes the ability of the officeholders to carry out their duties. In other words, the process of legitimating power is always a work in progress.

Scholars often categorize the strategies by which authority and legitimacy are established as either coercion or persuasion. Although coercion may work in the short term and over short distances, most methods of legitimation are persuasive and involve ideology, emotional attachment, and/or rational benefits. Recent scholarship has examined these persuasive strategies (Doyle 1986; Fleisher and Wynne-Jones 2010; Smith 2000; Schortman and Urban 2004). Since we have weak evidence for coercive methods of establishing authority among the Classic Maya, persuasive means must have been most important.

Schortman and Urban (2004) have described how legitimacy may be established using rational persuasive means: rulers convince the ruled that it is to their benefit to follow and obey them using some kind of system of economic rewards. In contrast, Adam Smith (2000) emphasizes that persuasive means of legitimation rely on emotive ties to rulers: Urartian "political ideologies . . . [strove] to create affective ties between regimes and those they rule by rendering the political aesthetic [beautiful on an emotional level]" (132). Smith finds that the political strategies for securing legitimacy in the Urartian empire of the Near East appear in both words (cuneiform texts) and images (pictorial representations in metal or stone artifacts) and appeal most to the emotions of "triumphalism" or "sacrality" rather than to "rational assessments of costs and benefits" (157).

Among the many possible persuasive ideological strategies, three come to the forefront: naturalizing the political structure (Bourdieu 1990; Kertzer 1988; Bauer 1996; McAnany 2010), creating a society-wide shared identity (Yaeger 2003a; Inomata 2006a, 2006b; Pauketat 2007; LeCount 2010), and transforming the landscape (A. Smith 2003).

These methods of legitimization need further explanation. Both Bourdieu (1990) and Kertzer (1988) explore how rulers and the ruling class use supernatural associations, powers, or origins to naturalize the political structure. This strategy enables them to claim that their political power has "natural" origins (see also McAnany 2008, 2010).[8] These supernatural associations are gained, performed, and remembered through rituals. Although texts and/or monuments may also record and speak of the supernatural powers of the rulers, the materialization of these associations in rituals brings full force to this process of legitimation.

A second method of legitimation is to create a shared identity across a society (Yaeger 2003a; Inomata 2006a, 2006b; Pauketat 2007). In his work at San Lorenzo near Xunantunich, Belize, Yaeger (2003a) discovered that specific rituals accompanied by feasts took place in this village and involved ruling elites (or their representatives) from the capital of Xunantunich. These rituals, which were hosted in a special nonresidential building, reinforced the shared experience of ruled and ruling, creating a feeling of common identity. Smith (2000) describes a similar strategy in his studies of the Urartian empire:

> Urartian political programs appealed to emotions in order to stimulate an embrace of and identification with charismatic triumph and a sense of reverence and deference towards the sacred. The product of such programs . . . is not consent to the state, but a profound interest in its continuance as it is the vehicle of "civilizing" the wastelands and making manifest the gods on earth. (157)

A third strategy for legitimating political leaders and their power is to transform the landscape. The built environment of political centers, fortresses, palatial and administrative edifices, and monuments is an active constituent of political power, not simply "a pale reflection of transformations in political organization" (A. Smith 2003, 76; see also Baines and Yoffee 2000, 15). These constructions functioned not only as ever-present symbols of the power to control human labor but were also the sites where political ceremonies, meetings, rulings, decisions, and so forth took place (see Smith 2003, 233–35). Because political institutions are manifested and made effective through political rituals, these events become the central arena where political power was created, reinforced, or contested (see Kertzer 1988; Dirks 1991; Lucero 2006). Baines and Yoffee (2006) also stress the importance of rituals to political power: "Without celebration, [political] order may be threatened; with it, everyone may internalize its significance" (16).

Maya Rituals of Politics: Performances of Political Power

By viewing the political process through rituals of politics, or performances of political power, we can study these phenomena archaeologically. Kertzer (1988) writes: "Ritualization entails the repetitive use of emotionally charged symbols in symbolically significant locations at symbolically appropriate times" (92). Ritualized events thus become visible archaeologically since repetitive action involving the same "symbols" at the same place and time will leave behind material patterns year after year or month after month, depending on the frequency of the political rituals (DeMarrais, Castillo, and Earle 1996; Lucero 2003, 2006; McAnany 2010).

However, this is where we run into an archaeological dilemma: the locations where these performances took place were also public spaces that were generally kept clean. Inomata (2006b) argues that the principal arenas for state political ceremonies were the large central plazas, where all or most of a state's population could attend, observe, and participate. Smaller political performances would have played out in the lesser courtyards associated with palaces and in the plazuelas of small (commoner) residential groups, where we can imagine that rituals involving lineage heads and the rest of the family were observed (Hutson, Magnoni, and Stanton 2004; Lucero 2003, 2006; Gonlin and Lohse 2007). Holding political performances inside Maya structures would have been ineffective, since only a small number of people could have fit in those spaces. (That is not to say that politicking wasn't done behind closed doors.)

In a recent contribution, Dahlin and colleagues (2009) looked at geochemical signatures in medium and large plazas at Chunchucmil and Trinidad (a secondary center under the control of Motul de San José). Their findings enabled them identify differences in the functions of these plazas. They found increased concentrations of phosphate in medium plazas that are indicative of feasting, and in the largest plazas they found extremely high phosphate concentrations that seem to correlate with nonfeasting market activities. Their research confirms that medium plazas had a role in performances, and in fact they suggest that feasting took place only in these smaller plazas. They posit that other ceremonies that did not include feasting were held in the larger central plazas where stelae are erected and that the larger central plazas that had no stelae were the locations of markets (see also Bair and Terry 2012). The medium-sized plazas and the adjoining elite palaces may have been places where political rituals happened, but their floors were generally swept clean and all remains of these festivities would have been dumped into middens.[9] Thus, it is not so easy to study the details of political events from material evidence, and we are left with the task of reconstructing them from depictions in art and descriptions in hieroglyphic texts.

As we turn to the artistic and hieroglyphic evidence of the nature of these political performances, a number of questions come to mind: Who was involved in these events? What rules did they follow? Who had power to affect these situations and rules? Depictions of reunions or meetings among several individuals (or even a whole royal court) that could be conceived as political rituals are not depicted frequently on Classic Maya stone monuments, but they are portrayed more frequently on art that was more private, such as the Bonampak murals (Miller 1986, 2001) and polychrome pottery (Reents-Budet 2001; Jackson 2009). I thus turn to polychrome pottery art to gather more details about Classic Maya political performances.

Before we enter the discourses found in Maya art, we need to consider the limitations of art, be it modern or ancient. Looper (2009) stresses that "images . . . in Maya art transcribed memories of performances into permanent media. As products of memory work, images provide an opportunity for montage, deletion, and creativity that radically alters the semantic and formal relationships between the image and the performance(s) that inspired them. . . . The images are not photographic records . . . but are carefully composed in order to crystallize the most important elements of the rites from the point of view of both patron and artist" (45). Central to this problem are a number of processes, including deletion and focalization; that is, some elements and/or participants of the performance are deleted and others become the focus, especially the main performer. The political valence of images comes from their role as a "reference point for the conceptualization of future performances. This function of images is profoundly political in that it ascribes an authority to a particular representation as a means of sustaining powerful emotions experienced during the event" (46). The permanent image is created as evidence of how things are done, should be done, and will always be done. In the Maya case, the political overtones of the image are even more powerful because of Maya beliefs that the self could be materialized in many places at the same time, such as in stelae, on murals, on pottery, and on other artifacts that depicted these individuals (Houston, Stuart, and Taube 2006).

Because political power was "what was seen" in premodern societies such as the Classic Maya, we can gain a more detailed understanding of these rituals from how they were depicted on polychrome vessels. These vases were used for serving, eating, and drinking during the feasting events that accompanied political rituals. Thus, they were highly visible to those who participated in these feasts. Members of the elite class were the audience for and the consumers of this imagery, and the concerns that we see in the iconography are the concerns of the elite (see further discussion below).

Since Classic k'uhul ajaws were political and religious leaders, the rituals recorded on Maya vases are both political and religious in nature. Although we cannot assume that these pottery scenes represent the full range of political performances that Maya elite engaged in, we can get a sense of the importance of different activities by considering how frequently they appear in pottery paintings. I have used Barbara and Justin Kerr's Maya

Table 6.1. Types of political events depicted on Ik' Style polychrome vessels

Depicted Event	Number of vessels	Frequency	Vessel Numbers
Dance	16	39%	K533, K534, K791, K1050, K1399, K1439, K1452, K1498, K1896, K3464, K4120, K4606, K4690, K6341, K6688, K6888
Presentation of captives	7	17%	K680, K2025, K2795, K3478, K3984, K5850, K6674
Small court reunion	8	20%	K1453, K2573 (wedding?), K2763, K3054, K4355, K5370, K6552, K6666
Adornment or preparation	5	12%	K1463, K8484, K8764, K8926, K9190
Presentation of tribute	5	12%	K1728 (Figure 5.1), K3203, K4996, K8790, K8889

Source: Maya Vase Database, www.mayavase.com.

Vase Database of rollout photographs of hundreds of Maya polychrome vases (available at www.mayavase.com) as a basis for my analysis, although this is not a complete set of all Maya pottery art. I selected only pots that were tied by style or text to the Ik' emblem glyph, which most epigraphers believe to refer to Motul de San José and its zone north of Lake Peten Itza. This produced a sample of 41 vessels. Only certain activities are recorded on these vases: 1) dances (39 percent, or 16 vessels)[10]; 2) presentation and/or sacrifice of captives (17 percent, or 7 vessels); 3) small court reunions (20 percent, or 8 vessels)[11]; 4) adornment in preparation for dance, war, or other state ritual (12 percent, or 5 vases); and 5) presentation of tribute (ca. 12 percent, or 5 vases).[12] Dance was by far the most common event, followed by presentations or sacrifice of captives and small meetings (or rituals involving drinking or enemas) (see Table 6.1). Scenes of adornment (or preparations for ritual, dancing or war) are less common, as are presentations of tribute. Based on these numbers, dance seems to have been the most important political ritual and tribute does not appear to have been a primary concern. However, war booty (and hence tribute) appears together with a captive presentation on one vase (K6674), on which the captive's outfit and weapons are placed on the throne in front of the ruler. Thus, the distinction between tribute scenes and captive presentation scenes may be more fluid that we suspect.[13]

Depictions of tribute may have been rare because the elite were not worried about their ability to extract it from commoners.[14] Alternatively, tribute may have been depicted only rarely because rulers and the elite promoted a specific ideological program to secure legitimacy that focused on the same emotive aspects that the Urartian state emphasized: "triumphalism" (because of their success in war) and "sacrality" (the ability of the king to "make manifest the gods on earth," or the sacred nature of the kings) (Smith 2000, 157).

Multiple actors were involved in these pottery scenes, but generally the most powerful actor (typically the *k'uhul ajaw*) was clearly marked and identified. The frequency with which individuals are portrayed indicates the existence of several "power blocs": 1) the *k'uhul ajaw*, who is placed in a central role, either sitting on a throne or standing in the middle of the scene (sometimes accompanied by his queen wife); 2) lower noble courtiers, who surround the *k'uhul ajaw* in more peripheral positions (these are often named by glyphic captions as *sajal, ajk'uhuun, ebet* or *muut ebet* messengers, dwarves, and other secondary administrators who are not always named); and 3) warriors, who are identified by their battle attire and weaponry.[15] Political power is clearly marked in these scenes by an individual's position (the higher the position, the higher the power), size, and symbols of political power (such as specific costume elements or actual objects that the power holders carry). The absence of ambiguity about who was the most powerful in many of these pottery scenes hints that ranking was a central concern for the Classic Maya, as it still is for their modern descendants: for example, even today, hosts and guests at ritual ceremonies in Zinacantan, Chiapas are carefully seated in the order of their social status (Vogt 2004, 2007). In addition, the absence of ambiguity about who was the most powerful in many (if not most) of these pottery scenes demonstrates the hierarchical organization of political power.

Vases, bowls, jars, and/or baskets full of food and drink are displayed prominently below the throne of the *k'uhul ajaw* in many pottery scenes, underscoring that political events involved feasting and rich displays of royal generosity through gifts of foods, drinks, and other goods (Wells and Davis-Salazar 2007; Schortman and Urban 2004; Wells 2006; Foias 2007). Landa describes how all rituals were accompanied by feasts and merriment (including dance and music) in Contact period Yucatan (see Tozzer 1941). Not surprisingly, musicians are also commonly depicted in pottery scenes, and figurine-whistles have been found in many Maya households (Foias 2007; Reents-Budet, Ball, and Kerr 1994; Reents-Budet 2001; Miller 2001;

Halperin 2007). Thus, when we think of political performances, we must remember that they involved feasting, dancing, music, and gift-giving. Witnessing these events must have been very important for Classic Maya states—the more public the ritual, the better, and the more prolonged the event, the more memorable. Witnessing was still important in Colonial times, as is revealed by Maya wills and court cases of the period, both of which always included a long list of witnesses (Restall 1997).

Political performances required significant amounts of food, drink, specialized paraphernalia, and possibly other items that were given as gifts. The elaborate paraphernalia involved in such political performances is exemplified by the huge costume-headdress of a supernatural bird that is twice as tall as its wearer, ruler Ahkal Mo' Nahb, depicted on the Palenque limestone panel found in Temple XIX (Stuart and Stuart 2008, 228, Plate 12). R. Joyce (2000), Tate (1999), and McAnany (2008, 2010) among others, explore the importance of women as the producers of the food, drinks, textiles, pottery, and other items that were used in political rituals and feasts. Political power cannot be disentangled from economic resources or from the gendered production of these resources. It is not surprising that elite households at Motul de San José were involved in more textile production than small or medium households (Halperin 2008), as cloth may have been one of the items given as gifts in these feasts. Foias et al. (2012) also document an extraordinary concentration of maize-grinding equipment (*manos* and *metates*) in Group D, one of the royal compounds at Motul de San José, presumably for the preparation of massive amounts of food for royal feasts. The largest and most dense middens at Motul were discovered adjacent to the Acropolis royal court, and evidence from them shows the court's major investment in feasting.

Dancing

As dance is the most commonly depicted activity on the Ik'-related pots, I discuss that topic in more detail here. The most extensive study of Classic Maya dance was carried out by Looper (2009). Rather than viewing it as an aesthetic performance or as a completely religious undertaking, Looper stresses how it functioned socially and politically as well as ritually (3–13). Dancing is recognized through textual evidence that includes the verb for dancing, *ahk'ot* (17), and through depictions of individuals in the process of dancing (with one foot lifted off the ground and/or with highly formal poses of knees, hands, wrists, and arms or in wilder positions for supernaturals). The dance verb *ahk'ot* often appears with another verb, *yahk'a (w)*, "to give" or "make an offering," underlining the ritual overtones of the performance as "a form of tribute or offering to the gods or to overlords" (18). In some texts, the dances are "received" by paramount lords together with tribute or offerings, evidence of the political role of dancing. In these cases, "dance is used as a means of bolstering [or sealing] alliances [or political ties] between rulers and their subordinates" (18–19). Looper intimates that some dances may have reembodied past events, such as war victories (20–21). For example, the ruler Itzamnah K'awil of Dos Pilas recorded a number of martial dances (involving God K scepters) on Stelae 11, 14, and 15, which may have reembodied and celebrated several of his war victories (22, 26). Interestingly, Stelae 2, 5, and 6 at Motul de San José are quite similar in style and scene to these three Dos Pilas monuments (Foias 1998, 1999), but the only one that is dated (MSJ Stela 2) commemorates a dance that took place a half-century later, in approximately 771 AD, between two rulers, the Motul ruler K'inich Lamaw Ek' and the Itsimte king Juun Tsak Took' (Tokovinine and Zender 2012). The other two Motul stelae may also portray dances involving the God K scepter because the positions of the individuals and the objects they are holding are similar in all three: a single ruler (in Stela 6) or paired rulers (in Stelae 2 and 5) hold(s) God K scepters, and each paired ruler is lifting a foot off the ground.

Yaxchilan, west of Motul and northwest of Dos Pilas, also has a long record of dance events dating to the second half of the eighth century (Looper 2009, 28). For example, Stela 11 records a flapstaff dance of the ruler Itzamnah B'ahlam II and his son Bird Jaguar IV, the ruler at that time.[16] The dance is recorded in a small secondary text next to the foot of Bird Jaguar IV; the main hieroglyphic texts recount his dedication of stelae, his accession to the throne, his parentage statements, and a pre-accession sacrificial ritual (30). As the dance was the first rite in this series of events, Looper concludes that it marked "the initiation of a transfer of power between father and son" (ibid.), which Bird Jaguar IV immortalized to gain legitimacy during his rise to the throne of Yaxchilan (Martin and Grube 2008, 128–29). Eight lintels in Temples 1, 33, and 42 also record dances performed by Bird Jaguar IV, most within a year of his accession (Looper 2009, 32–34). On Lintel 5 of Temple 33, Bird Jaguar IV performs the *xukpi* dance (named for the motmot bird staff that he carries in his hand), accompanied by his wife, Lady Wak Tun of Motul de San José (possibly the sister or daughter of one of the most successful of the Motul rulers, Yajawte' K'inich, who ruled in the mid-eighth century) (34; Tokovinine and Zender

2012). The Motul princess, interestingly enough, carries a tied bundle in her arms marked with the glyph *ikats*, "bundle or cargo" (Looper 2009, 34). Although most scholars see this bundle as containing important Yaxchilan ritual paraphernalia, Looper suggests that it may refer to the tribute burden that the Motul princess owed to the Yaxchilan ruler (her husband) because the glyph *ikats* is associated with tribute in other Classic texts (Stuart 1995; McAnany 2010). If Looper is correct, then marriage alliances involved a "dowry" of some kind or possible tribute rights that her home polity owed the princess.

The dances depicted on monuments are named for the objects manipulated by participants and have strong cosmological valences, as in the association of different dances with specific gods who are identified in the dancers' masks or headdress symbols (Looper 2009, 42–43).[17] For example, the flapstaff dance is named as the "clearer" dance and takes place around the summer solstice, when a dry spell (called *canicula*) begins in the Maya lowlands (37).

The pairing of dancers in the scenes found at Yaxchilan and its subsidiary sites (such as Site R) is paralleled at Motul de San José in its better-preserved Stelae 2 and 5. These double-actor dance performances at Yaxchilan and Motul de San José functioned as "a metonym of power sharing as well as political hierarchy. By dancing on formal occasions with subordinates, allies, wives and heirs, Maya rulers could demonstrate their sociopolitical unity, as well as status differences, through variations in costume, staging, or choreography" (43). This is what I call the double-edged sword of public performances: they can unify participants by creating a feeling of common identity, but they can also highlight hierarchical differences in power among the participants.

Although these dances were public performances, the positioning of the monuments that portray them at Yaxchilan in semi-private and private architectural contexts suggests an audience of elites only (43–44). This is not the case at Motul de San José, where all three stelae that depict dances are found in central, open plazas. In addition, the paired kings on Motul Stelae 2 and 5 are almost identical, so equality and alliance is the central message rather than hierarchy.

Dance has a particular relevance for the site of Motul de San José not only because it appears on its stone monuments but also because the great majority of Ik' Style vases depict dancing. Looper, Reents-Budet, and Bishop (2009) have examined in detail 66 whole vases in the Ik' Style (in museums and private collections), of which 47 have scenes related to dance

(132). According to Looper and his colleagues, the Motul dance performances "occurred during such important events as accession to the throne, successful war celebrations, and the observance of critical calendrical period-ending rites" (133).

Looper, Reents-Budet, and Bishop (2009) define a number of types of dance performances: dancing in X-ray–style costumes, with or without masks; dancing combined with drinking or with the ritual use of enemas; dancing combined with blood autosacrifice; dancing combined with divination; and dancing accompanied by presentation and sacrifice of captives (a practice that was related to the victory celebration dance).[18] It is noteworthy that the dances portrayed on these vessels are generally different from the dances found in the stone monuments. The only dances recorded on both stone monuments and in pottery scenes are war celebration dances.

Many of the dances that involved X-ray–style costumes and fantastic animal costumes materialized *wayob*, which have been interpreted as spiritual co-essences of particular individuals or as spiritual forces that are found in specific geographic points and are often tied to death and illness (Houston and Stuart 1989; Calvin 1997; Grube and Nahm 1994; Grube 2004; Looper, Reents-Budet, and Bishop 2009, 135). Two consecutive Motul de San José rulers (Yajawte' K'inich and K'inich Lamaw Ek') are named on a great majority of the Ik' vases painted with scenes of dances that invoke *wayob* (Looper, Reents-Budet, and Bishop 2009; Reents-Budet et al. 2012). Each ruler had a different royal artist, and these artists (together with their patron kings) chose to depict these performances in particular styles. While Yajawte' K'inich's scribe preferred to portray the king dancing together with secondary members of his court (*ajk'uhuunob* and female attendants, usually identified by secondary glyphic texts), the master artist of K'inich Lamaw Ek' chose to paint the supernaturals only through the wild contorted dancing of the participants who impersonated these deities. Secondary texts identify these deities as *wayob* of specific divine rulers (Looper, Reents-Budet, and Bishop 2009, 138). Genital bloodletting was integrated into the *way*-impersonation dances as intimated by "bloodletters dangling from dancers' groins" and blood-stained paper in bowls (ibid.). The dancing, the bloodletting, and scenes of *wayob* vomiting on some Classic Maya vessels all hint that impersonation of the *way* required participants to achieve altered states of consciousness (Freidel, Schele and Parker 1993, 265–67; Looper, Reents-Budet, and Bishop 2009, 140).

How did these dance performances relate to political power? First, dances are depicted so often because they pervaded political rituals. In fact, Looper and colleagues (2009) assert that these vases underscore "the necessity of public performance and dance rituals by the assembled nobility for the legitimation of political authority" (149). If this is true, a good performance was very important, while a poor performance may have detracted from the ruler's authority. In addition, the necessity of turning in a good performance conferred a degree of political power on the audience because they were the ones who assessed how successful the performance was. This is an inherent weakness of using performances to bolster the leaders' power.

However, an overview of these scenes suggests that the power of the audience was limited because audiences are rarely shown as more than a few individuals, and these were probably elites. Were this audience more powerful, I suspect that larger groups would have been depicted together with the *k'uhul ajaw*. The scenes are also generally hierarchical in that the main protagonist (usually the highest-ranking lord or the *k'uhul ajaw*) is almost always easily identified by either a higher position on a throne or bench, by a frontal presentation of the torso and/or by the largest body mass in the scene, or by his more elaborate wardrobe.

Nevertheless, working against this strongly hierarchical structure, some Ik' Style vessels with few protagonists show little to no differentiation between the *k'uhul ajaw* and his companions (e.g., K534, K1399, K3464, K3054, K8889) (see Figures 6.1–6.3). Two vases, K8889 and K3054, which pertain to Yajawte' K'inich, depict all participants in ways that indicate their equality. For example, K8889 (Figure 6.1) records a gift-giving or tribute-presentation scene in which Yajawte' K'inich and three other lords are all seated on the same level with equally simple costumes. Two other vessels, K534 and K1399 (Figures 6.2 and 6.3), are late and pertain to ruler Yeh Te'

Figure 6.1. K8889, example of an Ik' Style vessel displaying a heterarchical positioning of rulers and other elites. Photograph © Justin Kerr.

Figure 6.2. K534, a second example of an Ik' Style vessel displaying a heterarchical positioning of rulers and other elites. Photograph © Justin Kerr.

K'ihnich II (who reigned ca. 781–96) (Tokovinine and Zender 2012). Vase K534 (Figure 6.2) depicts three dancers, but the central one is not Yeh Te' K'ihnich II; instead, it is a high-ranking noble, Yopaat Bahlam, who also carries the Ik' emblem glyph. Yeh Te' K'ihnich II is to the viewer's left (Tokovinine and Zender 2012; Reents-Budet et al. 2012). This late vase shows lower levels of craftsmanship than other Ik' Style vases and may have been painted by scribes that Yopaat Bahlam patronized rather than for Yeh Te' K'inich II. If indeed this vessel was made for Yopaat, it presents a political discourse that gives him a claim to equal status with Yeh Te' K'inich II. (See below for additional discussion of competing claims to power.) Another vase, K1399 (Figure 6.3), which also depicts Yeh Te' K'inich II, places all the dancers on the same level, and they all wear equally elaborate costumes. The main protagonist seems to be a high noble who is carrying the Ik' emblem glyph, and the secondary main protagonist is Yeh Te' K'inich II (Tokovinine and Zender 2012). Here there is little to no distinction between the king and his high-ranking companions. The discourse of this vase presents a more equal relationship between the ruler and the secondary elite. However, since these are unprovenienced vases, it is also possible that they are presenting the claims to power of secondary elites or claimants to the throne of Motul de San José rather than the political perspective of the paramount ruler (Tokovinine and Zender 2012). Reents-Budet et al. (2007, 2012) interpret these vases as hinting that the Motul de San José polity may have been a confederacy of several allied k'uhul ajaws.

Figure 6.3. K1399, a third example of an Ik' Style vessel displaying a heterarchical positioning of rulers and other elites. Photograph © Justin Kerr.

A few Ik' vases with dance-related scenes include a larger number of individuals. For example, vase K6341 (Figure 6.4) shows the interior of a palace with a strong-red throne, pink pillars, and three steps fronting the palace (Looper, Reents-Budet, and Bishop 2009, 142–43).[19] The ruler stands in front of the throne in the typical dance pose of lifted heel and with his

Figure 6.4. K6341, an Ik' Style vase depicting a palace scene from the royal court of Motul de San José. Photograph © Justin Kerr.

head turned toward his right.[20] He is facing three assistants. One holds his hand, possibly to help him off the throne or to stabilize him because of his ingestion of drugs; a second one is kneeling directly in front of him and appears to be applying paint to his already red body; and the third assistant is also kneeling and is holding a divining mirror into which the ruler is presumably looking (143). All three of these males are dressed in white; two of them have long white skirts and a tight white wrap around the head that extends stiffly forward and upward. These may be priestly accoutrements, possibly identifying these three assistants as *ajk'uhuuns*, according to Zender (2004). The kneeling attendants have red paint (or blood?) splattered on their faces and chests and down their fronts. To the left of the ruler and adjacent to the throne are two other males also dressed in long white skirts and the stiff white head wrap. One may be kneeling behind the throne, while the second is holding a huge fan attached to a long thin handle. A dwarf, also dressed in white, crouches on the lowest of the three steps in front of the throne.

The scene then moves laterally toward the ruler's far right (but the viewer's far left). Here two more elaborately dressed nobles are quite likely dancing (Looper, Reents-Budet, and Bishop 2009, 143), as both are making formalized graceful hand gestures with flexed wrists. They are possibly carrying weapons in their extended arms. Both objects have long thin handles, and one has an attached projectile point, and the other has a hook. The second dancer also stands in the lifted-heel pose. These two individuals are positioned on the lowest level of the scene, outside in the plaza fronting the palace. Although their head wraps are white, the rest of their attire is not and contrasts starkly to the white attire of the ruler and his attendants. However, they do not wear the heavy costumes that we see on warriors in the battle scenes in the Bonampak murals. Their bodies are partly or completely painted red (as is the body of the ruler, leading one to think that he is getting ready to join them in dance) (ibid.). They wear kilts wrapped around their midsections that have elaborate designs in black and red, one with jaguar skin elements and the other with Lamat signs. Long pieces of fabric drop from these kilts in front of and behind them (similar to the ruler's outfit). Directly above them, partly hidden behind a platform or a white curtain, two robust ladies sit or stand. Both are painted red and are wearing white gowns with a bull's-eye design.

The six attendants on this vase occupy an important position because they are the closest to the *k'uhul ajaw*. However, they are placed below the ruler (either through their position or their actions), so we can infer that they were seen as subsidiary to the king. If Zender (2004) is correct in his interpretation of the white headdresses and long kilts as ecclesiastical "uniforms," they are all members of the priesthood. Interestingly enough, the two ladies are placed higher than the ruler and are very visible in this sense, even though their bodies are partly hidden. Women appear on several other Ik' vases with their royal spouses or as ladies-in-waiting for the royal spouse.[21] This high visibility of royal and elite females in the Ik' style polychrome pottery corpus implies that females had political roles (or power) and that marriage alliances may have been an important strategy of political cohesion (and power) for the Motul de San José royalty.

The two dancers on this vase can be seen as the other important protagonists (or "power bloc"). On other vases, their structural position is taken by warriors who stand to the ruler's right (e.g., K8790, K3984, K680, Dumbarton Oaks vase LC-cb2–443). For example, vase K3984 (Figure 6.5) shows another royal court scene at Motul. In this case, a throne is placed high above three steps that lead down into the plaza. In the highest position, the ruler (possibly Yajawte' K'inich) sits crossed-legged on a bench covered by a jaguar pelt. His head and headdress intrude into the hieroglyphic text at the rim of the vase. Below him in the plaza sit two captives. To the ruler's left, a courtier or attendant stands on the second step of the palace, wearing a long white skirt painted with red designs. The ruler is looking toward his

Figure 6.5. K3984, an Ik' Style vase depicting a war presentation scene in the royal court of Motul de San José. Photograph © Justin Kerr.

right at two warriors who carry spears and rectangular shields. Both warriors wear similar attire: gruesome necklaces (or belts?) made of human heads, headdresses with huge fantastical animal heads, and long strips of cloth hanging between their legs. These elements of the warriors' costumes suggest preparations for dancing. The headdresses remind one of the *way*-impersonation dances described by Looper and colleagues (2009); the long textile strips that swing and almost touch the ground are reminiscent of the attire of the two dancers on vase K6341. In this scene, the warriors occupy more visual space than the ruler: Yajawte' K'inich is quite small and his costume is not as flamboyant as that of the warriors. Similarly, the ruler's attendant is much larger than the ruler.[22] However, the hierarchical organization is maintained in the vertical direction: Yajawte' sits at the apex of the scene.

From these two representative examples of the few extant Ik' vessels that portray many individuals, we can surmise that the overlapping groups (or factions) of warriors, secondary elites, courtesans, and priests formed central power blocs that operated hierarchically on some occasions and in more equal ways in other instances (see further discussion below). The courtiers, wives, ladies-in-waiting, and warriors not only attended to the needs of the ruler (exhibiting a hierarchical arrangement) but also saw or witnessed (or, more important, watched) his political affairs (exhibiting a more heterarchical political arrangement).

Feasting as Political Performance

Ethnohistories and ethnographies of Conquest period, Colonial, and early twentieth-century Mayas of Yucatan speak of feasts that were celebrated at important rites of passage, political events, and points in the calendrical-ritual cycle (Tozzer 1941; Roys 1943; McAnany 1995; Redfield and Villa Rojas 1934; Foias 2002). Landa describes the enormous quantities of food involved in elite feasting in sixteenth-century Yucatan: "And to each guest they give a roasted fowl, bread and drink of cacao in abundance" (Tozzer 1941, 92; see also LeCount 2001). Maya commoners also engaged in feasting that took place at significant points in each individual's life and at important rituals that related to sacred cycles or ancestral celebrations that created and reproduced the identity of the kin group or of the community (Redfield and Villa Rojas 1934; McAnany 1995, 2010, 131–32).

Just like their descendants in Yucatan in the sixteenth century, the Classic Maya also engaged in feasting. As mentioned above, food and drink are depicted in palace or court scenes on many Classic polychrome pots, and the verb "to drink" appears in some of their texts (Reents-Budet 2000; Houston and Stuart 2001; Foias 2007). During these feasts, elite guests would have presumably been fed large amounts of food and drink, all served in polychrome vessels: vases for beverages, bowls for soups and stews, and tripod plates for solid foods such as tamales (Reents-Budet, Ball, and Kerr 1994; Houston, Stuart and Taube 1989). Massive middens that suggest rapid deposition after periodical feasting have been uncovered next to palaces, ball courts, and houses at a number of Maya sites (Reents-Budet 2000; LeCount 2001; Brown 2001; Hendon 2003; Wells 2007; Halperin and Foias 2010, 2012; Moriarty 2012).This evidence supports the theory that feasting was important in Classic Maya society.

I turn to polychrome pottery feasting scenes to consider how the Maya elite conceived of and portrayed them. One of the Ik' Style polychromes, K1453, records such a scene (Figure 6.6). The main protagonist (Sihyaj K'awiil, an eighth-century Motul de San José ruler who probably preceded Yajawte' K'inich) is seated on a bench with his back resting against a large pillow. He is surrounded by six courtier-attendants, of which two are dwarves and two others appear to be deformed. Three musicians are visible only through their instruments, which emerge into the scene on the far right: two long trumpets and a conch shell. The Motul k'uhul ajaw is remarkable both because of the simplicity of his costume (which contrasts with the elaborateness of the attire of rulers in monumental stone art) and the very lengthy nails on his right hand, which would certainly have prevented him from doing any kind of manual labor and are thus evidence of a life of leisure. A tiny dwarf (a statue?) kneels on the bench in front of the king and holds a mirror that may have been used for divination (Reents-Budet 2001). The king is facing three individuals. A second dwarf on the floor below the bench drinks from a wide bowl, and behind him (to the viewer's left) sit an older hunchbacked priest (his occupation marked by his white stiff headdress and white long skirt) and a younger man with a bunch of flowers in his hand and a stone pendant around his neck. Two attendants are positioned behind the king (to the viewer's right). A young man peeks from behind the king's pillow and may represent his bodyguard. The second attendant is another priest who is certainly older than the young man and may be deformed. He holds a bunch of feathers in his hand, as does the king. Four of these individuals have scribal pens stuck in their headdresses, another indication that they are ajk'uhuuns (Coe and Kerr 1997), although that identification is not spelled out in the hieroglyphs next to each figure.

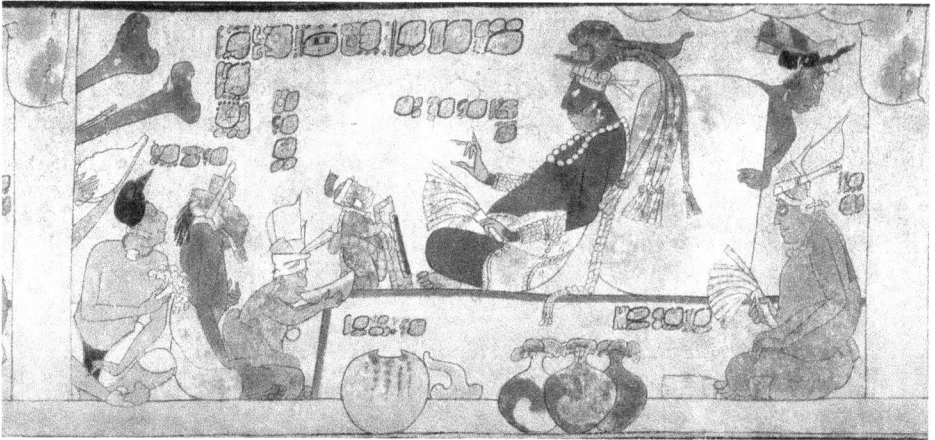

Figure 6.6. K1453, an Ik' Style vase showing a feast in the court of Motul's ruler Sihyaj K'awiil. Photograph © Justin Kerr.

Below the bench are the central elements of the feast: three jars with some foamy liquid emerging from the mouth of each and a large vessel with its lid removed and placed next to it. Another small vessel may be on the ground in front of the legs of the old priest on the viewer's far right. The small size of the gathering intimates that the actors with political and ritual power were few. The musicians don't even "deserve" to be depicted.

Gifts were given out at both elite and commoner feasts in Postclassic to modern times (Foias 2002, 239). Landa describes such gift-giving: "At the end of the repast, they were accustomed to give a manta to each to wear, and a little stand and vessel, as beautiful as possible" (Tozzer 1941, 92). Redfield and Villa Rojas (1934) record the types of gifts that were given by the groom's family to the bride's family in the early twentieth-century Yucatec village of Chan Kom: "a gold chain 'of two loops,' two rings of specified quality, two hair ribbons, one silk handkerchief, several meters of cotton cloth, two or three silver pesos, rum, bread, chocolate and cigarettes" (193; see also Foias 2002, 2007; LeCount 2001).

The Classic Maya may also have given similar gifts. The strongest evidence for this is that the most fancy of the polychrome vessels are generally found in restricted contexts (usually the tombs of the upper elite) at sites a long way from the homes of the scribes-artisans who painted them. The crafting of these valuables, which were likely given as gifts (including jade and marine shell jewelry which would be the pre-Hispanic antecedents of the "gold chain 'of two loops'" that Redfield and Villa Rojas recorded), involved specialized knowledge, major labor investments, and/or nonlocal raw materials, all of which suggests that they were produced or obtained via long-distance trade under the patronage of elites (Reents-Budet 1998, 2000; Inomata 2001b; Foias 2002, 2007; McAnany 2010). If these gifts were required at all feasts (both commoner and elite), the nobles' broader access to such restricted valuables would have given them significant social and political power over the non-elite (Foias 2002, 239–40; Rathje 1972, 1975, 2002; Saitta 1994; Graham 2002).

McAnany (2010) describes the significant political overtones of feasting: "Feasting is a performance not only of household productive capabilities but also of alliance structures between households. . . . [It] reveals political schisms and struggles for hegemony" (133; see also Foias 2007). Feasting mobilized labor and resources from many people, but the host of the feast controlled these resources and could decide to use them for his or her own purposes instead of in ways that benefited the community at large. The additional resources the host gained during these feasts were an added bonus to the social gain that came from the feast participants' perception that their host was very generous in giving the feast. This perception of generosity is most visible, while the host's more selfish uses of the additional resources gained is less visible, if not invisible (Wells 2007; Roscoe 1993).

In some cases, feasts could impoverish households for years (Vogt 1976; Cancian 1965), but the gains in power may have been substantial. Wells (2007) has emphasized that Maya feasting as a performance can assert and reinforce the social status (and social power) of the host. I have also argued that Classic Maya feasting as a performance could have elevated the power of the hosting k'uhul ajaw by tying the participants to him through the creation of debts to him or simply because of the intense desire of the attendees to be close to a divine ruler (Foias 2007; see also Schortman and Urban 2004; and a critique in Saitta 1994). Hendon (2003) has shown that feasting was practiced more frequently by lower-level nobles than higher-level elites at Copan as they attempted to gain more social status (and social power) than their high-level "cousins." In other words, feasting was another strategy that elite households could use to gain social (and presumably political) power.

Summary

Political rituals such as dancing and feasting served to institute (but could also redefine) the relations of power, the terms and rules through which power was achieved, and the arenas in which power was materialized.

Although most Ik' Style polychromes present a hierarchical perspective in which political power was held in the hands of the few, a small group of Ik' Style vases show little distinction between the *k'uhul ajaw* and his companions. The latter vases promote a competing discourse that highlights the high status of subsidiary elites or possibly an elite identity based on greater equality between the *k'uhul ajaw* and the other nobles. These vessels may have been commissioned by secondary elites who used them to present themselves in a more heterarchical relationship with the *k'uhul ajaw* as a way of subverting the dominant ideology (see further discussion below). These subsidiary aristocrats may have held their own feasts and given these pots as gifts to their guests.

All these performances, though, have economic costs. Dances, feasts, and gift-giving required considerable agricultural surplus, the creation of valuables to be given as gifts, women's labor to cook the food and prepare the beverages, and the construction of all the platforms, palaces, temples, pyramids where the performances took place (see discussion of these economic costs for modern Maya in Vogt 2007, Bunzel 1981). Therefore, political performances entail control over economic resources, but not necessarily control over all of the economy.

Collective Action and Councils in Classic Maya States

Current views that see political power as a relational phenomenon in the hands of all groups in human society bring back into focus the importance of examining collective action and the role of negotiation between the rulers and the ruled through the existence of elite councils, non-elite assemblies, and limits on the ruler's behavior in premodern societies. As discussed in Chapter 2, Blanton and Fargher (2008) found many societies with collective institutions in their cross-cultural survey of premodern, noncapitalist states. They call a society a "collective polity" "in which the government . . . provides services . . . in exchange for the revenues (including labor) provided by compliant taxpayers" (13). Blanton and Fargher argue that collective polities form when major negotiations are necessary between rulers and taxpayers over resources needed to support the state (14). If rulers depend significantly on internal revenue controlled by the taxpayers, commoners will be able to bargain with the rulers and demand a voice in the government of the polity (ibid.). If rulers depend mostly on external revenue, such as foodstuffs from state-controlled land, external warfare or taxation of international trade, they will be unwilling to bargain with the taxpayers, who will correspondingly have little or no voice in the political decision making (112–16).

We can attempt to assess if the Classic Maya depended on external revenue (or "free floating" resources, as Eisenstadt 1993 and Yoffee 2005 refer to them) or on internal income. As described in Chapter 5, the revenue base of Classic Maya states consisted of two major components: 1) production within the palace economy (production by members of the royal palace within the royal court at each capital city but also probably on estates controlled by the ruler); 2) a tax-tribute system in which a fraction of the agricultural or craft production or labor of each household or community is levied as tax to support political leaders (Webster 2001; Foias 2002; Rice 2009; McAnany 2010; Foias and Emery 2012). These components are distinct in that the palace economy of the rulers can be considered external revenue (independent of the taxpayers), while the tax-tribute system is internal revenue (dependent on the number of taxpayers, the amount of surplus production of the taxpayers, and the willingness of taxpayers to pay). It is imperative that we assess the significance of each of these components because they affected the power of the non-elite to bargain with rulers.

Pollock (1999) has considered the emergent royal palace and temple *oikoi* (great households) in Early Dynastic Mesopotamia as a strategy for survival in a political environment with high tribute volatility, presumably because of resistance by taxpayers. In other words, the *oikoi* were a much more stable form of state revenue than taxation. In addition, Blanton and Fargher (2008) assert that external revenue can be controlled by a small number of administrators, while internal revenue requires much larger bodies of officials (120). The excavation data from Motul de San José have given hints about the relative importance of the palace economy and tax-tribute revenues (Halperin 2008; Emery 2012; Foias et al. 2012). Halperin (2008) suggests that textiles were produced more frequently in the royal households than in the rest of the habitational groups, evidence that would put more weight on the side of the palace economy. However, Foias et al. (2012) and Emery (2012) have proposed that maize processing and hunting were more common among the smaller households than in the royal compounds, suggesting that corn flour and animal products were extracted through taxation from taxpayers and transferred into the royal coffers. This reconstruction suggests a balanced use of both external and internal revenues, and if we apply Blanton's and Fargher's argument, the evidence suggests that collective institutions such as councils were a component of the political arena of some Classic polities where the balance in revenue may have swung toward more internal sources (see below and Ringle and Bey 2001). Even though councils have generally been ignored by scholars because archaeological evidence in support of their existence is scarce, evidence of them has been found in some Classic and many later Maya polities.

We have archaeological evidence that councils existed as early as the Late Classic. Barbara Fash and her colleagues (1992) have identified Structure 10L-22A in the epicenter of Copan as a council house based on the prominent mat designs on its four facades. Council houses were called *popol na* (or *popol naah*) in Maya languages, or "house of the mat" (ibid.). The council house at Copan was probably built in the mid-eighth century by the fifteenth ruler of Copan, Smoke Monkey (K'ahk' Joplaj Chan K'awiil), who ruled following Quirigua's capture of the fourteenth ruler, 18 Rabbit (Waxaklahuun Ubaah K'awiil) (ibid.; Martin and Grube 2008, 200).[23] According to Fash and her colleagues, Smoke Monkey responded to this political crisis not by pursuing the "cult of personality" that characterized previous Copan rulers and most other Classic Maya polities but by building the council house "where the representatives of the polity's major subdivisions could have a voice" (437). In this manner, Smoke Monkey was committing the "'local chieftains' to supporting the centralized authority structure" and "was also holding them responsible for what was to come" (ibid.).

Eight powerful nobles are carved on the facades and sides of this building, sitting on top of eight different glyphs. These are not portraits of any Copan rulers, so they must have been other important figures, and the glyphs on which they sit hint at their identity. The glyphs appear to be place-names related to locations in the Copan Valley, and therefore it seems likely that they represent eight main divisions of the Copan polity and that the elite males sitting on the glyphs are portraits of the heads of these divisions. Fash and colleagues discuss the possible political office held by these eight nobles through ethnohistorical analogy with the Postclassic polities the Spanish conquistadors encountered in the sixteenth century. They may be *holpop* ("heads of the mat," or heads of small towns close to the capital) or they may be *batab* ("governors of large towns far afield from the center of the kingdom," similar to the Classic title of *sajal*) (439; see discussion of these titles in Chapter 4 and Table 4.1). Fash and colleagues prefer the first title because of the connection with the mat sign seen on Structure 10L-22A and on all council houses in the Maya area. They also intimate that these *holpops* may have had ritual functions in addition to their administrative or political roles: "One might argue that the individuals portrayed above the hieroglyphs . . . were charged with the rites and obligations needed for the perpetuation or care of certain designated supernatural realms" (432).They base this interpretation on ethnohistorical evidence that the *holpop* were closely tied to feasting cycles (including the organization of dances) and on textual evidence that one of the place glyphs on Structure 10L-22A is named on Quirigua Stela 10 as a supernatural locale (ibid.). The location of Structure 10L-22A in the epicore of Copan gives us a final clue to its role. Instead of being sited on the Main Plaza, which was much more public and more easily accessible to commoners, it was positioned in the more restricted and private East Court. Therefore, this was not a "democratic" institution that involved the participation of a wide segment of Maya society but one that was restricted to the elite rank drawn from all parts of Copan's realm. The interpretation of Fash and her colleagues of Copan Structure 10L-22A as a council house has not gone without critique: Wagner (2000) and Plank (2004) propose a ritual function for the building as an ancestral shrine based on the identification of the place-names on the facades with Underworld locations. Plank (2004) suggests that the depicted figures on top of the place-names are variants of the god Bolon K'awiil (104, 136–41). She concludes her critique with: "If the mat device signifies a house of assembly, it is probably an assembly-house for supernaturals, important ancestors and patron gods" (141).

Evidence for council houses becomes strong during the Terminal Classic and Postclassic periods at sites in the northern Maya lowlands. Ringle and Bey (2001) examine the architecture of Uxmal and Mayapan to illustrate how elite lineages (or "houses") and their councils were central to political organization. At Mayapan, temple assemblages or temple courtyards are important features in the epicenter, and Ringle and Bey argue that their number (11) is very close if not identical to the number of priests who ruled Mayapan (12), according to Bishop Landa (Tozzer 1941, 40).[24] Furthermore, the 23 colonnaded halls (open buildings supported by rows of pillars) clustered around the Main Group at Mayapan accords well with the number of provinces that were part of Mayapan's confederacy (Milbrath and Peraza Lope 2003, 9). These colonnaded halls, with their spacious and open interior spaces, may have hosted councils of the elite lineages (or houses) that were dominant in each province (ibid.; Ringle and Bey 2001). Landa

(Tozzer 1941) records oral traditions that describe the Mayapan council as consisting of the principal ruler and subsidiary dignitaries who represented towns, provinces, and/or provincial dominant elite lineages.

If indeed the colonnaded halls were council houses (*popol na*), the broad distribution of such buildings across the northern Maya lowlands would suggest that council institutions were common during the Terminal Classic and later times (Ringle and Bey 2001). This interpretation is also supported by Spanish ethnohistorical documents that record councils. Roys (1943) describes powerful councils in Yucatan composed of *ah cuch cabs*, who were individuals elected (or named by the *batabs*) as representatives of the *cuchteel* (wards or barrios in each town) (63; Ringle and Bey 2001, 270).[25] These councils advised the *batabs* (governors of the towns) within each Yucatan polity in the sixteenth century.

As mentioned in Chapter 4, Jones (1998, 83–107) also describes the important governing council of the Peten Itza Maya kingdom, whose capital was on the island of Nojpeten (modern Flores, Peten, Guatemala). This kingdom was not conquered by the Spanish until AD 1697–1704. A meeting hall, or *popol na*, was attached to the royal palace on the west side of the capital island (71). The governing council that met in this *popol na* consisted of 23 individuals: the paramount ruler (Ajaw Kan Ek'), the high priest (AjK'in Kan Ek'), eight provincial rulers (two for each of the four provinces of the Peten Itza realm), and 13 additional nobles bearing the title of *ach kat* (103–4). The eight provincial governors represented the four provinces of the core area of the Itza kingdom, while the 13 *ach kats* "represented outlying towns or territories as military chiefs and possibly as k'atun priests" (ibid.). Jones writes that the provincial governors also had the "role [of] high priests of deity cults" (104). This is supported by the number of temples and smaller shrines the Spanish found at Nojpeten (73). Nine temples, probably one for each of the eight provincial ruler-priests and one for the paramount ruler Ajaw Kan Ek' and the high priest AjK'in Kan Ek', were dispersed throughout the island. In addition, 12 smaller shrines were present, very close to the number of *ach kats* who served on the governing council.

Kowalski (2007) proposes that Chichen Itza also was ruled by a governing council that met in the Temple of Warriors and its antecedent, the Temple of the Chacmool. Large benches that could host several dozen dignitaries are a central feature of the inner chamber of the Temple of the Warriors, while within the Temple of the Chacmool, murals painted on similar benches depict 27 aristocratic figures, some dressed like dignitaries and priests (on the south bench) and others like warriors (on the north bench) (285–87). Many of the dignitaries on the south bench carry God K scepters that in the Classic world of the southern lowlands were the symbols of the k'uhul ajaw. Based on the resemblances between these figures and the composition of the Peten Itza governing council, Kowalski suggests that the dignitaries on the south bench were provincial governors, while the warriors on the north bench were military chiefs of conquered zones, like the ach kats of the Peten Itza Maya.[26]

Thus, councils were a feature of ancient Maya politics starting possibly in the Classic period, and became much more widespread in the Terminal Classic and Postclassic. If these councils existed in polities of the Classic period, they were another power bloc that would have competed with the other political factions of the k'uhul ajaw, nonroyal aristocrats, priests, and warriors (although there may have been some overlap between these groups).

Competing Claims to Power, Contested Political Power: From Figurines to Pots to Monuments

Political organizations are characterized by contestation between competitors and factions rather than static quantities of power and obedient individuals ("subjects") who always follow the rules and expectations of political institutions. To explore the nature of these contestations, I examine different forms of Classic Maya art, from tiny figurines to small polychrome vessels to public or monumental stonework. The themes found in these three art forms at each site provide evidence of the foundations of power of its blocs (or factions) and of competing discourses about power within each faction. Comparing the themes of the major stone monuments (stelae), small media (polychrome vases), and tiny media (figurines) will highlight competing depictions, discourses, and ideologies of power and legitimacy (Halperin 2007, 2012; Brumfiel 1996, 2006; Joyce 1993, 1996, 2000).

Figurines

Classic Maya figurines are found in many locations, from small households to large palaces. They were probably used in multiple ways, including in household rituals, in household performances of myths and/or historical events, or even as children's toys (Halperin 2007; Halperin et al. 2009; R. Joyce

2000; Triadan 2007). Because of their broad distribution and the likelihood that they were produced in both commoner and elite households, they are the best examples of the perspective of the populace and the themes they present were possibly closest to the concerns of Maya commoners.

In her now-classic study of figurines in the Aztec Empire, Brumfiel (1996) found that negative female gender ideologies of the Aztec state were resisted in conquered regions, where figurines highlighted females and their reproductive abilities.[27] Rosemary Joyce (1992, 1996, 2000) has examined gender ideologies among the Classic Maya, contrasting the gendered identities and practices promoted in state ideologies in public stone art with the household ideologies presented in figurines. While Classic Maya figurines present female social identity as defined by productive activities (such as weaving and grinding corn) or reproductive activities (such as caring for children), stone monuments present a distinct female identity for elite women through scenes in which queens participate in ritual activities, complementing the roles of their male companions and rulers (Joyce 1992).

However, there are differences in the images recorded in figurines from site to site, as exemplified by studies at Motul de San José and Aguateca. In contrast to Brumfiel's and Joyce's findings that figurines champion non-elites and women, Halperin's (2007) analysis of the figurine-whistles at Motul de San José found that one of "the most pervasive themes [among these tiny artifacts] . . . is ritual performance, a theme that cross-cuts and shows conceptual overlap between all . . . figurine categories" (224–25; see also Halperin 2012). The ritual performances portrayed over and over again in monumental stone art during the Classic period are without doubt the "public transcript" of the dominant state ideology (Scott 1990), but at Motul, this "public transcript" is replicated in the popular ideology promoted by figurines generally used in the more private contexts of the household. For example, one of the more common anthropomorphic figurine types at Motul shows rulers (or, less likely, high-status elites) wearing elaborate War Serpent headdresses; because such images are also immortalized on stelae, it is obvious that these figurines eulogize official state rituals (Halperin 2004, 2007).

Supplementing this penetration of state ideology into the discourse of the figurines is the discovery of 18 sets of matching figurines produced in the same mold. Their distribution across the landscape strongly suggests that Motul's Acropolis was the main distributor of these figurines to smaller sites across a six-kilometer radius, because 17 of these matched sets include one or more figurines from the site core (Halperin 2007, 282–83; Halperin et al. 2009). Thus, it appears that the royal elite of Motul de San José shared many of their figurines (which probably were used in rituals) with a broad spectrum of the polity's members, possibly in an attempt to create a common polity identity based on the performances involving these figurine-whistles (Halperin 2007; Triadan 2007; see also LeCount 2010 for the use of pottery to create a common polity identity at Xunantunich).

Although female figurines are found at many Maya sites, the dominant themes in this art form differ from site to site. For example, images of women cooking or weaving are absent in Motul's figurine corpus, although they were popular at other Maya sites. Instead, females are shown holding bowls of tamales (in nine cases), which can be seen as highlighting household food production and/or preparation. But this visual content may also refer to "activities of the market, or ceremonial food serving and consumption" (Halperin 2007, 225), especially since one of the more frequent female headdresses at Motul is the broad-brimmed hat (24 cases) known from iconographic, ethnohistorical and ethnographic studies to be worn by market women, traders, pilgrims, and hunters (Taube 1992; Halperin 2007).[28] It is worth noting here that research in soil chemistry has suggested that one of the main plazas at Motul de San José (Plaza II, see Figure 4.4) located north of the Acropolis was a market (Bair and Terry 2012). Furthermore, the largest plaza (Plaza V) at Trinidad, Motul's port on the north shore of Lake Peten Itza, may also have been a market (Dahlin et al. 2009). Thus, it is possible that marketing was an important activity at Motul and in its polity, which would have given commoner women public roles and venues for gaining status and possibly economic resources.

Even more significantly, there are differences between the "public transcript" promoted in stone monuments and the more popular or "hidden transcript" promoted in Motul figurines. Here we see hints of competing ideologies between the ruler and the ruled. Aside from the depiction of the ruler in some Motul figurines, most of the supernaturals and zoomorphs immortalized in these small objects "do not represent formal deities of Maya state religion . . . but appear to have been popular mythological characters, ritual clowns, and possibly spirit companions [wayob]" linked to the Uayeb New Year's Carnival-like ceremonies (Halperin 2007, 225–266; see also Taube 1989). Triadan (2007) suggests that in Aguateca, these figurines may have been used in household rituals that recounted important myths. They also likely played roles in wider festivals or rituals, since many of the figurines at Motul were found in public plazas or next to monumental public architecture (Halperin 2007, 290–91). However, most of the Motul figurines were found in household contexts. Because the household figurines emphasize different deities than the royal gods that are depicted in the Classic Maya "public transcripts," we can conclude that Maya households promoted their own rituals, and possibly these household rituals competed with state rituals in providing access to the supernatural.

A different constellation of themes is present in clay figurines of Aguateca, a Late Classic Maya center in the Petexbatun region. The figurines there depict males more than females, and most often these males are warriors (Triadan 2007). Triadan argues that this may be due to the increasing conflict in the Petexbatun region that culminated in the burning and rapid abandonment of Aguateca's core (see also Inomata 2008). The focus on male warriors among Aguateca's figurines suggests that state ideology pervaded household concerns to a significant degree, as it did at Motul de San José, or that rituals surrounding warfare and warriors were important to both the state and to members of both commoner and elite households.

Elaborate Polychrome Pottery

When we turn our attention to the polychrome vases painted with elaborate court scenes and texts (as in the Ik' Style produced at Motul de San José), we are entering another level of the competing political discourses and ideologies in Classic Maya states. While figurines were widely distributed in elite and commoner households and therefore present a broad popular ideology of power and legitimacy, elaborate polychrome vessels were produced by only a few elite scribe-artisans who were learned in the arts of writing, mythology, and religion. They were also consumed by a select group of elites and therefore expressed their ideology and concerns.[29]

Echoing Reents-Budet (2001; Reents-Budet, Ball, and Kerr 1994), Halperin (2007, 224) is struck by the simple dress and small headdresses of rulers on polychrome vases, in contrast to the heavy and elaborate costumes of rulers depicted on stone monuments. It is possible that the rulers understated their wealth and political influence on these vessels in an attempt to create a common identity among elites, in contrast to the imagery on stelae that portray the ruler in the larger-than-life role as a god. Alternatively, if secondary elites commissioned these pots, it is they who were understating the wealth and political influence of the ruler and claiming that their status was equal to that of the *k'uhul ajaw*. The individuals who painted these vessels were not the rulers themselves but the *ajk'uhuuns* or priestly scribes who are shown so often near or in attendance to their lord. The artist would have negotiated with the kingly patron about which scene to present and which individuals to depict, and this would have given the *ajk'uhuuns* a degree of power.

Depicting important courtiers with rulers with few differences in accoutrements (see Figures 5.3 and 6.1–6.6) not only created a common identity for the elite but also enhanced the position of these nonroyal elites. These depictions also served to bind these nobles to the ruler; members of the lower elite likely wanted constant reinforcement of their status and their connection to the ruler, and the best way to obtain it was through invited participation in the feasts and performances recorded on these vases (Foias 2007). The elaborateness of the pots suggests significant competition among the elites for the reward of being seen and being painted with the ruler, similar to the fierce competition among the Persian courtiers for the honor of sitting at the table of the Achaemenid emperor (Kuhrt 2001; Foias 2007).[30]

These vessels would have been critical "participants" in restricted (competitive) feasts given by the rulers and other members of the elite class. Not only were these vessels used to serve food and drink during the feasts, they were also given as gifts to guests at the ends of feasts (Tozzer 1941; Reents-Budet, Ball, and Kerr 1994; Reents-Budet 1998, 2000; Halperin and Foias 2010). Thus, Maya nobles needed artisans who could create these beautiful polychrome pots, which became symbols of political unity when they were given as gifts at the sumptuous feasts they hosted. Landa states that in the Postclassic, these elite feasts were competitive, status-enhancing, and status-reinforcing performances (Tozzer 1941), and this must also have been the case in the Late Classic polities. One piece of evidence that supports the notion of competitive feasting is the range of skill levels we see in these elaborate polychromes. For example, within the Ik' Style, Reents-Budet and colleagues (1994) have defined at least four subgroups. Groups 1 and 4 display the highest skill and were signed by the royal scribes of the two most successful Motul de San José divine rulers, Yajawte' K'inich and K'inich Lamaw Ek', who reigned during the eighth century AD. Groups 2 and 3 display less talent, and because of slight differences in the chemical composition of their pastes from those of Groups 1 and 4, they may have been made and painted by scribes attached to lower-level courts at secondary centers in Motul's realm or sphere of influence (Reents-Budet, Ball, and Kerr 1994; Reents-Budet et al. 2007; Reents-Budet et al. 2012). As mentioned above, we also have evidence for the competitiveness of feasting from Copan, where the lower-status elite households invested in more feasting than higher-status elite groups (Hendon 1991, 2003). These threads of evidence for elite competition suggest that the elaborate Late Classic Maya polychromes not only reflected but actively created and manipulated intense competition and factionalism among court elites (Halperin and Foias 2010). Certain elaborate vessels could be brought out to mark alliances with one group and then put away when another group visited and claims of allegiance to that group were presented in a different set of polychrome vessels.

Regardless of whether the understatement of the ruler's political power on polychrome vessels was due to his own intentional planning or to the machinations of aristocrats, I suggest that the end result was the same: the "public transcript" presented on these polychrome pots is one of a common unified elite identity. If this is true, these vessels tell us how the elite defined themselves and what their main concerns were. As described above, the most common scenes on the Ik' Polychrome Style vessels depict rituals, including dances of transformation into gods or celebrations of war victories, ritual dressing, presentations of captives or of tribute, and feasting. The political valence of these rituals cannot be denied, and so we can say that the elite identity was defined politico-ritually. This brings to mind modern Maya communities, such as Chichicastenango, where the civic officials saw their positions as embedded in both the political and religious realms. Political civic service was in many senses also religious service (Bunzel 1981).

It is important to note, though, that once we shift our purview to other Classic Maya polychrome pottery styles, such as the Holmul Style, the Tikal Dancer Style, the Turkey Vulture Plate Style, the Chama Style, the Altun Ha Style, and the Codex Style (Reents-Budet, Ball, and Kerr 1994), the palace or court scenes with more heterarchical power schemes just about disappear (with a few exceptions; for example, the Chama Style). Instead, the polychromes outside Motul de San José focus on just one figure (the ruler involved in rituals in some cases or a supernatural in other cases). Thus, the Ik' Style is an innovation in that it depicts so many secondary elites. This innovation probably accomplished two things: it created an elite identity and it gave secondary elites recognition and rewards for loyalty to and support of the king. So while the royals across the Maya lowlands generally expressed the same concerns in polychrome vessels as they did on stone monuments, the Motul royal family had another overarching concern: control over the elite, presumably through the creation of this common identity and through permanent recognition of secondary elites by depicting them on Ik' Style vessels. However, these pottery vessels could then be used by secondary elites to pursue their own political agenda, which may have differed from that of the Motul royal dynasty. Although this strategy may have worked initially to provide cohesion to a strong elite class, it failed over the long term because it diluted the power of the k'uhul ajaw. The symbols of power were slowly dispersed to the entire aristocratic rank.

Stone Monuments

The monumental art of the Classic Maya has been described in many treatises (Miller 1999; Miller and Martin 2004; Coe and Kerr 1997; Schele and Miller 1986; Schele and Freidel 1990; Freidel, Schele, and Parker 1993). This art portrays rulers and queens (and almost no one else) in stone stelae, altars, lintels, and panels found in public locales, such as plazas, or in more private ones, such as the interiors of palaces and temple-pyramids. It promotes a dominant ideology focused on the k'uhul ajaw, or divine ruler. For this reason, a number of Maya scholars have referred to these ideologies as "cults of personality" (Fash et al. 1992; Chase, Chase, and Smith 2009).

The images and texts on stone monuments inscribe the events and rituals of the lives of royals: birth and death, accession to the throne, bloodletting rituals and sacrifices of human captives, ritual (or triumphal) dances and processions, communication with the gods (by embodying or materializing these deities), and a variety of other religious events. Little or no mention is made of economic affairs or commoners. The exceptions are the rare references to tribute in images of bundles.

Of course there is variation among sites, as we saw in the case of figurines and polychromes. Yaxchilan and to a lesser degree Piedras Negras, both of which are major polities along the Usumacinta River, are exceptional in that their monuments depict subsidiary elites (Schele and Freidel 1990; Tate 1992; Martin and Grube 2008). For example, Yaxchilan Lintels 42, 6, and 8 show ruler Bird Jaguar IV and his first sajal (baah sajal) K'an Tok Wayib participating in different rituals and taking captives (see Schele and Freidel 1990, Figure 7.15; Martin and Grube 2008, 130–31). Schele and Freidel (1990) argue that Bird Jaguar IV was a relatively late son of his father and was quite unlikely to rise to the throne. However, he was successful in his intrigues, possibly in part due to his alliances with local sajals, who he then rewarded with monuments. Alliances made through marriage also figure prominently during Bird Jaguar IV's reign. Four queens are immortalized in monuments with Bird Jaguar, one from Hix Witz (the kingdom that encompassed Zapote Bobal, El Pajaral, and La Joyanca along the San

Pedro Martir River), two from Motul de San José (which was known to have been allied with Hix Witz; Tokovinine and Zender 2012), and a local lady from a powerful noble *sajal* lineage (Martin and Grube 2008, 131). The point to be drawn from Yaxchilan's monuments is that Maya monuments present several different discourses on power and legitimacy, just as figurines and polychromes do. In some polities, such as Tikal, cults of personality were dominant, while in other polities, such as Yaxchilan, cooperation between the divine rulers and secondary elites was depicted in the "public transcript."

In rare cases, Classic stone monuments depicted many actors. The most famous is probably Panel 3 of Piedras Negras, which portrays a dozen or so elites in a celebration for Ruler 4 in AD 749 but was created almost fifty years later by Ruler 7, his descendant (ibid., 149). The gathered aristocrats include not only local nobles but also foreign guests, who are carefully named on the panel. The local nobles are headed by a *baah sajal* and include an *aj k'uhuun*, while the foreign contingent hails from Yaxchilan, including presumably its ruler, Yopaat Bahlam. The celebration involved both dancing and the drinking of chocolate, or *kakaw*. Two other panels from Piedras Negras (Panel 12 and Panel 2) depict larger tableaux, the first of Ruler C with four captives and the second of another ruler (possibly Turtle Tooth) and his heir and subsidiary nobles who are kneeling before the ruler and his heir (ibid.). However, the rest of the Piedras Negras monuments conform to the dominant Late Classic pattern of depicting only the king or queen.

The six stelae of Motul de San José are typical of Classic monumental art. They portray one or two main royal figures, sometimes accompanied by tiny dwarves. Stelae 4 and 6 depict the Motul *k'uhul ajaw* standing and holding the God K scepter, a scene very similar (if not identical) to the scenes in Stelae 1, 14, and 15 at Dos Pilas (Houston 1993; discussed above in the section on dancing). Stelae 2 and 5 at Motul show paired lords richly attired with massive headdresses, heavy necklaces, and God C kilts, and they are also holding God K scepters and incense bags. A central text on these stelae is carved between the two lords. Tokovinine and Zender (2012) have deciphered the better-preserved section on Stela 2, which records the Itsimte lord Juun Tsak Took' and his participation in a dance with Motul's ruler, probably K'inich Lamaw Ek' (as mentioned above). Stela 5 may show the same scene or another dance of alliance between the *k'uhul ajaw* of Motul and the ruler of another polity. It is impossible to know what the remaining two Motul stelae recorded, as they are heavily fragmented and eroded. One of these, Stela 1, has a long, partially preserved text that describes one of the earliest known rulers of Motul, Yeh Te' K'inich, acceding to the throne under the patronage of Hasaw Chan K'awiil of Tikal (ibid.). The image of Yeh Te' K'inich may have been carved on the front side of Stela 1, but the carving is completely eroded.

Although Motul's stelae are typical in their focus on the figure of the divine king, the two stelae with paired rulers are less traditional and underscore the importance of alliances for Motul's dynasty. Even though the hieroglyphic texts are heavily eroded, the carved images on Motul's stelae portray more peaceful rituals undertaken by the divine kings and do not depict their involvement in warfare. However, Looper's (2009) argument that the dances with the God K scepter are victory celebrations suggests that the Motul monuments are also tied to war. Motul de San José has fewer stelae than other political capitals. It may be the case that this is not because of a low rate of preservation; it may be a consequence of the power of the elite families of Motul, who may have been able to limit the king's cult of personality and instead create an elite identity that was expressed through the Ik' Style polychrome vessels described above.

Discussion

In summary, the discourses revealed in the stone, polychrome pottery, and figurine art of the Classic period indicate a variety of constellations of power (*sensu* Smith 2003) because each polity had to deal with different configurations of political struggles and factions. Concerns about war with other polities (and possible military factions within polities?) seem to have been of great importance at Aguateca in the highly militarized southwestern part of Peten (Triadan 2007; Inomata 2007). In contrast, Motul de San José may have enjoyed more peaceful times (although it was not free of warfare; see Tokovinine and Zender 2012), and war themes are not as apparent in the six stelae at Motul. Instead, military concerns are replaced with strong representations of elite concerns in the Ik' Polychrome Style of pottery. One of these concerns is ritual, expressed in all three media: the Motul figurines, the Ik' Style vases that portray ritual dances by aristocrats and transformations of humans into *wayob*, and the Motul stelae that portray ritual dances. Each of these three media displays an overarching concern with religious matters. This overlap of discourses in these three types of art also portrays a society that was relatively well integrated: commoners shared the interests and concerns of the royalty and members of the elite.

However, the differences between the three media speak of an uneven integration and of significant competition and maneuvering for power and status by members of elite and non-elite groups.

The Maya evidence of competing discourses and ideologies of power presented here contributes to sociological debates about the role of ideology in integrating or fracturing human societies. Abercrombie, Hill, and Turner (1980) argue that the ideologies and concerns of dominant groups influenced the concerns and ideologies of subordinate groups very little or not at all. They present a view of human societies as highly fractured. For example, their study of feudalism in Western Europe found that the code of honor so pervasive among the aristocracy was basically unknown and of little import to the peasantry. Scott (1985, 1990) argues that multiple and competing ideologies exist in all societies. Dominant ideologies, those promoted by the elite group, are presented in "public transcripts" (such as in public monumental art, public political performances, and so on), while the ideologies of other groups will appear in "hidden transcripts" (such as folk traditions, myths, songs, gossip, poaching, household rituals, and pilfering). The fact that different Maya concerns are portrayed in stone monumental art, polychrome vessels, and figurines supports the proposition that dominant ideologies compete with alternate ideologies. But the Maya ideologies presented in Maya art are not completely divergent, intimating that Maya society was not as fractured as Abercrombie and colleagues reconstruct Western European medieval polities to be.

The Role of Commoners in Classic Maya Politics

The role of commoners in Classic Maya politics remains understudied (but see recent efforts in LeCount and Yaeger 2010a; Lohse and Valdez 2004; Gonlin and Lohse 2007). However, we do know something about the roles they played in ancient Maya civilization. Although there were different kinds of communities across the lowland landscape (Scarborough, Valdez, and Dunning 2003; Lohse and Valdez 2004; Iannone and Connell 2003; Graham 2011), the accumulated archaeological evidence suggests that commoners controlled a great part of the agricultural land and thus controlled the production of foodstuffs and everyday goods.

Many studies have shown that commoners as a group cannot be understood as a homogeneous mass of passive agriculturalists and taxpayers. Rather, their wealth and status, household composition, involvement in craft production, and investment in more elaborate architecture and ritual varied considerably (Gonlin and Lohse 2007; Scarborough, Valdez, and Dunning 2003; Lohse 2004; LeCount and Yaeger 2010a; Foias and Emery 2012). Because of these highly variable characteristics, the involvement of commoners in and their capacity for involvement in the political arena must have also been highly variable. Issues related to status must have always been a central concern, as they still are today among traditional Maya communities (Vogt 2007) and as is suggested by the fine distinctions in elite dress that are visible in Classic Maya art (Houston 1993; Hammond 1991a). Because status brought a degree of social and political power, commoners would have also been interested in pursuing higher status in multiple venues, including ritual life, the economic arena, and of course, politics.

A Variety of Political Arrangements

The variety of political arrangements that existed among small communities of commoners in the Maya lowlands is highlighted here through two examples, both drawn from Belize. Lohse (2007) examines the differences in commoner settlements in the supporting hinterland of Dos Hombres in northwestern Belize. His analysis of settlement patterns identifies two types of communities. The first type follows the "corporate group pattern" (generally found in zones with low to moderate agricultural fertility) characterized by a hierarchical arrangement of plaza groups or household clusters in which those with most elaborate architecture control the better lands (130–33). Lohse interprets this kind of community as representing "multi-family groups, perhaps arranged around lines of descent . . . but that almost certainly cohered through their common reliance on an agricultural resource base of limited scale" (132). For Lohse, these are the basic social units of Maya polities throughout the pre-Hispanic period. He argues that because of their control over land, they must "have operated as relatively autonomous . . . units" (ibid.). The second type of settlement Lohse found is called the "micro-community pattern." Communities of this type are located in very productive lands (in this case around an *aguada*) and are characterized by dense occupation, few differences in household size or elaboration, and increased frequency of boundary walls (133–34). Lohse interprets this nucleated village as a resource-specialized community (a term originally coined in Scarborough, Valdez, and Dunning 2003). Its members intensively exploited the resources of the *aguada*, and the absence of a household hierarchy suggests "a cooperative, communally based decision-making structure" (Lohse 2004, 134). Before accepting this conclusion, we should evaluate the alternative theory that this second type of community was the estate of a high elite from the nearby site of Dos Hombres. If this community was the estate of a non-resident aristocrat, I propose that it should have one large and elaborate household with little evidence of occupation; the "absentee" noble landlord would live there only during his or her visits. Since such a "manor" is missing, Lohse's proposition seems more valid.

What are the political implications of the existence of two types of communities? The *aguada* microcommunity Lohse described presents a distinct political arrangement in which decision making was communal rather than hierarchical, as found in the corporate group pattern. Even if the *aguada* microcommunity was politically tied to Dos Hombres through the extraction of tribute, it had enough collective power to limit such an intrusion because no evidence for political administration tied to Dos Hombres is found in this village. It is possible that the microcommunity's collective power came from its control over the desirable resource exploited within the *aguada*. Scarborough, Valdez, and Dunning (2003) have also argued that resource-specialized communities may have existed as independent political units outside the purview of the large hierarchical states and hegemonies of the Classic period, although they were probably impacted by these states periodically.

The second example of the variation in political arrangements between commoners and political elites comes from Yaeger (2003b), who compares the composition and historical trajectories of two minor sites in the Belize River Valley: San Lorenzo, a village in Xunantunich's hinterland, and Barton Ramie, down the river from Xunantunich. The divergent historical trajectories of these two mostly commoner settlements illuminate different strategies of political integration with regional elites. Yaeger finds major contrasts between San Lorenzo and Barton Ramie. First, Barton Ramie was continuously occupied from early times until after the collapse of the major cities of the Classic period, suggesting that its political links with the major polities were minor to nonexistent. In contrast, San Lorenzo's historical trajectory closely parallels that of Xunantunich, underscoring a tight political integration with the center. Second, ritual structures at the two sites were different: Barton Ramie had a temple-pyramid some 12 meters high that would have been the locale of ancestor worship. In contrast, San Lorenzo had no temple-pyramid, and its only ritual plaza group, SL-13, hosted feasts carried out probably under the supervision of representatives from Xunantunich (ibid.). Third, the largest plaza groups at the two sites, which represent the wealthiest households and possibly the households of local leaders, have distinct histories. At San Lorenzo, the wealthiest residents came first to the community, and thus their wealth and leadership is founded on kinship ties and agricultural wealth. This contrasts with the situation at Barton Ramie, where the three largest plazas were founded many centuries after the site was first occupied. The architectural features of the largest group were most similar to the site of Baking Pot, the nearby large center that began its growth at the time when Barton Ramie's large groups were built (the Early Classic). The wealth of the three largest Barton Ramie groups may have been legitimated via political affiliation with the Baking Pot elites (ibid.). The wealthiest households at San Lorenzo also acquired some power through their political association with the Xunantunich rulers, expressed through the display of gifts from these lords and through the adoption of architectural elements from the larger center.

Excavations at Barton Ramie and San Lorenzo revealed significant differences in wealth and status among the residents of these two sites and different ties to larger regional centers (ibid.). The fact that Barton Ramie retained most of its population after the Classic Maya collapse suggest that its inhabitants had a significant degree of independence, in spite of the community's earlier connections with nearby larger sites such as Baking Pot. In contrast, San Lorenzo was quickly abandoned when the paramount center at Xunantunich collapsed. Neither completely independent nor completely dependent, Barton Ramie has a history that suggests that some Classic Maya commoner communities had sufficient power to be able to form alliances and then break them without major consequences. In contrast, the historical trajectory of San Lorenzo is closely tied to its integration into the Xunantunich polity.

The Power of Commoners to Vote with Their Feet

There is increasing support for the hypothesis that commoners had the political power to vote with their feet. Inomata (2004) points to a number of factors that would have affected and shaped the mobility of Classic Maya commoners. One critical factor would be the amount of labor commoners invested in the preparation of their houses and agricultural fields. If the labor investment in houses and agriculture was great, they would not have been able to pick up and leave easily. Inomata describes how Maya commoners spent relatively little labor on their residences, which were usually made of perishable materials that were widely available. Although intensive agricultural systems existed among the Classic Maya, most commoners practiced slash-and-burn agriculture. This practice required a major labor investment at the beginning when the forest was cut down, but once that was accomplished it would have required a low level of work (182). The low labor investment of Maya commoners in house construction and agriculture suggests that they may have been relatively mobile. Cultural, landholding, and ideological practices may have also limited commoner mobility, but Contact period documents record that the Maya exhibited a high degree of mobility. The best evidence may come from the fact that "patronymic groups were distributed over wide areas, crosscutting local groups" (182). Inomata turns to the Classic site of Aguateca in the Petexbatun region to highlight the Classic period mobility patterns of commoners. Evidence that the population at Aguateca was small during the Early Classic contrasts with the community's rapid growth in the Late Classic at the same time that a foreign dynasty from Tikal founded the principal regional capital at nearby Dos Pilas. The growth in population at both centers was too rapid to be fully explained by an increase in the local birth rate, so immigration may have been the dominant means of growth. Although forced resettlement of commoners by the elite contingent arriving from Tikal is possible, Inomata remarks that it "seems unlikely that the newly established dynasty would have had enough coercive power to force such a large population to move to a new location" (186). Thus, it is more likely that the commoner population voluntarily resettled as they were attracted to this site either by the high prestige of the Dos Pilas and Aguateca rulers (ibid.), or by the rulers' offers of rewards. That the movement of commoners into Dos Pilas and Aguateca was voluntary is also suggested by the fact that the Dos Pilas rulers chose to settle in a zone in the Petexbatun that was relatively unoccupied because of the limited agricultural fertility of the land. Although most commoners may have moved willingly, not all of them did. At "least a certain number of non-elites, who worked as servants and close subjects of nobles, probably had little choice but to follow their masters" (186–87).

The fact that the rapid population expansion seen at Aguateca and Dos Pilas in the Late Classic is found at other sites broadens the applicability of Inomata's study. Both Xunantunich and Motul de San José fit the pattern (LeCount and Yaeger 2010a; Foias and Emery 2012). Rapid population growth is also coupled with rapid abandonment of these sites, which again suggests that commoners voted with their feet against the rulers. The most extreme example is found in the hinterland of Xunantunich, where small villages were abandoned when the rulers of Xunantunich began to experience problems before or at the beginning of the Tsak' phase (AD 780–890) (Ashmore 2010; LeCount and Yaeger 2010c; Robin, Yaeger, and Ashmore 2010). Epidemics and death could also precipitate rapid abandonment, but we have no evidence for major illnesses sweeping over the lowlands. Rather, Maya commoners appear to have picked up their things and headed for greener pastures in coastal Belize, highland Guatemala, and northern Yucatan, localities that experienced population growth during the Terminal Classic and Postclassic. Several authors have suggested that during these periods, commoners may have felt new freedoms as political and social bonds with the elites weakened (Joyce and Weller 2007; Joyce, Bustamente, and Levine 2001; Winter et al. 2007; Kepecs and Masson 2003).

The Ritual Power of Commoners

Because Maya political elites drew a great deal of their power from the religious sphere, commoners could also draw power from rituals if they were allowed to conduct them in their residences. Evidence that rituals took place in commoner households does exist, which suggests that the ruler and the ruled had competing arenas of ritual power. Lucero (2003, 2006) sees a continuum between the rituals carried out in Maya commoner households and those carried out as state rituals. McAnany and Plank (2001) describe three types of rituals found in Maya households: mortuary or ancestor worship, house dedication (and termination), and agricultural or calendrical rituals (see also Robin 2003). The fact that commoner household rituals such as these had parallels in elite rituals suggests that a modicum of ritual power was in the hands of commoners and that this could be converted into political power.

Commoner control over some rituals can also be seen in the presence of ritual arenas and ritual artifacts at commoner sites or in commoner households. For example, Joyce and Hendon (2000), Walling et al. (2006), and de Montmollin (1995) have reported ball courts in small sites in Honduras, Belize and Chiapas, where ruling elites do not appear to have supervised the ball game and other ritual activities that took place.

Gonlin (2007) considers commoner rituals in Late Classic Copan by reviewing the distribution of ritual structures (or shrines) and ritual artifacts in small residential groups in peripheral areas. Although only a few of the commoner groups in the hinterland of Copan had buildings that were used exclusively as shrines, all three types of household rituals described by

McAnany and Plank (2001) have been identified in commoner households through the presence of burials, caches, and ritual artifacts (Gonlin 2007). The discovery of ritual artifacts in commoner households such as frog-toad sculptures (which were used elsewhere in the Copan polity as part of agricultural water and fertility rituals), a miniature stone altar, small mirrors (which were important in divination rituals), and bark beaters (which were used to make paper used in bloodletting and ritual burning) is especially enlightening because it demonstrates that commoners had access to religious paraphernalia. Although these religious artifacts were not found in every commoner group that Gonlin (2007) tested, they are often found in the largest of these commoner households. This finding suggests that the ritual power of these commoners could be translated into economic power. As political power in the Classic period was founded mostly on religious power, it makes sense to conclude that the ritual power seen in these larger commoner households probably translated to political power.

Blackmore (2011) also found diversity in the distribution of ritual evidence in the commoner neighborhood called the Northeast Group at the site of Chan near Xunantunich, Belize. Although most household groups had evidence for rituals (such as ancestor worship through burials), some had considerably more evidence. For example, group NE-3, the most elaborate in the neighborhood, had substantially more and richer burials (some of which were multiple) and more special deposits (presumably related to house dedication and termination). Thick and large middens that were identified around group NE-3 and the higher density and diversity of serving vessels associated with this group also suggested "that its occupants were engaged in practices meant for neighborhood-wide [feasts of] display and consumption" (172). A high concentration of marine shells in this group may also imply ritual associations between its inhabitants and the underworld or fertility (172–73). In other words, this group appears to have had more ritual power than the other residents of the Northeast neighborhood, and this ritual power translated into economic power because the members of this group could build a more elaborate residence than everyone else in this neighborhood. In contrast, a second group, NE-1, the largest and among the first built in the neighborhood, also invested in rituals, but not as much as the NE-3 group. The occupants of NE-1 were close to most of the agricultural terraces in this zone, and because they were among the founders of the neighborhood, their claim to status (and power) was through "their ancestral ties to the land" or the "Principle of First Occupancy" (174). A high concentration of both jade and marine shells in this residential group suggests connections to the supernatural and external exchange networks, just as has been suggested for NE-3, but these valuables were found in more limited and in less visible ritual contexts (i.e., burials). Blackmore summarizes the distinction between these two commoner residential plaza groups: "In essence, those living at NE-1 had a historical authority and identity that did not require overt public performance while those at NE-3 needed visibility as a means to legitimate themselves within the social structure of the neighborhood" (174).

Classic Maya views of personhood and the soul also suggest that Maya commoners had ritual power that could be translated into economic and/ or political power. Every human had *ch'ulel*, or *k'uh* (divine energy or essence), so every individual had access to ritual power (Ringle 1990; Houston, Stuart, and Taube 2006). However, the royal *ch'ulel*, or *k'uh*, was much more powerful; the royal *ch'ulel*, or *k'uh*, was seen as hot, brilliant, or burning (Houston and Stuart 2001; Houston, Stuart, and Taube 2006, 79–80).

The Commoners' Power to Resist

Arthur Joyce and his colleagues (2001; Joyce and Weller 2007) have explored the evidence for commoner resistance that relates to the argument about whether commoners had political power. The ability of commoners to resist the demands of the elite would clearly have had an impact on political organization. I have mentioned previously that some scholars have suggested that the presence of royal *oikoi* in the Near East may have been the Sumerian kings' response to commoner resistance to providing tribute or corvee labor (Pollock 1999). Joyce, Bustamente, and Levine (2001; see also Joyce and Weller 2007) apply Scott's (1990) argument that in spite of dominant ideologies espoused by elites in every complex society, commoners are able to penetrate these and resist them, usually in very subtle "hidden transcripts," including rituals that took place in houses out of sight of the elites or through gossip or poaching or even delaying the provision of tribute with a never-ending list of excuses. Joyce and his associates propose that commoner resistance will be more visible at times of political disintegration such as the Classic Maya collapse, when elite control over commoners was loosened. Various sites from the Maya lowlands do indeed show signs of what could be interpreted as commoner resistance: "destruction, denigration and reuse of material symbols of the Late Classic state" (Joyce and Weller 2007, 168). At Dos Pilas, monuments were intentionally broken and some were reset in walls soon after the royal family abandoned the site (Palka 1997; Joyce and Weller 2007, 168). At Tikal during the Terminal Classic, commoners occupied royal palaces, tombs and caches were desecrated, and stelae and altars were reused (Culbert 1973; Harrison 1999; Joyce and Weller 2007, 169). Altun Ha provides similar evidence from the time of the Classic Maya collapse (Pendergast 1982; Joyce and Weller 2007). Although commoner revolutions are not suggested, Joyce and Weller believe that these types of desecration or destruction hint at commoner resentment of or resistance against Classic elites.

However, other explanations have been proposed for these instances of "desecration" during the Terminal Classic and Early Postclassic. The Classic Maya are known for rituals of termination in which buildings and monuments are destroyed to remove their soul power (or *ch'ulel*) so that they would not be dangerous anymore (Houston, Stuart, and Taube 2006; Mock 1998; Iannone 2005). Thus, it is possible that the buildings and monuments were terminated out of respect rather than as an act of desecration. Similarly, the reuse of Classic objects may not have been the result of desecration or resistance on the part of commoners: Linda Brown's (2000) research on modern Maya household ritual has highlighted that shamans use discarded objects, including archaeological ones, as ritually charged items.

Conclusions: Have We Reached the Bottom-Up Approach to Ancient Politics?

Political power is viewed today not as an essentialist quality of particular individuals or classes but rather as something that is contingent on individuals and their practices (Foucault 1979; Miller and Tilley 1984; Wolf 1999). Therefore, current perspectives on ancient politics imply that every member of a society has power (Fleisher and Wynne-Jones 2010), albeit not on the same scale as the ruling elite. Recent scholarship considers power as always composed at some level through agreement, compromise, or emotive ties among all or most factions and individuals involved rather than as primarily coercive or imposed from above (Guyer and Belinga 1995; Fleisher and Wynne-Jones 2010; Pauketat 2007; Joyce and Weller 2007).

Because of these perspectives on power, performances, discourses, and ideologies have become important to our understanding of political strategies. In the Maya case, the performances and discourses recorded in a variety of artistic media provide evidence of the political contestations and the various claims to power that are at the root of Classic Maya political dynamics. Although the ancient Maya are celebrated for their hieroglyphic texts and the unique insider's perspective that these texts present, the hieroglyphs are not much help here because they focus exclusively on the highest elite and a few members of their inner circle. The texts do not describe the different kinds of political events that took place or who was involved in these events. However, depictions in different media, from the "public transcripts" on large stone monuments to the small "transcripts" on polychrome feasting pottery to the tiny and more "hidden transcripts" of figurine-whistles provide windows on a variety of events and the claims to power of different "power blocs." While public stone monuments provide evidence of ritual concerns and a view of Maya society as dominated by the divine ruler (*k'uhul ajaw*), polychrome vessels and figurines provided alternative discourses. On pottery vessels, the *k'uhul ajaw* was not always dominant or "larger than life" but was rather a first among equals of a sort. The image of the *k'uhul ajaw* is rarely seen on figurines and instead a variety of supernaturals—*wayob* spirits, dwarves, and clowns—are prominent. These were probably the spiritual powers lower-status members of Maya society consulted and claimed. All in all, ritual is a common theme in these three media, suggesting that the ideologies of the "high and mighty" were not completely different from those of the poor.

Ceremonies involving dancing and feasting were an important element of political performances during the Late Classic, and dancers and pots full of food and drink are often shown in the palace scenes painted on polychrome pottery, especially on the Ik' Style vessels created at Motul de San José. As several scholars have remarked (e.g., Reents-Budet 2000; LeCount 2001; Foias 2007; Wells 2006, 2007; McAnany 2010), feasts would have showcased the generosity and wealth of the rulers and of other elites who hosted them. Because of this, banquets would have had significant economic costs, and producing the food, drink, and gifts given away during the celebrations would have required the sustained effort of the household and kin group of the host. Because the Motul de San José rulers invested so much labor in the Ik' Style pottery they used at feasts (Reents-Budet et al. 2012), it seems that the Motul *k'uhul ajaw* and his court were especially adept at using feasts to pursue their political goals (Halperin and Foias 2010): Ik' Style pots were distributed as far away from Motul as Altar de Sacrificios, Dos Pilas, Aguateca, Arroyo de Piedra, Uaxactun, and Altun Ha (Reents-Budet et al. 2012); these pots were permanent markers of the alliances formed between hosts and guests at the feasts.

Councils are another institution of pre-Hispanic Maya political life, but they are much more visible from the Terminal Classic on. We only have evidence for a Classic period council at Copan, but it is possible that other Classic centers had councils based on the indirect archaeological evidence that Maya rulers were dependent on the benevolence and support of the commoners. If councils were a widespread institution during the Classic period, they would have formed another power bloc with which the *k'uhul ajaw* would have had to engage. In sum, several power blocs seem to have risen to the top of Classic Maya polities apart from the divine ruler and his royal household and court: the political-ecclesiastical administrative hierarchy, the secondary elites, warriors, and possibly councils (although these may have had overlapping membership to some degree).

Classic Maya political life was dominated by the *k'uhul ajaw* and his court, but other groups also had claims to power. Among these are the members of the lower classes who shaped figurines in the form of the supernaturals that were important in their lives and who may also have had a political voice in councils. Secondary elites (priests, administrators, artisans, scribes, warriors, and courtiers) were another group that expressed their own claims to power through elaborate polychrome vessels that presented an almost equal status of royals and secondary elite individuals. The competing ideologies evident on figurines, polychrome pottery, and stone monuments at different sites suggest that political arrangements between power blocs varied by polity.

The range among Maya commoner communities in composition, wealth, involvement in ritual or craft specialization, and historical trajectories paints a mosaic of political landscapes, in which large polities peacefully intermixed with medium and small ones and sometimes engulfed them. If it is true that commoners could resist elite demands and vote with their feet, elites must have involved them in their political plans through promises and rewards, through major ceremonies designed to create emotional ties and a common identity, and possibly through councils. Alternatively, elites may have expanded their palace economies. This could be interpreted as a more coercive way of gaining authority because commoners may have been incorporated into the royal great households as serfs or dependents.

A great deal more research is needed to understand the roles commoners played in Classic Maya politics. But for now, there is sufficient evidence to argue that multiple power blocs existed in ancient polities that involved both elites and non-elites and that the arrangements, compromises, and resistances among these multiple factions would have impacted the power of the *k'uhul ajaw* and led to a dynamic system of shifting fortunes among the many states of the Classic southern lowlands.

Notes

1. Pauketat (2003, 2007) argues against coercion as an explanation for the movement of ancient populations in what is now the southeastern United States, although he sees such relocations as significant components of the creation of new political entities. However, according to Emerson and Pauketat (2002), these same relocated communities (called the Richland complex) are also characterized by resistance.

2. These titles are evidence against an interpretation of Maya warfare as purely ritualistic. If these wars were purely ritualistic for the purpose of obtaining captives for sacrifice, I would expect the title to be "he of X sacrifices."

3. The Classic Maya built landscape was not dominated by fortresses or by easily defensible sites, so it is unlikely that large-scale military action against population centers took place frequently. This changed during the Terminal Classic (Demarest 2006; Inomata 2007).

4. Sanchez (2005) compares the content of ruler portraits in Maya stelae in public plazas to those on pillars or lintels in more private contexts in palaces or acropolis courtyards. The more public depictions of the ruler, those on monuments, portrayed him as surrounded by supernatural imagery and deities, emphasizing his role as the mediator between humans and supernaturals. Although the more private monuments also depicted the rulers in religious activities, they offered more details about the actors, acts, and paraphernalia involved (264).

5. Pyburn (1997) groups small shrines together with temple-pyramids. This seems to muddy the waters, as small shrines reflect household-level investments rather than the labor investment of the whole community.

6. Lucero (2003) points out that royal rituals were appropriated and expanded versions of household practices of dedicating new houses, venerating ancestors, and ritually terminating domestic sacred spaces.

7. This scholarly interest in legitimacy is born out of the new perspective that states and any system of dominance are fragile and can be fractured by groups with different interests and goals than those of the dominant power. Therefore, what keeps states together or what provides social cohesion has become a central problem of archaeological studies of ancient states.

8. This does not impede the dominated groups from resisting the elite, as Scott's (1990) research has shown (71–107).

9. The only exception would be rapid abandonment of a site, as we see at Aguateca, Guatemala (because of an enemy attack) and at Ceren, El Salvador (because of a volcanic eruption).

10. Looper and colleagues (2009) place the vase, K791, in this category because it depicts the *wayob* (alter egos or animal spirits) of half a dozen *k'uhul ajaws* in contorted positions that are suggestive of dancing.

11. Vessel K2573 may depict a wedding.

12. Another vase (Miller and Martin 2004, 36, Plate 7) that was not included in Kerr and Kerr's *Maya Vase Book* is also a complex tribute scene involving Tayel Chan K'inich (Tokovinine and Zender 2012), another eighth-century ruler of Motul de San José. In the scene on this vessel, he is receiving bundles and stacks of textiles and feathers from two nobles dressed in long capes. This vase is not painted in the Ik' Polychrome Style.

13. Other vases, not in Ik' Style, depict tribute (or booty) together with the presentation of captives. Miller and Martin (2004) include a beautiful example in Plate 105 (187): a visiting war captain accompanied by three warriors and his palanquin are presenting two captives and tribute (two white bundles of cacao, possibly, and stacks of white shells and textiles) to a young ruler seated on a bench, while another lord who is seated slightly higher may be "the head courtier at work, the secretary who controlled access to the king and who organized courtly business" (ibid.).

14. To better gauge the frequency of tribute scenes in Maya pottery art in general, I searched the entire Maya Vase Database (www.mayavase.com) for images of "bundle, tribute, cache," one of the iconographic elements encoded in the database. Although this category is broader than tribute alone, the search produced only 145 vessels in a database that has close to 10,000 vases.

15. The k'uhul ajaw is not always the main figure in polychrome vessels. For example, K344 shows a scribe seated in the middle of a large throne, accompanied by a smaller individual.

16. The flapstaff dance is named for the object held in the hands of the dancers, a staff with cloth flaps attached to it.

17. The ancient Maya thought that dancing, like music and fragrant scents, brought an individual into contact with the supernatural realms. This activity enabled rulers to become the gods whose masks they wore (Looper 2009, 60; Houston and Stuart 1996).

18. Archaeologists use the term "X-ray costumes" to refer to costumes in which the costume and the individual within the costume were simultaneously visible, similar to the way an X-ray machine reveals concealed things (see Markman and Markman 1989, 70–73).

19. Looper, Reents-Budet, and Bishop (2009) identify this vessel as an Ik' Style Polychrome.

20. Looper, Reents-Budet, and Bishop (2009, 143) identify this ruler as Yajawte' K'inich, but the absence of glyphs on this vessel make this identification preliminary.

21. For example, vase K3054 portrays two ladies standing behind Yajawte' K'inich. The text identifies the first as a royal lady from Tsam, so presumably she is the wife of Yajawte'; the second is identified only as a female ajk'uhuun (Tokovinine and Zender 2012).

22. Miller and Martin (2004, 27) observe that attendants peeking behind the ruler's throne were depicted in polychrome vessels so often that they must be bodyguards. Thus, it seems likely that the king was attended by a personal retinue of bodyguards.

23. Plank (2004) suggests that Yax Pasaj, the final ruler of Copan, was the builder of Structure 10L-22A (140).

24. A temple assemblage is defined as a temple framed by a colonnaded hall on its left and an oratory to its right and a small platform shrine placed in the middle of the plaza or courtyard facing the hall (Proskouriakoff 1962).

25. These officials may also have been called ah kulels in other provinces (Ringle and Bey 2001, 270).

26. Boot (2005) offers the alternative explanation that these murals may depict dignitaries and warriors who were the ancestors of the Chichen Itza paramount ruler and that they hold the God K scepters because they were the previous rulers of Chichen.

27. Brumfiel notes that monumental art of the Aztec Empire presents females as sacrificial victims or as subordinate to and exploited by males. Thus, this art promotes a negative ideology of the female gender.

28. There are more females than males in the anthropomorphic figurines at Motul de San José. The frequency of females is between 54 and 83 percent, depending on how gender categories are identified (Halperin 2007, Table 7.3). Halperin (ibid.) also identified two figurines representing adults with children, but the gender of the adult is unclear.

29. I am referring here to elaborate polychromes. Simpler polychromes were found among commoner households also.

30. The intense competition among the Classic Maya elite is also attested to by the frequent depiction of bodyguards in palace scenes on polychrome pottery (Miller and Martin 2004). Miller and Martin describe the situation: "The Maya court was a place of pomp and splendor, but it was also one of danger and threat. Those fortunate enough to sit on the jaguar cushion kept themselves there by remaining ever vigilant" (27).

7

||||||||||||

Conclusions

Toward an Archaeology of Power

Politics arise in relationships between groups and individuals,
not fully grown from a repertoire of types.

A. Smith 2003, 101–2

The aim of this work is to present how archaeologists have reconstructed ancient Maya politics during the Classic period, the apogee of this most celebrated pre-Hispanic civilization. I hope that my summary of the various epistemological approaches and bodies of knowledge about this civilization has provided the foundation for further studies and discussions.

Just as political anthropologists have shifted their stance from sociocultural evolution and political economy, to processual-action models that focus on human actors, so archaeologists have moved to considerations of the fluidity of political power, the heterogeneity and conflictive nature of political institutions and factions, the importance of ideational strategies for negotiating conflicts, and the relational nature of power. Four recent archaeological projects in the Near East, North America, and Central America were used to illustrate the trends in how archaeologists theorize about political power, structure, and dynamics. An important lesson to be drawn from these studies is that we need to consider in more detail the manifestations of political power in the material world of archaeology at all levels of society, including the individual and the household, the village or local community, and the district or larger communal hinterland, not just the interactions between polities and suprapolities.

An archaeology of power (Stein 1998; A. Smith 2003) can be pursued by integrating these multiple scales with two types of analysis: 1) a regional analysis that examines "variation in 'nodes of [political, economic or religious] power' . . . [and] . . . in patterns of production, exchange, and consumption of different goods or forms of value (such as labor)" across the landscape of each polity (Stein 1998, 26–27) (in other words, what people do); and 2) an analysis that examines all lines of evidence of competing claims to political power and authority by different groups, factions, power blocs, or institutions in art or ritual (in other words, what people "say"). To accomplish this goal, I looked at how the macro-scale analysis of political power was distributed across interregional and regional landscapes. This was followed by a middle-scale study of internal institutions and dynamics at the intrapolity level and a micro-scale exploration of the claims to power and the flow of power among different factions, including commoners, royal and secondary elites, political-ecclesiastical officials, warriors, and courtiers.

To understand Maya political dynamics, we have to envision a plurality of political forms during pre-Hispanic times, and indeed, we have evidence of this plurality from Preclassic through Postclassic times. It is thus unnecessary to ask whether the Maya "state" was centralized or decentralized, even though this debate has influenced our research over the last thirty years. We now need to comprehend the nature and degree of variation among Maya polities. To understand Maya politics and dynamics, each Maya polity has to be studied on its own so that we can reconstruct its size and population, the nature of its administration and of the sources of power of the ruling elites, the number of political factions in the polity and the competing claims of such factions to legitimacy and power. The comparative approach I used in this book highlighted differences between Maya polities, and these differences are important aspects of political dynamics. At the same time, I drew upon my own research at Motul de San José, Guatemala.

Because the Classic period encompassed a variety of polities that ranged in size from as small as 150 square kilometers to a possible maximum of around 11,000 square kilometers, the political landscape must have been highly volatile. Smaller polities such as Motul de San José (which reached at most 150 square kilometers and encompassed at most 27,000 people) must have experienced intense pressures from larger and more powerful neighbors.[1] Tokovinine and Zender (2012) and Reents-Budet et al. (2012) reconstruct this volatility from the epigraphic records of Motul (fragmentary as they are), which document its alliances or wars with Tikal, Dos Pilas, La Florida (ancient Namaan), Zapote Bobal/El Pajarral/La Joyanca (ancient Hix Witz), and Yaxchilan. Although alliances tied the Motul dynasts with Yaxchilan, Tikal, Dos Pilas, and possibly the Caracol area (as shown in the celebration of marriages between the sites or in the gifting of Ik' Style pottery to the Petexbatun elites), these connections did not preclude conflicts within a few years after the formation of alliances or as soon as new dynasts acceded to the throne. However, Tokovinine and Zender (2012) remark that Motul had enduring amicable relations with the nearby small states of Namaan and Hix Witz, both of which were located to the west along the River San Pedro Martir (the tributaries of that river reach all the way to Motul). The reasons behind these enduring alliances remain opaque, but they may have included the need for assistance in conflicts with more powerful neighbors or the desire to control the trade that moved along the river into the Lakes region and then north and east (Tokovinine and Zender 2012). The enduring alliance between Motul and its western neighbors Namaan and Hix Witz reminds me of the alliances formed by the Mexicas of Tenochtitlan with Texcoco and Tacuba in their rebellion against their overlords, the Tepanecs. This alliance, of course, became the Triple Alliance or the Aztec Empire (Conrad and Demarest 1984). In its early history, the Roman city-state also relied on alliances with other neighboring Latin city-states (forming the Latin League) to defend itself against enemies, such as the Gauls and other Etruscan kingdoms (Raaflaub 1996). Could it be that Motul was also involved in some kind of league with its neighbors Namaan and Hix Witz?

The rapidly changing relations between Motul and the more powerful Maya states suggest a multipolar and dynamic international system (see Kaufman 1997 and Doyle 1986 for a discussion of international systems). This international system was overshadowed at times by a bipolar system that involved the archrivals Tikal and Calakmul (Martin and Grube 1995, 2000).

We also find evidence of the political volatility of the Maya lowlands in the multiple types of arrangements that existed within hegemonies (or multistate networks) like the ones dominated by Tikal, Calakmul, Caracol, and Naranjo (to name the best-known cases). Connections between the paramount state and the smaller subsidiary polities included loose patron-client relationships, tighter alliances (in which the smaller states were independent or dependent vassals), and direct incorporation with major reorganization of the dominated polities. Despite these political arrangements, some scholars champion the dominated polities as the critical forces (or actors) in the rise and fall cycles of Maya geopolitics (Marcus 1993, 1998).

The Motul de San José Archaeological Project has provided a glimpse into the internal political dynamics of one of these subsidiary polities because Motul was a vassal of Tikal off and on during the Late Classic. Although I have not dwelled much on the importance of the environment in this work, those who wish to reconstruct ancient Maya political dynamics must be able to understand the relationships of humans with their environment. However, that is for another book. Here, I only want to mention two elements that had an impact on the political history of Motul de San José in the Classic period. Based on climatic studies in nearby regions (Vilma Fialko, personal communication, 2000; Scarborough, Valdez, and Dunning 2003; Scarborough and Valdez 2003) and commentaries from local informants, we suspect that this zone was more humid during the Late Classic period and was crossed by flowing rivers, including the Riachuelo K'ante't'u'ul, which probably drained into the Akte River, which then connected into the west-flowing San Pedro Martir River (Figure 4.3; see Moriarty 2004a; Foias and Emery 2012). Water transportation may have connected Motul with areas far removed in the west toward Yaxchilan and in the east to northeast toward Tikal and Belize. We suspect this because hieroglyphic texts on monuments and polychrome vessels at those sites mention the Ik' polity (Tokovinine and Zender 2012; Reents-Budet et al. 2012). Water transportation routes may have led to the use of Motul de San José and its principal port Trinidad as centers of trade, and preliminary studies suggest that both had marketplaces (Dahlin et al. 2009; Bair and Terry 2012; Halperin et al. 2009). Ecological studies within the Motul zone have indicated that human settlement correlated with fertile soils on high plateaus or hillocks, but these soils were vulnerable to rapid loss of nutrients if they weren't fertilized (Jensen et al. 2007; Webb et al. 2007; Webb and Schwarcz 2012). Geochemical studies of the regional soils have found that little agriculture was taking place in Motul proper, even though the soils there were the most fertile in the zone (Webb et al. 2007; Jensen et al. 2007; Webb and Schwarcz 2012; see also Emery and Foias 2012). The capital center, therefore, was either a garden "city" (with fruit trees among the residences) or a natural forest preserve (Richard Terry, personal communication, 2009) or a combination of the two. This ecological evidence from Motul suggests that its power was founded less on agricultural wealth and more on political power and possibly trade.

We have gained insights into the political structure of this small polity through settlement pattern surveys, excavations, and decipherments of hieroglyphic texts. We have identified subsidiary centers, each with one or several pyramids between two and five kilometers away from Motul, that may have been occupied by subsidiary elites who had political administrative functions (Moriarty 2004a, 2004b; Moriarty 2012; Yorgey and Moriarty 2012). The evidence of religious or economic specialization at some of these minor centers implies that the political hierarchy was not identical to the economic hierarchy or the religious hierarchy. For example, Motul had no ball court, but there was one at Trinidad, the second largest center in the polity. Buenavista–Nuevo San José, La Estrella–Nuevo San José, and Trinidad, all of which are located along the north shore of Lake Peten Itza, were situated close to chert sources and appear to have specialized in the production of chert blanks and tools. In contrast, little chert tool production occurred at Motul de San José. Preliminary soil carbon isotope studies at Chachaklu'um suggest that this secondary center located approximately five kilometers east of Motul may have specialized in non-agricultural pursuits, such as the cultivation of fruit trees (Bair and Terry 2012). These signs of specialization imply that a system of integration was in place. On the economic level, markets could have provided the mechanism of integration where goods produced in different sites could be exchanged. As already mentioned, the identification of possible marketplaces in Plaza II at Motul and in Plaza V at Trinidad suggest that both the political capital and the port had such economic functions (Bair and Terry 2012; Dahlin et al. 2009; Moriarty 2012). On the religious plane, we can imagine that religious ceremonies would have taken polity elites to the different sites, including the ball court at Trinidad, and that this mobility could have integrated the population of the peripheries. The occurrence of large politico-ritual ceremonies, presumably under the direction of Motul's royalty and elite, at peripheral sites within the Motul polity is supported by Moriarty's (2012) discovery of rich middens next to the Trinidad ball court that may represent the remains of periodic feasts for large numbers of people.

Although some scholars argue that Classic Maya political administrations were bureaucratic, a comparison of Classic Maya officialdom with early to modern bureaucracies found few similarities. Three critical features characterize Classic Maya administration: 1) Maya officials were political-ecclesiastical or noble priests who were promoted to increasingly higher levels of political office during their lifetimes; 2) the system was hierarchical with two to four levels of elite officials, including the divine ruler (the *k'uhul ajaw*), the *ti'sakhuun*, the *sajal*, the *ajk'uhuun*, the *yajawk'ahk'*, the *lakam* (the only possibly non-elite post); and 3) the system was intensely personal; superior elite sponsors or patrons "owned" lower officials or priests even after the sponsors had died.[2]

Epigraphy provides details about differences in Classic political administration among lowland polities. Several polychrome vases depict divine lords of Motul with two *ajk'uhuuns*, one shows a divine lord with a *sajal*, and another shows a divine lord with three *lakams*. In contrast, Palenque texts record not only that the *k'uhul ajaw* had a *ti'sakhuun*, several *sajals*, and multiple *ajk'uhuuns* but also that *sajals* could have several *ajk'uhuuns* under their control (Zender 2004). The reconstruction at Palenque suggests parallel and noncentralized administrative hierarchies. In contrast, at Motul de San José, we have no such statements of hierarchy among the *ajk'uhuuns*, *sajals*, and *lakams*, and they may have all been directly under the supervision of the divine ruler. *Lakams* may have been found only within the large settlements, such as Motul de San José, because we believe they were district or neighborhood officials in charge of levying taxes (Lacadena 2008). In contrast to the situation at Motul, the *lakam* title does not appear at Palenque. The *ajk'uhuuns* may have been the divine lord's "prime ministers" because they are the most visible on polychrome vessels, especially on Ik' Style vessels (Coe and Kerr 1997; Tokovinine and Zender 2012). As such, they may have resided within the royal courts, such as in the Acropolis of Motul. In contrast, the *sajals* (which have been interpreted as governors of secondary centers) may have been located in subsidiary centers such as Trinidad, Kante't'u'ul, Buenavista–Nuevo San José, and Chakokot within the Motul polity, either as full- or part-time residents. However, further investigation is needed to answer the question of whether *sajals*, *ajk'uhuuns*, or other types of officials lived in secondary centers.

Two major institutions supported Classic Maya political administration: the *oikoi*, or great royal households, which varied in composition and size in each polity; and the tribute-tax system, which consisted of goods levied from commoners as tax and items (probably social valuables) extracted from conquered polities as tribute.

Archaeological evidence from Motul de San José uncovered further details of the *oikos* and of the tribute-tax economies. We have found evidence that members of three social ranks lived in the capital based on an analysis of architectural volume: Rank 1 royal elites, Rank 2 secondary elites, and Rank 3 commoners (Foias et al. 2012). A number of ritual economic activities took place in all households, but evidence of ritual activity was especially prominent in the royal houses (Rank 1). Members of these royal *oikoi* generally produced social valuables, and they obtained staples (such as corn flour and wild animal meat) through taxation of the commoner stratum (Foias et al. 2012; Emery 2012). The tax system is revealed in a low density of grinding tools in the royal and secondary-elite households at Motul and a higher density at commoner plaza groups (Foias et al. 2012). This suggests that taxes in Motul consisted at least in part of ground corn or cornmeal that passed from low-level households to royal compounds. A similar pattern suggests that commoners hunted wild animals and paid tax in meat to the royal households (Emery 2012). In contrast, cloth production at Motul was more common in the royal and secondary-elite groups than in lower-rank ones, supporting the importance of the palace economy in which royal ladies, ladies-in-waiting, kin members, or attached individuals would create wealth in cloth for the ruling and elite households (Halperin 2008; Emery 2012).

Instead of being static and timeless, ancient political institutions were built on contestations and compromises between different competitors and factions. Some Classic polities, such as Copan and Chichen Itza may have had councils, and these councils may have formed another power bloc in addition to the *k'uhul ajaw* and his royal household, the political-ecclesiastical administration (where the concerns of the priesthood might have been foremost), and the warriors and courtiers who were also of aristocratic rank. Contention among these power blocs might have affected the success of polities during the Classic period.

Public performances were especially important to ancient Maya politics because, as Inomata (2006) writes, the state was what was visible in "the tangible images of the ruler's body, state buildings, and collective acts" (805). Significant competition within the Late Classic aristocracy reinforced the need for public performance to sustain claims to power. The Classic Maya did not leave a complete record in their writings or art of the types or nature of political ceremonies. Public stone monuments rarely show more than one main figure (the divine ruler), so we are left with only fragmentary scenes painted on polychrome vases like the Ik' Style vessels produced at Motul de San José and the (still-unique) palace murals from Bonampak. Only certain ceremonies are recorded on the polychrome vases: dances, presentations and/or sacrifices of captives, small court reunions, adornment ceremonies (in preparation for dance, war, or other state ritual), and tribute offerings. These present a narrow range of concerns and claims to power of Classic Maya elites (see Reents-Budet, Ball, and Kerr 1994; Reents-Budet et al. 2012; Halperin and Foias 2010). Religious themes dominate this art, while captive presentation and tribute presentation are secondary concerns. However, there may be a fine line between the latter two; in one case, the warriors' regalia are placed on the throne in front of the victorious *k'uhul ajaw*.

More important, Ik' Style vessels were used as a strategy to form an elite group identity; the ruler is depicted in much more equal terms with his courtiers than in stone monuments. The ruler is portrayed in simple attire, often sitting or standing on the same level with the members of his court. This visual relative equality served a double purpose. First, it understated the political, economic, and social differences between the royal figure and the rest of the nobles, thus creating a unity and a recognition of the high status of elites. Second, it tied the nobles to the king because they may have competed for the recognition and honor of being seen and painted with the divine ruler (see also Foias 2007). This understatement of the political, economic, and social power of the ruler in the Ik' Style vases stands in stark contrast to the great wealth controlled by Motul's royals that has been uncovered in our excavations (Foias et al. 2012).

Performances and discourses recorded in Classic Maya art media, including large stone monuments, small polychrome painted vases, and tiny figurines, provide evidence of political maneuvering through slightly different claims to power. Tiny figurines found in many Motul households display many different animals and supernaturals that are generally distinct from those identified in stone monuments (Halperin 2007). Often, these figurines immortalize nonroyal women (and to a lesser extent nonroyal men) from different walks of life. The two most common female figurine types at Motul portray a woman wearing a broad-brimmed hat characteristic of traders and pilgrims or a woman holding a basket/bowl of tamales. The figure of the *k'uhul ajaw* is also present, but it is not dominant. In contrast to these figurines, Ik' Style polychromes depict the elite "class" on more equal terms with the divine king. Finally, the "public transcript" of stone monuments is almost exclusively about the *k'uhul ajaw* and his religious power. But ritual themes appear in all three media. Although themes representing state ideology occur in household art, they are not the only ones seen there. The different themes found in stone monuments, polychrome vessels, and figurines lead us to conclude that Classic Maya society at Motul de San José was partly, but unevenly, integrated. Differences between the themes in figurines and polychrome pottery excavated at different sites are also worthy of notice. For example, at Aguateca, a Petexbatun site that was burned and abandoned in the ninth century AD, male warrior imagery is the most common theme of household figurines (Triadan 2007), which may suggest that conflict was of great concern to everyone, not just the ruler and the state.

Commoners are generally not viewed as being central to the political process, but recent research has brought to light a variety of types of commoner households and communities and the different degrees of involvement of these groups with other political entities. If the lowest political position of *lakam* was indeed non-elite, as Lacadena (2008) suggests, then some commoners were formally included in the political process. Councils and assemblies were a common feature of Postclassic Maya kingdoms, and they may also have existed during the Classic period; the possible council house at Copan provides intriguing evidence of this. Councils may have included commoner representatives who had a voice in the political process. However, regardless of whether non-elite administrative positions or commoner assemblies existed, archaeological evidence shows that commoners had political power through their control over a majority of agricultural land (Pyburn et al. 1998) and over a large portion of the manufacture of daily items (Foias 2002, 2004; McAnany 2010). Even more important, the distribution of ritual objects among commoner households at Copan and at other Maya sites intimates that some non-elite had a modicum of ritual power, which possibly could be translated into political power (Gonlin 2007; Blackmore 2011). Other evidence of the political power of commoner communities is provided by settlements such as Barton Ramie, which had the capacity to survive for long periods after breaking off from more dominant sites (Yaeger 2003b). Another line of inquiry into the political power of commoners considers signs of resistance from low-status groups during the transition from the Classic to the Postclassic (Joyce, Bustamente, and Levine 2001; Joyce and Weller 2007). A final thread looks at commoner mobility (their power to vote with their feet) during the Classic period as another form of political power (Inomata 2004). In light of this recent research, the interconnections between commoners and political institutions deserve a great deal more attention in the future.

Although it is quite likely that the political life of the ancient Maya was much more rich and colorful than the picture I have painted in this book, I hope that I have been able to at least impart two points: the archaeological, epigraphic, and ethnohistorical records are full of political evidence and archaeologists can reconstruct a great deal from that evidence, although much remains to be discovered.

Archaeology is the only social science that can provide direct evidence for long-term processes of change in noncapitalist societies for which few or no written documents have survived. No other area of the world has the richness of data that is available for the Classic Maya, and this affords us a unique opportunity to reconstruct the details and dynamics of the politics of different Classic kingdoms along multiple scales, from the micro scale of commoner individuals and households to the macro scale of polity and suprapolity interactions.

What have we learned about the Classic Maya? We know that both cooperation and competition were at work, paralleling what political anthropologists call "power to" and "power over." Although the Late Classic political history of the southern Maya lowlands was volatile, long-term patterns of cooperation also existed. For example, over several generations Motul de San José allied itself with nearby polities along the San Pedro Martir River. But the conflicts that Classic stone monuments chronicle illuminate competition between the royal families of different polities and fierce competition among secondary elites within some (if not all) polities. Such competition led to the creation of the elaborate and beautiful Ik' Style polychromes in the Motul de San José realm. These vases depicted the involvement of a variety of nonroyal aristocrats with Motul's dynasts. The heavy concentration of Classic Maya artistic and textual records on rituals brings to the forefront not only efforts of active political power blocs to legitimize their power through persuasion but also the fractures among these power blocs: the state ideology promoted in stone monuments referred mostly to different gods from those immortalized in either the Ik' Style polychromes or Motul's figurines.

Ancient Maya elites used a number of strategies to achieve their political goals. Some of these were more successful than others, and these variable degrees of success are responsible for the dynamics of the Classic period. Although the religious foundations of divine kingship were quite strong, Maya rulers also relied on economic and military sources of power. Their control of segments of the economy gave Maya rulers and/or elites access to a fund that could be used to pursue more political power or centralize their power. Polities and aristocrats were involved in the economy in various ways, for example through the landed estates they controlled, through the tax-tribute system, or through the sponsoring of master artist-scribes who produced highly charged and hypertrophic valuables (e.g., Ik' Style polychromes). And of course rulers and elites had varying degrees of access to each of these avenues to power. Although we do not know how Maya armies were organized during the Classic period, military power is relevant because many monuments show rulers standing over captives or capturing the enemy. Nevertheless, the low impact of war during the Classic period and the ability of Maya commoners to vote with their feet hint that military power was not as important as religious prowess. Just as important, Maya dynasts gained power through their control over an administrative cadre of officials that probably varied in size and structure from state to state and over time within the same state. The ability to maintain such control also varied by rulers and over time.

Although the latest models of Maya dynamics envision political history as cycling between fragmentation and unification (e.g., Marcus 1993), the present study shows that different sizes and different kinds of states coexisted in the Classic period and probably also in the preceding Preclassic and subsequent Postclassic periods. All in all, the present study makes clear that the political power of the Classic Maya was precarious and fragile because so many political actors were involved, and the dynamics of political power in this period were shaped by this fragility. Political power emerged from the practices of individuals and groups, rather than from "a repertoire of [fully grown] types" (A. Smith 2003, 101–2). Examining political power at different scales—from the micro scale of individuals, households, communities to the middle scale of power blocs, administrations, tax-tribute systems, and palace economies to the macro scale of the polity itself and its relations with other similar entities—can illuminate the complexities and intricacies of political power, and the contention for power between different individuals, factions, and institutions in each Maya state of the Classic period. Although many questions remain, I hope this work opens the door to further study of an archaeology of power.

Notes

1. It is possible that the size of the Motul polity fluctuated, contracting and expanding with the successes and failures of its Late Classic rulers, whose feats are described in detail by Tokovinine and Zender (2012) and Reents-Budet et al. (2012).

2. Tokovinine and Zender (2012) also remark that each new ruler probably named his own *ajk'uhuuns*, so the entire top administration at Motul de San José changed with each ruler.

References Cited

Abercrombie, N., S. Hill, and B. S. Turner
1980   *The Dominant Ideology Thesis*. Allen & Unwin, London.
Abrams, E. M.
1994   *How the Mayas Built Their World: Energetics and Ancient Architecture*. University of Texas Press, Austin.
Adams, R. E. W.
1986   Rio Azul. *National Geographic* 169:420–51.
1999   *Rio Azul: An Ancient Maya City*. University of Oklahoma Press, Norman.
Adams, R. E. W., and R. C. Jones
1981   Spatial Patterns and Regional Growth among Classic Maya Cities. *American Anthropologist* 46:301–22.
Adams, R. E. W., and W. D. Smith
1981   Feudal Models for Classic Maya Settlement. In *Lowland Maya Settlement Patterns*, edited by W. Ashmore, pp. 335–49. University of New Mexico Press, Albuquerque.
Adams, R. McC.
1966   *The Evolution of Urban Society: Early Mesopotamia and Prehispanic Mexico*. Aldine, Chicago.
Adánez, J. Pavón, A. Lacadena García-Gallo, A. Ciudad Ruiz, and M. J. Iglesias Ponce de Leon
2009   La identificación de unidades socio-administrativas en las ciudades Mayas clasicas: El caso de Tikal (Peten, Guatemala). Paper given at the XIX Encuentro Internacional de los Investigadores de las Cultura Maya. Universidad Autonoma de Campeche, Campeche, Mexico.
Adánez, J. Pavón, A. Ciudad Ruiz, M. J. Iglesias Ponce de Leon, and A. Lacadena García-Gallo
2011   La identificación de unidades socio-administrativas en las ciudades Mayas clasicas: De Tikal al sureste de Peten. In *XXIV Simposio de Investigaciones Arqueologicas en Guatemala*, edited by B. Arroyo, L. Paiz Aragon, A. Linares Palma, and A. L. Arroyave, pp. 517–30. Ministerio de Cultura y Deportes, IDAEH and Asociacion Tikal, Guatemala.
Aimers, J.
2007   What Maya Collapse? Terminal Classic Variation in the Maya Lowlands. *Journal of Archaeological Research* 15:329–77.

Ambrosino, J. N., T. Ardren, and T. W. Stanton
2003   The History of Warfare and Yaxuná. In *Ancient Mesoamerican Warfare*, edited by M. K. Brown and T. W. Stanton, pp. 109–23. AltaMira, Walnut Creek.

Andrews, A. P.
1983   *Maya Salt Production and Trade*. University of Arizona Press, Tucson.
1990   The Fall of Chichen Itza: A Preliminary Hypothesis. *Latin American Antiquity* 1:258–67.

Andrews, A. P., and F. Robles Castellanos
2004   An Archaeological Survey of Northwest Yucatan, Mexico. *Mexicon* 26:714.

Andrews, A. P., T. Gallereta N., F. Robles C., R. Cobos, and P. Cervera R.
1988   Isla Cerritos: An Itza Trading Port of the North Coast of Yucatan, Mexico. *National Geographic Research* 4:196–207.

Arens, W., and I. Karp (editors)
1989   *Creativity of Power: Cosmology and Action in African Societies*. Smithsonian Institution Press, Washington, D.C.

Arnold, J. E.
1995   Social Inequality, Marginalization and Economic Process. In *Foundations of Social Inequality*, edited by T. D. Price and G. M. Feinman, pp. 87–103. Plenum, New York.

Ashmore, W.
1986   Peten Cosmology in the Maya Southeast: An Analysis of Architecture and Settlement Patterns at Classic Quirigua. In *The Southeast Maya Periphery*, edited by P. A. Urban and E. M. Schortman, pp. 35–49. University of Texas Press, Austin.
1991   Site-Planning Principles and Concepts of Directionality among the Ancient Maya. *Latin American Antiquity* 2(3):199–226.
1992   Deciphering Maya Architectural Plans. In *New Theories on the Ancient Maya*, edited by E. C. Danien and R. J. Sharer, pp. 173–84. University Museum Monograph 77. University Museum, University of Pennsylvania, Philadelphia.
1998   Monumentos políticos: Sitio, asentamiento, y paisaje alrededor de Xunantunich, Belice. In *Anatomia de una civilizacion: Aproximaciones interdisciplinarias a la cultura Maya,* edited by A. Ciudad Ruiz, Y. Fernandez Marquinez, J. M. Garcia Campillo, M. J. Iglesias Ponce de Leon, A. Lacadena Garcia-Gallo, and L. T. Sanz Castro, pp. 161–83. Publicaciones de la S.E.E.M. No. 4. Sociedad Española de Estudios Maya, Madrid.
2002   Distinguished Lecture: "Decisions and Dispositions": Socializing Spatial Archaeology. *American Anthropologist* 104(4):1172–83.
2010   Antecedents, Allies, Antagonists: Xunantunich and Its Neighbors. In *Classic Maya Provincial Politics: Xunantunich and Its Hinterlands*, edited by L. J. LeCount and J. Yaeger, pp. 46–64. University of Arizona Press, Tucson.

Ashmore, W., and J. Sabloff
2002   Spatial Order in Maya Civic Plans. *Latin American Antiquity* 13:201–15.

Ashmore, W., J. Yaeger, and C. Robin
2004   Commoner Sense: Late and Terminal Classic Social Strategies in the Xunantunich Area. In *The Terminal Classic in the Maya Lowlands: Collapse, Transition, and*

Transformation, edited by A. A. Demarest, P. M. Rice and D. S. Rice, pp. 302–23. University Press of Colorado, Boulder, Colorado.

Atran, S.

1993   Itza Maya Tropical Agro-Forestry. *Current Anthropology* 34(5):633–700.

Bailey, F. G.

1969   *Stratagems and Spoils: A Social Anthropology of Politics*. Schocken Books, New York.

Baines, J., and N. Yoffee

2000   Order, Legitimacy, and Wealth: Setting the Terms. In *Order, Legitimacy, and Wealth in Ancient States*, edited by J. Richards and M. van Buren, pp. 13–17. Cambridge University Press, Cambridge.

Bair, D. A., and R. E. Terry

2012   In Search of Markets and Fields: Soil Chemical Investigations at Motul de San José. In *Motul de San José: Politics, History, and Economy in a Classic Maya Polity*, edited by A. E. Foias and K. F. Emery, pp. 357–385. University Press of Florida, Gainesville.

Ball, J. W.

1993   Pottery, Potters, Palaces, and Politics: Some Socioeconomic and Political Implication of Late Classic Maya Ceramic Industries. In *Lowland Maya Civilization in the Eighth Century A.D.*, edited by Jeremy A. Sabloff, and John S. Henderson, pp. 243–72. Dumbarton Oaks, Washington, D.C.

Ball, J. W., and J. T. Taschek

1991   Late Classic Lowland Maya Political Organization and Central Place Analysis: Insights from the Upper Belize Valley. *Ancient Mesoamerica* 2:149–65.

2003   Reconsidering the Belize Valley Preclassic: A Case for Multiethnic Interactions in the Development of a Regional Culture Tradition. *Ancient Mesoamerica* 14:179–217.

2001   The Buenavista-Cahal Pech Royal Court: Multi-Palace Court Mobility and Usage in a Petty Lowland Maya Kingdom. In *Royal Courts of the Ancient Maya*. Vol. 2, *Data and Case Studies*, edited by T. Inomata and S. Houston, 165–200. Westview Press, Boulder, Colorado.

Barrett, J.

2000   A Thesis on Agency. In *Agency in Archaeology*, edited by M. A. Dobres and J. E. Robb, pp. 61–68. Routledge, London.

Barth, F.

1959   *Political Leadership among Swat Pathans*. Athlone Press, London.

2007   Overview: Sixty Years in Anthropology. *Annual Review of Anthropology* 36:1–16.

Baudez, C.-F., and N. Latsanopoulos

2010   Political Structure, Military Training, and Ideology at Chichen Itza. *Ancient Mesoamerica* 21:1–20.

Bauer, B. S.

1996   Legitimization of the State in Inca Myth and Ritual. *American Anthropologist* 98(2):327–37.

Beach, T.

1998   Soil Constraints in Northwest Yucatán, Mexico: Pedoarchaeology and Maya Subsistence at Chunchucmil. *Geoarchaeology* 13:759–91.

Becker, M. J.

1971   The Identification of a Second Plaza Plan at Tikal, Guatemala and Its Implications for Ancient Maya Social Complexity. PhD dissertation, University of Pennsylvania, Philadelphia.

Beliaev, D.

2004   Wayaab' Title in Maya Hieroglyphic Inscriptions: On the Problem of Religious Specialization in Classic Maya Society. In *Continuity and Change: Maya Religious Practices in Temporal Perspective*, edited by D. Graña-Behrens, C. M. Prager, F. Sachse, S. Teufel, and E. Wagner, pp. 121–30. Acta Mesoamericana vol. 14. Verlag Anton Saurwein, Markt Schwaben.

Berlin, H.

1958   El Glifo "Emblema" en las Inscripciones Mayas. *Journal de la Societe des Americanistes* 47:111–19.

Bey, G.

2003   The Role of Ceramics in the Study of Conflict in Maya Archaeology. In *Ancient Mesoamerican Warfare*, edited by M. K. Brown and T. W. Stanton, pp. 19–29. AltaMira, Walnut Creek, California.

Blackmore, C.

2011   Ritual among the Masses: Deconstructing Identity and Class in an Ancient Maya Neighborhood. *Latin American Antiquity* 22(2):159–77.

Blanton, R. E.

1998   Beyond Centralization: Steps toward a Theory of Egalitarian Behavior in Archaic States. In *Archaic States*, edited by G. M. Feinman and J. Marcus, pp. 135–72. School of American Research, Santa Fe.

Blanton, R. E., and L. Fargher

2008   *Collective Action in the Formation of Pre-Modern States.* Springer, New York.

Blanton, R. E., G. M. Feinman, S. A. Kowalewski, and P. M. Peregrine

1996   A Dual-Processual Theory for the Evolution of Mesoamerican Civilization. *Current Anthropology* 38(1); 1–14.

Bloch, M.

1983   *Marxism and Anthropology: The History of a Relationship.* Clarendon Press, Oxford.

Boot, E.

2005   *Continuity and Change in Text and Image at Chichen Itza, Yucatan, Mexico: A Study of the Inscriptions, Iconography, and Architecture of a Late Classic to Early Postclassic Maya Site.* CNWS Publications 135. Research School CNWS, Leiden.

Borstein, J. A.

2005   Epiclassic Political Organization in Southern Veracruz, Mexico. *Ancient Mesoamerica* 16:11–21.

Boucher, S., and L. Quiñones

2007   Entre mercados, ferias y festines: Los murales de la Sub 1–4 de Chiik Nahb, Calakmul. *Mayab* 19:27–50.

Bourdieu, P.

1977   *Outline of a Theory of Practice.* Cambridge University Press, Cambridge.

1990   *The Logic of Practice.* Stanford University Press, Stanford.

Bradbury, R. E.

1967   The Kingdom of Benin. In *West African Kingdoms in the Nineteenth Century*, edited by C. D. Forde and P. M. Kaberry, pp. 1–35. International African Institute, Oxford University Press.

Brady, J. E.

1997   Settlement Configurations and Cosmology: The Role of Caves at Dos Pilas. *American Anthropologist* 99(3):602–18.

Brady, J. E., and W. Ashmore

1999   Mountains, Caves, Water: Ideational Landscapes of the Ancient Maya. In *Archaeologies of Landscape*, edited by W. Ashmore and A. B. Knapp, pp. 124–45. Blackwell, London.

Braswell, G. E.

1997   El Intercambio Preshispanico en Yucatan, Mexico. In *X Simposio de Investigaciones Arqueologicas en Guatemala, 1996*, edited by J. P. Laporte and H. L. Escobedo, pp. 545–55. Museo Nacional de Arqueologia y Etnologia, Guatemala City.

2001   Post-Classic Maya Courts of the Guatemalan Highlands: Archaeological and Ethnohistorical Approaches. In *Royal Courts of the Ancient Maya: 2. Data and Case Studies*, edited by T. Inomata and S. Houston, pp. 308–34. Westview Press, Boulder, Colorado.

Braswell, J. B.

2010   Elite Craft Production of Stone Drills and Slate at Group D, Xunantunich. In *Classic Maya Provincial Politics: Xunantunich and Its Hinterlands*, edited by L. J. LeCount and J. Yaeger, pp. 161–83. University of Arizona Press, Tucson.

Brown, L. A.

2000   From Discard to Divination: Demarcating the Sacred through the Collection and Curation of Discarded Objects. *Latin American Antiquity* 11:319–33.

2001   Feasting on the Periphery: The Production of Ritual Feasting and Village Festivals at the Ceren Site, El Salvador. In *Feasts: Archaeological and Ethnographic Perspectives on Food, Politics, and Power*, edited by M. Dietler and B. Hayden, pp. 368–90. Smithsonian Institution Press, Washington, D.C.

Brown, M. K., and T. W. Stanton (editors)

2003   *Ancient Mesoamerican Warfare*. AltaMira, Walnut Creek, California.

Brumfiel, E. M.

1983   Aztec State Making: Ecology, Structure, and the Origin of the State. *American Anthropologist* 85 (2):261–284.

1992   Distinguished Lecture in Archaeology: Breaking and Entering the Ecosystem: Gender, Class, and Faction Steal the Show. *American Anthropologist* 94 (3):551–67.

1996   Figurine and the Aztec State: Testing the Effectiveness of Ideological Domination. In *Gender in Archaeology: Research in Gender and Practice*, edited by R. P. Wright, pp. 143–66. University of Pennsylvania Press, Philadelphia.

2006   Cloth, Gender, Continuity, and Change: Fabricating Unity in Anthropology. *American Anthropologist* 108(4):862–77.

Brumfiel, E. M., and J. W. Fox

1994   *Factional Competition and Political Development in the New World*. Cambridge University Press, Cambridge.

Bullard, W. R., Jr.

1960   Maya Settlement Pattern in Northeastern Peten, Guatemala. *American Antiquity* 25(3):355–72.

Bunzel, R.

1981   *Chichicastenango.* Translated into Spanish by F. Gall. Seminario de Integracion Social Guatemalteca Publication no. 41. Ministry of Education, Guatemala City.

Calvin, I.

1997   Where the Wayob Live: A Further Example of Classic Maya Supernaturals. In *The Maya Vase Book*, vol. 5, edited by J. Kerr and B. Kerr, pp. 868–83. Kerr Associates, New York.

Cancian, F.

1965   *Economics and Prestige in a Maya Community: The Religious Cargo System of Zinacantan.* Stanford University Press, Stanford, California.

Carmack, R. M.

1981   *The Quiché Maya of Utatlan: The Evolution of a Highland Guatemala Kingdom.* University of Oklahoma Press, Norman.

Carrasco Vargas, R., V. A. Vasquez Lopez, and S. Martin

2009   Daily Life of the Ancient Maya Recorded on Murals at Calakmul, Mexico. *Proceedings of the National Academy of Science* 106(46):19245–49.

Caso Barrera, L.

2002   *Caminos en la selva: Migración, comercio y resistencia, Mayas yucatecos e itzaes, siglos XVII–XIX.* Colegio de México, Fondo de Cultura Económica, México City.

Castellanos, J.

2007   *Buenavista Nuevo San José, Petén, Guatemala: Otra Aldea del Preclásico Medio (800–400 a.c.).* Report submitted to the Foundation for the Advancement of Mesoamerican Studies, Inc. Available at www.famsi.org/reports/05039es/index.html.

Chapman, A. C.

2003   *Archaeologies of Complexity.* Routledge, London.

Chase, A. F., and D. Z. Chase

1992   Mesoamerican Elites: Assumptions, Definitions and Models. In *Mesoamerican Elites: An Archaeological Assessment*, edited by D. Z. Chase and A. F. Chase, pp. 3–17. University of Oklahoma Press, Norman.

1996   More than Kin and King: Centralized Political Organization among the Late Classic Maya. *Current Anthropology* 37(5):803–10.

1998   The Architectural Context of Caches, Burials, and Other Ritual Activities for the Classic Maya period. In *Function and Meaning in Classic Maya Architecture*, edited by S. D. Houston, pp. 299–328. Dumbarton Oaks, Washington, D.C.

2003   Minor Centers, Complexity and Scale in Lowland Maya Settlement Archaeology. In *Perspectives on Ancient Maya Rural Complexity,* edited by G. Iannone and S. V. Connell, pp. 108–18. Cotsen Institute of Archaeology Monograph 49. University of California, Los Angeles.

Chase, A. F., D. Z. Chase, and M. E. Smith

2009   States and Empires in Ancient Mesoamerica. *Ancient Mesoamerica* 20:175–82.

Chase, A. F., N. Grube, and D. Z. Chase

1991   *Three Terminal Classic Monuments from Caracol, Belize.* Research Reports on Ancient Maya Writing 36. Center for Maya Research, Washington, D.C.

Chase, D. Z., and A. F. Chase

1992   An Archaeological Assessment of Mesoamerican Elites. In *Mesoamerican Elites: An Archaeological Assessment,* ed. by D. Z. Chase and A. F. Chase, pp. 303–17. University of Oklahoma Press, Norman.

2003   Texts and Contexts in Maya Warfare: A Brief Consideration of Epigraphy and Archaeology at Caracol, Belize. In *Ancient Mesoamerican Warfare,* edited by M. K. Brown and T. W. Stanton, pp. 171–88. AltaMira Press, Walnut Creek.

Chase, D. Z., A. F. Chase, and W. A. Haviland

1990   The Classic Maya City: Reconsidering the "Mesoamerican Urban Tradition." *American Anthropologist* 92:499–506.

Chase-Dunn, C., and P. Grimes

1995   World-Systems Analysis. *Annual Review of Sociology* 21:387–417.

Chase-Dunn, C., and T. D. Hall

1997   *Rise and Demise: Comparing World-Systems.* Westview Press, Boulder, Colorado.

Cheetham, D. T.

2005   Cunil: A Pre-Mamom Horizon in the Southern Maya Lowlands. In *New Perspectives on Formative Mesoamerican Cultures,* edited by T. G. Powis, pp. 27–38. BAR International Series 1377. Archaeopress, Oxford.

Cheetham, D. T., D. W. Forsyth, and J. E. Clark

2003   La ceramica pre-Mamom de la Cuenca del Rio Belice y del centro de Peten: Las correspondencias y sus implicaciones. In *XVI Simposio de Investigaciones Arqueologicas en Guatemala, 2002,* edited by J. P. Laporte, B. Arroyo, H. Escobedo and H. Mejia, pp. 615–34. Museo Nacional de Arqueologia y Etnologia, Guatemala City.

Christaller, W., and C. W. Baskin

1966   *Central Places in Southern Germany.* Prentice Hall, Englewood Cliffs, New Jersey.

Ciudad Ruiz, A.

2001   El sistema politico hegemonico en el sur de las tierras bajas Mayas a finales del Postclasico. In *Anales de la Academia de Geografia e Historia de Guatemala* 76:191–238. Guatemala.

Claessen, H. J. M., and J. G. Oosten (editors)

1996   *Ideology and the Formation of Early States.* E. J. Brill, New York.

Claessen, H. J. M., and P. Skalnik (editors)

1978   *The Early State.* Mouton Publishers, The Hague, Netherlands.

1981   *The Study of the State.* Mouton Publishers, The Hague, Netherlands.

Claessen, H. J. M., and P. van de Velde (editors)

1987   *Early State Dynamics.* E. J. Brill, Leiden, Netherlands.

1991   *Early State Economics.* Political and Economic Anthropology vol. 8. Transaction Publishers, New Brunswick, N.J.

Claessen, H. J. M., P. van de Velde, and M. E. Smith (editors)

1985   *Development and Decline: The Evolution of Sociopolitical Organization.* Bergin and Garvey, South Hadley, Massachusetts.

Clark, J. E.

1996   Reply to Forum on "Agency, Ideology, and Power in Archaeological Theory." *Current Anthropology* 37(1):51–52.

Clark, J. E., and M. Blake

1994   The Power of Prestige: Competitive Generosity and the Emergence of Rank Socie-
       ties in Lowland Mesoamerica. In *Factional Competition and Political Development
       in the New World*, edited by E. M. Brumfiel and J. W. Fox, pp. 17–30. Cambridge
       University Press, Cambridge.

Clark, J. E., and R. D. Hansen

2001   Architecture of Early Kingship: Comparative Perspectives on the Origins of the
       Maya Royal Court. In *Royal Courts of the Ancient Maya: 2, Data and Case Studies*,
       edited by T. Inomata and S. Houston, pp. 1–45. Westview Press, Boulder, Colorado.

Clark, J. E., R. D. Hansen, and T. Pérez Suárez

2000   La Zona Maya en el Preclasico. In *Historia Antigua de Mexico*. Vol. 1, *El Mexico
       Antiguo, sus Areas Culturales, los Origenes y el Horizonte Preclasico*, edited by L.
       Manzanilla and L. Lopez Lujan, pp. 437–510. Instituto Nacional de Antropologia
       e Historia, Mexico, DF.

Clark, J. E., and W. J. Parry

1990   Craft Specialization and Cultural Complexity. In *Research in Economic Anthropo-
       logy*, vol. 12, edited by B. Isaac, pp. 289–346. JAI Press, Greenwich, Connecticut.

Cobos Palma, R.

2004   Chichen Itza: Settlement and Hegemony during the Terminal Classic Period. In
       *The Terminal Classic in the Maya Lowlands: Collapse, Transition, and Transforma-
       tion*, edited by A. Demarest, P. Rice, and D. Rice, pp. 517–44. University of Colo-
       rado Press, Boulder.

2007   Multepal or Centralized Kingship? New Evidence on Governmental Organization
       at Chichen Itza. In *Twin Tollans: Chichen Itza, Tula, and the Epiclassic to Early
       Postclassic Mesoamerican World*, edited by J. K. Kowalski and C. Kristan-Graham,
       pp. 315–43. Dumbarton Oaks, Washington, D.C.

Coe, M. D., and J. Kerr

1997   *The Art of the Maya Scribe*. Harry N. Abrams, New York.

Coe, M. D., and M. Van Stone

2005   *Reading the Maya Glyphs*. 2nd ed. Thames & Hudson, New York.

Coggins, C. C.

1975   Painting and Drawing Style at Tikal: An Historical and Iconographic Reconstruc-
       tion. PhD dissertation, Department of Fine Arts, Harvard University, Cambridge.

1983   *The Stucco Decoration and Architectural Assemblage of Structure 1-Sub, Dzibilchal-
       tun, Yucatan, Mexico*. MARI Publication 40. Tulane University, New Orleans.

Conlon, J. M., and A. F. Moore

2003   Identifying Urban and Rural Settlement Components: An Examination of Classic
       Period Plazuela Group Function at the Ancient Maya Site of Baking Pot, Belize.
       In *Perspectives on Ancient Maya Rural Complexity*, edited by G. Iannone and S. V.
       Connell, pp. 59–70. Cotsen Institute of Archaeology Monograph 49. University of
       California, Los Angeles.

Connell, S. V.

2003   Making Sense of Variability among Minor Centers: The Ancient Maya of Chaa
       Creek, Belize. In *Perspectives on Ancient Maya Rural Complexity*, edited by G. Ian-
       none and S. V. Connell, pp. 27–41. Cotsen Institute of Archaeology Monograph 49.
       University of California, Los Angeles.

2010   A Community to be Counted: Chaa Creek and the Emerging Xunantunich Polity. In *Classic Maya Provincial Politics: Xunantunich and Its Hinterlands*, edited by L. J. LeCount and J. Yaeger, pp. 295–314. University of Arizona Press, Tucson.

Conrad, G. W., and A. A. Demarest
1984   *Religion and Empire: The Dynamics of Aztec and Inca Expansionism.* Cambridge University Press, New York.

Conrad, G. W., and A. A. Demarest (editors)
1986   *Ideology and Pre-Columbian Civilizations.* School of American Research Press, Santa Fe.

Cook, P. M.
1997   Basal Platform Mounds at Chau Hiix Belize: Evidence for Ancient Maya Social Structure and Cottage Industry Manufacturing. PhD dissertation, Department of Anthropology, University of Arizona. University Microfilms, Ann Arbor.

Cortes, H.
1908   *The Letters of Cortes to Charles V.* Translated by F. A. MacNutt. 2 vols. Oxford University Press, New York.

Cowgill, G. L.
1977   On Causes and Consequences of Ancient and Modern Population Changes. *American Anthropologist* 77:505–25.

1993   Distinguished Lecture in Archaeology: Beyond Criticizing New Archaeology. *American Anthropologist* 95(3):551–73.

Crumley, C. L.
1976   Toward a Locational Definition of State Systems of Settlement. *American Anthropologist* 78:59–73.

1979   Three Locational Models: An Epistemological Assessment of Anthropology and Archaeology. In *Advances in Archaeological Method and Theory*, vol. 2, edited by M. B. Schiffer, pp. 141–73. Academic Press, New York.

1987   A Dialectical Critique of Hierarchy. In *Power Relations and State Formation*, edited by T. C. Patterson and C. Ward Gailey, pp. 155–69. American Anthropological Association, Washington, D.C.

1995   Heterarchy and the Analysis of Complex Societies. In *Heterarchy and the Analysis of Complex Societies,* edited by R. M. Ehrenreich, C. L. Crumley, and J. E. Levy, pp. 1–6. Archaeological Papers 6. American Anthropological Association, Arlington, Virginia.

2001   Communication, Holism and the Evolution of Sociopolitical Complexity. In *From Leaders to Rulers*, edited by J. Haas, pp. 19–33. Kluwer Academic/Plenum, New York.

Culbert, T. P.
1973   The Maya Downfall at Tikal. In *The Classic Maya Collapse*, edited by T. P. Culbert, pp. 63–92. University of New Mexico Press, Albuquerque.

1988a   Political History and the Decipherment of Maya Glyphs. *Antiquity* 62:135–52.

1988b   The Collapse of Classic Maya Civilization. In *The Collapse of Ancient States and Civilizations*, edited by N. Yoffee and G. Cowgill, pp. 69–101. University of Arizona Press, Tucson.

1991   Polities in the Northeast Peten, Guatemala. In *Classic Maya Political History: Hi-*

eroglyphic and Archaeological Evidence, edited by T. P. Culbert, pp. 128–46. Cambridge University Press, New York.

1992   La escala de las entidades politicas mayas. In *V Simposio de Investigaciones Arqueologicas en Guatemala*, edited by J. P. Laporte, H. Escobedo, and S. Villagran de Brady, pp. 261–67. Ministerio de Cultura y Deportes, IDAEH, Asociacion Tikal, Guatemala City.

Culbert, T. P., and D. Rice (editors)

1990   *Precolumbian Population History in the Maya Lowlands*. University of New Mexico Press, Albuquerque.

Dahlin, B. H.

2003   Chunchucmil: A Complex Economy in NW Yucatán. *Mexicon* 25:129–38.

Dahlin B. H., and T. Ardren

2002   Modes of Exchange and Their Effects on Regional and Urban Patterns at Chunchucmil, Yucatán, Mexico. In *Ancient Maya Political Economies*, edited by M. A. Masson and D. Freidel, pp. 249–84. AltaMira Press, Walnut Creek, California.

Dahlin, B. H., A. P. Andrews, T. Beach, C. Bezanilla, P. Farrell, S. Luzzadder-Beach, and V. McCormick

1998   Punta Canbalam in Context: A Peripatetic Coastal Site in Northwest Campeche, Mexico. *Ancient Mesoamerica* 9:1–15.

Dahlin, B. H., D. Bair, T. Beach, M. Moriarty, and R. Terry

2009   The Dirt on Food: Ancient Feasts and Markets among the Lowland Maya. In *Pre-Columbian Foodways: Landscapes of Creation and Origin*, edited by J. E. Staller and M. B. Carrasco, pp. 191–232. Springer, New York.

Dahlin, B. H., T. Beach, S. Luzzadder-Beach, D. Hixson, S. Hutson, A. Magnoni, E. Mansell, and D. Mazeau

2005   Reconstructing Agricultural Self-Sufficiency at Chunchucmil, Yucatán, Mexico. *Ancient Mesoamerica* 16(2):1–19.

Dahlin, B. H., C. T. Jensen, R. E. Terry, D. R. Wright, and T. Beach

2007   In Search of an Ancient Maya Market. *Latin American Antiquity* 18(4):363–84.

D'Altroy, T. N.

1996   Reply to Forum on "Agency, Ideology, and Power in Archaeological Theory." *Current Anthropology* 37(1):55–56.

D'Altroy, T. N., and T. K. Earle

1985   Staple Finance, Wealth Finance, and Storage in the Inka Political Economy. *Current Anthropology* 26:187–206.

De Montmollin, O.

1989   *The Archaeology of Political Structure: Settlement Analysis in a Classic Maya Polity*. Cambridge University Press, Cambridge.

1995   *Settlement and Politics in Three Classic Maya Polities*. Prehistory Press, Madison, Wisconsin.

Demarest, A. A.

1992   Ideology in Ancient Maya Cultural Evolution: The Dynamics of Galactic Polities. In *Ideology and Pre-Columbian Civilizations,* edited by A. A. Demarest and G. Conrad, pp. 135–58. School of American Research Press, Santa Fe, New Mexico.

1996a   Closing Comment to Forum on Theory in Anthropology, The Maya State: Centralized or Segmentary? *Current Anthropology* 37(5):821–24.

1996b   War, Peace, and the Collapse of a Native American Civilization: Lessons for Contemporary Systems of Conflict. In *A Natural History of Peace*, edited by T. Gregor, pp. 215–48. Vanderbilt University Press, Nashville, Tennessee.

1996c   Reply to Forum on "Agency, Ideology, and Power in Archaeological Theory." *Current Anthropology* 37(1):56.

1997   The Vanderbilt Petexbatun Regional Archaeological Project, 1989–1994: Overview, History, and Major Results of a Multidisciplinary Study of the Classic Maya Collapse. *Ancient Mesoamerica* 8:209–227.

2004   *Ancient Maya: The Rise and Fall of a Rainforest Civilization*. Cambridge University Press, Cambridge and New York.

2006   *The Petexbatun Regional Archaeological Project: A Multidisciplinary Study of the Maya Collapse*. Vanderbilt Institute of Mesoamerican Archaeology Series No. 1. Vanderbilt University Press, Nashville, Tennessee.

Demarest, A. A., and A. E. Foias

1993   Mesoamerican Horizons and the Cultural Transformations of Maya Civilization. In *Latin American Horizons: Symposium at Dumbarton Oaks, 11th and 12th October 1986*, edited by D. Rice, pp. 147–192. Dumbarton Oaks Research Library and Collection, Washington, DC.

Demarest, A. A., P. M. Rice, and D. S. Rice (editors)

2004   *The Terminal Classic in the Maya Lowlands: Collapse, Transition and Transformation*. University Press of Colorado, Boulder.

DeMarrais, E.

2005   *Rethinking Materiality: The Engagement of Mind with the Material World*. McDonald Institute for Archaeological Research, Cambridge.

DeMarrais, E., L. J. Castillo, and T. Earle

1996   Ideology, Materialization and Power Strategies. *Current Anthropology* 37:15–31.

2004   The Materialization of Culture. In *Rethinking Materiality: The Engagement of Mind with the Material World*, edited by E. DeMarrais, C. Gosden and C. Renfrew, pp. 11–22. McDonald Institute for Archaeological Research, Cambridge.

Diakonoff, I. M.

1974   *Structure of Ancient Society and State in Early Dynastic Sumer*. Monographs of the Ancient Near East 1 (3). Undena Publications, Malibu, California.

Dirks, N. B.

1991   Ritual and Resistance: Subversion as a Social Fact. In *Contesting Power: Resistance and Everyday Social Relations in South Asia*, edited by D. Haynes and G. Prakash, pp. 213–38. University of California Press, Berkeley.

Dobres, M.-A., and J. E. Robb (editors)

2000   *Agency in Archaeology*. Routledge, London.

Donham, D. L.

1999   *History, Power, Ideology: Central Issues in Marxism and Anthropology*. University of California Press, Berkeley.

Doyle, M.

1986   *Empires*. Cornell University Press, Ithaca, New York.

Dunning, N.
1992   *Lords of the Hills: Ancient Maya Settlement in the Puuc Region, Yucatan, Mexico.* Monographs in World Archaeology 15. Prehistory Press, Madison, Wisconsin.

Earle, T. K.
1991   The Evolution of Chiefdoms. In *Chiefdoms: Power, Economy and Ideology*, edited by T. Earle, pp. 1–15. Cambridge University Press, Cambridge.
1997   *How Chiefs Come to Power: The Political Economy in Prehistory.* Stanford University Press, Stanford, California.
2001   Institutionalization of Chiefdoms: Why Landscapes Are Built. In *From Leaders to Rulers*, edited by J. Haas, pp. 105–24. Kluwer Academic/Plenum, New York.
2004   Distinguished Lecture: Culture Matters in the Neolithic Transition and Emergence of Hierarchy in Thy, Denmark. *American Anthropologist* 106(1):111–25.

Edmonson, M. S.
1979   Some Postclassic Questions about the Classic Maya. In *Tercera Mesa Redonda de Palenque*, vol. 4, edited by M. Greene Robertson and D. C. Jeffers, pp. 9–18. Pre-Columbian Art Research Center, Palenque, Mexico.
1982   *The Ancient Future of the Itza: The Book of Chilam Balam of Tizimin.* University of Texas Press, Austin.
1986   *Heaven Born Merida and Its Destiny: The Book of Chilam Balam of Chumayel.* University of Texas Press, Austin.

Ehrenreich, R. M., C. L. Crumley, and J. E. Levy (editors)
1995   *Heterarchy and the Analysis of Complex Societies.* Archaeological Papers of the American Anthropological Association No. 6. American Anthropological Association, Washington, D.C.

Eisenstadt, S. N.
1993   *The Political Systems of Empires.* 2nd ed. Transaction Publishers, New Brunswick, New Jersey.

Emerson, T. E.
1997   *Cahokia and the Archaeology of Power.* University of Alabama Press, Tuscaloosa.

Emerson, T. E., and T. R. Pauketat
2002   Embodying Power and Resistance at Cahokia. In *The Dynamics of Power*, edited by M. O'Donovan, pp. 105–25. Center for Archaeological Investigation Occasional Papers No. 30. Southern Illinois University, Carbondale.

Emery, K. F.
2003a   Natural Resource Use and Classic Maya Economics: Environmental Archaeology at Motul de San José, Guatemala. *Mayab* 16:33–48.
2003b   Animals from the Maya Underworld: Reconstructing Elite Maya Ritual at the Cueva de los Quetzales, Guatemala. In *Behavior behind Bones: The Zooarchaeology of Religion, Ritual, Status and Identity*, edited by S. Jones O'Day, W. Van Neer and A. Ervynck, pp. 101–13. Oxbow Books, Oxford, U.K.
2012   Zooarchaeology of Motul de San Jose: Animals in Environmental and Economic Perspective. In *Motul de San José: Politics, History, and Economy in a Classic Maya Polity*, edited by A. E. Foias and K. F. Emery, pp. 291–325. University Press of Florida, Gainesville.

Emery, K., and A. E. Foias

2012   Landscape, Economies, and the Politics of Power in the Motul de San José Zone. In *Motul de San José: Politics, History, and Economy in a Classic Maya Polity*, edited by A. E. Foias and K. F. Emery, pp. 401–18. University Press of Florida, Gainesville.

Estrada-Belli, F.

2011   *The First Maya Civilization: Ritual and Power before the Classic Period*. Routledge, New York.

Estrada-Belli, F., A. Tokovinine, J. M. Foley, H. Hurst, G. A. Ware, D. Stuart, and N. Grube

2009   A Maya Palace at Holmul, Peten, Guatemala, and the Teotihuacan "Entrada": Evidence from Murals 7 and 9. *Latin American Antiquity* 20(1):228–59.

Farriss, N. M.

1984   *Maya Society under Colonial Rule: The Collective Enterprise of Survival*. Princeton University Press, Princeton, New Jersey.

Fash, B., W. Fash, S. Lane, R. Larios, L. Schele, J. Stomper, and D. Stuart

1992   Investigations of a Classic Maya Council House at Copan, Honduras. *Journal of Field Archaeology* 19:419–42.

Fash, W. L.

1991   *Scribes, Warriors and Kings: The City of Copán and the Ancient Maya*. Thames and Hudson, London.

Fash, W. L., and D. Stuart

1991   Dynastic History and Cultural Evolution at Copan, Honduras. In *Classic Maya Political History: Hieroglyphic and Archaeological Evidence*, edited by T. P. Culbert, pp. 147–79. Cambridge University Press, New York.

Fedick, S. (editor)

1996   *The Managed Mosaic: Ancient Maya Agriculture and Resource Use*. University of Utah Press, Salt Lake City.

Feinman, G. M.

1995   The Emergence of Inequality: A Focus on Strategies and Processes. In *Foundations of Social Inequality* edited by T. D. Price and G. M. Feinman, pp. 255–79. Plenum Press, New York.

1998   Scale and Social Organization: Perspectives on the Archaic State. In *Archaic States*, edited by G. M. Feinman and J. Marcus, pp. 95–133. School of American Research, Santa Fe.

2001   Mesoamerican Political Complexity: The Corporate-Network Dimension. In *From Leaders to Rulers*, edited by J. Haas, pp. 151–75. Kluwer Academic/Plenum, New York.

Feinman, G. M., and J. Marcus (editors)

1998   *Archaic States*. School of American Research Press, Santa Fe, New Mexico.

Feinman, G. M., and J. Neitzel

1984   Too Many Types: An Overview of Sedentary Prestate Societies in the Americas. *Advances in Archaeological Method and Theory* 7:39–102.

Feinman, G. M., and L. M. Nicholas

2004   Unraveling the Prehispanic Highland Mesoamerican Economy: Production, Exchange, and Consumption in the Classic Period Valley of Oaxaca. In *Archaeological Perspectives on Political Economies*, edited by G. M. Feinman and L. M. Nicholas, pp. 167–88. University of Utah Press, Salt Lake City.

Fitzsimmons, J.
2006   Kings of Jaguar Hill: Monuments and Caches at Zapote Bobal. Report to the Foundation for the Advancement of Mesoamerican Studies, Inc. Available at www.famsi.org/reports/05047/. Accessed September 1, 2012.

Flannery, K. V.
1972   The Cultural Evolution of Civilizations. *Annual Review of Ecology and Systematics* 3:399–426.
1998   The Ground Plans of Archaic States. In *Archaic States*, edited by G. M. Feinman and J. Marcus, pp. 15–57. School of American Research, Santa Fe, New Mexico.

Fleisher, J., and S. Wynne-Jones
2010   Authorisation and the Process of Power: The View from African Archaeology. *Journal of World Prehistory* 23:177–93.

Foias, A. E.
2000   History, Politics, and Economics at Motul de San José. Paper presented at the 2000 Maya Hieroglyphic Meetings at University of Texas, Austin, entitled Core-Periphery Interactions in Mesoamerica: Tikal and Its Neighbors. Manuscript on file, Department of Anthropology & Sociology, Williams College, Williamstown, Massachusetts.
2002   At the Crossroads: The Economic Basis of Political Power in the Petexbatun Region. In *Ancient Maya Political Economies,* edited by M. A. Masson and D. Freidel, pp. 239–40. AltaMira Press, Walnut Creek, California.
2003   Perspectivas Teóricas en las Dinámicas del Estado Clásico Maya: Resultados Preliminares del Proyecto Eco-arqueológico Motul de San José, 1998–2003. *Mayab* 16:15–32.
2004   The Past and Future of Maya Ceramic Studies. In *Continuities and Changes in Maya Archaeology: Perspectives at the Millennium*, edited by C. Golden and G. Borgstede, pp. 143–75. Routledge Press, New York.
2007   Pots, Sherds and Glyphs: Pottery Production and Exchange at the Twin Capitals of the Petexbatun Polity, Petén, Guatemala. In *Pottery Economics in Mesoamerica: Integrated Approaches*, edited by C. A. Poole and G. J. Bey, III, pp. 212–36. University of Arizona Press, Tucson.

Foias, A. E. (editor)
1998   *Proyecto Arqueológico Motul de San José: Informe Preliminar #1: Temporada de Campo 1998*. Report submitted to Williams College, Williamstown, and the Institute of Anthropology and History, Guatemala City. Available at www.motul-archaeology.williams.edu.
1999   *Proyecto Arqueológico Motul de San José: Informe Preliminar #2: Temporada de Campo 1999*. Report submitted to Williams College, Williamstown and the Institute of Anthropology and History, Guatemala City. Available at www.motul-archaeology.williams.edu.

Foias, A. E., and K. F. Emery (editors)
2012   *Motul de San José: Politics, History, and Economy in a Classic Maya Polity*. University Press of Florida, Gainesville.

Foias, A. E., C. T. Halperin, E. Spensley, and J. Castellanos
2012   Architecture, Volumetrics and Social Stratification at Motul de San José during the

Late and Terminal Classic. In *Motul de San José: Politics, History, and Economy in a Classic Maya Polity*, edited by A. E. Foias and K. F. Emery, pp. 94–138. University Press of Florida, Gainesville.

Folan, W. J., E. R. Kintz, and L. A. Fletcher

1983   *Coba: A Classic Maya Metropolis*. Academic Press, New York.

Ford, A.

2004   Integration among Communities, Centers, and Regions: The Case from El Pilar. In *The Ancient Maya of the Belize Valley: Half a Century of Archaeological Research*, edited by James F. Garber, pp. 238–56. University Press of Florida, Gainesville.

Ford, A., and R. Nigh

2009   Origins of the Maya Forest Garden: Maya Resources Management. *Journal of Ethnobiology* 29(2):213–36.

Foucault, M.

1978a   *The History of Sexuality*, vol 1. Translated by Robert Hurley. Pantheon Books, New York.

1978b   *The History of Sexuality*, vol 3. Translated by Robert Hurley. Pantheon Books, New York.

1979   *Discipline and Punish: The Birth of the Prison*. Translated by Alan Sheridan. Vintage Books, New York.

1991   Governmentality. In *The Foucault Effect: Studies in Governmentality*, edited by G. Burchell, C. Gordon, and P. Miller, pp. 87–104. University of Chicago Press, Chicago.

Fourquin, G.

1978   *The Anatomy of Popular Rebellion in the Middle Ages*. Elsevier, Amsterdam.

Fox, J. W.

1977   *Urban Anthropology: Cities in Their Cultural Settings*. Prentice Hall, Englewood Cliffs, New Jersey.

1987   *Maya Post-Classic State Formation: Segmentary Lineage Migration in Advancing Frontiers*. Cambridge University Press, Cambridge.

Fox, J., G. W. Cook, A. F. Chase, and D. Z. Chase

1996   Questions of Political and Economic Integration: Segmentary versus Centralized States among the Ancient Maya. *Current Anthropology* 37(5):795–801.

Freidel, D.

1986   Terminal Classic Lowland Maya: Successes, Failures, and Aftermaths. In *Late Lowland Maya Civilization*, edited by J. A. Sabloff and A. E. Wyllys, pp. 409–30. School of American Research, University of New Mexico Press, Albuquerque.

Freidel, D. A., and J. A. Sabloff

1984   *Cozumel: Late Maya Settlement Patterns*. Academic Press, New York.

Freidel, D., B. MacLeod, and C. K. Suhler

2003   Early Classic Maya Conquest in Words and Deeds. In *Ancient Mesoamerican Warfare*, edited by M. Kathryn Brown and Travis W. Stanton, pp. 189–215. AltaMira Press, Walnut Creek, California.

Freidel, D., L. Schele, and J. Parker

1993   *Maya Cosmos: Three Thousand Years on the Shaman's Path*. William Morrow, New York.

Fried, M. H.

1967   *The Evolution of Political Society: An Essay in Political Anthropology.* Random House, New York.

1978   The State, the Chicken, and the Egg; or, What Came First? In *Origins of the State,* edited by R. Cohen and E. Service, pp. 35–47. Institute of Study of Human Issues, Philadelphia.

Gailey, C. W.

1987   *Kinship to Kingship: Gender Hierarchy and State Formation in the Tongan Islands.* University of Texas Press, Austin.

Garber, J. F, M. K. Brown, and C. J. Hartman

2002   The Early/Middle Formative Kanocha Phase (1200–850 B.C.) at Blackman Eddy, Belize. Report submitted to the Foundation for the Advancement of Mesoamerican Studies, Inc. Available at www.famsi.org/reports/00090/index.html. Accessed September 1, 2012.

Garber, J. F, M. K. Brown, J. Awe, and C. J. Hartman

2004   Middle Formative Prehistory of the Central Belize Valley: An Examination of Architecture, Material Culture, and Sociopolitical Change at Blackman Eddy. In *The Ancient Maya of the Belize Valley: Half a Century of Archaeological Research*, edited by J. F. Garber, pp. 25–47. University Press of Florida, Gainesville.

Garcia Campillo, J.

1991   Edificios y dignitarios: La historia escrita de Oxkintok. In *Oxkintok: Una ciudad maya de Yucatan*, edited by M. R. Dorado, pp. 55–78. Mision Arqueologica de Espana en Mexico, Madrid.

1992   Informe epigrafico sobre Oxkintok y la ceramica Chocholá. *Oxkintok* 4:185–200.

Garnsey, P., and R. Saller

1987   *The Roman Empire: Economy, Society and Culture.* University of California Press, Berkeley.

Garraty, C. P.

2000   Ceramic Indexes of Aztec Eliteness. *Ancient Mesoamerica* 11:323–40.

Geertz, C.

1980   *Negara: The Theater State in Nineteenth-Century Bali.* Princeton University Press, Princeton, New Jersey.

Gerth, H. H., and C. Wright Mills (translators and editors)

1960   *From Max Weber: Essays in Sociology.* Oxford University Press, New York.

Giddens, A.

1979   *Central Problems in Social Theory: Action, Structure, and Contradiction in Social Analysis.* University of California Press, Berkeley.

1981   *A Contemporary Critique of Historical Materialism.* Macmillan, London.

1984   *The Constitution of Society: Outline of the Theory of Structuration.* University of California Press, Berkeley.

Gill, R. B.

2000   *The Great Maya Droughts: Water, Life and Death.* University of New Mexico Press, Albuquerque.

Gillespie, S. D.

2000   Rethinking Ancient Maya Social Organization: Replacing "Lineage" with "House." *American Anthropologist* 102(3):467–84.

2001   Personhood, Agency, and Mortuary Ritual: A Case Study from the Ancient Maya. *Journal of Anthropological Archaeology* 20:73–112.

Gilman, A.
1996   Reply to Forum on "Agency, Ideology, and Power in Archaeological Theory." *Current Anthropology* 37(1):56–57.

Godelier, M.
1978   Infrastructures, Societies, and History. *Current Anthropology* 19:763–71.
1988   *The Mental and the Material: Thought, Economy and Society.* Verso, London.

Golden, C.
2003   The Politics of Warfare in the Usumacinta Basin: La Pasadita and the Realm of Bird Jaguar. In *Ancient Mesoamerican Warfare*, edited by M. K. Brown and T. W. Stanton, pp. 31–48. AltaMira, Walnut Creek, California.

Golden, C., A. K. Scherer, A. R. Muñoz, and R. Vasquez
2008   Piedras Negras and Yaxchilan: Divergent Political Trajectories in Adjacent Maya Polities. *Latin American Antiquity* 19:249–74.

Gómez-Pompa, A., J. S. Flores, M. Aliphat Fernandez
1990   The Sacred Cacao Groves of the Maya. *Latin American Antiquity* 1(3):247–57.

Gómez-Pompa, A., and A. Kaus
1990   Traditional Management of Tropical Forests in Mexico. In *Alternatives to Deforestation: Steps towards Sustainable Use of the Amazon Rain Forest*, edited by A. Anderson, pp. 45–64. Columbia University Press, New York.

Gonlin, N.
2007   Ritual and Ideology among Classic Maya Rural Commoners at Copan, Honduras. In *Commoner Ritual and Ideology in Ancient Mesoamerica*, edited by N. Gonlin and J. C. Lohse, pp. 83–122. University Press of Colorado, Boulder.

Gonlin, N., and J. C. Lohse (editors)
2007   *Commoner Ritual and Ideology in Ancient Mesoamerica.* University Press of Colorado, Boulder.

Graham, E.
2002   Perspectives on Economy and Theory. In *Ancient Maya Political Economies*, edited by Marilyn A. Masson and David Freiden, pp. 398–418. AltaMira Press, Oxford.
2011   *Maya Christians and Their Churches in Sixteenth-Century Belize.* University Press of Florida, Gainesville.
2012   Control without Controlling: Motul de San José and Its Environs from an Outsider's Perspective. In *Motul de San José: Politics, History, and Economy in a Classic Maya Polity*, edited by A. E. Foias and K. F. Emery, pp. 419–30. University Press of Florida, Gainesville.

Graña-Behrens, D.
2006   Emblem Glyphs and Political Organization in Northwestern Yucatan in the Classic Period (A.D. 300–1000). *Ancient Mesoamerica* 17:105–23.

Grazioso Sierra, L., T. P. Culbert, V. Fialko, T. Sever, J. Murphy, and C. Ramos
2001   Arqueología en el Bajo La Justa, El Petén, Guatemala. In *XIV Simposio de Investigaciones Arqueológicas en Guatemala, 2000*, edited by J. P. Laporte, A. C. de Suásnavar, and B. Arroyo, pp. 205–9. Museo Nacional de Arqueología y Etnología, Guatemala

Grube, N.

1994   Hieroglyphic Sources for the History of Northwestern Yucatan. In *Hidden Among the Hills: Maya Archaeology of the Northwest Yucatan Peninsula,* edited by Hanns J. Prem, pp. 316–58. Acta Mesoamericana vol. 7. Verlag von Flemming, Mockmuhl.

2000   The City-States of the Maya. In *A Comparative Study of Thirty City-State Cultures,* edited by M. H. Hansen, pp. 547–65. The Royal Danish Academy of Sciences and Letters, Copenhagen.

2004   Akan: The God of Drinking, Disease and Death. In *Continuity and Change: Maya Religious Practices in Temporal Perspective*, edited by D. Graña-Behrens, N. Grube, C. M. Prager, F. Sachse, S. Teufel, and E. Wagner, pp. 59–76. Acta Mesoamericana 14. Verlag Anton Saurwein, Markt Schwaben.

Grube, N., and R. Krochock

2007   Reading between the Lines: Hieroglyphic Texts from Chichen Itza and Its Neighbors. In *Twin Tollans: Chichen Itza, Tula, and the Epiclassic to Early Postclassic Mesoamerican World*, edited by Jeff K. Kowalski and Cynthia Kristan-Graham, pp. 205–49. Dumbarton Oaks, Washington, D.C.

Grube, N., and W. Nahm

1994   A Census of Xibalba: A Complete Inventory of "Way" Characters on Maya Ceramics. In *The Maya Vase Book*, vol.4, edited by J. Kerr and B. Kerr, pp. 686–715. Kerr Associates, New York.

Guderjan, T.

1996   Investigations at the Blue Creek Ruin, Northwestern Belize. In *Los investigadores de la cultura maya*, vol. 3, pp. 330–54. Universidad Autonoma de Campeche, Mexico.

1998   The Blue Creek Jade Cache: Early Classic Ritual in Northwest Belize. In *The Sowing and the Dawning*, edited by S. Boteler Mock, pp. 101–11. University of New Mexico Press, Albuquerque.

Guderjan, T. H., J. Baker, and R. J. Lichtenstein

2003   Environmental and Cultural Diversity at Blue Creek. In *Heterarchy, Political Economy, and the Ancient Maya: The Three Rivers Region of the East-Central Yucatán Peninsula*, edited by V. L. Scarborough, F. Valdez, Jr., and N. P. Dunning, pp. 77–91. University of Arizona Press, Tucson.

Guderjan, T. H., R. J. Lichtenstein, and C. C. Hanratty

2003   Elite Residences at Blue Creek, Belize. In *Maya Palaces and Elite Residences: An Interdisciplinary Approach*, edited by J. Joyce Christie, pp. 13–45. University of Texas Press, Austin.

Guyer, J. I., and S. M. Belinga

1995   Wealth in People as Wealth in Knowledge: Accumulation and Composition in Equatorial Africa. *Journal of African History* 36:91–120.

Haas, J.

2001a   Cultural Evolution and Political Centralization. In *From Leaders to Rulers,* edited by J. Haas, 13–16. Kluwer Academic/Plenum, New York.

Haas, J. (editor)

2001b   *From Leaders to Rulers.* Kluwer Academic/Plenum, New York.

Haggett, P.

1966   *Locational Analysis in Human Geography.* St. Martin's Press, New York.

Hall, T. D.

1997   The Millennium before the Long Sixteenth Century: How Many World-Systems Were There? In *Economic Analysis beyond the Local System,* edited by R. Blanton, P. N. Peregrine, T. D. Hall, and D. Winslow, pp. 47–78. University Press of America, Lanham, Maryland.

1998   The Rio de la Plata and the Greater Southwest: A View from World System Theory. In *Contested Ground: Comparative Frontiers on the Northern and Southern Edges of the Spanish Empire,* edited by D. J. Guy and T. E. Sheridan, pp. 150–66. University of Arizona Press, Tucson.

1999   World-Systems and Evolution: An Appraisal. In *World Systems Theory in Practice: Leadership, Production, and Exchange,* edited by P. N. Kardulias, pp. 1–23. Rowman & Littlefield, New York.

Hall, T. D., and C. Chase-Dunn

1993   The World-Systems Perspective and Archaeology: Forward into the Past. *Journal of Archaeological Research* 1:121–43.

1994   Forward into the Past: World-Systems before 1500. *Sociological Forum* 9:295–306.

Halperin, C. T.

2004   Realeza maya y figurillas con tocados de la Serpiente de Guerra de Motul de San José, Guatemala. *Mayab* 17:45–60.

2007   Materiality, Bodies, and Practice: The Political Economy of Late Classic Maya Figurines from Motul de San Jose, Peten, Guatemala. PhD dissertation, Department of Anthropology, University of California-Riverside.

2008   Classic Maya Textile Production: Insights from Motul de San José, Petén, Guatemala. *Ancient Mesoamerica* 19:111–25.

2009   Figurines as Bearers of and Burdens in Late Classic Maya State Politics. In *Mesoamerican Figurines: Small-Scale Indices of Large-Scale Phenomena,* edited by C. T. Halperin, K. A. Faust, R. Taube, and A. Giguet, pp. 378–403. University Press of Florida, Gainesville.

2012   Figurine Economies at Motul de San José: Multiple and Shifting Modes of Valuation. In *Motul de San José: Politics, History, and Economy in a Classic Maya Polity,* edited by A. E. Foias and K. F. Emery, pp. 139–66. University Press of Florida, Gainesville.

Halperin, C. T., and A. E. Foias

2010   Pottery Politics: Late Classic Maya Palace Production at Motul de San José, Petén, Guatemala. *Journal of Anthropological Archaeology* 29(3):392–411.

2012   Motul de San José Palace Pottery Production: Reconstructions from Wasters and Debris. In *Motul de San José: Politics, History, and Economy in a Classic Maya Polity,* edited by A. E. Foias and K. F. Emery, pp. 167–93. University Press of Florida, Gainesville.

Halperin, C. T., R. L. Bishop, E. Spensley, and M. J. Blackman

2009   Late Classic (A.D. 600–900) Maya Market Exchange: Analysis of Figurines from the Motul de San José Region, Guatemala. *Journal of Field Archaeology* 34(4):457–80.

Hammond, N.

1972   Obsidian Trade Routes in the Mayan Area. *Science* 178:1092–93.

1974   The Distribution of Late Classic Maya Major Ceremonial Centers in the Central Area. In *Mesoamerican Archaeology: New Approaches*, edited by N. Hammond, pp. 313–34. University of Texas Press, Austin.

1975a   Maya Settlement Hierarchy in Northern Belize. In *Studies in Ancient Mesoamerica*, vol. 2, edited by J. A. Graham, pp. 40–55. Contributions of the University of California Archaeological Research Facility no. 27. Department of Anthropology, University of California, Berkeley.

1975b   *Lubaantun: A Classic Maya Realm*. Peabody Museum Monographs no. 2. Peabody Museum of Archaeology and Ethnology, Harvard University, Cambridge, Massachusetts.

1991a   Inside the Black Box: Defining Maya Polity. In *Classic Maya Political History*, edited by T. P. Culbert, pp. 253–84. Cambridge University Press, New York.

2005   Review of *Maya Political Science: Time, Astronomy, and the Cosmos* by Prudence M. Rice. *Journal of Anthropological Research* 61(2):254–56.

2007   Recovering Maya Civilisation. *Proceedings of the British Academy* 151:361–85.

Hammond, N. (editor)

1991b   *Cuello: An Early Maya Community in Belize*. Cambridge University Press, Cambridge.

Hansen, M. H.

2000   The Hellenic *Polis*. In *A Comparative Study of Thirty City-State Cultures*, edited by M. H. Hansen, pp. 141–88. The Royal Danish Academy of Sciences and Letters, Copenhagen.

Hansen, R. D.

1990   *Excavations in the Tigre Complex, El Mirador, Peten, Guatemala*. Papers of the New World Archaeological Foundation no. 62. Brigham Young University, Provo.

1994   Las dinamicas culturales y ambientales de los origenes mayas: Estudios recientes del sitio arqueologico Nakbe. In *VII Simposio de Investigaciones Arqueologicas en Guatemala, 1993*, edited by J. P. Laporte and H. L. Escobedo, pp. 369–87. Ministerio de Cultura y Deportes, IDAEH, Asociacion Tikal, Guatemala City.

1998   Continuity and Disjunction: The Pre-Classic Antecedents of Classic Maya Architecture. In *Function and Meaning in Classic Maya Architecture*, edited by S. Houston, pp. 49–122. Dumbarton Oaks and Harvard University Press, Washington, D.C.

Hansen, R. D., S. Bozarth, J. Jacob, D. Wahl, and T. Schreiner

2002   Climatic and Environmental Variability in the Rise of Maya Civilization: A Preliminary Perspective from the Northern Peten. *Ancient Mesoamerica* 13:273–95.

Hansen, R. D., E. Suyuc Ley, C. Morales Aguilar, T. P. Schreiner, A. Morales Lopez, E. Hernandez, and D. Mauricio

2007   La cuenca Mirador: Avances de la investigacion y conservacion del Estado Kan en los periodos Preclasico y Clasico. In *XX Simposio de Investigaciones Arqueologicas en Guatemala, 2006*, edited by J. P. Laporte, B. Arroyo, and H. E. Mejia, pp. 349–61. Ministerio de Cultura y Deportes, IDAEH, Asociacion Tikal, and NWAF, Guatemala City.

Hare, T. S.

2000   Between the Household and the Empire: Structural Relationships within and among Aztec Communities and Polities. In *The Archaeology of Communities: A New World Perspective*, edited by M. Canuto and J. Yaeger, pp. 78–101. Routledge, New York.

Harrison, P. D.

1999   *The Lords of Tikal: Rulers of an Ancient Maya City*. Thames and Hudson, London.

Hatch, M. P. de

1997   *Kaminaljuyu/San Jorge: Evidencia arqueologica de la actividad economica en el Valle de Guatemala, 300 AC a 300 DC*. Universidad del Valle, Guatemala City.

Haviland, W. A.

1981   Dower Houses and Minor Centers at Tikal, Guatemala: An Investigation into the Identification of Valid Units in Settlement Hierarchies. In *Lowland Maya Settlement Patterns,* edited by W. Ashmore, pp. 89–117. University of New Mexico Press, Albuquerque.

1992   Status and Power in Classic Maya Society: The View from Tikal. *American Anthropologist* 94:937–40.

1997   On the Maya State. *Current Anthropology* 38:443–45.

Helms, M. W.

1993   *Craft and the Kingly Ideal: Art, Trade and Power*. University of Texas Press, Austin.

1998   *Access to Origins: Affines, Ancestors, and Aristocrats*. University of Texas Press, Austin.

Hendon, J. A.

1991   Status and Power in Classic Maya Society: An Archaeological Study. *American Anthropologist* 93:894–918.

2003   Feasting at Home: Community and House Solidarity among the Maya of Southeastern Mesoamerica. In *The Archaeology and Politics of Food and Feasting in Early States and Empires*, edited by T. L. Bray, pp. 203–33. Kluwer Academic/Plenum, New York.

Hodder, I.

1986   *Reading the Past: Current Approaches to Interpretations in Archaeology*. Cambridge University Press, Cambridge.

Hodge, M. G.

1984   *Aztec City-States*. Museum of Anthropology Memoirs vol. 18. University of Michigan, Ann Arbor.

Houk, B. A.

2003   The Ties that Bind. In *Heterarchy, Political Economy, and the Ancient Maya: The Three Rivers Region of the East-Central Yucatán Peninsula*, edited by V. L. Scarborough, F. Valdez, Jr., and N. Dunning, pp. 52–63. University of Arizona Press, Tucson.

Houston, S. D.

1986   *Problematic Emblem Glyphs: Examples from Altar de Sacrificios, El Chorro, Río Azul, and Xultun*. Research Reports on Ancient Maya Writing 3. Center for Maya Research, Washington, D.C.

1989   *The Way Glyph: Evidence for "Co-Essences" among the Classic Maya*. Research Reports on Ancient Maya Writing no. 30. Center for Maya Research, Washington D.C.

1993   *Hieroglyphs and History at Dos Pilas: Dynastic Politics of the Classic Maya.* University of Texas Press, Austin.

2008   A Classic Maya Bailiff? Available at decipherment.wordpress.com. Accessed May 10, 2012.

2012   The Good Prince: Transition, Texting and Moral Narrative in the Murals of Bonampak, Chiapas, Mexico. *Cambridge Archaeological Journal* 22(2):153–175.

Houston, S. D. (editor)

1998   *Function and Meaning in Classic Maya Architecture, A Symposium at Dumbarton Oaks, 7th and 8th October 1994.* Dumbarton Oaks, Washington, D.C.

Houston, S. D., and T. Inomata

2009   *The Classic Maya.* Cambridge University Press, New York.

Houston, S. D., and D. Stuart

1996   Of Gods, Glyphs, and Kings: Divinity and Rulership among the Classic Maya. *Antiquity* 70:289–312.

2001   Peopling the Classic Maya Court. In *Royal Courts of the Ancient Maya: 1. Theory, Comparison, and Synthesis,* edited by T. Inomata and S. D. Houston, pp. 54–83. Westview Press, Boulder, Colorado.

Houston, S., D. Stuart, and J. Robertson

2000   The Language of Classic Maya Inscriptions. *Current Anthropology* 41(3):321–56.

Houston, S., D. Stuart, and K. Taube

1989   Folk Classification of Classic Maya Pottery. *American Anthropologist* 91(3):720–26.

2006   *The Memory of Bones: Body, Being, and Experience among the Classic Maya.* University of Texas Press, Austin.

Hutson, S.

2010   *Dwelling, Identity and the Maya: Relational Archaeology at Chunchucmil.* AltaMira Press, Lanham, Maryland.

Hutson, S. R., B. H. Dahlin, and D. Mazeau

2010   Commerce and Cooperation among the Classic Maya: The Chunchucmil Case. In *Cooperation in Economy and Society*, edited by R. Marshall, pp. 81–103. AltaMira Press, Lanham, MD.

Hutson, S. R., A. Magnoni, D. E. Mazeau, and T. W. Stanton

2006   The Archaeology of Urban Houselots at Chunchucmil, Yucatán. In *Lifeways in the Northern Maya Lowlands: New Approaches to Archaeology in the Yucatán Peninsula*, edited by J. P. Mathews and B. A. Morrison, pp. 77–92. University of Arizona Press, Tucson.

Hutson, S. R., A. Magnoni, and T. W. Stanton

2004   House Rules? The Practice of Social Organization in Classic-period Chunchucmil, Yucatan, Mexico. *Ancient Mesoamerica* 15(1):75–92.

Hutson, S. R., T. W. Stanton, A. Magnoni, R. Terry, and J. Craner

2007   Beyond the Buildings: Formation Processes of Ancient Maya Houselots and Methods for the Study of Non-Architectural Space. *Journal of Anthropological Archaeology* 26:442–73.

Iannone, G.

2002   Annales History and the Ancient Maya State: Some Observations on the "Dynamic Model." *American Anthropologist* 104 (1):68–78.

2003   Rural Complexity in the Cahal Pech Microregion: Analysis and Implications. In *Perspectives on Ancient Maya Rural Complexity*, edited by G. Iannone and S. Connell, pp. 13–26. Cotsen Institute of Archaeology Monograph 49. University of California, Los Angeles.

2005   The Rise and Fall of an Ancient Maya Petty Royal Court. *Latin American Antiquity* 16(1):26–44.

Iannone, G., and S. V. Connell (editors)

2003   *Perspectives on Ancient Maya Rural Complexity*. Cotsen Institute of Archaeology Monograph 49. University of California, Los Angeles.

Inomata, T.

2001a   King's People: Classic Maya Courtiers in a Comparative Perspective. In *Royal Courts of the Ancient Maya: 1. Theory, Comparison, and Synthesis*, edited by T. Inomata and S. Houston, pp. 27–53. Westview Press, Boulder, Colorado.

2001b   The Power and Ideology of Artistic Creation: Elite Craft Specialists in Classic Maya Society. *Current Anthropology* 42(3):321–49.

2004   The Spatial Mobility of Non-Elite Populations in Classic Maya Society and Its Political Implications. In *Ancient Maya Commoners*, edited by J. C. Lohse and F. Valdez, Jr., pp. 175–96. University Press of Texas, Austin.

2006a   Politics and Theatricality in Mayan Society. In *Archaeology of Performance: Theaters of Power, Community, and Politics*, edited by T. Inomata and L. S. Coben, pp. 187–222. AltaMira Press, Lanham, Maryland.

2006b   Plazas, Performers, and Spectators: Political Theaters of the Classic Maya. *Current Anthropology* 47(5):805–42.

2007   Knowledge and Belief in Artistic Production by Classic Maya Elites. In *Rethinking Craft Specialization in Complex Societies: Archaeological Analyses of the Social Meaning of Production*, edited by Z. X. Hruby and R. K. Flad, pp. 129–41. Archaeological Papers of the American Anthropological Association no. 17. American Anthropological Association and University of California Press, Berkeley, California.

2008   *Warfare and the Fall of a Fortified Center: Archaeological Investigations at Aguateca.* Vanderbilt Institute of Mesoamerican Archaeology Series vol. 3. Vanderbilt University Press, Nashville, Tennessee.

Inomata, T., and K. Aoyama

1996   Central-Place Analyses in the La Entrada Region, Honduras: Implications for Understanding Classic Maya Political and Economic Systems. *Latin American Antiquity* 7(4):291–312.

Inomata, T., and S. Houston (editors)

2001   *Royal Courts of the Ancient Maya.* 2 vols. Westview Press, Boulder, Colorado.

Inomata, T., and D. Triadan

2000   Craft Production by Classic Maya Elites in Domestic Settings: Data from Rapidly Abandoned Structures at Aguateca, Guatemala. *Mayab* 13:57–66.

2009   Culture and Practice of War in Maya Society. In *Warfare in Cultural Context: Practice, Agency, and the Archaeology of Violence*, edited by A. E. Nielsen and W. H. Walker, pp. 56–84. University of Arizona Press, Tucson.

Inomata, T., D. Triadan, E. Ponciano, E. Pinto, R. E. Terry, R. E., and M. Eberl
2002   Domestic and Political Lives of Classic Maya Elites: The Excavation of Rapidly Abandoned Structures at Aguateca, Guatemala. *Latin American Antiquity* 13:305–30.

Isendahl, C.
2006   Review of *Water and Ritual: The Rise and Fall of Classic Maya Rulers* by Lisa J. Lucero. *Journal of Latin American Anthropology* 11(2):457–59.

Jackall, R.
1988   *Moral Mazes: The World of Corporate Managers*. Oxford Press, New York.

Jackson, S. E.
2004   Un entendimiento de la jerarquía de los Mayas a través de las élites cortesanas: Algunas reflexiones basadas en datos jeroglíficos y arqueológicos. In *XVII Simposio de Investigaciones Arqueológicas en Guatemala, 2003*, edited by J. P. Laporte, B. Arroyo, H. Escobedo, and H. Mejía, pp. 749–63. National Museum of Archaeology and Ethnology, Guatemala.
2009   Imagining Courtly Communities: An Exploration of Classic Maya Experiences of Status and Identity through Painted Ceramic Vessels. *Ancient Mesoamerica* 20 (1):71–85.

Jackson, S., and D. Stuart
2001   The *Aj K'uhun* Title: Deciphering a Classic Maya Term of Rank. *Ancient Mesoamerica* 12:217–28.

Jamison, T. R.
2010   Monumental Building Programs and Changing Political Strategies at Xunantunich. In *Classic Maya Provincial Politics: Xunantunich and Its Hinterlands*, edited by L. J. LeCount and J. Yaeger, pp. 122–44. University of Arizona Press, Tucson.

Jensen, C., M. D. Moriarty, K. D. Johnson, R. E. Terry, K. F. Emery, and S. D. Nelson
2007   Settlement Agriculture at a Late Classic Maya Center: Connections between Soil Classification and Settlement Patterns at Motul de San José, Guatemala. *Geoarchaeology* 22:337–57.

Johnson, A., and T. Earle
1987   *The Evolution of Human Societies*. Cambridge University Press, Cambridge.

Johnson, G. A.
1980   Rank-Size Convexity and System Integration: A View from Archaeology. *Economic Geography* 56:234–47.
1987   The Changing Organization of Uruk Administration on the Susiana Plain. In *The Archaeology of Western Iran*, edited by F. Hole, pp. 107–39. Smithsonian Institution Press, Washington, D.C.

Johnston, K. J.
2003   The Intensification of Pre-Industrial Cereal Agriculture in the Tropics: Boserup, Cultivation Lengthening and the Classic Maya. *Journal of Anthropological Archaeology* 22:126–61.

Jones, G.
1989   *Maya Resistance to Spanish Rule: Time and Resistance on a Colonial Frontier*. University of New Mexico Press, Albuquerque.
1998   *The Conquest of the Last Maya Kingdom*. Stanford University Press, Stanford, California.

2009   The Kowoj in Ethnohistorical Perspective. In *The Kowoj: Identity, Migration, and Geopolitics in the Late Postclassic Peten, Guatemala*, edited by P. M. Rice and D. S. Rice, pp. 55–69. University Press of Colorado, Boulder.

Joyce, A. A.

2000   The Founding of Monte Alban: Sacred Propositions and Social Practices. In *Agency in Archaeology*, edited by M. A. Dobres and J. E. Robb, pp. 71–91. Routledge, London.

Joyce, A. A., and E. T. Weller

2007   Commoner Rituals, Resistance, and the Classic to Postclassic Transition in Ancient Mesoamerica. In *Commoner Ritual and Ideology in Ancient Mesoamerica*, edited by N. Gonlin and J. C. Lohse, pp. 143–84. University Press of Colorado, Boulder.

Joyce, A. A., L. Arnaud Bustamente, and M. N. Levine

2001   Commoner Power: A Case Study from the Classic Period Collapse on the Oaxaca Coast. *Journal of Archaeological Method and Theory* 8(4):343–85.

Joyce, R. A.

1993   Women's Work: Images of Production and Reproduction in Pre-Hispanic Southern Central America. *Current Anthropology* 34:255–74.

1996   The Construction of Gender in Classic Maya Monuments. In *Gender in Archaeology*, edited by Rita P. Wright, pp. 167–95. University of Pennsylvania Press, Philadelphia.

2000   *Gender and Power in Prehispanic Mesoamerica*. University of Texas Press, Austin.

2004   Unintended Consequences? Monumentality as a Novel Experience in Formative Mesoamerica. *Journal of Archaeological Method and Theory* 11(1, Part 1):5–29

Joyce, R. A., and S. D. Gillespie (editors)

2000   *Beyond Kinship: Social and Material Reproduction in House Societies*. University of Pennsylvania Press, Philadelphia.

Joyce, R. A., and J. A. Hendon

2000   Heterarchy, History, and Material Reality: "Communities" in Late Classic Honduras. In *The Archaeology of Communities: A New World Perspective*, edited by M. A. Canuto and J. Yaeger, pp. 143–60. Routledge Press, New York.

Kardulias, P. N. (editor)

1999   *World Systems Theory in Practice: Leadership, Production, and Exchange*. Rowman & Littlefield, New York.

Kaufman, S. J.

1997   The Fragmentation and Consolidation of International Systems. *International Organization* 51(2):173–208.

Kaufman, T. S., and W. M. Norman

1984   An Outline of Proto-Cholan Phonology, Morphology, and Vocabulary. In *Phoneticism in Mayan Hieroglyphic Writing*, edited by J. S. Justeson, and L. Campbell, pp. 77–166. Institute for Mesoamerican Studies Publication 9. State University of New York Press, Albany.

Keller, A.

2010   The Social Construction of Roads at Xunantunich, from Design to Abandonment. In *Classic Maya Provincial Politics: Xunantunich and Its Hinterlands*, edited by L. J. LeCount and J. Yaeger, pp. 184–208. University of Arizona Press, Tucson.

Kelley, D. H.

1962   Glyphic Evidence for a Dynastic Sequence at Quirigua, Guatemala. *American Antiquity* 27:323–35.

Kepecs, S., and M. A. Masson

2003   Political Organization in Yucatan and Belize. In *The Postclassic Mesoamerican World*, edited by M. E. Smith and F. F. Berdan, pp. 40–44. University of Utah Press, Salt Lake City.

Kepecs, S., G. Feinman, and S. Boucher

1994   Chichen Itza and Its Hinterland: A World-Systems Perspective. *Ancient Mesoamerica* 5:141–58.

Kerr, J., and B. Kerr (editors)

1989–2001   *The Maya Vase Book: A Corpus of Rollout Photographs of Maya Vases.* 6 vols. Kerr Associates, New York.

Kertzer, D. I.

1988   *Ritual, Politics and Power.* Yale University Press, New Haven, Connecticut.

Kimmel, M. S.

1989   Review of *Ritual, Politics, and Power* by David I. Kertzer. *American Journal of Sociology* 94(5):1273.

King, E. M., and D. Potter

1994   Small Sites in Prehistoric Maya Socioeconomic Organization: A Perspective from Colha, Belize. In *Archaeological Views from the Countryside: Village Communities in Early Complex Societies*, edited by G. M. Schwartz and S. E. Falconer, pp. 10–18. Smithsonian Institution Press, Washington, D.C.

King, E. M., and L. C. Shaw

2003   A Heterarchical Approach to Site Variability. In *Heterarchy, Political Economy, and the Ancient Maya: The Three Rivers Region of the East-Central Yucatan Peninsula*, edited by V. L. Scarborough, F. Valdez, and N. Dunning, pp. 64–76. University of Arizona Press, Tucson.

Kiser, E., and Y. Cai

2003   War and Bureaucratization in Qin China: Exploring an Anomalous Case. *American Sociological Review* 68(4):511–39.

Klein, C., E. Guzman, E. C. Mandell, and M. Stanfield-Mazzi

2002   The Role of Shamanism in Mesoamerican Art: A Reassessment. *Current Anthropology* 43(3):383–419.

Knapp, A. B., and W. Ashmore

1999   Archaeological Landscapes: Constructed, Conceptualized, Ideational. In *Archaeologies of Landscape: Contemporary Perspectives*, edited by W. Ashmore and A. B. Knapp, pp. 1–30. Blackwell, Oxford.

Kolb, M. J.

1996   Reply to Forum on "Agency, Ideology, and Power in Archaeological Theory." *Current Anthropology* 37(1):59–60.

Kovacevich, B.

2007   Ritual, Crafting, and Agency at the Classic Maya Kingdom of Cancuen. In *Mesoamerican Ritual Economy: Archaeological and Ethnological Perspectives*, edited by E. C. Wells and K. L. Davis-Salazar, pp. 67–114. University of Colorado Press, Boulder, Colorado.

Kowalski, J. K.

1990 A Preliminary Report on the 1988 Field Season at the Nunnery Quadrangle, Uxmal, Yucatan, Mexico. *Mexicon* 12:27–33.

2007 What's Toltec at Uxmal and Chichen Itza? Merging Maya and Mesoamerican Worldviews and World Systems in Terminal Classic to Early Postclassic Yucatan. In *Twin Tollans: Chichen Itza, Tula, and the Epiclassic to Early Postclassic Mesoamerican World*, edited by J. K. Kowalski and C. Kristan-Graham, pp. 251–313. Dumbarton Oaks, Washington, D.C.

Kowalski, J. K., and C. Kristan-Graham (editors)

2007 *Twin Tollans: Chichén Itza, Tula, and the Epiclassic to Early Postclassic Mesoamerican World*. Dumbarton Oaks, Washington D.C.

Krejci, E., and T. P. Culbert

1995 Preclassic and Classic Burials and Caches in the Maya Lowlands. In *The Emergence of Lowland Maya Civilization: The Transition from the Preclassic to the Early Classic*, edited by N. Grube, pp. 103–16. Acta Mesoamericana 8. Verlag von Flemming, Berlin.

Kristiansen, K.

2001 Rulers and Warriors: Symbolic Transmission and Social Transformation in Bronze Age Europe. In *From Leaders to Rulers*, edited by J. Haas, pp. 85–104. Kluwer Academic/Plenum, New York.

Krochock, R. J.

1988 The Development of Political Rhetoric at Chichen Itza, Yucatan, Mexico. Ph.D. dissertation, Department of Anthropology, Southern Methodist University.

Kuhrt, A.

2001 The Achaemenid Persian Empire (c. 550–c. 330 BCE): Continuities, Adaptations, Transformations. In *Empires: Perspectives from Archaeology and History*, edited by Susan A. Alcock, pp. 93–123. Cambridge University Press, New York.

Kurjack, E. B., and S. Garza T.

1981 Pre-Columbian Community Form and Distribution in the Northern Maya Area. In *Lowland Maya Settlement Patterns*, edited by W. Ashmore, pp. 287–310. University of New Mexico Press, Albuquerque.

Kurtz, D. V.

1996 Hegemony and Anthropology: Gramsci, Exegetes, Transformations. *Critique of Anthropology* 15:103–35.

2001 *Political Anthropology: Power and Paradigms*. Westview Press, Boulder, Colorado.

Kus, S.

1989 Sensuous Human Activity and the State: Towards an Archaeology of Bread and Circuses. In *Domination and Resistance*, edited by D. Miller, M. Rowlands, and C. Tilley, pp. 140–54. One World Archaeology Series no. 3. Routledge, London.

Lacadena García-Gallo, A.

2004 The Glyphic Corpus from Ek' Balam, Yucatan, Mexico. Report to the Foundation for the Advancement of Mesoamerican Studies, Inc. Available at http:/www.famsi. org/reports/01057/. Accessed September 20, 2010.

2008   El Título *Lakam*: Evidencia Epigráfica Sobre la Organización Tributaria y Militar Interna de los Reinos Mayas del Clásico. *Mayab* 20:23–43.

Lacadena García-Gallo, A., and A. Ciudad Ruiz

1998   Reflexiones Sobre La Estructura Politica Maya Clasica. In *Anatomia de una civilizacion: Aproximaciones interdisciplinarias a la cultura Maya,* edited by A. Ciudad Ruiz, Y. Fernandez Marquinez, J. M. García Campillo, M. J. Iglesias Ponce de Leon, A. Lacadena García-Gallo, and L. T. Sanz Castro, pp. 31–64. Publicaciones de la S.E.E.M. No. 4. Sociedad Española de Estudios Maya, Madrid.

Laporte, J. P., and V. Fialko

1990   New Perspectives on Old Problems: Dynastic References for the Early Classic at Tikal. In *Vision and Revision in Maya Studies*, edited by F. Clancy and P. Harrison, pp. 33–66. University of New Mexico Press, Albuquerque.

1995   Un reencuentro con mundo perdido, Tikal, Guatemala. *Ancient Mesoamerica* 6:41–94.

Laporte, J. P., H. Mejia, J. Adanez, J. Chocon, L. Corzo, A. Ciudad Ruiz, M. J. Inglesias

2004   Aplicación del Sistema de Informacion Geografico (SIG) a la interpretacion del asentamiento del Sureste de Peten: Primeros resultados. In *XVII Simposio de Investigaciones Arqueologicas en Guatemala*, edited by J. P. Laporte, B. Arroyo, H. Escobedo, and H. Mejia, pp. 93–113. Ministerio de Cultura y Deportes, IDAEH, Asociacion Tikal, Guatemala.

Laporte, J. P., M. A. Reyes, and J. E. Chocon

2004   Catálogo de figurillas y silbatos de baro del Atlas Arqueológico de Guatemala. In *Reconocimiento y excavaciones arqueológicas en los municipios de La Libertad y Dolores y Poptun, Peten*, edited by J. P. Laporte and H. Mejía, pp. 295–344. Atlas Arqueológico de Guatemala y Área de Arqueología, Guatemala City.

Lasswell, H., and A. Kaplan

1950   *Power and Society*. Yale University Press, New Haven, Connecticut.

Lawton, C.

2007   Excavaciones residenciales en el Grupo O: Operaciones 1O1, 6A, 6B y 6D. In *Proyecto arqueológico Motul de San José, Informe #7: Temporada de Campo 2005–2006.*, edited by M. D. Moriarty, E. Spensley, J. E. Castellanos and A. E. Foias, pp. 177–98. Report submitted to the Instituto de Antropología e História de Guatemala.

LeCount, L. J.

1999   Polychrome Pottery and Political Strategies in Late and Terminal Classic Lowland Maya Society. *Latin American Antiquity* 10:239–58.

2001   Like Water for Chocolate: Feasting and Political Ritual among the Late Classic Maya of Xunantunich, Belize. *American Anthropologist* 103 (4):935–53.

2004   Looking for a Needle in a Haystack: The Early Classic Period at Actuncan. In *Archaeological Investigations in the Eastern Maya Lowlands: Papers of the 2003 Belize Archaeology Symposium*, vol. 1, edited by J. Awe, J. Morris, and S. Jones, pp. 27–36. Institute of Archaeology, Belmopan, Belize.

2005   The Actuncan Early Classic Maya Project: Progress Report on the Second Season. In *Papers of the 2004 Belize Archaeology Symposium*, vol. 2, edited by J. Awe, J. Morris, S. Jones, and C. Helmke, pp. 67–78. Institute of Archaeology, Belmopan, Belize.

2010   Mount Maloney People? Domestic Pots, Everyday Practice, and the Social Forma-
        tion of the Xunatunich Polity. In *Classic Maya Provincial Politics: Xunantunich and
        Its Hinterlands*, edited by L. J. LeCount and J. Yaeger, pp. 209–30. University of
        Arizona Press, Tucson.

LeCount, L. J., and J. Yaeger (editors)

2010a   *Classic Maya Provincial Politics: Xunantunich and Its Hinterlands*. University of
        Arizona Press, Tucson.

LeCount, L.J., and J. Yaeger

2010b   Provincial Politics and Current Models of the Maya State. In *Classic Maya Provin-
        cial Politics: Xunantunich and Its Hinterlands*, edited by L. J. LeCount and J. Yaeger,
        pp. 20–45. University of Arizona Press, Tucson.

2010c   Conclusions: Placing Xunantunich and Its Hinterland Settlements in Perspective.
        In *Classic Maya Provincial Politics: Xunantunich and Its Hinterlands*, edited by L.
        J. LeCount and J. Yaeger, pp. 337–69. University of Arizona Press, Tucson.

Leventhal, R. M., W. Ashmore, L. J. LeCount, and J. Yaeger

2010   The Xunantunich Archaeological Project, 1991–97. In *Classic Maya Provincial Poli-
        tics: Xunantunich and Its Hinterlands*, edited by L. J. LeCount and J. Yaeger, pp.
        1–19. University of Arizona Press, Tucson.

Lewis, A.

1982   *Royal Succession in Capetian France: Studies on Familial Order and the State*. Har-
        vard University Press, Cambridge.

Liendo Stuardo, R.

2003   Access Patterns in Maya Royal Precincts. In *Maya Palaces and Elite Residences: An
        Interdisciplinary Approach,* edited by J. Joyce Christie, pp. 184–203. University of
        Texas Press, Austin.

Lincoln, C.

1986   The Chronology of Chichen Itza: A Review of the Literature. In *Late Lowland
        Maya Civilization: Classic to Postclassic*, edited by J. Sabloff and E. W. Andrews V.,
        pp. 141–96. University of New Mexico Press, Albuquerque.

1990   Ethnicity and Social Organization at Chichen Itza, Yucatan, Mexico. Ph.D. dis-
        sertation, Department of Anthropology, Harvard University.

1994   Structural and Philological Evidence for Dual Rulership at Chichen Itza, Yucatan,
        Mexico. In *Hidden among the Hills: Maya Archaeology of the Northwest Yucatan
        Peninsula*, edited by H. J. Prem, pp. 164–96. Acta Mesoamericana vol. 7. Verlag von
        Flemming, Mockmuhl.

Lind, M.

2000   Mixtec City-States and Mixtec City-State Culture. In *A Comparative Study of Thir-
        ty City-State Cultures,* edited by M. H. Hansen, pp. 567–80. Royal Danish Academy
        of Sciences and Letters, Copenhagen.

Liverani, M.

1996   Reconstructing the Rural Landscape of the Ancient Near East. *Journal of the Eco-
        nomic and Social History of the Orient* 39(1):13.

Loewe, M.

1986   The Former Han Dynasty. In *The Cambridge History of China: 1. The Ch'in and Han
        Empires, 221 B.C.–A.D. 220*, edited by D. Twitchett and M. Loewe, pp. 103–222.
        Cambridge University Press, Cambridge.

Lohse, J. C.

2004   Intra-Site Settlement Signatures and Implications for Late Classic Maya Common-
        er Organization at Dos Hombres, Belize. In *Ancient Maya Commoners*, edited by
        J. C. Lohse and F. Valdez, Jr., pp. 117–45. University of Texas Press, Austin.

2007   Commoner Ritual, Commoner Ideology: (Sub-)Alternate Views of Social Com-
        plexity in Prehispanic Mesoamerica. In *Commoner Ritual and Ideology in Ancient
        Mesoamerica*, edited by N. Gonlin and J. C. Lohse, pp. 1–32. University Press of
        Colorado, Boulder.

2010   Archaic Origins of the Lowland Maya. *Latin American Antiquity* 21(3):312–52.

Lohse, J. C., J. Awe, C. Griffith, R. N. Rosenswig, and F. Valdez, Jr.

2006   Preceramic Occupations in Belize: Updating the Paleoindian and Archaic Record.
        Latin American Antiquity 17(2):209–26.

Lombard, J.

1967   The Kingdom of Dahomey. In *West African Kingdoms in the Nineteenth Century*,
        edited by C. D. Forde and P. M. Kaberry, pp. 70–92. International African Institute,
        Oxford University Press, London.

Looper, M. G.

2009   *To Be Like Gods: Dance in Ancient Maya Civilization*. University of Texas Press,
        Austin.

Looper, M. G., D. Reents-Budet, and R. L. Bishop

2009   Dance in Classic Maya Ceramics. In *To Be Like Gods: Dance in Ancient Maya
        Civilization*, by M. G. Looper, pp. 113–50. University of Texas Press, Austin.

Lopez Varela, S., and A. E. Foias (editors)

2005   *Geographies of Power: Understanding the Nature of Terminal Classic Pottery in the
        Maya Lowlands*. British Archaeological Reports International Series no. 1447. Ar-
        chaeopress, Oxford.

Love, M.

2002   Domination, Resistance, and Political Cycling in Formative Period Pacific Guate-
        mala. In *The Dynamics of Power*, edited by M. O'Donovan, pp. 214–37. Center for
        Archaeological Investigation Occasional Papers no. 30. Southern Illinois Univer-
        sity Press, Carbondale.

Lucero, L.

1999a   Classic Lowland Maya Political Organization: A Review. *Journal of World Prehis-
        tory* 13(2):211–63.

1999b   Water Control and Maya Politics in the Southern Maya Lowlands. In *Complex
        Societies in the Ancient Tropical World*, edited by E. A. Bacus and L. J. Lucero, pp.
        35–49. Archaeological Papers of the American Anthropological Association no. 9.
        American Anthropological Association, Washington, D.C.

2002   The Collapse of the Classic Maya: A Case for the Role of Water Control. *American
        Anthropologist* 104(3):814–26.

2003   The Politics of Ritual: The Emergence of Classic Maya Rulers. *Current Anthropol-
        ogy* 44(4):523–58.

2006   *Water and Ritual: The Rise and Fall of Classic Maya Rulers*. University of Texas
        Press, Austin.

2007   Classic Maya Temples, Politics, and the Voice of the People. *Latin American An-
        tiquity* 18(4):407–27.

Luttwak, E. N.

1976   *The Grand Strategy of the Roman Empire: From the First Century A.D. to the Third.* Johns Hopkins University Press, Baltimore, Maryland.

MacLeod, B., and A. Stone

1995   The Hieroglyphic Inscriptions of Naj Tunich. In *Images from the Underworld: Naj Tunich and the Tradition of Maya Cave Painting*, edited by A. Stone, pp. 155–84. University of Texas Press, Austin.

Maisels, C. K.

1999   *Early Civilizations of the Old World: The Formative Histories of Egypt, the Levant, Mesopotamia, India and China.* Routledge, London.

Malinowski, B.

1961 [1922]   *Argonauts of the Western Pacific.* Routledge, London.

Mann, M.

1986   *The Sources of Social Power.* Vol. 1, *A History of Power from the Beginning to A.D. 1760.* Cambridge University Press, New York.

Manzanilla, L. (editor)

1997   *Emergence and Change in Early Urban Societies.* Plenum Press, New York.

Marcus, J.

1973   Territorial Organization of the Lowland Classic Maya. *Science* 180:911–16.

1976   *Emblem and State in the Classic Maya Lowlands: An Epigraphic Approach to Territorial Organization.* Dumbarton Oaks, Washington, D.C.

1983   Lowland Maya Archaeology at the Crossroads. *American Antiquity* 48(3):454–88.

1993   Ancient Maya Political Organization. In *Lowland Maya Civilization in the Eighth Century A.D.: A Symposium at Dumbarton Oaks, 7th and 8th October 1989*, edited by J. A. Sabloff and J. S. Henderson, pp. 111–183. Dumbarton Oaks, Washington, D.C.

1998   The Peaks and Valleys of Ancient States: An Extension of the Dynamic Model. In *Archaic States*, edited by G. M. Feinman and J. Marcus, pp. 59–94. School of American Research, Santa Fe, New Mexico.

Marcus, J., and Flannery, K. V.

1996   *Zapotec Civilization: How Urban Society Evolved in Mexico's Oaxaca Valley.* Thames and Hudson, London.

Markman, Peter T., and Roberta H. Markman

1989   *Masks of the Spirit: Image and Metaphor in Mesoamerica.* University of California Press, Berkeley.

Martin, S.

2001   Court and Realm: Architectural Signatures in the Classic Maya Southern Lowlands. In *Royal Courts of the Ancient Maya.* Vol. 1, *Theory, Comparisons, and Synthesis*, edited by T. Inomata and S. D. Houston, pp. 168–194. Westview Press, Boulder, Colorado.

Martin, S., and N. Grube

1995   Maya Superstates: How A Few Powerful Kingdoms Vied for Control of the Maya Lowlands during the Classic Period (A.D. 300–900). *Archaeology* 48(6):41–46.

2000   *Chronicle of the Maya Kings and Queens: Deciphering the Dynasties of the Ancient Maya.* Thames and Hudson, London.

2008   *Chronicle of the Maya Kings and Queens: Deciphering the Dynasties of the Ancient Maya*. 2nd ed. Thames and Hudson, New York.

Marx, K.

1966 [1857–58]   *Pre-Capitalist Economic Formations*. International Publishers, New York.

Masson, M. A., and D. A. Freidel (editors)

2002   *Ancient Maya Political Economies*. AltaMira Press, Walnut Creek, California.

Masson, M. A., T. S. Hare, and C. Peraza Lope

2006   Postclassic Maya Society Regenerated at Mayapan. In *After Collapse: The Regeneration of Complex Societies*, edited by G. M. Schwartz and J. J. Nichols, pp. 188–207. University of Arizona Press, Tucson.

Matheny, R. T.

1986   Early States in the Maya Lowlands during the Late Preclassic Period: Edzna and El Mirador. In *City States of the Maya: Art and Architecture*, edited by E. P. Benson, pp. 1–44. Rocky Mountain Institute for Pre-Columbian Studies, Denver.

1987   An Early Maya Metropolis Uncovered: El Mirador. *National Geographic* 172(3):317–39. Washington, D.C.

Mathews, P.

1985   Early Classic Monuments and Inscriptions. In *A Consideration of the Early Classic Period in the Maya Lowlands*, edited by G. R. Willey and P. Mathews, pp. 5–55. Institute for Mesoamerican Studies Publication no. 10. State University of New York Press, Albany.

1991   Classic Maya Emblem Glyphs. In *Classic Maya Political History: Hieroglyphic and Archaeological Evidence*, edited by T. P. Culbert, pp. 19–29. Cambridge University Press, Cambridge.

McAnany, P. A.

1993a   The Economics of Social Power and Wealth among Eighth-Century Maya Households. In *Lowland Maya Civilization in the Eighth Century A.D.: A Symposium at Dumbarton Oaks, 7th and 8th October 1989,* edited by J. A. Sabloff and J. S. Henderson, pp. 65–89. Dumbarton Oaks, Washington, D.C.

1993b   Resources, Specialization and Exchange in the Maya Lowlands. In *The American Southwest and Mesoamerica*, edited by J. E. Ericson and T. G. Baugh, pp. 213–45. Plenum Press, New York.

1995   *Living with the Ancestors: Kinship and Kingship in Ancient Maya Society*. University of Texas Press, Austin.

2008   Shaping Social Difference: Political and Ritual Economy of Classic Maya Royal Courts. In *Dimensions of Ritual Economy*, edited by E. C. Wells and P. A. McAnany, pp. 219–47. Research in Economic Anthropology vol. 27. Emerald Publishing, Bradford.

2010   *Ancestral Maya Economies in Archaeological Perspective*. Cambridge University Press, New York.

McAnany, P. A., and S. Plank

2001   Perspectives on Actors, Gender Roles, and Architecture at Classic Maya Courts and Households. In *Royal Courts of the Ancient Maya: 1. Theory, Comparisons, and Synthesis,* edited by T. Inomata and S. D. Houston, pp. 84–129. Westview Press, Boulder, Colorado.

McAnany, P., and N. Yoffee (editors)

2010   *Questioning Collapse: Human Resilience, Ecological Vulnerability, and the Aftermath of Empire.* Cambridge University Press, New York.

McFarlane, B., S. Cooper, and M. Jaksic

2005   The Asiatic Mode of Production: A New Phoenix (Part 2). *Journal of Contemporary Asia* 35(4):499–536.

McGuire, R. H.

1992   *A Marxist Archaeology.* Academic Press, New York.

McKillop, H.

2004   *The Ancient Maya: New Perspectives.* W. W. Norton, New York.

Meillasoux, C.

1981   *Maidens, Meal and Money: Capitalism and the Domestic Community.* Cambridge University Press, Cambridge.

Meskell, L. M.

1999   *Archaeologies of Social Life.* Routledge, London.

2005   *Archaeologies of Materiality.* Wiley-Blackwell, New York.

Milbrath, S., and C. Peraza Lope

2003   Revisiting Mayapan: Mexico's Last Maya capital. *Ancient Mesoamerica* 14:1–46.

Miller, D. (editor)

2005   *Materiality.* Duke University Press, Durham, N.C.

Miller, D., and C. Tilley

1984   Ideology, Power and Prehistory: An Introduction. In *Ideology, Power and Prehistory*, edited by D. Miller and C. Tilley, pp. 1–15. Cambridge University Press, Cambridge.

Miller, M. E.

1986   *The Murals of Bonampak.* Princeton University Press, Princeton, New Jersey.

1999   *Maya Art and Architecture.* Thames & Hudson, London.

2001   Life at Court: The View from Bonampak. In *Royal Courts of the Ancient Maya: 2. Data and Case Studies*, edited by T. Inomata and S. Houston, pp. 201–22. Westview Press, Boulder, Colorado.

Miller, M. E., and S. Martin

2004   *Courtly Art of the Ancient Maya.* Thames & Hudson, New York.

Millon, R.

1981   Teotihuacan: City, State, and Civilization. In *Handbook of Middle American Indians*, Supplement, vol. 1, edited by V. R. Bricker, pp. 198–243. University of Texas Press, Austin.

Mock, S. B. (editor)

1998   *The Sowing and the Dawning: Termination, Dedication, and Transformation in the Archaeological and Ethnographic Record of Mesoamerica.* University of New Mexico Press, Albuquerque.

Moertono, S.

1968   *State and Statecraft in Old Java: A Study of the Later Mataram Period, 16th to 19th Century.* Cornell University Press, Ithaca, New York.

Moriarty, M. D.

2001   Notas preliminares sobre la clasificación indígena de suelos en San José, Petén,

Guatemala. In *Proyecto Arqueologico Motul de San José Informe #4: Temporada de Campo 2001*, edited by A. Foias, pp. 131–35. Report submitted to Williams College, Williamstown, and the Institute of Anthropology and History, Guatemala City. Available at http://motul-archaeology.williams.edu/excavation.

2004a Settlement Archaeology at Motul de San José, Petén, Guatemala: Preliminary Results from the 1998–2003 Seasons. *Mayab* 17:21–44.

2004b *Investigating an Inland Maya Port: The 2003 Field Season at Trinidad de Nosotros, El Petén, Guatemala.* Report submitted to the Foundation for the Advancement of Mesoamerican Studies, Inc. Available at www.famsi.org/reports/02061/.

2012 History, Politics, and Ceramics: The Ceramic Sequence of Trinidad de Nosotros, El Peten, Guatemala. In *Motul de San José: History, Politics and Economy at a Classic Maya Center*, edited by A. E. Foias and K. F. Emery, pp. 194–228. University Press of Florida, Gainesville.

n.d. Notes on Indigenous Soil Classification and Agricultural Potential in San José, Petén, Guatemala Region. Unpublished manuscript. Available upon request from Antonia Foias, Department of Anthropology and Sociology, Williams College, Williamstown, Massachusetts.

Moriarty, M. D., F. Ramirez, E. Spensley, and J. Buechler

2001 Reconocimiento, mapeo y sondeos in la periferia de Motul de San José: El transecto este. In *Proyecto Arqueologico Motul de San José Informe #4: Temporada de Campo 2001*, edited by A. E. Foias, pp. 86–103. Report submitted to Williams College and the Institute of Anthropology and History, Guatemala City. Available at http://motul-archaeology.williams.edu/excavation.

Moriarty, M. D, E. Spensley, J. Castellanos, and A. Foias (editors)

2007 *Proyecto Arqueologico Motul de San José: Informe #7, Temporada de Campo 2005–2006.* Report submitted to Tulane University and IDAEH, Guatemala City. Available at http://motul-archaeology.williams.edu/excavation.

Moriarty, M. D., and A. Wyatt

2001 Reconocimiento Preliminar de Algunos Sitios Menores en la Zona de Motul de San José. In *Proyecto Arqueologico Motul de San Jose Informe #4, Temporada de Campo 2001*, edited by A. E. Foias, pp. 104–7. Report submitted to Williams College and the Institute of Anthropology and History, Guatemala City. http://motul-archaeology.williams.edu/excavation.

Munson, J. L., and M. J. Macri

2009 Sociopolitical Network Interactions: A Case Study of the Classic Maya. *Journal of Anthropological Archaeology* 28:424–38.

Murdock, G. P.

1957 Review of "Oriental Despotism: A Comparative Study of Total Power." *American Anthropologist* 59:545–47.

Nyerges, A. E.

1992 The ecology of wealth-in-people: Agriculture, settlement, and society on the perpetual frontier. *American Anthropologist* 94:860–81.

O'Donovan, M.

2002a The Dynamics of Power. In *The Dynamics of Power*, edited by M. O'Donovan, pp. 3–16. Center for Archaeological Investigation Occasional Papers No. 30. Southern Illinois University, Carbondale.

2002b   Grasping Power: A Question of Relations and Scales. In *The Dynamics of Power*, edited by M. O'Donovan, pp. 19–33. Center for Archaeological Investigation Occasional Papers No. 30. Southern Illinois University, Carbondale.

O'Donovan, M. (editor)

2002   *The Dynamics of Power*. Center for Archaeological Investigation Occasional Papers No. 30. Southern Illinois University, Carbondale.

Offner, J.

1981   On the Inapplicability of "Oriental Despotism" and the "Asiatic Mode of Production" to the Aztecs of Texcoco. *American Antiquity* 46(1):43–61.

O'Neill, T., and G. Hymel

1995   *All Politics is Local, And Other Rules of the Game*. Adams Media Co.

Palka, J.

1997   Reconstructing Classic Maya Socioeconomic Differentiation and the Collapse at Dos Pilas, Peten, Guatemala. *Ancient Mesoamerica* 8:293–306.

Parkinson, W. A., and M. L. Galaty

2007   Secondary States in Perspective: An Integrated Approach to State Formation in the Prehistoric Aegean. *American Anthropologist* 109(1):113–29.

Parmington, A.

2003   Classic Maya Status and the Subsidiary "Office" of Sajal: A comparative Study of Status as Represented in Costume and Composition in the Iconography of Monuments. *Mexicon* 25(2):46–53.

Parsons, T.

1960   *Structure and Process in Modern Societies*. Free Press, New York.

Pauketat, T. R.

2000   The Tragedy of the Commoners. In *Agency in Archaeology*, edited by M.-A. Dobres and J. E. Robb, pp. 113–29. Routledge, London.

2001   Practice and history in archaeology: An emerging paradigm. *Anthropological Theory* 1(1):73–98.

2003   Resettled Farmers and the Making of a Mississippian Polity. *American Antiquity* 68:39–66.

2007   *Chiefdoms and Other Archaeological Delusions*. AltaMira Press, Lanham, Maryland.

Pendergast, D. A.

1981   Lamanai, Belize: Summary of Excavation Results, 1974–80. *Journal of Field Archaeology* 8:29–53.

1982   *Excavations at Altun Ha, Belize, 1964–1970*, vol. 2. Royal Ontario Museum, Toronto.

Plank, S. E.

2004   *Maya Dwellings in Hieroglyphs and Archaeology: An Integrative Approach to Ancient Architecture and Spatial Cognition*. BAR International Series 1324. Archaeopress, Oxford.

Plog, S.

1995   Equality and Hierarchy: Holistic Approaches to Understanding Social Dynamics in the Pueblo Southwest. In *Foundations of Social Inequality*, edited by T. D. Price and G. M. Feinman, pp. 189–206. Plenum Press, New York.

Pohl, J.

1994   *The Politics of Symbolism in the Mixtec Codices.* Vanderbilt University Publications in Anthropology 46. Vanderbilt University, Nashville.

Pohl, M., D. R. Piperno, K. O. Pope, J. G. Jones

2007   Microfossil Evidence for Pre-Columbian Maize Dispersals in the Neotropics from San Andres, Tabasco, Mexico. *Proceedings of the National Academy of Sciences of the USA* 104:6870–75.

Pohl, M. D., K. O. Pope, J. G. Jones, J. S. Jacob, D. R. Piperno, S. D. DeFrance, D. L. Lentz, J. A. Gifford, M. E. Danforth, and J. K. Josserand

1996   Early Agriculture in the Maya Lowlands. *Latin American Antiquity* 7:355–72.

Pohl, M. E. D., and J. M. D. Pohl

1994   Cycles of Conflict: Political Factionalism in the Maya Lowlands. In *Factional Competition and Political Development in the New World*, edited by E. M. Brumfiel and J. W. Fox, pp. 138–157. Cambridge University Press, Cambridge.

Polanyi, K.

1957   The Economy as an Instituted Process. In *Trade and Market in the Early Empires*, edited by K. Polanyi, C. W. Arensberg, and H. W. Pearson, pp. 243–70. Free Press, New York.

Polanyi, K., C. M. Arensberg, and H. W. Pearson (editors)

1957   *Trade and Market in Early Empires: Economies in History and Theory.* Free Press, Glencoe, Illinois.

Pollock, S.

1999   *Ancient Mesopotamia: The Eden that Never Was.* Cambridge University Press, Cambridge.

Potter, D. R., and E. M. King

1995   A Heterarchical Approach to Lowland Maya Socioeconomies. In *Heterarchy and the Analysis of Complex Societies,* edited by R. M. Ehrenreich, C. L. Crumley and J. E. Levy, pp. 17–32. Archaeological Papers of the American Anthropological Association no. 6. Washington, D.C.

Preucel, R. (editor)

1991   *Processual and postprocessual Archaeologies.* Center for Archaeological Investigations Occasional Paper No. 10. Southern Illinois University, Carbondale.

Price, T. D., and G. M. Feinman (editors)

1995   *Foundations of Social Inequality.* Plenum Press, New York.

Proskouriakoff, T.

1962   *Mayapan, Yucatan, Mexico.* Carnegie Institution Publication no. 619. Carnegie Institution of Washington, Washington, D.C.

Pyburn, K. A.

1997   The Archaeological Signature of Complexity in the Maya Lowlands. In *The Archaeology of City-States: Cross-Cultural Approaches*, edited by D. L. Nichols and T. H. Charlton, pp. 155–68. Smithsonian Institution, Washington, D.C.

Pyburn, K. A., B. Dixon, P. Cook, A. McNair

1998   The Albion Island Settlement Pattern Project: Domination and Resistance in Early Classic Northern Belize. *Journal of Field Archaeology* 25(1):37–62.

Quezada, S.

1993   *Pueblos y caciques yucatecos, 1550–1580.* El Colegio de Mexico, Mexico, D. F.

Raaflaub, K.A.

1996   Born to Be Wolves? Origins of Roman Imperialism. In *Transitions to Empire: Essays in Greco-Roman History, 360–146 B.C., in Honor of E. Badian,* edited by R. W. Wallace and E. M. Harris, pp. 273–314. University of Oklahoma Press, Norman.

Radcliffe-Brown, A. F.

1965 [1952]   *Structure and Function in Primitive Society.* Free Press, New York.

Rathje, W. L.

1972   Praise the Gods and Pass the Metates: A Hypothesis of the Development of Lowlands Rainforest Civilizations in Mesoamerica. In *Contemporary Archaeology: A Guide to Theory and Contributions,* edited by M. P. Leone, pp. 365–92. Southern Illinois University Press, Carbondale.

1975   The Last Tango in Mayapan: A Tentative Trajectory of Production-Distribution Systems. In *Ancient Civilizations and Trade,* edited by J. Sabloff and C. C. Lamberg-Karlovsky, pp. 409–48. University of New Mexico Press, Albuquerque.

2002   The Nouveau Elite Potlatch: One Scenario for the Monumental Rise of Early Civilizations. In *Ancient Maya Political Economies,* edited by Marilyn A. Masson and David Freiden, pp. 31–40. AltaMira Press, Oxford.

Recinos, A., and D. Goetz

1953   *The Annals of the Cakchiquels.* University of Oklahoma Press, Norman.

Redfield, R., and A. Villa Rojas

1934   *Chan Kom: A Maya Village.* University of Chicago Press, Chicago.

Reents-Budet, D.

1998   Elite Maya Pottery and Artisans as Social Indicators. In *Craft and Social Identity,* edited by C. L. Costin and R. P. Wright, pp. 71–89. Archaeological Papers of the American Anthropological Association No. 8. American Anthropological Association, Arlington, Virginia.

2000   Feasting among the Classic Maya: Evidence from the Pictorial Ceramics. In *The Maya Vase Book,* vol. 6, edited by Justin Kerr, pp. 1022–37. Kerr Associates, New York.

2001   Classic Maya Conceptualizations of the Royal Court: An Analysis of Palace Court Renderings on the Pictorial Ceramics. In *Royal Courts of the Ancient Maya,* edited by S. Houston and T. Inomata, 195–233. Westview Press, Boulder, Colorado.

Reents-Budet, D., J. W. Ball, and J. Kerr

1994   *Painting the Maya Universe: Royal Ceramics of the Classic Period.* Duke University Press, Durham.

Reents-Budet, D., A. Foias, D. R. Bishop, J. Blackman, and S. Guenter

2007   Interacciones Politicas y el Sitio Ik' (Motul de San Jose): Datos de la Ceramica. In *XX Simposio de Investigaciones Arqueologicas en Guatemala,* edited by J. P. Laporte and B. Arroyo, pp. 1141–1159. Ministerio de Cultura y Deportes, Museo Nacional de Antropologia e Etnologia, Guatemala City.

Reents-Budet, D., S. Guenter, R. L. Bishop, and M. J. Blackman

2012   Identity and Interaction: Ceramic Styles and Social History of the Ik' Polity, Guatemala. In *Motul de San José: History, Politics and Economy in a Classic Maya Cen-*

ter, edited by A. E. Foias and K. F. Emery, pp. 67–93. University Press of Florida, Gainesville.

Reina, R. E., and R. M. Hill II

1980   Lowland Maya Subsistence: Notes from Ethnohistory and Ethnography. *American Antiquity* 45(1):74–79.

Renfrew, C.

1974   Beyond a Subsistence Economy: The Evolution of Social Organization in Prehistoric Europe. In *Reconstructing Complex Societies: An Archaeological Colloquium*, edited by C. B. Moore, pp. 69–95. Supplement to the Bulletin of the American Schools of Oriental Research, No. 20.

1975   Trade as Action at a Distance: Questions of Integration and Communication. In *Ancient Civilization and Trade*, edited by J. A. Sabloff and C. C. Lamberg-Karlovsky, pp. 3–59. School for American Research Advanced Seminar Series, University of New Mexico Press, Albuquerque.

1982   Polity and Power: Interaction, Intensification and Exploitation. In *An Island Polity: The Archaeology of Exploitation in Melos*, edited by C. Renfrew and M. Wagstaff, pp. 264–90. Cambridge University Press, Cambridge.

1986   Introduction: Peer Polity Interaction and Socio-Political Change. In *Peer Polity Interaction and Socio-Political Change*, edited by C. Renfrew and J. Cherry, pp. 1–18. Cambridge University Press, Cambridge.

Renfrew, C., and J. F. Cherry (editors)

1986   *Peer Polity Interaction and Socio-Political Change*. Cambridge University Press, Cambridge.

Restall, M.

1997   *The Maya World: Yucatec Culture and Society, 1550–1850*. Stanford University Press, Stanford.

1998   *Maya Conquistador*. Beacon Press, Boston.

2001   The People of the Patio: Ethnohistorical Evidence of Yucatec Maya Royal Courts. In *Royal Courts of the Ancient Maya: 2, Data and Case Studies*, edited by T. Inomata and S. Houston, pp. 335–90. Westview Press, Boulder, Colorado.

2003   *Seven Myths of the Spanish Conquest*. Oxford University Press, Oxford.

Rice, D. S., and T. P. Culbert

1990   Historical Contexts for Population Reconstruction in the Maya Lowlands. In *Precolumbian Population History in the Maya Lowlands*, edited by T. P. Culbert and D. S. Rice, pp. 1–36. University of New Mexico Press, Albuquerque.

Rice, D. S., P. M. Rice, R. Sanchez-Polo, and G. D. Jones

1996   *Proyecto Maya-Colonial: Geografía Política del Siglo XVII en el Centro de Petén, Guatemala*. Preliminary report submitted to the Institute of Anthropology and History. Available at the Institute of Anthropology and History, Guatemala City.

Rice, P. M.

2004   *Maya Political Science: Time, Astronomy, and the Cosmos*, 25–28. University of Texas Press, Austin.

2008   Time, Power, and the Maya. *Latin American Antiquity* 19(3):275–298.

2009   On Classic Maya Political Economies. *Journal of Anthropological Archaeology* 28:70–84.

Rice, P. M., and D. S. Rice (editors)

2009   *The Kowoj: Identity, Migration, and Geopolitics in the Late Postclassic Peten, Guatemala.* University Press of Colorado, Boulder, Colorado.

Ringle, W. M.

1990   Who Was Who in Ninth-Century Chichen Itza. *Ancient Mesoamerica* 1:233–43.

1999   Pre-Classsic Cityscapes: Ritual Politics among the Early Lowland Maya. In *Social Patterns in Pre-Classic Mesoamerica: A Symposium at Dumbarton Oaks 9 and 10 October 1993*, edited by D. C. Grove and R. A. Joyce, pp. 183–223. Dumbarton Oaks, Washington D.C.

Ringle, W. M., and G. J. Bey III

2001   Post-Classic and Terminal Classic Courts of the Northern Maya Lowlands. In *Royal Courts of the Ancient Maya.* Vol. 2, *Data and Case Studies,* edited by T. Inomata and S. Houston, pp. 266–307. Westview Press, Boulder, Colorado.

Ringle, W. M., T. Gallereta Negrón, and G. J. Bey III

1998   The Return of Quetzalcoatl: Evidence for the Spread of a World Religion during the Epiclassic Period. *Ancient Mesoamerica* 9:183–232.

Ringle, W. M., G. J. Bey, III, T. B. Freeman, C. A. Hanson, C. W. Houck, and J. G. Smith

2004   The Decline of the East: The Classic to Postclassic Transition at Ek Balam, Yucatan. In *The Terminal Classic in the Maya Lowlands: Collapse, Transition, and Transformation*, edited by A. Demarest, P. Rice, and D. Rice, pp. 485–516. University of Colorado Press, Boulder.

Robertshaw, P.

2010   Beyond the Segmentary State: Creative and Instrumental Power in Western Uganda. *Journal of World Prehistory* 23:255–69.

Robin, C.

2003   New Directions in Classic Maya Household Archaeology. *Journal of Archaeological Research* 11:307–56.

Robin, C., J. Yaeger, and W. Ashmore

2010   Living in the Hinterlands of a Provincial Polity. In *Classic Maya Provincial Politics: Xunantunich and Its Hinterlands*, edited by L. J. LeCount and J. Yaeger, pp. 315–33. University of Arizona Press, Tucson.

Robles C. F., and A. P. Andrews

1986   A Review and Synthesis of Recent Postclassic Archaeology in Northern Yucatan. In *Late Lowland Maya Civilization: Classic to Postclassic*, edited by J. Sabloff and A. E. Wyllys, pp. 53–98. SAR and University of New Mexico Press, Albuquerque.

Roscoe, P. B.

1993   Practice and Political Centralisation: A New Approach to Political Evolution. *Current Anthropology* 34(2):111–40.

Rosenswig, R. M., and M. A. Masson

2001   Seven New Preceramic Sites Documented in Northern Belize. *Mexicon* 23:138–40.

Rothman, M.

2004   Studying the Development of Complex Society Mesopotamia in the Late Fifth and Fourth Millennia BC. *Journal of Archaeological Research* 12(1):88, 90–91.

Rothman, M. (editor)

2001   *Uruk Mesopotamia and Its Neighbors: Cross-Cultural Interactions in the Era of State*

Formation. Advanced Seminar Series, School of American Research Press, Santa Fe, New Mexico.

Rouse, J.

2005   Power/Knowledge. In *The Cambridge Companion to Foucault*, edited by G. Gutting, pp. 95–122. 2nd ed. Cambridge University Press, New York.

Roys, R. L.

1943   *The Indian Background of Colonial Yucatan*. Carnegie Institution of Washington Publication 548. Washington, D.C.

1957   *The Political Geography of the Yucatan Maya*. Carnegie Institution Publication No. 613. Carnegie Institution of Washington, Washington, D.C.

1967   *The Book of Chilam Balam of Chumayel*. University of Oklahoma Press, Norman.

Runggaldier, A., and N. Hammond

In press   Maya states: The theoretical background in historical overview. In *Origins of Maya States, Papers from the International Conference on the Maya States at the University of Pennsylvania, 2007*, edited by L. Traxler and R. Sharer. University of Pennsylvania Museum, Philadelphia.

Sabloff, J. A.

1986   Interaction among Maya Polities: A Preliminary Examination. In *Peer Polity Interaction and Socio-political Change*, edited by C. Renfrew and J. F. Cherry, pp. 109–16. Cambridge University Press, Cambridge.

Sahlins, M. D.

1963   Poor Man, Rich Man, Big Man, Chief: Political Types in Melanesia and Polynesia. *Comparative Studies in Society and History* 5:285–303.

1972   *Stone Age Economics*. Aldine, Chicago.

1985   *Islands of History*. University of Chicago Press, Chicago.

Sahlins, M., and E. Service (editors)

1960   *Evolution and Culture*. University of Michigan Press, Ann Arbor.

Saitta, D.

1994   Agency, Class, and Archaeological Interpretation. *Journal of Anthropological Archaeology* 13:1–27.

Sanchez, J. L. J.

2005   Ancient Maya Royal Strategies: Creating Power and Identity through Art. *Ancient Mesoamerica* 16:261–75.

Sanders, W. T.

1981   Classic Maya Settlement Patterns and Ethnographic Analogy. In *Lowland Maya Settlement Patterns*, edited by W. Ashmore, 351–69. University of New Mexico Press, Albuquerque.

Sanders, W. T., and B. J. Price

1968   *Mesoamerica: The Evolution of a Civilization*. Academic Press, New York.

Sanders, W. T., and D. Webster

1988   The Mesoamerican Urban Tradition. *American Anthropologist* 90:521–46.

Saturno, W. A.

2006   The Dawn of Maya Gods and Kings. *National Geographic* 209(1):68–77.

2009   High Resolution Documentation of the Murals of San Bartolo, Guatemala. In *Maya Archaeology 1*, edited by C. Golden, S. Houston, and J. Skidmore, pp. 8–27. Precolumbia Mesoweb Press, San Francisco.

Saturno, W. A., K. Taube, and D. Stuart

2005   *The Murals of San Bartolo, El Peten, Guatemala. Part 1: the North Wall. Ancient America.* Center for Ancient American Studies, Barnardsville, North Carolina.

Saturno, W. A., D. Stuart, and B. Beltran

2006   Early Maya Writing at San Bartolo, Guatemala. *Science* 311:1281–83.

Scarborough, V. L.

1993   Water Management in the Southern Maya Lowlands: An Accretive Model for the Engineered Landscape. *Research in Economic Anthropology* 7:17–69.

1998   Ecology and Ritual: Water Management and the Maya. *Latin American Antiquity* 9:135–59.

2003   *The Flow of Power: Ancient Maya Systems and Landscapes.* School of American Research Press, Santa Fe, New Mexico.

Scarborough, V. L., and F. Valdez, Jr.

2003   The Engineered Environment and Political Economy of the Three Rivers Region. In *Heterarchy, Political Economy, and the Ancient Maya: The Three Rivers Region of the East-Central Yucatán Peninsula,* edited by V. L. Scarborough, F. Valdez, Jr., and N. Dunning, pp. 3–13. University of Arizona Press, Tucson.

Scarborough, V. L., F. Valdez, Jr., and N. Dunning (editors)

2003   *Heterarchy, Political Economy, and the Ancient Maya: The Three Rivers Region of the East-Central Yucatán Peninsula.* University of Arizona Press, Tucson.

Schele, L., and D. Freidel

1990   *A Forest of Kings: The Untold Story of the Ancient Maya.* William Morrow, New York.

Schele, L., and P. Mathews

1998   *The Code of Kings: The Language of Seven Sacred Maya Temples and Tombs.* Scribner, New York.

Schele, L., and M. Miller

1986   *The Blood of Kings: Dynasty and Ritual in Maya Art.* 2nd ed. Kimbell Art Museum and George Braziller, New York.

Scherer, A. K., and C. Golden

2009   Tecolote, Guatemala: Archaeological Evidence for a Fortified Late Classic Maya Political Border. *Journal of Field Archaeology* 34:285–305.

Schieber de Lavarreda, C., and M. Orrego Corzo

2001   Mil años de historia en Abaj Takalik. *Utz'ib* 3(1):1–31. Asociacion Tikal, Guatemala City.

Schiera, P.

1995   Legitimacy, Discipline, and Institutions: Three Necessary Conditions for the Birth of the Modern State. In "The Origins of the State in Italy, 1300–1600," supplement, *Journal of Modern History* 67:S11–S33.

Schmidt, P. J.

2007   Birds, Ceramics, and Cacao: New Excavations at Chichen Itza, Yucatan. In *Twin Tollans: Chichen Itza, Tula, and the Epiclassic to Early Postclassic Mesoamerican World,* edited by J. K. Kowalski and C. Kristan-Graham, pp. 151–203. Dumbarton Oaks and Harvard University Press.

Schoenbrun, D.

1999   The (In)Visible Roots of Bunyoro-Kitara and Buganda in the Lakes Region, AD 800–1300. In *Beyond Chiefdoms: Pathways to Complexity in Africa*, edited by S. K. McIntosh, pp. 136–50. Cambridge University Press, Cambridge.

Scholes, F. V., and R. L. Roys

1968   *The Maya Chontal Indians of Acalan-Tixchel: A Contribution to the History and Ethnography of the Yucatan Peninsula.* 2nd ed. University of Oklahoma Press, Norman.

Schortman, E. M.

2010   Provincial Politics at Xunantunich: Power, Differentiation, an Identity in a Classic-Period Maya Realm. In *Classic Maya Provincial Politics: Xunantunich and Its Hinterlands*, edited by L. J. LeCount and J. Yaeger, pp. 370–83. University of Arizona Press, Tucson.

Schortman, E. M., and P. A. Urban

2004   Modeling the Roles of Craft Production in Ancient Political Economies. *Journal of Archaeological Research* 12(2):185–226.

Schortman, E. M., P. A. Urban, and M. Ausec

1996   Reply to Forum on "Agency, Ideology, and Power in Archaeological Theory." *Current Anthropology* 37(1):61–63.

Schwartz, G. M., and S. E. Falconer (editors)

1994a   *Archaeological Views from the Countryside: Village Communities in Early Complex Societies.* Smithsonian Institution Press, Washington, D.C.

1994b   Rural Approaches to Social Complexity. In *Archaeological Views from the Countryside: Village Communities in Early Complex Societies*, edited by G. M. Schwartz and S. E. Falconer, pp. 1–9. Smithsonian Institution Press, Washington, D.C.

Scott, J.

1985   *Weapons of the Weak: Everyday Forms of Peasant Resistance.* Yale University Press, New Haven, Connecticut.

1990   *Domination and the Arts of Resistance: Hidden Transcripts.* Yale University Press, New Haven, Connecticut.

Service, E.

1962   *Primitive Social Organization: An Evolutionary Perspective.* Random House, New York.

1975   *Origins of the State and Civilization.* Harper and Row, New York.

Sewell, W. H. Jr.

1992   A Theory of Structure: Duality, Agency, and Transformation. *American Journal of Sociology* 98(1):1–29.

Shanks, M., and C. Tilley

1987   *Social Theory and Archaeology.* University of New Mexico Press, Albuquerque.

Sharer, R. S.

1991   Diversity and Continuity in Maya Civilization: Quirigua as a Case Study. In *Classic Maya Political History: Hieroglyphic and Archaeological Evidence*, edited by T. P. Culbert, pp. 180–98. Cambridge University Press, New York.

Sharer, R. S., and C. W. Golden

2004   Kingship and Polity: Conceptualizing the Maya Body Politic. In *Continuities and*

Changes in Maya Archaeology: Perspectives at the Millennium, edited by Charles W. Golden and Greg Borsgstede, pp. 23–50. Routledge: New York.

Sharer, R. S., and L. P. Traxler

2006 *The Ancient Maya.* 6th ed. Stanford University Press, Stanford.

Small, D. B.

2009 The Dual-Processual Model in Ancient Greece: Applying a Post-Neoevolutionary Model to a Data Rich Environment. *Journal of Anthropological Archaeology* 28:205–21.

Smith, A. T.

2000 Rendering the Political Aesthetic: Political Legitimacy in Urartian Representations of the Built Environment. *Journal of Anthropological Archaeology* 19:131–63.

2003 *The Political Landscape: Constellations of Authority in Early Complex Polities.* University of California Press: Berkeley.

Smith, M. Estellie

1991 The ABCs of Political Economy. In *Early State Economics,* edited by H. J. M. Claessen and P. van de Velde, pp. 31–74. Political and Economic Anthropology vol. 8. Transaction Publishers, New Brunswick.

Smith, M. E.

1989 Cities, Towns, and Urbanism: Comment on Sanders and Webster. *American Anthropologist* 91:454–60.

1996 The Strategic Provinces. In *Aztec Imperial Strategies,* edited by F. F. Berdan, R. E. Blanton, E. H. Boone, M. G. Hodge, M. E. Smith, and E. Umberger, pp. 137–50. Dumbarton Oaks, Washington, D.C.

2004 The Archaeology of Ancient State Economies. *Annual Reviews of Anthropology* 33:73–102.

2008 *Aztec City-State Capitals.* University Press of Florida, Gainesville, Florida.

Smith, M. E., and L. Montiel

2001 The Archaeological Study of Empires and Imperialism in Pre-Hispanic Central Mexico. *Journal of Anthropological Archaeology* 20:245–84.

Smith, M. E., and K. J. Schreiber

2005 New World States and Empires: Economic and Social Organization. *Journal of Archaeological Research* 13:189–229.

2006 New World States and Empires: Politics, Religion, and Urbanism. *Journal of Archaeological Research* 4(1):1–52.

Smyth, M., C. D. Dore, and N. P. Dunning

1995 Interpreting Prehistoric Settlement Patterns: Lessons from the Maya Center of Sayil, Yucatan. *Journal of Field Archaeology* 22:321–47.

Smyth, M. P., and C. D. Dore

1992 Large Site Archaeological Methods at Sayil, Yucatan, Mexico: Investigation Community Organization at a Prehispanic Maya Center. *Latin American Antiquity* 3:3–21.

1994 Maya Urbanism in Sayil, Yucatan. *Research and Exploration* 10:38–55.

Southall, A. W.

1956 *Alur Society: A Study in Processes and Types of Domination.* Heffer, Cambridge.

1988 The Segmentary State in Africa and Asia. *Comparative Studies in Society and History* 30:52–82.

Spores, R.

1984   *The Mixtecs in Ancient and Colonial Times.* University of Oklahoma Press, Nor-
        man.

Stein, G.

1994   Segmentary States and Organizational Variation in Early Complex Societies: A
        Rural Perspective. In *Archaeological Views from the Countryside: Village Commu-
        nities in Early Complex Societies,* edited by G. M. Schwartz and S. E. Falconer, pp.
        12–15. Smithsonian Institution Press, Washington, D.C.

1998   Heterogeneity, Power, and Political Economy: Some Current Research Issues in
        the Archaeology of Old World Complex Societies. *Journal of Archaeological Re-
        search* 6(1):1–44.

1999   *Rethinking World-Systems: Diasporas, Colonies, and Interaction in Uruk Mesopota-
        mia.* University of Arizona Press, Tucson.

2001   Understanding Ancient State Societies in the Old World. In *Archaeology at the
        Millennium: A Sourcebook,* edited by G. M. Feinman and T. D. Price, pp. 353–80.
        Kluwer, New York.

Stein, G., and M. S. Rothman (editors)

1994   *Chiefdoms and Early States in the Near East: The Organizational Dynamics of Com-
        plexity.* Prehistoric Press, Madison.

Steward, J. H.

1955   *Theory of Culture Change.* University of Illinois Press, Urbana.

1956   Cultural Evolution. *Scientific American Reprints,* pp. 9–17. W. H. Freeman.

Stuart, D.

1992   Hieroglyphs and Archaeology at Copan. *Ancient Mesoamerica* 3(1):169–84.

1995   A Study of Maya Inscriptions. PhD dissertation, Department of Anthropology,
        Vanderbilt University, Nashville, TN.

1998   "The Fire Enters His House": Architecture and Ritual in Classic Maya Texts. In
        *Function and Meaning in Classic Maya Architecture, A Symposium at Dumbarton
        Oaks, 7th and 8th October 1994,* edited by S. D. Houston, pp. 373–425. Dumbarton
        Oaks, Washington, D.C.

2000   "Arrival of Strangers": Teotihuacan and Tollan in Classic Maya History. In *Me-
        soamerica's Classic Heritage: Teotihuacan to the Aztecs,* edited by D. Carrasco, L.
        Jones, and S. Session, pp. 465–513. University Press of Colorado, Niwot.

2004   The Beginnings of the Copan Dynasty: A Review of the Hieroglyphic and His-
        torical Evidence. In *Understanding Early Classic Copan,* edited by E. E. Bell, M. A.
        Canuto, and R. J. Sharer, pp. 215–48. University of Pennsylvania Museum, Phila-
        delphia.

2007   The Origin of Copan's Founder. Available at http://decipherment.wordpress.
        com/2007/06/25/the-origin-of-copans-founder/. Accessed January 21, 2011.

Stuart, D., and S. D. Houston

1994   *Classic Maya Place Names.* Studies in Pre-Columbian Art & Archaeology No. 33.
        Dumbarton Oaks Research Library and Collection, Washington, D.C.

Stuart, D., and G. Stuart

2008   *Palenque: Eternal City of the Maya.* Thames & Hudson, New York.

Suhler, C. K., T. Ardren, and D. Johnstone

1998   The Chronology of Yaxuna: Evidence from Excavation and Ceramics. *Ancient Mesoamerica* 9:176–82.

Swartz, M. J., V. W. Turner, and A. Tuden (editors)

1966   *Political Anthropology.* Aldine, Chicago.

Tambiah, S. J.

1976   *World Conqueror and World Renouncer: A Study of Buddhism and Polity in Thailand against a Historical Background.* Cambridge Studies in Social Anthropology 15, Cambridge.

1977   The Galactic Polity: The Structure of Traditional Kingdoms in Southeast Asia. In *Anthropology and the Climate of Opinion,* edited by S. A. Freed, 69–97. Annals of the New York Academy of Science 293. New York.

Taschek, J. T., and J. Ball

1999   Las Ruinas de Arenal: Preliminary Report on a Subregional Major Center in the Western Belize Valley (1991–1992 Excavations). *Ancient Mesoamerica* 10:215–35.

2003   Nohoch Ek Revisited: The Minor Center as Manor. *Latin American Antiquity* 14(4):371–80.

Tate, C. E.

1992   *Yaxchilan: The Design of a Maya Ceremonial City.* University of Texas Press, Austin.

1999   Writing on the Face of the Moon: Women's Products, Archetypes, and Power in Ancient Maya Civilization. In *Manifesting Power: Gender and the Interpretation of Power in Archaeology,* edited by T. L. Sweely, pp. 81–102. Routledge, London.

Taube, K. A.

1992   *The Major Gods of Ancient Yucatan.* Dumbarton Oaks, Washington D.C.

Taussig, M. T.

1980   *The Devil and Commodity Fetishism in South America.* University of North Carolina Press, Chapel Hill

1987   *Shamanism, Colonialism and the Wild Man: A Study in Terror and Healing.* University of Chicago Press, Chicago.

Tedlock, D. (translator and commentator)

1986   *Popul Vuh: The Definitive Edition of the Mayan Book of the Dawn of Life and the Glories of Gods and Kings.* Touchstone, Simon & Schuster, New York.

Terray, E.

1971   *Marxism and Primitive Societies.* Monthly Review Press, New York.

Thompson, J. Eric S.

1970   *Maya History and Religion.* University of Oklahoma Press, Norman.

Thornton, E. K.

2012   Animal Resource Use and Exchange at an Inland Maya Port: Zooarchaeological Investigations at Trinidad de Nosotros. In *Motul de San José: Politics, History and Economy in a Classic Maya Polity,* edited by A. E. Foias and K. F. Emery, pp. 326–356. University Press of Florida, Gainesville.

Tilley, C.

1994   *A Phenomenology of Landscape: Places, Paths, and Monuments.* Berg, Oxford.

Tokovinine, A. A.

2008   The Power of Place: Political Landscape and Identity in Classic Maya Inscriptions, Imagery, and Architecture. PhD dissertation, Department of Anthropology, Harvard University.

Tokovinine, A., and M. Zender

2012   Lords of Windy Water: The Royal Court of Motul de San José in Classic Maya Inscriptions. In *Motul de San José: Politics, History, and Economy in a Classic Maya Polity*, edited by A. E. Foias and K. F. Emery, pp. 30–66. University Press of Florida, Gainesville.

Tourtellot, G., III

1988   *Excavations at Seibal: Peripheral Survey and Excavation, Settlement, and Community Patterns*. Memoirs of the Peabody Museum of Archaeology and Ethnology vol. 16. Harvard University Press, Cambridge.

1993   A View of Ancient Maya Settlements in the Eighth Century. In *Lowland Maya Civilization in the Eighth Century A.D.*, edited by J. Sabloff and J. Henderson, pp. 219–42. Dumbarton Oaks, Washington, D.C.

Tourtellot, G., F. Estrada Belli, J. J. Rose, and N. Hammond

2003   Late Classic Maya Heterarchy, Hierarchy, and Landscape at La Milpa, Belize. In *Heterarchy, Political Economy, and the Ancient Maya: The Three Rivers Region of the East-Central Yucatán Peninsula*, edited by V. L. Scarborough, F. Valdez, Jr., and N. P. Dunning, pp. 37–51. University of Arizona Press, Tucson.

Tourtellot, G., M. Wolf, F. Estrada Belli, and N. Hammond

2000   Discovery of two predicted Ancient Maya sites in Belize. *Antiquity* 74:481–82.

Tourtellot, G., M. Wolf, S. Smith, K. Gardella, and N. Hammond

2002   Exploring Heaven on Earth: Testing the Cosmological Model at La Milpa, Belize. *Antiquity* 76:634.

Tozzer, A. M. (editor and translator)

1941   *Landa's Relación de las cosas de Yucatán*. Papers of the Peabody Museum of Archaeology and Ethnology, Vol. 18. Harvard University, Cambridge, MA.

Triadan, D.

2000   Elite Household Subsistence at Aguateca, Guatemala. *Mayab* 13:46–56. Madrid, Spain.

2007   Warriors, Nobles, Commoners and Beasts: Figurines from Elite Buildings at Aguateca, Guatemala. *Latin American Antiquity* 18(3):269–94.

Trigger, B. G.

1974   The Archaeology of Government. *World Archaeology* 6(1):95–106.

1998   *Sociocultural Evolution: Calculation and Contingency*. Blackwell Publishers, New York.

Turner, E. S., N. I. Turner, and R. E. W. Adams

1981   Volumetric Assessment, Rank Ordering, and Maya Civic Centers. In *Lowland Maya Settlement Patterns*, edited by W. Ashmore, pp. 37–70. University of New Mexico Press, Albuquerque.

Upham, S. (editor)

1990   *The Evolution of Political Systems: Sociopolitics in Small-Scale Sedentary Societies*. Cambridge University Press, Cambridge.

Urban, P., and E. Schortman

2004 Opportunities for Advancement: Intra-community Power Contests in the Midst of Political Decentralization in Terminal Classic Southeastern Mesoamerica. *Latin American Antiquity* 15(3):251–72.

Valdes, J. A.

1995 Desarrollo cultural y señales de alarma entre los mayas: El preclasico tardio y la transicion hacia el clasico temprano. In *The Emergence of Lowland Maya Civilization: The Transition from the Preclassic to the Early Classic,* edited by N. Grube, pp. 71–85. Acta Mesoamericana 8. Verlag Anton Saurwein, Markt Schwaben.

Valdes, J. A., and M. P. de Hatch

1996 Evidencias de poder y control social en Kaminaljuyu: Proyecto Arqueologico Miraflores II. In *IX Simposio de Investigaciones Arqueologicas en Guatemala, 1995,* edited by J. P. Laporte and H. Escobedo, pp. 377–96. Ministerio de Cultura y Deportes, IDAEH, Asociacion Tikal, Guatemala City.

Velásquez García, E.

2010 Los Señores de la Entidad Politica de Ik'. *Estudios de Cultura Maya* 21:45–87.

Vincent, J.

1990 *Anthropology and Politics: Visions, Traditions, and Trends.* University of Arizona Press, Tucson.

Vogt, E. Z.

1976 *Tortillas for the Gods: A Symbolic Analysis of Zinacanteco Rituals.* Harvard University Press, Cambridge.

2007 Daily Life in a Highland Maya Community: Zinacantan in Mid-Twentieth Century. In *Ancient Maya Commoners,* edited by J. C. Lohse and F. Valdez, Jr., pp. 23–47. University of Texas Press, Austin.

Wagner, E.

2000 An Alternative View on the Meaning and Function of Structure 10L-22a, Copán, Honduras. In *The Sacred and the Profane: Architecture and Identity in the Maya Lowlands,* edited by P.R. Colas, K. Delvendahl, M. Kuhnert, and A. Schubart, pp. 25–49. Acta Mesoamericana 10. Verlag Anton Saurwein, Markt Schwaben.

Wahl, D., R. Byrne, T. Schreiner, and R. Hansen

2006 Holocene vegetation change in the Northern Peten and its implications for Maya prehistory. *Quaternary Research* 65:380–89.

Wailes, B.

1995 A Case Study of Heterarchy in Complex Societies: Early Medieval Ireland and Its Archaeological Implications. In *Heterarchy and the Analysis of Complex Societies,* edited by Robert M. Ehrenreich, Carole L. Crumley and Janet E. Levy, pp. 55–69. Archaeological Papers of the American Anthropological Association no. 6. American Anthropological Association, Arlington, Virginia.

Wallerstein, I.

1974 *The Modern-World System I: Capitalist Agriculture and the Origins of European World-Economy in the Sixteenth Century.* Academic Press, New York.

1980 *The Modern-World System II: Mercantilism and the Consolidation of the European World-Economy, 1600–1750.* Academic Press, New York.

1989   *The Modern-World System III: The Second Era of Great Expansion of the Capitalist World-Economy, 1730–1840s.* Academic Press, New York.

Walling, S.

2005   Archaeological investigations of Prehispanic Maya residential terraces, commoner housing and hydrology at Chawak But'o'ob, Belize. *Antiquity* 79 (304). http://antiquity.ac.uk/progall/walling/index.html.

Walling, S., P. Davis, J. Hanna, L. Matthews, N. Prasarn, and C. Taylor

2006   Residential Terracing, Water Management, Matrix Analysis, and Suburban Ceremonialism at Chawak But'o'ob, Belize: Report of the 2005 Rio Bravo Archaeological Survey. In *Programme for Belize Archaeological Project: Report of Activities from the 2005 Field Season*, edited by F. Valdez, Jr., pp. 41–88. Occasional Papers No. 6. Mesoamerican Archaeological Research Laboratory, University of Texas, Austin.

Webb, E. A., and H. P. Schwarcz

2012   Stable Carbon Isotope Evidence of Ancient Maize Cultivation on the Soils of Motul de San José. In *Motul de San José: Politics, History, and Economy in a Classic Maya Polity*, edited by A. E. Foias and K. F. Emery, pp. 386–400. University Press of Florida, Gainesville.

Webb, E. A., H. P. Schwarcz, C. T. Jensen, R. E. Terry, M. D. Moriarty, and K. F. Emery

2007   Stable Carbon Isotope Signature of Ancient Maize Agriculture in the Soils of Motul de San José, Guatemala. *Geoarchaeology* 22(3):291–312.

Weber, M.

1964 [1947]   *The Theory of Social and Economic Organization*, transl. by A. M. Henderson and T. Parsons. Oxford University Press, New York.

Webster, D. L.

1978   Three Walled Sites of the Northern Maya Lowlands. *Journal of Field Archaeology* 5:375–90.

1992   Maya Elites: The Perspective from Copan. In *Mesoamerican Elites: An Archaeological Assessment*, edited by D. Z. Chase and A. F. Chase, pp. 135–56. University of Oklahoma Press, Norman.

2000   The Not so Peaceful Civilization: A Review of Maya War. *Journal of World Prehistory* 14(1):65–119.

2001   Spatial Dimensions of Maya Courtly Life: Problems and Issues. In *Royal Courts of the Ancient Maya, vol. 1: Theory, Comparison, and Synthesis*, edited by T. Inomata and S. Houston, pp. 130–67. Westview Press, Boulder, Colorado.

2002   *The Fall of the Ancient Maya: Solving the Mystery of the Maya Collapse.* Thames & Hudson, London.

Webster, D. L. (editor)

1989   *The House of the Bacabs, Copan, Honduras.* Dumbarton Oaks, Washington, D.C.

Wells, E. C.

2006   Recent Trends in Theorizing Prehispanic Mesoamerican Economies. *Journal of Archaeological Research* 14:265–312.

2007   Faenas, Ferias, and Fiestas: Ritual Finance in Ancient and Modern Honduras. In *Mesoamerican Ritual Economy: Archaeological and Ethnological Perspectives*, edited by E. C. Wells and K. L. Davis-Salazar, pp. 29–65. University Press of Colorado, Boulder.

Wells, E. C., and K. L. Davis-Salazar

2007 Mesoamerican Ritual Economy: Archaeological and Ethnological Perspectives. In *Mesoamerican Ritual Economy: Archaeological and Ethnological Perspectives*, edited by E. C. Wells and K. L. Davis-Salazar, pp. 1–26. University Press of Colorado, Boulder.

White, C. D., M. W. Spence, F. J. Longstaffe, H. Stuart-Williams, K. R. Law

2002 Geographic Identities of the Sacrificial Victims from the Feathered Serpent Pyramid, Teotihuacan: Implications for the Nature of State Power. *Latin American Antiquity* 13(2):217–36.

White, L.

1959 *The Evolution of Culture: The Development of Civilization to the Fall of Rome*. McGraw-Hill, New York.

Whitmeyer, J. M.

1997 Mann's Theory of Power—A (Sympathetic) Critique. *The British Journal of Sociology* 48(2):210–25.

Whitmore, T. M., and B. L. Turner II

1992 Landscapes of Cultivation in Mesoamerica on the Eve of the Conquest. In "The Americas before and after 1492," special edition, *Annals of the Association of American Geographers* 82(3):402–25.

Wiesehofer, J.

1996 *Ancient Persia: From 550 B.C. to 650 A.D.* Translated by Azizeh Azodi. I. B. Tauris, London, New York.

Willey, G. R.

1986 The Postclassic of the Maya Lowlands: A Preliminary Overview. In *Late Lowland Maya Civilization: Classic to Postclassic*, edited by J.A. Sabloff and E. W. Andrews V., pp. 17–51.University of New Mexico Press, Albuquerque.

Williams-Beck, L. A., B. Liljefors Persson, and A. Anaya Hernadez

In press Back to the Future for Predicting the Past: Cuchcabal-Batabil-Cuchteel and May Ritual Political Structures across Archaeological Landscapes, in Ethnohistoric Texts, and through Cosmological Time. Paper presented at the European Conference of Mayanists, November 2009, Central European University, Cracow, Poland.

Winter, M., R. Markens, C. Martinez Lopez, and A. Herrera Muzgo T.

2007 Shrines, Offerings and Postclassic Continuity in Zapotec Religion. In *Commoner Ritual and Ideology in Ancient Mesoamerica*, edited by N. Gonlin and J. C. Lohse, pp. 185–212. University Press of Colorado, Boulder.

Wittfogel, K. A.

1957 *Oriental Despotism: A Comparative Study of Total Power*. Yale University Press, New Haven, Connecticut.

Wolf, E. R.

1964 *Anthropology: Humanistic Scholarship in America. Princeton Studies*. Prentice-Hall, Englewood Cliffs, New Jersey.

1982 *Europe and the Peoples without History*. University of California Press, Berkeley.

1990 Facing Power, Old Insights, New Questions. *American Anthropologist* 92:586–96.

1999 *Envisioning Power: Ideologies of Dominance and Power*. University of California Press, Berkeley.

Wren, L. H.

1994 Ceremonialism in the Reliefs of the North Temple, Chichen Itza. In *Seventh Palenque Round Table, 1989*, edited by Virginia Fields, pp. 25–31. The Pre-Columbian Art Research Institute, San Francisco.

Wright, L.

2005 In Search of Yax Nuun Ayiin I: Revisiting the Tikal Project's Burial 10. *Ancient Mesoamerica* 16:89–100.

2006 *Diet, Health, and Status among the Pasión Maya: A Reappraisal of the Collapse.* Vanderbilt Institute of Mesoamerican Archaeology Series no. 2. Vanderbilt University Press, Nashville.

Wright, L., and C. White

1996 Human Biology in the Classic Maya Collapse: Evidence from Paleopathology and Paleodiet. *Journal of World Prehistory* 10:147–98.

Yaeger, J.

2003a Untangling the Ties that Bind: The City, the Countryside, and the Nature of Maya Urbanism at Xunantunich, Belize. In *The Social Construction of Ancient Cities*, edited by Monica L. Smith, pp. 121–55. Smithsonian Institution Press, Washington, D.C.

2003b Small Settlements in the Upper Belize River Valley: Local Complexity, Household Strategies of Affiliation, and the Changing Organization. In *Perspectives on Ancient Maya Rural Complexity*, edited by G. Iannone and S. V. Connell, pp. 42–58. Cotsen Institute of Archaeology Monograph 49. University of California, Los Angeles.

2010 Shifting Political Dynamics as Seen from the Xunantunich Palace. In *Classic Maya Provincial Politics: Xunantunich and Its Hinterlands*, edited by L. J. LeCount and J. Yaeger, pp. 145–60. University of Arizona Press, Tucson.

Yoffee, N.

2005 *Myths of the Archaic State: Evolution of the Earliest Cities, States, and Civilizations.* Cambridge University Press, Cambridge.

Yorgey, S. C.

2005 Rural Complexity in the Central Peten: A View from Akte, El Petén, Guatemala. MA thesis, Department of Anthropology, Tulane University.

Yorgey, S. C., and M. D. Moriarty

2012 Akte: Small Secondary Center to the Northeast of Motul de San José. In *Motul de San José: Politics, History, and Economy in a Classic Maya Polity*, edited by A. E. Foias and K. F. Emery, pp. 250–74. University Press of Florida, Gainesville.

Zeitlin, R. N., and J. F. Zeitlin

2000 The Paleoindian and Archaic cultures of Mesoamerica. In *The Cambridge History of the Native Peoples of the Americas: 2. Mesoamerica*, edited by R. E. W. Adams and M. J. McLeod, pp. 45–121. Cambridge.

Zender, M.

2004 *A Study of Classic Maya Priesthood*. PhD dissertation, Department of Archaeology, University of Calgary. ProQuest/University Microfilms, Ann Arbor, Michigan.

Zier, C. J.

1992 Intensive Raised-Field Agriculture in a Post-Eruption Environment, El Salvador. In *Gardens in Prehistory*, edited by T. W. Killion, pp. 217–33. University of Alabama Press, Tuscaloosa.

Index

The letter *f* following a page number denotes a figure. The letter *t* following a page number denotes a table.

Antonia E. Foias is professor of anthropology at Williams College. She is the coeditor, with Kitty Emery, of *Motul de San José: Politics, History, and Economy in a Classic Maya Polity* and the coauthor, with Ronald Bishop, of *Ceramics, Production, and Exchange in the Petexbatun Region: The Economic Parameters of the Classic Maya Collapse*. Since 1998 she has directed the multifaceted archaeological research at the site of Motul de San José, located in the central Peten jungle of Guatemala.

Salt: White Gold of the Ancient Maya, by Heather McKillop (2002)

Archaeology and Ethnohistory of Iximché, by C. Roger Nance, Stephen L. Whittington, and Barbara E. Borg (2003)

The Ancient Maya of the Belize Valley: Half a Century of Archaeological Research, edited by James F. Garber (2003; first paperback edition, 2011)

Unconquered Lacandon Maya: Ethnohistory and Archaeology of the Indigenous Culture Change, by Joel W. Palka (2005)

Chocolate in Mesoamerica: A Cultural History of Cacao, edited by Cameron L. McNeil (2006; first paperback printing, 2009)

Maya Christians and Their Churches in Sixteenth-Century Belize, by Elizabeth Graham (2011)

Chan: An Ancient Maya Farming Community, edited by Cynthia Robin (2012; first paperback edition, 2013)

Motul de San José: Politics, History, and Economy in a Maya Polity, edited by Antonia E. Foias and Kitty F. Emery (2012)

Ancient Maya Pottery: Classification, Analysis, and Interpretation, edited by James John Aimers (2013; first paperback edition, 2014)

Ancient Maya Political Dynamics, by Antonia E. Foias (2013; first paperback edition, 2014)